ROMANS

You, God, and a KJV Bible

By Eric Neumann

Copyright 2017

Quotations

The only material quoted in this book is the Word of God in the King James Version. No commentaries or scholars are quoted, because God's Word is important, not man's word. As such, I encourage all readers to be good Bereans by searching the scriptures to see if what I have said is true (Acts 17:11). It is okay if you do not agree with what I say, but it is not okay if your disagreement is not based upon the Word of God in its proper context, which involves "rightly dividing the Word of Truth" (II Timothy 2:15).

Goal

The goal of this Bible study is to cast "down imaginations, and every high thing that exalteth itself against the knowledge of God and [bring] into captivity every thought to the obedience of Christ" (II Corinthians 10:5) so that members of the body of Christ may "come unto the knowledge of the truth" (I Timothy 2:4).

Contact the author

Therefore, the author encourages any disagreements be brought to his attention so that future versions of this Bible study can be changed if deemed necessary.

You may e-mail the author at Bibledivider@gmail.com.

Go to www.amazon.com/author/bibledivider to order the author's books.

Books by Eric Neumann

All books are available in paperback and in Kindle formats by going to: www.amazon.com/author/bibledivider. You may also access the author's sermons by going to: http://www.youtube.com/user/bibledivider/videos.

Eric's Bible study guides on the following books are now available:

Matthew
Mark
Luke
John
Acts
Romans
Hebrews
James & I Peter

In addition, the following books are available:

A Bible Believer's Bible Summary: How to Understand the Bible – Section 1 is a narrative of the Bible from beginning to end, while section 2 gives a one-sentence summary and a key verse from each book of the Bible. (84 pages)

Bible Per-VERSIONS: How Satan Changes God's Word to Lead You Astray – Over 850 Bible verses are listed in the KJV, NIV, NKJV, and NLT with comments to show how modern versions stray from the truth of God found in the KJV. A topical guide and an explanation of why modern versions are perverted are given. (248 pages)

How to Be Led by the Holy Spirit: Discerning God's Will for Your Life – This book examines a megachurch pastor's decision-making process, compares this process to scripture, and shows God's way to be led by the Spirit in making decisions in your life. (34 pages)

A Bible Believer's Critique of Ironside's "Wrongly Dividing the Word of Truth": A Defense of Paul's Mystery – (150 pages)

NOTE: The author highly recommends that you read his book entitled "A Bible Believer's Bible Summary" before you read this book on Romans, because you need to understand where Romans fits into God's edification process for today before you read the details of what Romans is all about. Nevertheless, I will now give you a very brief explanation of terms to give you some basic knowledge of where Romans fits into God's master plan.

Terms defined

In order to understand the foundational doctrine of Romans, we need to understand some fundamental terms that will be used in this book.

Dispensation: This is a "dirty" word among most Christians. However, all Christians are dispensationalists, whether they admit it or not. Moreover, it is not dirty, because it is a Biblical word. Paul uses the word in I Corinthians 9:17 to show that God committed to him "a dispensation of the gospel." (The word is also found in Ephesians 1:10, Ephesians 3:2, and Colossians 1:25.) As Paul uses it, God "dispensed" some new information to him that was not dispensed to man before given to Paul (Romans 16:25-26).

Most Christians will say that God gave some information to man in Genesis, and then He merely expanded on that same information throughout scripture. This idea is known as progressive revelation. In other words, Christianity says that God gave part A of the story in Genesis, part B later, part C later, etc., and that there is only one story told throughout scripture. While progressive revelation is a good doctrine and the idea of "one story" is true in a very broad sense, God "dispensed" different instructions to different people at different times.

It is impossible to follow all of these instructions. For example, in Genesis 1:29, God says that man may only eat fruits and vegetables. In Genesis 9:3, God says that man may eat fruits, vegetables, and any animal that he wants to. In Leviticus 11:4-43, God prohibits man from eating certain types of animals. In I Timothy 4:3-4, God says that man may eat any meat that he wants to. Therefore, you must recognize which dispensation in which you live in order to understand what you may eat.

Therefore, in order to understand scripture, it is absolutely essential that we recognize when God dispensed new instructions and to whom He dispensed these instructions. Otherwise, we will try to follow instructions that were not written to us and may end up never receiving eternal life, as a result. For example, in Genesis 2:17, God told Adam that the only way he would not have eternal life is if he ate of the tree of the knowledge of good and evil. If we believe God wrote this instruction to us today, we will believe that all people ever born after Adam will have eternal life with God, since the tree of the knowledge of good and evil does not exist today. Christians do not believe this today, which shows that, in practice, they believe dispensationalism is true, even if they will not admit this.

Another example is found in Genesis 15:4-6. There, God told Abram that He would make his seed as innumerable as the stars in heaven. We are then told that Abram "believed in the Lord; and He counted it to him for righteousness." Thus, Abram received the gift of eternal life here, but Christians today do not tell people that they will live forever in heaven if they believe that God will make their seed as innumerable as the stars in heaven. That is because Christians know that the gospel, that God has given us today, is different from the gospel that God gave to Abram. If we do not recognize this, we will think we have eternal life by believing Abram's gospel, and we will go to hell, as a result. Therefore, it is critical that we follow the command of II Timothy 2:15 to rightly divide the word of truth. This simply means that we need to divide the Bible into sections based upon the different dispensations of instructions that God has given man.

Prophecy and mystery; Israel and the body of Christ: When we divide the Bible into these sections, we find that the two main sections of scripture are "prophecy" and "mystery." Prophecy instructions are found in Genesis – Acts and Hebrews – Revelation, and mystery instructions are found in Romans – Philemon.

"In the beginning, God created the heaven and the earth. And the earth" (Genesis 1:1-2a). The very first verse of the Bible tells you that God created two realms, and the second verse tells you that He will now tell you about the earth. In Genesis 12:1-3, God calls Abram and promises to make of him a great nation. That nation ends up being Israel, and God says that He will make Israel a kingdom of priests to reconcile the earth back to Himself (Exodus 19:5-6). God continues to talk about the earth until we get to Acts 9. There, Paul is saved, and the Lord tells him a secret. That secret is that God also planned to reconcile the heaven back to Himself, and He will do so through a new group of people He is now going to save called "the body of Christ." This term is only found in Paul's epistles, which are Romans through Philemon ("Body of Christ" is found in Romans 7:4, I Corinthians 10:16, I Corinthians 12:27, and Ephesians 4:12), and Paul says that he was the first one placed into that body after Jesus' crucifixion (I Timothy 1:16). Therefore, those saved in Matthew, Mark, Luke, John, and Acts 1-8 are not part of the body of Christ. Thus, a new dispensation began with Paul in Acts 9.

Why did God keep this a secret until then? Because, had Satan and his forces known that God would reconcile the heaven back to Himself through Jesus' death on a cross, "they would not have crucified the Lord of glory" (I Corinthians 2:8). Thus, before Acts 9, God had prophets speak about His program to reconcile the earth back to Himself. Beginning with Acts 9, God had Paul, and others after him, proclaim the mystery about God's program to reconcile the heaven back to Himself. I use the term "mystery" in this book, because Paul uses "mystery" 10 times to describe God's instructions to us today (Romans 16:25, I Corinthians 2:7, Ephesians 3:3,4,9, 6:19,

Colossians 1:26-27, 2:2, 4:3).

Therefore, I will use the term "prophecy dispensation" or "Israel's program" to describe the set of instructions that God gives in His Word regarding reconciling the earth back to Himself. I will use the term "mystery dispensation" or the "body of Christ's program" to describe the set of instructions that God has given to us today in His Word regarding reconciling the heaven back to Himself. This distinction is most clearly recognized by seeing that Peter proclaimed that "which God hath spoken by the mouth of all His holy prophets since the world began" (Acts 3:21) (prophecy), while Paul proclaimed "the mystery, which was kept secret since the world began" (Romans 16:25). These are clearly two, different messages, or else God just lied to you, which He cannot do (Titus 1:2). Therefore, Paul did not preach the same message that Peter preached. This means that the great division in your Bible is not between the Old and New Testaments, but it is between the prophecy and mystery dispensations. (I recognize that there are other dispensations in the Bible than these two. However, in light of the subject matter of this book on Romans, a discussion of the other dispensations would not be that beneficial. If you understand the difference between prophecy and mystery, you are ahead of almost 100% of all Christians, and you will understand your Bible just by reading and believing it.)

Paul says, "consider what I say; and the Lord give thee understanding in all things" (II Timothy 2:7). Therefore, you must understand Paul's epistles before you can understand the rest of the Bible. Since Romans gives foundational doctrine, Romans is the first book you need to read and understand before you can understand the rest of the Bible. Therefore, you need to understand this introductory material before reading Romans. Otherwise, your preconceived notions from Christianity will lead you to incorrect conclusions regarding Romans, and you will spend all of your Bible study time "ever learning, and never able to come to the knowledge of the truth" (II Timothy 3:7).

Introduction

With this understanding, we can conclude that Romans through Philemon is the ONLY section of scripture that is written directly TO us today as members of the body of Christ. Since Romans begins this section, it gives foundational doctrine that you MUST understand before you try to understand any other book of the Bible. That is not to say that we should not read any other scripture outside of Romans through Philemon, because II Timothy 3:16 says that "ALL scripture is given by inspiration of God, and is profitable for doctrine, for reproof, for correction, for instruction in righteousness." Therefore, all scripture is profitable FOR us today, even though only Romans through Philemon was written directly TO us today.

II Timothy 3:16 also provides a basic outline of the Pauline epistles. Romans gives the DOCTRINE of justification by faith in the Lord Jesus Christ and that our sanctification is accomplished through allowing the Holy Spirit to teach us sound doctrine as we study God's Word rightly divided (II Timothy 2:15). I & II Corinthians then provides the REPROOF, or the error in living life apart from the sound doctrine of Romans. Galatians then provides the CORRECTION, which is correcting bad doctrine with the sound doctrine provided in Romans. Then, the cycle is repeated with Ephesians, Philippians, and Colossians. Ephesians gives the DOCTRINE of the Body of Christ in heavenly places, Philippians provides the REPROOF of error from not living out the sound doctrine concerning the Body of Christ, and Colossians CORRECTS false doctrine concerning the Body of Christ. I & II Thessalonians provides sound DOCTRINE concerning the rapture of the Body of Christ. There is no reproof or correction, since the rapture marks the end of the current dispensation of grace. I Timothy – Philemon are then provided as "instruction in righteousness" (II Timothy 3:16) in a church setting.

Romans – Galatians tells us how to live in Christ (faith).
Ephesians – Colossians gives us the motivation for living in Christ (charity).
I & II Thessalonians is when our living in Christ is fully realized (hope).
I Timothy – Philemon shows how godliness is manifest in the local church, with godliness being the combination of faith, charity, and hope (I Corinthians 13:13).

As such, Romans is foundational doctrine for those recently saved. **No one today can go on to deeper doctrine without first understanding the sound doctrine provided in Romans.** This sound doctrine consists of salvation by grace through faith in the Lord Jesus Christ and all that salvation entails, primarily that the flesh is buried with Christ upon receiving salvation (Romans 6) so that our sanctification can be accomplished by walking in the Spirit (Romans 8) and not fulfilling the lusts of the flesh (Romans 7).

Romans gives doctrine of what the cross of Christ means to people today. Romans 1:1 – 3:20 shows that all people are worthy of eternal damnation in the lake of fire. At least 90% of all people who attend church on a regular basis probably never learn this. Romans 3:21 – 5:21 shows that Jesus Christ's death, burial, and resurrection ALONE atone for the sins of all of those who believe this gospel, and that, upon believing, a person has "NOW [been] justified by His blood" and has "NOW received the atonement" (5:9,11). At least 90% of all people who understand Romans 1:1 – 3:20 probably never learn this. Romans 6 – 8, then, teaches that we have been baptized into Jesus' death and raised with Him into eternal life. Thus, we have the ability to allow the Holy Spirit to live through us so that we serve God, rather than serving our own flesh. At least 90% of all people, who understand Romans 1:1 – 5:21, probably never learn this.

Therefore, by my very conservative estimate, only 1 out of every 1,000 people, who regularly attend church for many years, will ever learn the foundational doctrine for today that is found in Romans 1-8. Since Paul says, "consider what I say; and the Lord give thee understanding in all things" (II Timothy 2:7), I conclude that no more than 0.1% of "Christians" use the mind of Christ necessary (Philippians 2:5) to understand spiritual truths found outside of Romans 1-8! Therefore, it is vital that we cover these chapters in detail in this commentary so that the reader will have the necessary foundation to learn advanced doctrine.

Romans 9 – 11 addresses what happened to Israel's program and brings both Israel's program and today's programs full circle, showing that, once "the fulness of the Gentiles be come in" (11:25), i.e., once the rapture takes place, Israel's program will pick back up, such that "all Israel shall be saved" (11:26). It also teaches us that we should have a sense of urgency to do God's will, since the dispensation of grace can end at any time (11:21). Romans 12:4-5 teaches that all people saved today are part of the body of Christ. Romans 12 – 16 shows how the practical application of Romans 1 – 8 doctrine is lived out, such that, if a local group of believers follow it, God will bruise Satan under their feet (16:20), regardless of how small that group of believers is. After all, one man, the Lord Jesus Christ bruised Satan's head (Genesis 3:15), and we are in Christ. Therefore, Christ can use us to bruise Satan under our feet.

Summary: Romans begins the section that is written to us today, and it explains that the cross means that we can have justification (3:21-31) and live in Christ (chapters 6-8) right now (5:9,11) by faith in Jesus' death, burial, and resurrection.

Key passage: 3:21-25 (21) But now the righteousness of God without the law is manifested, being witnessed by the law and the prophets; (22) Even the righteousness of God which is by faith of Jesus Christ unto all and upon all them that believe: for there is no difference: (23) For all have sinned, and come short of the glory of God; (24) Being justified freely by his grace through the redemption that is in Christ Jesus: (25) Whom God hath set forth to be a propitiation through faith in his blood, to declare his righteousness for the remission of sins that are past, through the forbearance of God;

1 Paul recognizes the Romans as saints (v. 7) because of what Jesus Christ did for them (vs. 3-4). Therefore, he wants to impart to them the "spiritual gift" (v. 11) of sound doctrine for today so that they are established in the faith (v. 12). The first step is to tell them that God's wrath will be poured out upon the world (v. 18), if they do not have the righteousness of God (v. 17). This is not a good situation for the Gentiles, because God: 1) Gave them up to adultery with the opposite sex due to their exaltation of creation above God (vs. 23-24), 2) Gave them up to homosexuality because they changed God's truth into a lie (vs. 25-27), and 3) Gave them over to all kinds of evil because they rejected everyone but themselves as God (vs. 28-32), thus, rebelling against the consciences God gave them. As such, chapter 1 brings the Gentiles guilty before God, subject to God's judgment of death against them (v. 32).

1:1 All those, who believe the gospel of grace today, are "called of Jesus Christ" (1:6). However, the Lord Jesus Christ specifically called Paul "to be an apostle." Specifically, he was called to be "the apostle of the Gentiles" (11:13), because God is now saving Gentiles through the gospel. Therefore, he was not the twelfth apostle to replace Judas Iscariot. Acts 1:20 says that the Psalms says that someone was to take Judas' position as the twelfth apostle. Therefore, they appointed two candidates (Acts 1:23), and the Lord Himself chose Matthias (Acts 1:24-26) as that twelfth apostle. This makes Paul an apostle outside of Israel's program, who is not of the 12 (I Corinthians 15:8-10).

Paul also says that he was "separated unto the gospel." Paul was called by God's grace and then separated by God to preach the gospel to the heathen, which are the Gentiles and unsaved Jews (Galatians 1:15-16). "The gospel of God" means the good news of God for the eternal life of man. As such, this is a general term that applies to all gospels that God gives to man in order to receive eternal life.

1:2 When Paul says that the gospel of God was "promised afore by His prophets in the holy scriptures," it does not mean that the gospel of grace was revealed in the Old Testament. Rather, it just means that God promised in the Old Testament to give eternal life to those who believe God's gospel to them. Regardless of what God required man to believe, in order to give man eternal life, the Lord Jesus Christ had to die for man's sins. In fact, when man first sinned, God promised to bring a redeemer to save man from his sin (Genesis 3:15). Therefore, from man's first sin in Genesis 3 and throughout the Old-Testament scriptures, God promised to give eternal life to those who believe Him, and that eternal life is only accomplished through the death of the Redeemer, the Lord Jesus Christ. Therefore, the promise of God, found in the Old Testament, is of that coming Redeemer.

1:3 Paul now explains that the Redeemer, promised by the Old-Testament prophets, turned out to be God's "Son, Jesus Christ our Lord." To redeem man, He had to be a man; therefore, He was of "the flesh." He was also "of the seed of David" to fulfill God's promises to the nation of Israel that the throne of David's son will be established forever (II Samuel 7:13). Jesus Christ also had to live a perfect life as a man, which means that He also had to be God. (Old-Testament prophecy said that He would be "God with us" (Isaiah 7:14 and Matthew 1:23).) Therefore, He is also God's Son.

1:4 As God, the Lord Jesus Christ has no beginning nor ending (Revelation 1:8). As man, He was born of a virgin (Matthew 1:23). That is why, "according to the flesh," He was "MADE" (1:3), but, as God, He was

"DECLARED to be the Son of God" (1:4). He has always been the Son of God (John 1:1-2), but it was not until His resurrection that God said, "This day have I begotten Thee" (Acts 13:33) as "His only begotten Son" (John 3:16). In other words, the Lord Jesus Christ was not "declared to be the Son of God" (1:4) until His resurrection. Jesus usually called Himself the "Son of man" (Matthew 8:20, 9:6, 10:23, etc.), and you will not see Jesus refer to Himself as the Son of God in Matthew – Luke. In fact, even when asked the direct question: "Art Thou then the Son of God?" Jesus responded, "YE SAY that I am" (Luke 22:70). That is because it was not until His resurrection that the Lord Jesus Christ had the power over death (I Corinthians 15:20,55-57). By living a perfect life ("the spirit of holiness"), the justice of God demanded that the Lord Jesus Christ not stay dead (Psalm 16:10). Therefore, He conquered death (Ephesians 1:19-20), giving Him power over death, as demonstrated by His "resurrection from the dead" (I Corinthians 15:20,55-57), such that God could now declare Him to be the Son of God.

Also, note that Jesus Christ had "the spirit of holiness" (1:4). He was holy because He had never sinned. God commanded Israel to "Be ye holy; for I am holy" (Leviticus 20:7 and I Peter 1:16). Jesus is the only One to ever fulfill that command. Therefore, when He went to the grave, He had "the spirit of holiness," which meant that the grave could not hold Him.

1:5-6 Ephesians 2:5, in referring to our pre-belief status, says that "we were dead in sins." However, because of the Lord Jesus Christ's power over death (1:4), once we believe, He raises us to life with Christ (Ephesians 2:5) by His grace.

The term apostle means "sent one." Once we are saved by grace, we are God's apostles. That is, we are sent to everyone we meet to reconcile them back to God (II Corinthians 5:18-20). That is why Paul modifies the word "apostleship" with "for obedience to the faith among all nations." "Among all nations" does not mean that we are to be missionaries to third-world countries. Rather, it just means that today's gospel is not confined to Israel, as it was for the 12 apostles (Matthew 10:5-6) in their dispensation. In other words, the gospel of the grace of God (Acts 20:24) is given today to all nations without respect of person (1:16).

Once we believe the gospel, we are raised from the dead, we receive eternal life, and we are sent by God to give the gospel to all people so that they also may receive eternal life (Believing the gospel is what is meant by "obedience to the faith." (See Romans 6:17 which says that, by believing the gospel, the Romans had "obeyed from the heart." Also see Romans 16:26, which says that the mystery has been "made known to all nations for the obedience of faith.")). This is our calling (1:6). Therefore, God does not confine the term "apostle" to the 12 of Israel's program or to Paul, but every believer, in the dispensation of grace, is called to be God's apostle.

"For His name" (1:5) should remind us of Philippians 2:9-11, which says that "every knee should bow...and...every tongue should confess that Jesus Christ is Lord," giving Jesus "a name which is above every name." WHEN you change your mind about Jesus determines your eternal state. If you change your mind while on the earth and trust in Jesus' death, burial, and resurrection as atonement for your sins, you have the gift of eternal life (6:23). If you change your mind and believe that Jesus Christ is Lord at the Great White Throne Judgment, you have eternal damnation in the lake of fire. Either way, God the Father is glorified in Jesus Christ's name being higher than everyone else. When you glorify God the Father on earth by believing the gospel, God gets the glory immediately, instead of having to wait to be glorified at the Great White Throne Judgment by sending you to hell for your unbelief. Of course, the former is a much better situation for you, as well.

1:7 Jesus Christ is God's beloved Son (Luke 9:35). Before we are saved, we are dead due to Adam's transgression (5:14-18). Once we believe the gospel, we are placed into Christ's death, burial, and resurrection, making us alive unto God (6:3-5,11). We are now "in Christ," instead of being "in Adam" (I Corinthians 15:22). Specifically, our lives are "hid with Christ in God" (Colossians 3:3). Therefore, we are "accepted in the beloved" (Ephesians 1:6), who is Christ, which makes us "beloved of God" (1:7).

We are also "called to be saints" (1:7). The word "called" is one of those magic words that Calvinists like to re-define to fit their belief system. We will go into detail in 8:30 about what "called" means. For now, we can recognize that the context tells us that the "called" are those who "have received grace and apostleship" (1:5). This means that the "called" are all saved individuals. A saint is someone holy, who has been separated from unbelievers by God. We are holy (Colossians 3:12) based upon Christ's death, burial, and resurrection for us. Therefore, all believers today are "called to be saints," not based on any work we did, but based exclusively on what Christ did for us and our trust in His work.

From Romans through II Thessalonians (Romans 1:7; I Corinthians 1:3; II Corinthians 1:2; Galatians 1:3; Ephesians 1:2; Philippians 1:2; Colossians 1:2; I Thessalonians 1:1; II Thessalonians 1:2), Paul starts every one of his epistles with the greeting of "grace and peace." ("Mercy" is added to the church epistles because church leaders also need God's mercy (I Timothy 1:2; II Timothy 1:2; Titus 1:4).) Christianity will tell you that "grace" was a common Greek greeting, and "peace" was a common Hebrew greeting. Therefore, "grace and peace" is just Paul's way of saying "hi" to his audience, both Gentile and Jew. However, this is NOT the case.

"Grace and peace" is an incredibly significant and surprising greeting, in light of the prophecy program. When Jesus Christ ascended to His Father, prophecy said that He was to sit at His Father's right hand "UNTIL I make Thy foes Thy footstool" (Acts 2:34-35; Psalm 110:1). In Acts 7:55, Stephen sees Jesus "standing on the right hand of God." Isaiah 3:13 says that "the

Lord standeth up to plead, and standeth to judge the people." Also, James 5:9 sees Jesus, as the judge, standing before the door of the sheepfold of Israel. Therefore, according to PROPHECY, when Jesus stood, He stood to bring judgment upon unbelievers. However, judgment did not come, because the world has continued on in unbelief to this day.

Rather, God had another plan, which was "the mystery, which was kept secret since the world began, But now is made manifest" (16:25-26). This mystery is "that the Gentiles should be fellowheirs, and of the same body, and partakers of His promise in Christ by the gospel" (Ephesians 3:6). In other words, when Jesus stood up, instead of dispensing judgment and wrath upon unbelievers, He began dispensing grace and peace. Specifically, He called Paul and committed unto him "a dispensation of the gospel" (I Corinthians 9:17). Because it was a mystery, Paul received the gospel, not "of man...,but by the revelation of Jesus Christ" (Galatians 1:11-12).

Therefore, when Paul starts his epistles with "grace and peace," he is not just saying "hi." Rather, he is proclaiming glad tidings that, instead of being cast into hell, God, in His grace, is giving peace (5:1) to all, who believe Paul's gospel for the gift of eternal life (6:23).

1:8 The Romans met in house churches, as at least five house churches are mentioned at the end of this epistle: 1) Priscilla and Aquilla (16:3-5), 2) Aristobulus (16:10), 3) Narcissus (16:11), 4) Brethren in 16:14, and 5) Brethren in 16:15. The point is that this epistles is written to various small groups of believers in Rome, yet Paul says that their "faith is spoken of throughout the whole world" (1:8)! He also says that God will bruise Satan under their feet shortly (16:20). This shows that there is such power in the gospel (1:16) that God can make a worldwide impact with a small group of believers.

1:9 Paul says that he serves God with his "spirit in the gospel of His Son" (1:9). Today, Christians say things like: "Christ died for me; the least I can do is live for Him." However, you cannot live for Him in the energies of your flesh. The flesh cannot please God (8:8), because in your flesh dwells NO good thing (7:18), not even after you are saved, because you still have a vile body (Philippians 3:21). You must walk in the Spirit to avoid following the lusts of your flesh (Galatians 5:16). You do this by believing God's Word, allowing the Holy Spirit to teach it to you (I Corinthians 2:9-14), and then obeying it by praying without ceasing (I Thessalonians 5:17), which means to talk constantly to God in your renewed mind (12:2) to work out everyday situations (Ephesians 6:17-18). Therefore, Paul does not say, "I serve God by what I do." Rather, he reckons his flesh to be dead (6:11; Colossians 3:3), recognizes that "Christ liveth in" him (Galatians 2:20), and serves God with his "spirit in the gospel of His Son" by praying for the Romans.

1:10 Paul's prayer to God is that he might see the Romans. Because of this constant prayer, Jesus told him that He would grant his request (Acts

23:11). Paul did finally make it to Rome in Acts 28:16 and spent two years receiving the Romans in his house (Acts 28:30-31).

1:11-12 Note that Paul's prayer is not a selfish one. He did not ask God for a nice vacation in Italy. Rather, he wants to come to Rome to impart unto them "some spiritual gift" (1:11). When the term "spiritual gift" is used, Christians automatically think of speaking in tongues, physical healings, or other gifts mentioned in I Corinthians 12-14. However, the "spiritual gift," that Paul wants to impart to the Romans, is one that will establish them, so that they are not "tossed to and fro, and carried about with every wind of doctrine" (Ephesians 4:14). This gift cannot be speaking in tongues, because no one is established in that. Rather, the "spiritual gift" is the "mutual faith" (1:12) of both Paul and the Romans in mystery doctrine for today.

This sets the purpose of the book of Romans as foundational doctrine for the current dispensation. Thus, Paul will cover our sin (1:1-3:20), our justification (3:21-5:21), and our sanctification (chapters 6-8) in the first, eight chapters of Romans, in order to impart this spiritual gift. Unfortunately, some Christians will seek to find out how they are "gifted" from God with something mentioned in Romans 12:6-8 or I Corinthians 12:8-10, while having no regard for the spiritual gift, that God seeks to give them in Romans 1-8, of be doctrinally established in Christ.

1:13 Paul had been wanting to come to the Romans but had been unable to do so. This is to our benefit, since he had to write down foundational, mystery doctrine, instead of speaking it to them. God preserved this for us, so that we also may be established in this doctrine. Also, note that Paul refers to "other Gentiles," which implies that the Romans are Gentiles, too.

1:14 The Greeks and the Barbarians were all Gentiles. The difference is that "the Greeks" were Gentiles with an education, while "the Barbarians" were uneducated Gentiles, as the last past of this verse defines the terms for you. The reason Paul is a debtor to all Gentiles is because "a dispensation of the gospel" was committed unto Paul. As such, "necessity is laid upon" him to preach the gospel (I Corinthians 9:16-17). Therefore, he owes a debt to all unsaved people to preach the gospel to them. This also shows that God is willing to save all people, regardless of how smart they are. In fact, it is often the unwise people, who believe the gospel, because "the world by wisdom knew not God" (I Corinthians 1:21).

1:15 Although Paul wrote to the saints in Rome, there were many lost people in Rome, and he has been commissioned by Christ to preach the gospel. Therefore, he wants to come to Rome for two purposes: 1) To show the saints that they need to count the flesh as dead and walk in the Spirit (chapters 6-8), and 2) To give the gospel to the unsaved in Rome (chapters 1-5).

1:16 Christians like to use this verse to say that we should proudly proclaim the gospel and not be ashamed that we are Christians. However, Paul's statement, that he is "not ashamed of the gospel of Christ," speaks more of the gospel's contents, than of Paul's boldness. In other words, in presenting the gospel, Paul is not like a used-car salesman trying to sell a lemon. Rather, his gospel "is the power of God unto salvation" (1:16). He has the best product ever! Therefore, there is no shame in proclaiming the gospel.

The reason, that Paul says that the gospel is "to the Jew first, and also to the Greek" (1:16), is because Jesus Christ sent Paul to all unsaved people (Acts 9:15). From Acts 9 until Acts 28, unsaved Jews were "diminishing" away (11:12), meaning that they still had an opportunity to hear and believe the gospel. When Paul went to a city, his "manner was" (Acts 17:1-2) to go to the Jewish synagogue first and then go to the Gentiles. Since Paul probably wrote the book of Romans around Acts 20:1-3, he was still following this pattern, which is why he says that the gospel is "to the Jew first, and also to the Greek" (1:16). (After Acts 28, he no longer followed this pattern.)

Paul uses the term "Gospel of Christ" (1:16), because the glad tidings are to trust in what Christ did—His death, burial, and resurrection—as atonement for sins. By contrast, the "gospel of God," from 1:1, is a general term that applies to all gospels for all dispensations. That is why the "gospel of God" was "promised afore by His prophets in the holy scriptures" (1:2), while no such notation is made regarding the gospel of Christ.

1:17-18 Paul is willing to use foolish looking preaching (I Corinthians 1:21) in proclaiming the gospel because of the predicament the world is in. "The wrath of God is revealed from heaven against all ungodliness and unrighteousness." Note that it is "revealed." It is revealed in His Word, but it is not actually on people yet, because, as believers, God has "delivered us from the wrath to come" (I Thessalonians 1:10). The way to avoid this wrath is to get God's righteousness, and the only way to get God's righteousness is by believing the gospel. Therefore, Paul does not mind using preaching, since it means that some people will believe the gospel and become righteous and not receive God's wrath upon them. Those, who never believe the gospel, will experience God's wrath upon them at the Great White Throne Judgment (Revelation 20:11-15).

The "faith to faith," in 1:17, refers to the two faiths necessary for salvation. When you place your faith in Christ, Who was faithful to go to the cross, you are saved. Thus, the righteousness of God comes upon man when man places HIS faith in CHRIST'S faith. The quote of "the just shall live by faith" comes from Habakkuk 2:4 in relation to not trusting in your own righteousness. Habakkuk 2:4 actually says, "the just shall live by HIS faith," which may indicate that a person becomes just by believing the gospel, and the reason that justification occurs is because of the faith of Jesus Christ. So, the verse may mean: "the just man shall live by Christ's faith." This means that the way you live for Christ is by Christ living in you. Galatians

2:20 conveys this same idea by saying, "Christ liveth in me: and the life which I now live in the flesh I live by the faith OF the Son of God, Who loved me, and gave Himself for me." Therefore, "the just shall live by faith" speaks both of the salvation of the person, i.e., his justness, and his sanctification, i.e., the way he lives, and BOTH are accomplished by Jesus Christ's faith. All we have to do is trust (our faith) in what He did for us, and Jesus Christ takes care of the rest (His faith).

The note, in 1:18, about holding "the truth in unrighteousness" refers to man's status before believing the gospel for salvation. Regardless of the dispensation, men have the opportunity to have faith in God, because God has revealed Himself to man, both externally and internally. God has revealed Himself to ALL men, as 1:19-20 and John 1:9. Therefore, all men hold the truth. Then, if they do not have faith in God, they are unrighteousness. Therefore, they "hold the truth in unrighteousness."

1:18-3:20 When God created Lucifer, he was "full of wisdom, and perfect in beauty" (Ezekiel 28:12). He was the anointed cherub over God's throne (Ezekiel 28:14). Then, his heart was lifted up, and he corrupted his wisdom because of his beauty (Ezekiel 28:17).

Man was created with even more beauty than Lucifer, because he was created in the image of God, which gave him a clothing of light (Psalm 104:2). He was also crowned with glory and honour, because God put him over His entire creation on earth (Genesis 1:26-27 and Psalm 8:5-8). This included having dominion over Satan, since Satan's fall made him a "beast of the field" (Genesis 3:1).

God told Adam that he would die the very day that he ate of the tree of the knowledge of good and evil (Genesis 2:17). Adam did die right then, because he lost his clothing of light, as seen by him being naked and ashamed after his sin (Genesis 3:7) when he was naked and unashamed before his sin (Genesis 2:25). At that time, Adam went from being a child of light to having darkness enter his soul via the sin nature. He also gained the knowledge of good and evil.

When Adam fell, God said that He would bring a redeemer to bruise Satan for him (Genesis 3:15). However, that redemption will only take place if man has faith in what God tells him (Hebrews 11:6). Just like with Lucifer, when man sinned, he corrupted his wisdom by reason of his beauty. If God left man alone with his sin nature, man would never have faith in God, because of man's corrupted wisdom. Therefore, at the same time that man received the sin nature he also received the knowledge of good and evil (After all, the fruit he ate came from that tree.). Man now has two choices. He can either listen to his conscience or listen to his sin nature. If he listens to his conscience, he will see that he is a sinner (7:13) and trust in God to redeem him. If he listens to his sin nature, he will deceive himself into thinking he is okay with God by doing "good" things that somehow cancel out the "evil" things (Jeremiah 17:9).

In 1:18-3:20, Paul will now prove to both Jew and Gentile that they need to listen to their conscience, rather than to their sin nature.

1:19-20 Unbelievers like to say that the gospel of believing in Jesus' death as atonement for your sins is unfair because it is unfair for God to throw into hell those who never hear this gospel. Christians respond by saying, "That is why we have got to send the gospel to the unreached nations. Once all nations hear the gospel, then Jesus Christ can come back. After all, Matthew 24:14 says, 'This gospel of the kingdom shall be preached in all the world for a witness unto all nations; and THEN shall the end come.' So, be sure to give every spare dime you have to missions so all the unreached people groups may hear the gospel." This "Christian" mentality takes a verse out of its context as an excuse to get more money into the pockets of the church leaders. If both unbelievers and Christians merely believe what is said in 1:19-20, their arguments would go away.

These verses state that, for those who never hear that Jesus died, was buried, and rose again as atonement for their sins, they are still accountable to God because God has given an internal gospel to every man. According to these verses, EVERY person, who has ever existed, knows that there is a God, that He created the world, that He has eternal power, and that there is a Godhead. (Revelation 14:6-7 calls this "the everlasting gospel.") The way that man verifies that this internal gospel is true is by examining the external evidence from creation. That is what is meant by "the invisible things of Him from the creation of the world are clearly seen, being understood by the things that are made" (1:20). In other words, God made the world as a pattern to represent the things of God. For example, the sun represents "the Sun of righteousness," Jesus Christ (Malachi 4:2), Who is "the true Light" (John 1:9). The moon, as a reflection of the sun's light, represents the bride of Christ, Israel. The stars represent the angels (Revelation 1:20). Therefore, man understands the invisible things of God and knows they exist by seeing the things in creation, such as the sun, moon, and stars, that represent those invisible things.

Many people will argue that there is no internal knowledge of God and that creation just happened by chance. In making such a statement, they are calling God a liar, because God says in these two verses that He has given this knowledge to all men. Since God cannot lie (Titus 1:2), I suggest believing what God says here. Therefore, billions of dollars do not need to be given to churches in order to get the gospel of grace to the unreached nations, because even a man on a deserted island can worship God as the Creator and God will give him eternal life for doing so. In fact, such a man is probably better off not being reached by Christian missionaries, because most missionaries will not present a clear gospel to him. Therefore, if he believes what the missionaries say, he will go to hell for believing a false gospel, when he could have at least believed the internal gospel he had from

God and be saved. The fact, that all men know there is a God, also proves that those, who claim to be atheists, are the liars, not God. They "oppose themselves" (II Timothy 2:25), keeping themselves from receiving the free gift of eternal life from God by, in their pride, emphatically denying what they know to be true.

1:21-32 The rest of chapter 1 presents a three-step, progressive slide away from God. It occurred in history, as seen in the Tower of Babel in Genesis 11. However, it also can be seen in the fall of societies over time.

1:21 In spite of the internal and external evidence of God, man did not worship God as the Creator. The reason is because of man's pride. He became vain in his imaginations. Jesus called the Pharisees children of the devil (John 8:44). The reason is because the devil was the first to become vain in his imaginations, making five "I will" statements in Isaiah 14:12-14, culminating in his declaration that he will be "like the most High," Who is the "possessor of heaven and earth" (Genesis 14:19). Man, in his vain imaginations, does the same thing, ignoring the evidence for God and declaring himself to be god. It is no coincidence, then, that, as Christians, when we bring "into captivity every thought to the obedience of Christ," we are "casting down imaginations, and every high thing that exalteth itself against the knowledge of God" (II Corinthians 10:5).

When man refused to believe God, his "foolish heart was darkened" (1:21). So, the light of God, that everyone is created with (John 1:9), became dark because his "foolish heart" said there is no God (Psalm 14:1 and 53:1). Note that this verse does not say that man stopped knowing God. It just says that his "foolish heart was darkened," meaning that there was now darkness with the light in man's heart. This means that man can still be saved if he repents of this first step in the downward spiral of sin.

1:22-23 Man chose to continue to follow his sin nature ("became vain in their imaginations") rather than believing the message of his conscience that he is a sinner. This sin-nature path presents a problem because man knows he must answer to his conscience due to the external witness of creation and the internal witness that there is a God Who is higher than man (1:19-20). Therefore, all three steps of the downward spiral of sin have to do with getting rid of God and replacing Him with the self.

Since God made creation, man's first step in getting rid of God is making his own creation. Christians will say that this verse refers to physical idols. That way, they can say that they do not do that themselves because they do not make and bow down to physical idols. However, this verse says that they turn "the uncorruptible God into AN IMAGE made like to corruptible man, and to birds, and four-footed beasts, and creeping things" (1:23). If physical idols were in view, this verse would say "images made like...," not "AN IMAGE made like...." Therefore, the image, that man makes, is one of the entire creation being God. That is why the theory of evolution is so prevalent in the "civilized world" today. Man has turned the uncorruptible God into an image of the world evolving out of nothing. Thus, man uses his "wisdom" (1:22) to make his own creation so that the external matches his own internal vain imaginations. In other words, man says, "I am God, because, in my mind, I can create whatever I want to create."

1:24 Man is "desperately wicked" (Jeremiah 17:9), which means that, left to himself, man will "work all uncleanness with greediness" (Ephesians 4:19). Left to himself, man will just continue to get more and more vile and more and more wicked. The result would be that man would completely destroy himself. Therefore, God holds back man's wickedness. The reason we know this is that, at each stage of the downward spiral of sin, God's response is to give them up (1:24), give them up (1:26), and give them over (1:28) to further sin. Therefore, the implication is that God, in His grace, must be restraining man's sin somehow. Then, when man falls to a new level, God gives man over to more sin so that he can fall to a newer low, hoping that he will allow his conscience to recognize this new low. He will then see his depravity and listen to his conscience, rather than his sin nature, resulting in having faith in what God has told him. In other words, if God fully gave man over to his sin nature right away, man would destroy himself and all would go to hell. By giving man over to sin in stages, God wants man's conscience to be triggered so that his pride is crushed and he trusts in God for his salvation.

Now, remember that man elevated himself to god status. Therefore, God will have to lower man's status at each stage in hopes that man sees that man is not God. I Corinthians 6:18 says, "Flee fornication. Every sin that a man doeth is without the body; but he that committeth fornication sinneth against his own body." Therefore, the only way to sin against your own body, thereby lowering your status, is by committing fornication, which is sexual sin.

So, now, we need to define sexual sin. I Corinthians 6:15-16 says that, when two people have sex, even when a man has sex with a harlot, the two people become one. In Matthew 19:6, Jesus says that, when this happens, God actually joins the two together. In other words, by having sex, two people agree to join themselves together for life, and so God joins them together when they have sex. Romans 7:2-3 says that this union is in effect until one of them dies. Furthermore, Genesis 2:23-24 and Matthew 19:4-5 define this union as being in effect only between a man and a woman. Therefore, the first time that a man and a woman have sex, God joins them together as husband and wife for life. Therefore, sexual sin is having sex outside of this relationship. (I realize there are issues and reasons for marriage beyond a first marriage. However, since the purpose of our discussion is to define sexual sin, we will not go into those issues at this time.)

We have now established that: 1) God is going to punish man by lowering man's status, 2) Man's status can only be lowered by sexual sin, and 3) Sexual sin is sex that is not between a husband and a wife. Therefore, God's punishment at the first stage of sin is to give man over to adultery with members of the opposite sex. That is what is described here in 1:24.

In other words, God says, "Because you have replaced 'the uncorruptible God' with an image made like creation (1:23), I will corrupt your image further by allowing your sin nature to make you sin against your own body by committing adultery with members of the opposite sex."

1:25 1:20 told us that, the way that man knew the truth of God, was through His creation. Because man chose to follow his sin nature, he made his own creation of an image that is like creation. Man now sees that image, and so, in his mind, he has "changed the truth of God into a lie" (1:25). Since he has eliminated God from his mind, man now has to replace God with something else. Because this is just the first stage of the downward spiral of sin, man is not yet egotistical enough to declare himself alone to be God. Instead, he thinks that the opposite sex is God. Therefore, he determines that he will be more godlike if he is with multiple members of the opposite sex. Now, I realize that, if you ask a person who has committed adultery why they did it, they will not give you that answer. But, that is because they have a deceitful heart (Jeremiah 17:9). God gives us the real reason here, and we need to believe God above man.

Thus, man worships the creature by having sex with another creature like himself that he has deemed to be more godlike than he is, because the other creature is of the opposite gender.

So, in the first step of sin, man makes his own creation in his mind to replace the knowledge of the true creation that God has given him. Since he has now effectively eliminated God from his thinking, in the second step of sin, he creates the god of the opposite sex.

1:26-27 Due to this second type of sin by man, God gives man a second punishment, which is a progression of the first. First, man rejected the true God and accepted the opposite sex as God. However, because men and women think differently and man is prideful in thinking that he is God, it does not take long for man to realize that the opposite sex is not God. Yet, in his pride, man still thinks that he is God. Therefore, God's punishment for man's second step of sin is homosexuality. Man now rejects the opposite sex as God and embraces the same sex as God. Therefore, men think other men are God, and women think other women are God. Now, they may not be consciously thinking this or admit to it, but, spiritually speaking, that is what they are doing by committing the sin of homosexuality. Therefore, you see homosexual relationships prevailing. This is a further lessening of the value of man's body, because a homosexual relationship is having sex with a member of the same gender, when the only sexual relationship that is not a sin is marriage between a man and a woman.

1:28-31 After awhile though, man realizes that, although members of the same sex think like they do, they still do things that get on their nerves. The fault, of course, must be with the other person, not with themselves. Therefore, the final step is that man rejects other members of the same sex as being God, and each man thinks of himself as God. Therefore, the transformation from God being God to each person being his own god is now complete.

Since each individual man alone is God, he can now do whatever he wants to do. Since, "the heart is deceitful above all things, and desperately wicked" (Jeremiah 17:9), man does wicked things, which are listed, in part, in verses 29-31. Man gives no regard to others, because man is his own god; therefore, others are inferior and not important.

This is the state that the world fell into during the days of Noah. Genesis 6:5 says, "And GOD saw that the wickedness of man [was] great in the earth, and [that] every imagination of the thoughts of his heart [was] only evil continually." Thus, we see the progression of rebellion against God from verse 22 through verse 31. First, man says he is God; therefore, he makes his own creation in his mind and goes into sexual sin. Second, man says only his gender is God; therefore, he goes into homosexuality. Third, man says that he alone is God; therefore, he does not obey anyone and only does the wicked desires of his heart.

Note that 1:24 says that "God also gave them up to uncleanness," and 1:26 says that "God gave them up unto vile affections." However, 1:28 says that "God gave them OVER to a reprobate mind." In other words, once a society has the widespread acceptance of homosexuality, they have gone as low as they can go. Therefore, the last punishment is that God gives them over completely to their sinful minds. There is nothing more that God can do. That is why, when Sodom and Gomorrah were completely involved in homosexuality (Genesis 19:4-5), God destroyed them (Genesis 19:24-25).

In the United States, in the 1950s and 1960s, we saw the first step take place, where man engaged in sexual fornication, sleeping with multiple partners of the opposite sex. Today, in 2017, homosexuality has been accepted by society as a whole, which shows that we are close to the final stage, when God gives society over to a reprobate mind. This results in complete rebellion against God as each person thinks he is his own god, entitling him to do whatever he wants to do. However, we should note that, while society as a whole has accepted homosexuality, that does not mean that everyone is doomed to fall prey to it. For example, Lot did not involve himself in that sin, and God spared him from being destroyed along with Sodom and Gomorrah. Therefore, even in a society filled with reprobate minds, individuals can still recognize their sin, believe the gospel, and receive the gift of eternal life.

We should also note the error of the modern argument that homosexuality should be accepted because homosexuals are born that way. Being "born that way" is not an excuse to engage in sinful behavior. Since we are all born with a sin nature, if we do what we are born to do, all we will do is sin. However, since society recognizes that homosexuals are born that way, rather than trying to disprove that assertion, we should try to get them to see that they are also born sinners. They will then see that they cannot receive eternal life on their own merits, and so they need to believe the gospel instead. Therefore, rather than trying to say that no one is born a homosexual, we should, instead, say that all of us are born sinners, and we need to trust in Jesus' death, burial, and resurrection alone to atone for our sins so that we may receive the free gift of eternal life from God.

In the introduction to this section, I mentioned that, historically speaking, the three steps of the downward spiral of sin happened in Genesis 11 with the Tower of Babel. What I mean by that is that, at the time, man had gone through all three steps of the downward spiral of sin. Man did this in Noah's day, as well. God destroyed man, at that time, and man was now in the same predicament in Genesis 11, as he was in Noah's day. Since destroying man did not stop the sin cycle from happening again, God did something different at this time. He created nations, scattering man across the whole earth (Genesis 11:7-8). Five generations later, God began a new nation from Abram. This nation was the nation of Israel, which is not to be reckoned among the nations (Numbers 23:9).

Therefore, when God says that he "gave them over to a reprobate mind" (1:28), historically speaking, God gave the whole world over to a reprobate mind at the Tower of Babel in Genesis 11. His creation of nations added a level of authority to keep the entire world from being united in their rebellion against God again (However, united man will rebel against God one more time, and that time is under the Antichrist's rule for the last 3 ½ years of the tribulation period.). Then, five generations later, God started His nation, the nation of Israel, with Abram. Therefore, historically speaking, 1:21-32 applies to the Gentiles. This is important to note because, in chapter 2, Paul will address the Jews (2:17), showing that they are also guilty before God. Then, in chapter 3, he will be able to reach his conclusion that all the world is guilty before God (3:19).

1:29-31 In this list of 23 things, "disobedient to parents" may stand out as something that is not nearly as bad as the others. However, when we see the context is rebellion, we can see that being disobedient to parents is one of the greater sins on the list. The other sins show a lack of respect of the laws of the land, but being disobedient to your parents is a higher level of disrespect and lawlessness, rebelling, not just against mankind as a whole, but against the very people who brought you into this world. This means that you will teach a new level of immorality to the next generation, who, when they disobey you, will introduce yet another new level of immorality to their generation.

That is why "Honour thy father and thy mother" (Exodus 20:12) is "the first commandment with promise" (Ephesians 6:2). That promise is that Israel's days may be long upon the land which God gives them (Exodus 20:12). On the other hand, if Israel disobeys their parents, each generation will introduce a new level of immorality, which will cause God to kick them out of their land more quickly.

Another item to note from this list is "haters of God" (1:30). "They did not like to retain God in their knowledge" (1:28). Therefore, they declared that "there is no God" (Psalm 14:1 and 53:1). Yet, they really know that there is a God, because they hate God, and you cannot hate someone who does not exist! As such, they are "haters of God," not "haters of the idea of God," as they would have you believe.

"Implacable" (1:31) is a great word to sum up those, who God has given over to a reprobate mind. They have such anger toward God that their anger cannot be stopped. Yet, "God is love" (I John 4:8). I John 4:8 does not say that God is loving, but it says that God is love. He defines what love is. "God commendeth His love toward us, in that, while we were yet sinners, Christ died for us" (5:8). Yet, man becomes implacable toward God. This shows how truly evil man can become when he determines to follow his sin nature, such that he is unstoppably angry at love.

And, that is why God gives up on them. People will say, "Oh, God never gives up on anyone." But, 1:28-31 says otherwise. Granted, we do not know if God has given up on someone, and so we should not give up on a person's salvation. However, God, in His wisdom, knows if a person's anger toward Him will never be stopped. Note the statement by God regarding mankind at the Tower of Babel: "Now nothing will be restrained from them, which they have imagined to do" (Genesis 11:6). In other words, they have reached the point of no return, where they will always do evil things, in spite of God's love. Therefore, the only thing God can do is give them over to a reprobate mind (1:28).

1:32 In spite of man's great fall from God, man still has the knowledge of God that He placed within man of His eternal power and Godhead and outside of man with His creation (1:19-20). Therefore, although man has convinced himself that he is God, he still knows that the sins he commits against God have made him worthy of God's judgment of death against him. Remember that man never forgets God; he just becomes a hater of God (1:30). Thus, no matter how bad off man gets, the knowledge of God still remains with him. This is seen in that, before the tribulation period is over, man blasphemes the name of God (Revelation 16:9,11). Then, shortly after, at Jesus' second coming, these same men proclaim: "Hide us from the face of Him that sitteth on the throne, and from the wrath of the Lamb: For the great day of His wrath is come; and who shall be able to stand?" (Revelation 6:16-17). Therefore, in spite of all of his efforts, man, even at his worst, still knows he is worthy of death because of his sin.

The final thing that man can do to try to get rid of that guilty conscience is to "have pleasure in them that do them" (1:32). In other words, man tries to justify his sins against God by saying that what he is doing is okay because "everyone else does it." Thus, the pleasure he obtains from others' sins is that it helps ease his guilty conscience so that he can continue sinning. This is the human evil side of things. This is why the news media talks about all of the bad things that are happening, but they rarely mention any good things. The human good side, where man tries to justify himself in the sight of God by the good things he does, is seen in the religion that man creates. In other words, the human good side of man says that he is okay, although he has done some sins, because they are cancelled out by the good things of his religion.

People say that the two things you do not want to talk about with others are politics and religion. The reason is because politics talks about the human evil side of man (what is wrong with society), and religion deals with the human good side of man (what man can do to rise above society's evils). So, each person has it worked out in his own mind how to deal with both sides. Then, someone comes along with a different point of view, and man is offended because the view is against his own view. So, he vehemently defends his own view, starting an argument. And, all of this started with man not glorifying God (1:21).

2 Those, not believing the gospel given to them by God, whatever gospel that may be, will be judged according to the law (v. 6). They must keep the law perfectly to receive eternal life (v. 7). Consequently, no man will be saved by keeping the law (3:20,23). This applies to the Jew, as well as the Gentile (v. 9). The Gentile has the law of the conscience (vs. 14-15), while the Jew also has the Mosaic law. Jews have the problem of resting in the law (v. 17), rather than learning the lesson of the law that they are sinners so that God may circumcise their hearts (vs. 28-29). Thus, the Jews have blasphemed God's name among the Gentiles (v. 24), instead of bringing glory to God.

2:1 Through the three-step progression into sin that we read about in 1:22-32, we saw man judging. He judged God not to be God, he judged members of the opposite sex not to be God, and he judged members of the same sex not to be God. Man now thinks that he alone is God. Therefore, Paul seeks to correct this faulty thinking. In this one verse, Paul condemns man by his own thinking. In other words, since man judged all others as not being God, man now must judge himself not to be God, because he is guilty of committing the same sins that all others committed. Therefore, no member of the human race is God.

However, each man still thinks he is okay with God. Why? Because "the heart is deceitful above all things, and desperately wicked: who can know it?" (Jeremiah 17:9). Man cannot know his own heart, and so man's heart will deceive himself into thinking he is okay with God. For example, man will hear of someone who raped someone else and say in his heart, "I am okay

23

because I have never done that." Yet, he will lust after a woman in his heart, committing rape with her in his heart, which Jesus says makes him guilty of adultery (Matthew 5:28). This man will also hear of someone who has killed another person and say in his heart, "I am okay because I have never done that." Yet, he will be angry with someone without a cause, and Jesus says that anger causes him to be in danger of the judgment, as if he actually killed the person (Matthew 5:22). In other words, man justifies his own sin by seeing someone commit something he deems as being worse than his sin, making himself okay in his own sight. Yet, God says that "whosoever shall keep the whole law, and yet offend in one point, he is guilty of all" (James 2:10).

Man deceives himself into thinking he is okay (Jeremiah 17:9). But, "all things are naked and opened unto the eyes of Him [God] with Whom we have to do" (Hebrews 4:13). Therefore, God sees "that every imagination of the thoughts of [man's] heart [is] only evil continually" (Genesis 6:5). Man needs to see this, as well, so that he may see his wickedness and believe the gospel, that God has given him, so that he receives eternal life. Hebrews 4:12 tells us that "the Word of God...is a discerner of the thoughts and intents of the heart." Man used his own thoughts to try to get rid of his knowledge of God that God gave him in his heart (1:19-20). Now, in 2:1-15, Paul will show that, in doing so, man broke the law of the conscience, which means that he is guilty before God.

"Wherein thou judgest another, thou condemnest thyself; for thou that judgest doest the same things" (2:1). This is a great statement against society regarding whatever evil they want to push. Today, we are told that we cannot judge homosexuals and transgenders as sinners. However, in telling us that, such people are condemning themselves, because they are judging us by saying that we cannot judge them. On the other hand, we do have the right to judge them because God is the judge (Psalm 50:6), and we are in Christ (Colossians 3:3). Therefore, we can judge all things and be judged of no man ourselves (I Corinthians 2:15), while they have no right to judge because they are not in Christ, and "the natural man receiveth not the things of the Spirit of God" (I Corinthians 2:14).

2:2-3 Since no man is God, God must be God. Therefore, man is subject to the judgment of God, and the judgment of God is against all of mankind, because all have broken the law of the conscience that God wrote into man's heart (2:14-15).

Note how "the judgment of God is according to truth" (2:2), and all men "hold the truth" (1:18), because God "hath shewed it unto them" (1:19) "so that they are without excuse" (1:20). Therefore, God's judgment is fair. When God judges unbelievers to the lake of fire, not a single person will be able to say: "But I did not know. Missionaries from America never came to my nation, and so I never heard about Jesus' death as atonement for my sins." Rather, all people know of God and that He is worthy of their worship.

If they choose to ignore this truth, God will fairly judge them into the lake of fire.

2:4 Now that Paul has established that all men are subject to the judgment of God, the natural question from man is, "Where is this judgment of God? I haven't been judged by God." That is why Paul now says that God has been good in forbearing His judgment, leading man into repentance. "The Lord is not slack concerning His promise, as some men count slackness; but is longsuffering to us-ward, not willing that any should perish, but that all should come to repentance" (II Peter 3:9).

The problem is that man looks at God's delay of judgment and says that judgment is not coming. "Because sentence against an evil work is not executed speedily, therefore the heart of the sons of men is fully set in them to do evil" (Ecclesiastes 8:11). However, God's delay is His mercy, not His lack of power to judge man. Paul says in I Timothy 1:16 that the whole dispensation of grace is the longsuffering of God "to them which should hereafter believe on Him to life everlasting." If not for God's longsuffering, He would have destroyed this world a LONG time ago!

2:5-6 An "impenitent heart" is one that does not repent. Therefore, the men Paul is talking about are those who have never believed the gospel because they never changed their mind. Therefore, they are relying upon their own righteousness to have eternal life, and not relying upon God's righteousness for salvation. Therefore, they will be part of the Great White Throne Judgment of Revelation 20:11-15. This judgment is "according to their works," according to Revelation 20:12-13, which matches what Paul says here that God "will render to every man according to his deeds." This is the "righteous" judgment of God, because God does what is right. Those meeting a perfect, holy standard receive eternal life, while those not meeting this standard receive eternal death. Revelation 20:14 says that every person, who is part of this judgment, will be "cast into the lake of fire."

2:5 says that those, who use their "impenitent heart," are treasuring up for themselves wrath. This shows that there are varying degrees of punishment in hell, as seen in Luke 20:47, where Jesus says that the religious leaders, "which devour widows' houses, and for a shew make long prayers: the same shall receive GREATER damnation." Therefore, while all unbelievers will be cast into hell because of their sin, those, who follow their impenitent heart more than others, will receive a greater punishment in hell than the others will. Thus, they are treasuring up for themselves wrath. The natural assumption may be that murderers, rapists, and child molesters would receive more wrath than others. However, the standard is not how "bad" the sins are. The standard is how much the impenitent heart is used by the person. This means that, the more a person shuts out the witness of God, the more that person will receive God's wrath. The people, who do this the most, are religious people. The murderer knows he is a bad person and may believe the gospel if you present it to him. However, the Pope would never believe the gospel because, doing so would mean he would lose his job, which means he would lose his power, money, and lifestyle. Therefore, the Pope will use his impenitent heart, more than the murderer will, because he justifies himself more by putting up the front that he is a good person. Thus, the Pope will receive more of God's wrath in hell than the man executed by the government for his great crimes against society will receive.

2:7 Paul will show, in 3:28, that justification is by faith alone, apart from works. Those, who try to throw works into the mix, usually respond to 3:28 by saying that Paul does not mean that salvation is received apart from works because of what he says here in 2:7. However, that is taking these verses out of context, mixing a complete-works salvation (2:7) with a complete-faith salvation (3:28). In 1:18 - 3:20, Paul is establishing that no one is righteous on his own (3:10), so that man will see that he needs God's imputed righteousness for eternal life. Therefore, the context, here, is God's righteous judgment of those who rely upon their own works to receive eternal life.

"Patient continuance in well doing" means not once straying away from worshipping God as Creator and perfectly obeying the law of the conscience (2:14-15). In other words, it means living a perfect life. Anyone, who lives a perfect life, will receive eternal life. The point is that no one meets this perfect standard, as God says in Revelation 20:14. Therefore, the only way man has eternal life is by receiving it as a gift from God (6:23), rather than by earning it.

As a side note, this verse is important to show why Jesus Christ's soul was not left in hell after He died on the cross (Psalm 16:10). He went to hell to pay the wages of our sin (6:23), but Jesus Christ Himself "did no sin" (I Peter 2:22). Therefore, Jesus Christ is the only man who never sinned, which means that He had "patient continuance in well doing," which means that the justice of God demanded that He be raised from the dead to receive eternal life. Since all believers have been "baptized into Jesus" Christ's death (6:3), all believers have eternal life in Christ, as a result of Christ's perfect life and sacrifice for us.

2:8-9 Those, who do not believe the gospel, do not receive Christ's life. Therefore, they will be judged on whether or not they lived a perfect life. Because "there is none righteous, no, not one" (3:10), all people judged by their works, except Jesus Christ, will receive "indignation and wrath, tribulation and anguish." The point Paul is making is that, if the reader takes an HONEST look at himself, he will realize that, what is said about him in 1:21-32, is true, making him worthy of death. Essentially, he has now been told that God will judge him to death. Therefore, the honest man knows by now that he is in a status of eternal separation from God. This makes him primed to receive the gospel of salvation by grace through the faith of Christ that Paul presents in Romans 3.

Note that the people, who receive "indignation and wrath, tribulation and anguish," are those who "do not obey the truth" (2:8). Remember, from 1:5, that we said that believing the gospel is what is meant by "obedience to the faith," as also seen in 6:17. 1:18-20 says that all men "hold the truth" because God has shewed the truth to them. Therefore, obeying the truth simply means believing what God has shown them. This means that all people, even those who have never heard the gospel of grace and have never heard or read any passage of scripture, may receive the gift of eternal life by just believing what God has already shown to them in their heart and in creation. Therefore, those, who "do not obey the truth" (2:8), are all unbelievers, because obeying the truth has nothing to do with our works, but it has everything to do with faith. Therefore, all believers obey the truth, and all unbelievers do not obey the truth. They "obey unrighteousness" (2:8).

If we do not understand this now, it will be very difficult to understand justification by faith alone when we get to 3:28. We have to abandon the mentality that God is pleased or displeased by the works we do. Hebrews 11:6 says that God is only pleased by faith. We have also seen, from 1:18-32, that wickedness stems from unbelief in the heart. Jesus said, "for from within, out of the heart of men, proceed evil thoughts, adulteries, fornications, murders....All these evil things come from within, and defile the man" (Mark 7:21-23). Therefore, the cause of man's sin is a defiled heart, and the gift of eternal life comes from an undefiled heart. The undefiled heart is the one that believes the truth that God has shown man. Therefore, eternal life is a heart issue, not a works issue. If man believes the truth, he receives eternal life. If man does not believe, he receives eternal damnation.

2:9-10 The Gentiles were only given the law of the conscience (2:14-15). The Jews were also given "the oracles of God" (3:2), which is the Mosaic law. This gave the Jews an advantage because they have more opportunities to see their sin (7:13).

Now, in the dispensation of grace, the middle wall of partition between Jew and Gentile has come down (Ephesians 2:14), which means that God treats all men equally. However, at the time that Romans was written, the Jewish religion was still in existence, and they were the only ones who read God's Word in their religious services. They did not believe the Bible, because they crucified their Messiah (Matthew 27:25), but they would, at least, let someone read and explain the Bible in their synagogues (Acts 13:15). Since God sent Paul to all people—both Jews and Gentiles—(Acts 9:15), Paul would go into a Jewish synagogue first (Acts 17:2), where he could explain Jesus as the Messiah, using Old-Testament scriptures. Then, after the Jews kicked him out, he would go to the Gentiles. If he went to the Gentiles first, they would have associated him with the Jews, since Paul was an Old-Testament toting Jew (Acts 22:3), and would not have listened to him. But, if he went to the Gentiles last, he could tell them that the Jews kicked him out. This would tell the Gentiles that his message was not something the Jews believed, and so the Gentiles would then listen to what he said, realizing that it was a new thing (Acts 17:19-20). Thus, in Acts 9-28, before Israel had diminished away, Paul would go to the Jews with the gospel and then he would go to the Gentiles. That is why these verses say, "of the Jew first, and also of the Gentile."

An equivalent to this today would be if we went into a Christian church to speak the gospel. They would kick us out because God's gospel does not conform to the Christian religion. Then, we could go to people outside of the church. If those people try to stop us from speaking by saying, "I don't believe that because Christians are prideful hypocrites," we can let them know that what we are saying is banned from XYZ church. Maybe they will then at least listen to what we have to say.

As mentioned in the commentary on 2:8-9, the heart is the issue. So, unbelievers are said to do evil (2:9), because they have an evil heart. Believers have faith in God, but that does not mean that they will never sin, because they still have the sin nature with them. However, they do have the gift of eternal life (6:23), a live spirit (Ephesians 2:1), and the Holy Spirit in them (5:5). When they believe God's Word, they walk in the Spirit (8:4-5), and their spirits "worketh good" (2:10) within them. These would be the works of faith. They may not necessarily "do good" because of their vile bodies (Philippians 3:21). That is why "WORKETH good" is used for believers, but "DOETH evil" is used of unbelievers, because their spirits are dead, meaning that there is no one inside them to work good within them. In other words, because unbelievers are dead in their sins, they always do evil, but believers have the Holy Spirit working good within them, and they also do good if they walk in the Spirit.

2:11 Regardless of dispensation, God has never been a respecter of persons. Granted, God gave the Mosaic law to Israel only (3:2). Deuteronomy 4:8 says, "what nation is there so great, that hath statutes and judgments so righteous as all this law." However, that does not mean that God gives eternal life to Jews and eternal damnation to Gentiles, just because the Jews have the Mosaic law. The law is given to teach people to have faith in God (Galatians 3:24). If the Gentiles learn that lesson with just the law of the conscience (2:14-15), then they are saved. If the Jews do not learn that lesson, in spite of having both the conscience and the Mosaic law, they are not saved (2:22-24). Again, faith is the issue, not works. Therefore, although God treated Jews and Gentiles in time past differently, by setting up the middle wall of partition between them with circumcision and the Mosaic law, when it comes to judgment, God will judge all people based upon faith. If they believed whatever God told them, they will receive eternal life. If they did not believe whatever God told them, they will receive eternal damnation. The information that God told them is not the issue, and their works are not the issue. Faith is the issue.

2:12 "Sin is not imputed when there is no law" (5:12). Therefore, "without law" (2:12) does not mean that the Gentiles had no law to follow. If that were the case, they will not receive punishment for sin. As will be explained in 2:13-15, they had the law of the conscience. Since they disobeyed that law, sin will be imputed to them for their disobedience of the law of their conscience, if they did not have faith in what God told them about Himself (1:18-20). Thus, "law," in this verse, is a reference to the Mosaic law. Therefore, the Gentiles sin by not obeying the law of the conscience and so they will perish without the law. The Jews "sinned in the law," and so they will perish for their disobedience of the Mosaic law. Either way, all unbelievers perish because they failed to believe God's gospel to them, in spite of the evidence God gave them through law, whether conscience or Mosaic, that they were not righteous on their own. Thus, God is no respecter of persons.

The reason Paul brings up the Mosaic law is because the Jews rested in it (2:17). They thought they were saved just because God gave them the law. Therefore, Paul has to show that the Jews do not receive eternal life just because God gave them the Mosaic law. Even religious Jews can still be children of the devil (John 8:44)!

2:13-15 In time past, the Jews had an advantage over the Gentiles because "unto them were committed the oracles of God" (3:2). In other words, they had an enhanced opportunity to see their sin so that they might believe God's gospel to them. However, instead of allowing the law to show them that their sin nature is "exceeding sinful" (7:13), they rested in the law (2:17), thinking that they would make it into God's kingdom just because they were given God's law. (This is akin to thinking that God will give you eternal life because you have the knowledge of good and evil from the fruit that Adam ate!) They also thought that the Gentiles would automatically not be a part of God's kingdom because they did not have the law. Both conclusions are incorrect.

Paul clears this up, saying that it is the doers of the law who shall be justified, not the hearers of the law. So, having the Mosaic law committed unto them does not give the Jews a free pass into God's kingdom. Meanwhile, the Gentiles have "the work of the law written in their hearts," which means that they do the things contained in the law, i.e., they disobey the law. (This concept will be explained in 7:8-13. In summary, the sin nature works with the law to cause you to sin, so that you will see your sin and your need for a Saviour. This is "the work of the law" (2:15).) Therefore, the Gentiles are not excused from hell, because they are not ignorant of their sin, just like the Jews are not excused. Also, without ever picking up a Bible, the Gentiles know about God as creator, His eternal power, and the Godhead (1:20). Therefore, the Gentiles are in the same boat as the Jews are. That is, the Jews know they are sinners, based upon the Mosaic law, and they have been given the gospel to trust in God to give them eternal life through the Mosaic law, i.e., Jesus' fulfillment of that law. Similarly, the

Gentiles know they are sinners, based upon the law of the conscience, and they have been given the gospel to trust in their Creator to give them life by recognizing Him as God. Thus, when it comes to God's judgment of Jews and Gentiles, all are judged into eternal life or eternal damnation based upon their faith in, or lack of faith in, what God has told them. Therefore, the Jews' idea, that they all will have eternal life with God and the Gentiles will all receive eternal damnation, is incorrect.

We should also note that, while God gave specific laws to the Jews, He did not do so with the Gentiles. He just gave them a conscience, and it is up to the parents, society, and the person to determine what is in that conscience. For example, 50 years ago, the United States would condemn homosexuals. Today, that is not the case. God does not cause people to believe one way or the other. He just allows man to decide what goes into the conscience. The reason is because it does not matter. All that God cares about is that man has a conscience that tells him that certain things are right and certain things are wrong. Regardless of which specific things are wrong, the conscience will still show "the work of the law" (2:15), and "the law worketh wrath" (4:15). In other words, because the wages of sin is death (6:23) and the law (conscience) works with the sin nature to cause people to sin (7:5,8-11), the conscience shows all people that they need a Saviour. Therefore, specific sins are not the issue with God. The issue is that God has given man a conscience so that he recognizes that he is a sinner so that he will have faith in God to save him.

Instead, because man is wicked, unbelievers will use their knowledge of good and evil to justify themselves so that they do not have to give up their pride and trust in God's gospel to save them. That is what is meant by, "their thoughts the mean while accusing or else excusing one another" (2:15). When Adam and Eve ate of the tree of the knowledge of good and evil, they received the knowledge of good and evil (Genesis 3:5-7). Then, instead of having faith in what God told them, they began to use that knowledge to make decisions. Because God's ways and thoughts are higher than our ways and thoughts (Isaiah 55:8-9), those decisions were used to cover up sin, rather than acknowledge sin. So, man uses his knowledge of human evil to accuse one another. For example, most unbelievers rationalize that they will go to heaven because they have not done anything really bad, i.e., they have never gone to prison. In other words, they accuse prisoners with their thoughts to say that, although they themselves have done some bad things, they are not "bad enough" to deserve eternal damnation. At the same time, man also uses his knowledge of human good to excuse one another. For example, most unbelieving religious folks rationalize that they will go to heaven because of all of the good things they did, i.e., became a church member, paid tithes, were nice to people, tried to help the less fortunate, etc. In other words, they excuse themselves with their thoughts to say that they are "good enough" to deserve eternal life. Thus, man's argument for receiving eternal life by his own righteousness involves accusing others of evil and excusing himself due to his own good. Both are relative righteousness, using man as the standard, which is a problem, since the standard is God's standard of perfect holiness. Either way, man is prideful, thinking that he knows better than God does, which is why eating of the tree of the knowledge of good and evil resulted in man continuing in sin.

2:16 "The day" refers to the Great White Throne Judgment. God will judge all according to their works, which are what are on the inside of man. Jesus said: "From within, out of the heart of men, proceed evil thoughts, adulteries, fornications, murders....All these evil things come from within, and defile the man" (Mark 7:21-23). When Jesus said in Matthew 5:20 that, "except your righteousness shall exceed the righteousness of the scribes and Pharisees, ye shall in no case enter into the kingdom of heaven," He went on to show that it is the thoughts of the heart that are judged, not the outward actions (Matthew 5:21-48). For example, man commits adultery by lusting after a woman, not by actually committing the physical act (Matthew 5:27-28). Therefore, God's judgment of man according to works is judging the intents of the heart to determine if they were always pure (eternal life) or evil (lake of fire). That is what is meant by "the secrets of men."

This does not mean that all the evil things a believer did will be revealed for all the world to see on judgment day, because, for believers, we are no longer under the law but under grace (Romans 6:14) because the Lord Jesus Christ nailed the law and our works to His cross (Colossians 2:14 and Galatians 2:19). The believers' judgment comes at a different time and is based upon sound doctrine built upon the foundation of salvation built by the Lord Jesus Christ (I Corinthians 3:11-15). Therefore, if you are afraid that, on judgment day, the whole world will see what a terrible person you are, you need to make sure you have trusted in Jesus' death, burial, and resurrection as atonement for your sins so that God will not reveal your secret sins for all to see.

Getting back to the judgment of unbelievers, the reason that it is "by Jesus Christ" is because "the Father...hath committed all judgment unto the Son," "because He is the Son of man" (John 5:22,27). In other words, only Jesus Christ is qualified to judge men because He is fully God, and God is the judge (Psalm 50:6 and 75:7), and He is also fully man and is the only man who ever lived a sin-free life.

How did Jesus Christ live a sin-free life? In 2:13-15, we mentioned that "the work of the law" (2:15) is to make your sin nature exceeding sinful so that you will recognize your need for a Saviour. Because Jesus was born of a virgin (Matthew 1:21-25), He was born without a sin nature, which means He "knew no sin" (II Corinthians 5:21). Therefore, He had no sin nature to work in Him "all manner of concupiscence" (7:8), as we do. Every time that He was tempted, He chose not to sin (Hebrews 4:15). Therefore, He lived a perfect life, which means that He "did no sin" (I Peter 2:22). In other words, Jesus lived a perfect life because He chose to live a perfect life. We cannot fathom how that is possible because our sin nature precludes us from even having the choice not to sin, that is, until we are given Christ's life by faith.

2:16 goes on to say that this judgment is "according to my gospel." In order to understand this, we need to first learn what the term "my gospel" means. "My gospel" is only found three times in scripture (2:16, 16:25, and II Timothy 2:8). It always relates to Paul's gospel, which is to trust in Jesus' death, burial, and resurrection as atonement for sin (I Corinthians 15:3-4). This term makes it clear that Paul's gospel is different from the gospel of the 12 apostles.

We should also note that 2:12 says that the judgment of unbelievers will be "by the law," but 2:16 says that the judgment is "according to my gospel." Since God cannot lie (Titus 1:2), it must be both. God looks at man to see if he is in Christ, by believing the gospel given to him, or if he is in Adam, by not believing God. If he has not believed whatever gospel God gave him, he is judged according to his own works ("judged by the law" (2:12)), rather than according to the Lord Jesus Christ's works. Therefore, he is judged into the lake of fire.

Now, being judged by "my gospel" does NOT mean that the person had to believe in Jesus' death, burial, and resurrection as atonement for his sins, because most people in history have never heard that gospel, which would make such a judgment unfair, and "the Judge of all the earth [will] do right" (Genesis 18:25). We have previously stated that Paul's gospel was not revealed to man until revealed to Paul in Acts 9. When we studied Matthew - John, we demonstrated from scripture that the 12 apostles did not preach a gospel of believing in Jesus' death, burial, and resurrection for atonement of sins. (For example, the twelve apostles preached the gospel in Luke 9:6. Then, in Luke 18:32-33, which is AFTER Luke 9:6, Jesus told them that He would be put to death and rise again the third day. We are then told that "they understood none of these things: and this saying was hid from them, neither knew they the things which were spoken" (Luke 18:34). Therefore, they could not have been preaching Jesus' death, burial, and resurrection as the gospel in Luke 9 when, nine chapters later, they did not know anything about those things.) They also did not preach Jesus' death, burial, and resurrection as good news in the first 7 chapters of Acts. Rather, Peter preached it as bad news: "Jesus of Nazareth ... ye have taken, and by wicked hands have crucified and slain" (Acts 2:22-23). "Ye denied the Holy One and the Just,... and killed the Prince of life" (Acts 3:14-15).

"The gospel which was preached of [Paul] is not after man. For [he] neither received it of man, neither was [he] taught it, but by the revelation of Jesus Christ" (Galatians 1:11-12). Therefore, Paul was the first to preach Jesus Christ's death, burial, and resurrection as good news, which is why Paul calls it, "my gospel." Therefore, since no one in the first 4,000 years of mankind's history ever heard Paul's gospel and many since then have also not heard it, how can God fairly judge those people by Paul's gospel? The answer is that all people are judged based upon the gospel that God has given them to believe. If they believe that gospel, they receive eternal life with God.

Since God is holy, those dwelling with God must also be holy (I Peter 1:16). Otherwise, God will become unholy. The only way a man earns his own holiness is by obeying the law perfectly. The only one to do that was the Lord Jesus Christ. Therefore, all those receiving eternal life must have Jesus Christ's death as a substitute for their own death in order to satisfy the justice of God and make believers holy. That is why Old Testament saints were in Abraham's bosom in the heart of the earth (Luke 16:22) and were not joined to God until after Jesus' death when He took them out of Abraham's bosom and put them in heaven, i.e., "He led captivity captive" (Psalm 68:18 and Ephesians 4:8). Therefore, all those receiving eternal life receive it through Jesus' death, burial, and resurrection, which is Paul's gospel, even though they may have believed a different gospel in order to receive eternal life. For example, Noah received eternal life by obeying God's command to him to build the ark. That was the gospel given to Noah, yet Noah could not enter into eternal life until Jesus died for his sins, which is Paul's gospel. Another example is Abraham, who had God's righteousness imputed unto him by believing that God would make his seed as numerable as the stars in heaven (Genesis 15:5-6). Thus, by believing whatever gospel God gives to a person, Jesus Christ's death atones for his sins, which is Paul's gospel. Therefore, Paul's gospel makes eternal life possible with God, even if the gift of eternal life comes by man believing a different gospel.

In summary, at the Great White Throne Judgment, God judges the secrets of men and finds that all men deserve eternal punishment in the lake of fire. (This is the judgment by the law that is mentioned in 2:12). He then looks to see if that punishment has been paid by Jesus' death on the cross. (This is the judgment by "my gospel" that is mentioned in 2:16.) If it has not, they are judged to hell, according to the law. If it has, they receive eternal life, according to "my gospel." Because all those at the Great White Throne Judgment did not believe the gospel given to them, they are all cast into the lake of fire (Revelation 20:13-14).

2:17 Paul says, "thou art CALLED a Jew" (2:17). He does not say "thou art a Jew." That is because, "they are not all Israel, which are of Israel" (9:6). They have to be "the Israel of God" (Galatians 6:16) in order to be saved. In other words, Jesus said that physical Jews are children of the devil, unless they do the works of Abraham, which means that they have to believe the gospel given to them in order to be a true Jew (John 8:39-44).

Therefore, the fact that Paul says "thou art CALLED a Jew" (2:17) tells us that he will now address the condition of the Jewish religion. In 2:13, Paul said that, just because God gave them the law, does not mean that they will be saved by the law. He said that "the doers of the law shall be justified," "not the hearers of the law." The Jewish religious leaders of Paul's day would step up and say, "Wait a minute. We will make it into God's kingdom, because we do the law." Therefore, Paul now shifts his focus to these Jews to show that they do not obey the law perfectly, which means that they will not be justified by the law. In other words, their resting in the law is in vain.

Because they rest in the law, they make their "boast of God" (2:17). Paul will soon conclude that all are "under sin" (3:9), because "there is none that doeth good, no, not one" (3:12). Therefore, the law causes all underneath it to have their mouths stopped from boasting because all are guilty before God (3:19). Yet, here is the person who calls himself a Jew, resting in the law, making his boast of God. He says, "God, I thank Thee, that I am not as other men are extortioners, unjust, adulterers" (Luke 18:11). He is self-righteous, and God says that his righteousness is as filthy rags (Isaiah 64:6). Therefore, his "boast of God" (2:17) is incorrect.

2:18-20 I Timothy 2:4 says that God's will is for "all men to be saved, and to come unto the knowledge of the truth." 2:18 says that the Jews know God's will. This cannot mean the same thing as I Timothy 2:4. The reason is because Paul says that Jesus Christ gave His life "a ransom for all, to be testified in due time" (I Timothy 2:6). This was not testified until Paul, as Jesus said that He gave "His life a ransom for many," not for all (Matthew 20:28). Therefore, the Jew, in the law, did not know God's will was for all men to be saved. Rather, the way the Jews knew God's will is explained in 2:18-20. They knew God wanted them to approve of the more excellent things (2:18), be a light to those in darkness (2:19), and teach babes (2:20).

The things that are more excellent come from the way of the righteous (Proverbs 12:26). Therefore, the Jewish religious leaders were to put themselves under the law to be an example to the rest of the Jews of how they should live. With the Jews believing God, they could then be a light to the Gentiles (Isaiah 42:6), so that the Gentiles would also learn the law (Isaiah 2:2-3). They were also to teach babes, who are new believers in Israel's program. (This is seen in Jesus' application of "babes" from Psalm 8:2 to those who said "Hosanna to the Son of David" as He entered Jerusalem to be crucified (See Matthew 21:15-16).) Thus, the Jewish religious leaders were to use the law to lead people to God.

Note that they had "the FORM of knowledge and of the truth in the law" (2:20). That is because the law was "a shadow of things to come; but the body is of Christ" (Colossians 2:17). In other words, the law was very limited in what it could do. It was meant to be a schoolmaster to teach the world that they need to believe God (Galatians 3:24). Since God committed the law to the Jews, their job was to teach people to put themselves under the law so that they would recognize their sin so that they would believe the gospel that God gave them.

Therefore, what Paul is saying in these verses is that God gave the Jews an advantage by giving them the law. Since they were to teach the law, they certainly should know the lesson of the law themselves, i.e., to have faith in

God. As Paul will now demonstrate, they had not learned this lesson.

2:21-23 Verse 23 lists the Jewish religious leaders' problem. They made their boast of the law. God gave Israel the law so that they would see that they do not perfectly obey it. They would then learn the lesson of the law that they need to trust in God to give them His righteousness apart from their obedience of the law. In other words, having faith in God would give the Jews life in Christ Jesus and make them "free from the law of sin and death" (8:2).

Instead, the Jews took God's perfect law and modified it so that they would appear to be holy in the eyes of men. Jesus said that: "Full well ye reject the commandment of God, that ye may keep your own tradition" (Mark 7:9). For example, they said it was okay to curse their own father and mother when the law said they were to be killed for doing so (Mark 7:10-12). Another example is that they took tithing down to the minute level of the giving of their spices so that people would focus on how holy they were for doing so, while they neglected "the weightier matters of the law, judgment, mercy, and faith" (Matthew 23:23). Therefore, when people asked them about eternity, they would say, "We will make into God's kingdom because we are Jews and have kept God's law."

However, Jesus said they will not make it into God's kingdom: "Except your righteousness shall exceed the righteousness of the scribes and Pharisees, ye shall in no case enter into the kingdom of heaven" (Matthew 5:20). Jesus also said that, "the scribes and the Pharisees sit in Moses' seat," but "they say, and do not" (Matthew 23:2-3). That is because they had changed God's law so that they could fulfill the lusts of their flesh. Therefore, Paul takes the Jews back to God's law. He asks them if they steal, commit adultery, or profane the things of God, i.e., "commit sacrilege" (2:21-22). In other words, since the Jews represent God and make their "boast of the law" (2:23), they must obey the law perfectly in order to honor God by their performance of the law. Instead, they dishonour God because they break His law (2:23). This shows that the Jews' boast was in the wrong place as seen by this statement by Paul: "But God forbid that I should glory, save in the cross of our Lord Jesus Christ" (Galatians 6:14). Paul brought glory to God because he recognized that he was a lawbreaker (I Timothy 1:13), while the Jews blasphemed God's name (2:24) by saying that they were righteous by their own performance of the law.

The law was given to Israel so that they would glory in the Lord, not in themselves. In fact, God told the Jews: "But let him that glorieth glory in this, that he understandeth and knoweth Me, that I am the Lord which exercise lovingkindness, judgment, and righteousness, in the earth: for in these things I delight" (Jeremiah 9:24). If the Jews had faith in the Lord, they would glory in Him, rather than in the law. They would then have eternal life and bring glory to God by leading others to have the correct attitude of I "cannot serve the Lord" (Joshua 24:19). "God will have to redeem me Himself" (Psalm 103:1-6). Instead, they gloried in their own performance of the law. Since they represented God, relied upon themselves, and broke the law, they dishonoured God and blasphemed His name (2:24). God had told Israel: "I will not give My glory unto another" (Isaiah 48:11 and 42:8). Therefore, He defended His name by setting Israel aside and by starting the dispensation of grace.

2:24 Because the Jewish religious leaders boast in the law, God's name is blasphemed through their breaking the law. The Gentiles look at those moralizing Jews and say, "I am not going to believe God, because you commit the very acts that you say God will judge me for." In other words, they were hypocrites, and Jesus called them such at least 16 times (Matthew 6:2,5,16, 15:7, 16:3, 22:18, 23:13,14,15,23,25,27,29, Mark 7:6, Luke 11:44, 13:15). Because the Jews boast in the law and connect God with the law (2:17), the Gentiles curse God when they see the Jews break the law, and the Jews WILL break the law because of their sin nature. Instead, they should boast in what God has done for them, not in the filthy-rags righteousness that they have created for themselves (Isaiah 64:6). Today, we are to boast in the cross of Christ, because it never fails in bringing salvation to mankind.

The phrase "as it is written" means that the Old Testament talks about how the Jews blasphemed God's name among the Gentiles as a result of boasting in and then breaking the law. Paul is referring to Ezekiel 36:19-21, which says that the Jews profaned God's holy name, when they were scattered among the heathen. In other words, the Gentiles associated the Jews with Jehovah God, because of their boast in God's law, which caused the Gentiles to blaspheme Jehovah God because they associated Him with the sins of the Jews.

2:25 When God called Abram and started the nation of Israel, He gave the law of circumcision (Genesis 17:10). Those circumcised would be part of the nation of Israel, while those not circumcised would be "cut off from his people" (Genesis 17:13-14). About 400 years later, Israel was given the Mosaic law or "the oracles of God" (3:2 and Exodus 20). All unbelievers will be judged by their deeds (2:5), and only those, who have "patient continuance in well doing," will receive eternal life (2:7). Therefore, a physically circumcised Jew is only given eternal life if he keeps the law. This means that physical circumcision alone cannot save the Jew, which is why Paul says that his "circumcision is made uncircumcision" (2:25) when he breaks the law. Therefore, "in Jesus Christ neither circumcision availeth any thing, nor uncircumcision" (Galatians 5:6), which means that the Jews' boast, in being physical Jews, is a vain one.

2:26-27 In other words, the Jews are looking at the wrong thing. They should not judge someone's standing before God based upon whether or not he has been circumcised. (By the way, if physical circumcision mattered, no women could be saved, not even Jewish women!) After all, if uncircumcised

36

people kept the law, God's justice would require Him to give them eternal life (2:7), and those uncircumcised Gentiles would be in God's eternal kingdom, while circumcised Jews, who did not keep the law, would actually be judged by the uncircumcision!

2:27-29 It is vital to note that Paul says that the Jews, "by letter and circumcision dost transgress the law" (2:27). How do they transgress the law, when male Jews make sure they are physically circumcised? Because "circumcision is of the heart, in the spirit, and not in the letter" (2:29).

The only reason God gave the physical law of circumcision was so that Jews would see their need for heart circumcision. In fact, He told them in the law that true circumcision is of the foreskin of the heart (Deuteronomy 10:16). This means that true Israel would use the law to recognize that their heart is "desperately wicked" (Jeremiah 17:9), such that they would trust in God to give them eternal life as a gift, which is how they would circumcise the foreskin of their heart.

This is why Paul says that, without this true circumcision, Jews were only God's people if they kept the law (2:25). Their being physically circumcised meant nothing if they did not keep the law, as God says in Genesis 17:11, circumcision is "a TOKEN of the covenant betwixt Me and you;" it is NOT what saves them. In other words, God gave physical circumcision to Israel merely as a sign of the spiritual circumcision of the heart that He wanted to perform on them. Since circumcision is of the heart, this means that true circumcision is not confined to Jewish males. Jewish women and all Gentiles could also recognize their sin and trust in the gospel that God had revealed to them, which would result in them being circumcised in the heart and receiving the gift of eternal life, as well.

For the unbelieving Jews, whom Paul is addressing in this passage, it means that they are not saved just because they have the law. They also must be doers of the law in order to be justified (2:13). Since all "are under sin" (3:9), "by the deeds of the law there shall no flesh be justified in His sight" (3:20). Therefore, a true Jew is one who is a Jew inwardly (2:29). Having the outward sign of a Jew means absolutely nothing to God. This means that, God views "Israel" as all believers in the prophecy program, regardless of if they are physical Jews or not. That is why Paul will later say, "For they are not all Israel, which are of Israel" (9:6). The true Israel is "the Israel of God" (Galatians 6:16) who have had the foreskins of their hearts circumcised by believing the gospel God gave to them. That is how Jesus could call Pharisees, children of the devil (John 8:44), while James could say that a Gentile harlot was justified in Israel's program (James 2:25). This also shows how "ALL Israel shall be saved" (11:26), when some physical Jews in the tribulation period are of "the synagogue of Satan" (Revelation 2:9 and 3:9).

Note also that 2:29 says that true circumcision is of the spirit and receives praise of God, while physical circumcision is of the letter and receives praise of men. That is because "man looketh on the outward appearance, but the Lord looketh on the heart" (I Samuel 16:7), because "God is a spirit" (John 4:24). Thus, the Jewish leaders, with their phylacteries and enlarged garment borders (Matthew 23:5), cannot "escape the damnation of hell" (Matthew 23:33), while it is God's good pleasure to give the kingdom to the little flock of Israel (Luke 12:32), who will be poor and starving for food (Matthew 5:3,6).

3 In verses 3-8, Paul shows that the flesh's arguments against salvation being possible by faith alone in what God has told us to believe are false. This leads to the conclusion that none are righteous, because the whole world is guilty of sin (vs. 9-19). Therefore, the law cannot save us; it just lets us know that we are sinners (v. 20). The good news is that God has now manifested His righteousness apart from the law (vs. 21-23). We are now justified freely by Christ's death on the cross (vs. 24-26). This excludes our boasting and gives all the glory to God (v. 27). This salvation is available to all, but it is only upon all who believe (v. 22), because it takes an individual's belief to establish Jesus' death as the fulfillment of the law on his behalf (v. 31), meaning that others cannot keep us from being justified (vs. 3-4).

3:1-2 Since the Gentiles have the conscience as their law (Romans 2:14-15) and the Jews are not automatically saved because they have circumcision and God's written law, the question is what advantage does a Jew have? In other words, what good was it to be a Jew and have God's written law, when both Jews and Gentiles are sinners? The advantage is that God's written law, which Paul calls "the oracles of God" (3:2), gave the Jews a heightened awareness of their sin nature. In 7:12-14, Paul explains how the sin nature works with the conscience. He says that the law is holy, and the conscience is holy, just, and good (7:12). "But I am carnal, sold under sin" (7:14). Therefore, the sin nature works with the conscience to make me "exceeding sinful" (7:13). My sin now exceeds my pride so that I recognize my sin, giving me the opportunity to have faith in what God has told me, so that I might receive the gift of eternal life. The Jew not only had the conscience on the inside, but also had God's written law on the outside. While the Gentile has internal forces to let him know he is a sinner, the Jew has both external and internal forces to let him know he is a sinner. Therefore, the advantage that the Jew has is "the oracles of God" (3:2), which is an extra opportunity to see his sin and need for a Saviour. The advantage of the law is not that it will make the Jews righteous, as they thought it did. The advantage of the law is that it shows the Jews that they need a Saviour. In other words, if all men objectively believed God's witnesses to them, Jews would feel more wretched and vile than Gentiles would, because of the extra witness of the law. Therefore, the law was given to the Jews so that they would believe God's Word to them and be saved. This is seen in the question of 3:3: "What if some did not believe?"

Instead, the Jews combated the witness of the law with their pride, such that they made their boast of God in how well they supposedly kept the law (2:17). Thus, instead of learning the lesson of the law, they became more entrenched in their sin nature. For example, a Pharisee said: "God, I thank Thee, that I am not as other men are....I fast twice in the week, I give tithes of all that I possess" (Luke 18:11-12). Note how he said "I am not as other men are." In other words, the Pharisee claimed that, because he had supposedly obeyed the law, he was righteous by his own merits and did not need God to save him. This kind of thinking made each subsequent generation of proud Jews, "twofold more the child of hell" than the previous generation (Matthew 23:15). Therefore, instead of being a kingdom of priests to the Gentiles (Exodus 19:5-6), they became Satan's lawful captive (Isaiah 49:24-25), culminating in them rejecting God the Father by beheading John the Baptist (Matthew 14:10), rejecting God the Son by crucifying Jesus Christ (Matthew 27:25), and rejecting God the Holy Ghost by stoning Stephen (Acts 7:55-60). Therefore, God put Israel's program on hold and started the dispensation of grace with Paul in Acts 9.

3:3-4 Said a different way, the question of 3:3 is: "Did the unbelief of most Jews cause all Jews to go to hell?" Note how 3:3 says "the faith OF God." God had faith that the Mosaic law would cause the Jews to believe. Since most did not believe, does that mean that God's plan failed and that His faith will not save those who did believe? The answer is "God forbid" (3:4).

3:4 shows that God will deal with each Jew on an individual basis. In other words, the entire nation did not have to believe in God to save them from their sins in order for those, who did believe, to receive eternal life from God. Therefore, the law still worked in that some Jews saw their wretchedness and believed that God would save them. Hebrews 3:16 points this out: "For some, when they had heard, did provoke: howbeit not all that came out of Egypt by Moses." Only the unbelievers did not enter into God's rest, while the believers did (Hebrews 3:18-19).

The quote, here, is of Psalm 51:4. The context is David's sin with Bathsheba and Uriah, and we must understand the first three verses of Psalm 51 before we can understand verse 4. First, David asks God to have mercy on him and blot out his transgressions (Psalm 51:1-2). The reason God should do this is because David has acknowledged his transgressions, and David's sin is ever before David (Psalm 51:3). In other words, David acknowledges that there is no way that he can have eternal life with God unless God forgives him of his sins. Then, David says that his sin is only against God, not anyone else (Psalm 51:4). Since his sin is against God only, God is justified in forgiving him of his sin. In other words, if David's sin was against someone else, God would be an unjust God in forgiving David's sin. However, because David's sin is only against God, He is not unjust in forgiving David's sin. Therefore, God is justified in His sayings and overcomes the argument that He is not just.

Now, we will apply to 3:3-4 what we just learned in Psalm 51:1-4. Because every person's sin is only against God, the unbelief of the Jews, as a whole, cannot affect those Jews who trusted in God to save them. God made the promise to all Jews that, if they learned the lesson of the Mosaic law to trust in God, then God would save them. However, because each individual's sin is only between him and God, the sin of unbelief by the nation as a whole cannot stop God from being faithful to forgive the sins of the individual Jews, who did trust in God to save them.

Therefore, when Paul says, "let God be true, but every man a liar" (3:4), he is saying that God is true to His Word in justifying individual believing Jews. At the same time, every man is a liar in the sense that every man's flesh lies about his own sinful condition because they are all born in sin (Psalm 51:5) and will only do sin in their flesh (7:18). This means that the only way man can have eternal life is if God is true to His promise to give him eternal life when his soul recognizes that his flesh is lying about how good he is. This means that only God can save man's soul. When man has faith in God to save him, God upholds his soul by His "free spirit" (Psalm 51:12), i.e., His "Holy Spirit" (Psalm 51:11). In doing so, God is shown to be true to His Word, and every man, in his flesh, is shown to be a liar. Therefore, Paul is saying, "Do not try to stop God from justifying individual, believing Jews. Instead, let the justification process continue by letting God be true, but every man a liar."

3:5-6 Since every man is a liar (3:4), every man's flesh is unrighteous. When we recognize this in our soul and seek for God to save us, God imparts His righteousness unto us. Therefore, "our unrighteousness [commends] the righteousness of God" (3:5). Can we then say that God is unrighteous for taking vengeance against those who do not believe? Note that Paul adds "(I speak as a man)" (3:5) to this question. In other words, such a question is not of God. Such a question comes only from man's deceptive flesh in his attempt to thwart the soul from recognizing his need of a Saviour.

In just two words ("God forbid" (3:6)), this doctrine of universal salvation is said to be false. Why? God cannot lie (Titus 1:2); His Word is true (John 17:17). God's Word says that "God is judge Himself" (Psalm 50:6) "of all the earth," (Genesis 18:25), and He is "the righteous judge" (II Timothy 4:8). In order to be a righteous judge, He must judge according to the law. The law says that "the wages of sin is death" (6:23). For believers, Christ was made sin for us (II Corinthians 5:21). For unbelievers, Christ was not made sin, because they allowed their flesh to keep their souls from accepting His sin payment as atonement for their sin. This means that their "sin remaineth" (John 9:41) on their souls. This means that they have earned death. God, as "the righteous judge" (II Timothy 4:8), must take vengeance upon them by giving them death in hell. Therefore, Paul says that, if God cannot take vengeance upon unbelievers, then God cannot judge the world. In other words, rather than God being unrighteous in taking vengeance upon unbelievers as the question claims, God would actually be unrighteous if He did not take vengeance upon unbelievers.

3:7 First, we need to remember that "let God be true, but every man a liar" (3:4) means that the only way believers can receive eternal life is that God has to abound over the lie of my flesh when my soul recognizes my sin and need for a Saviour. He then makes my spirit alive by His Spirit. In this situation, the truth of God abounds OVER my lie. But, the scenario of God being unrighteous in taking vengeance upon unbelievers (3:5) would mean that "the truth of God hath MORE abounded THROUGH my lie" (3:7). In other words, "let God be true, but every man a liar" (3:4) says that God intervenes to change my soul through the sacrifice of Christ. However, "the truth of God hath more abounded through my lie" (3:7) says that my soul believes the lie of my flesh that I am self-righteous, and God still takes my soul and makes it alive. Therefore, rather than God getting the victory OVER my lie, He gets the victory THROUGH my lie, meaning that I had a part in my salvation and that part was my lie. This means that I have eternal life BECAUSE of my sin nature, rather than IN SPITE OF my sin nature!

Such a view may seem crazy, but it actually goes along with Mormon doctrine. Mormons say that God's plan all along was for Adam to sin, because, had he not sinned, he would not have become mortal, which means there would have been no eternal progress of man. Therefore, Mormons believe that Adam's sin was part of God's will, causing the truth of God to abound THROUGH Adam's lie. Since this argument is present in modern-day Christianity and the sin nature is just as depraved now as it was 2,000 years ago, we can see why Paul addresses this crazy argument here.

If this argument is true, then "why yet am I also judged as a sinner?" (3:7). In other words, if this argument is true, then God has judged me to have eternal life based upon the fact that my sin nature worked with God to give me eternal life. So, why would God ALSO pronounce a second judgment upon me, which is that I am a sinner? God would not judge my sin worthy of death (6:23). Rather, He would be thrilled that I am a sinner, because, if I were not a sinner, I would not have lied. And, since I needed to lie in order for God's truth to abound, then I could never have eternal life with God if I were never a sinner. Therefore, God should be glad that Adam ate the fruit of the tree of the knowledge of good and evil, as Mormons claim that He is! This shows just how deceitful our desperately wicked heart can become (Jeremiah 17:9)!

In summary, what Paul has done, in 3:3-7, is that he has proven that each individual makes his choice about where he will spend eternity. If man recognizes his sin and believes what God has told him, God is just in forgiving him of his sin, because God's truth abounded over man's lie. At the same time, God is just in condemning unbelievers to hell because God's truth does not more abound through man's lie. This makes God "just," in condemning the unbeliever, "and the justifier of him which believeth in Jesus" (3:26).

3:8 Since man cannot get out of God's judgment by arguing that God is unrighteous, man then argues that the way God imparts His imputed righteousness to man is unrighteous. This is the argument that Christianity today uses most against the gospel of grace. Paul's gospel is that we are saved by grace through the faith of Jesus Christ (Ephesians 2:8-9) when we recognize we are sinners and trust in Jesus' death, burial, and resurrection as atonement for our sins (I Corinthians 15:3-4). Since we are not saved by the law, we are not kept saved by the law, which means that "all things are lawful for me" (I Corinthians 10:23). This means that I can do whatever I want to do after I am saved, and I still have eternal life.

In practice, it is very rare to find a church that will teach this. Granted, Baptists and non-denominationalists say that they believe in eternal security. But, if you commit adultery or murder someone, they would say that you were never saved in the first place, because a Christian would never do these things. In other words, over 99% of Christian churches, including those that proclaim on their doctrinal statement that eternal security is true, believe you must work to maintain your salvation. The difference among the denominations is how much you can get away with before they label you as "not saved" or "backslidden." Therefore, even churches, that teach eternal security, do not really teach it, because they will say that someone is not saved if he does a "big" sin, like murder and adultery. Their rational is that God has changed us so that we no longer have the desire to sin after we are saved. All saved people know this is not true, because, to our flesh, sin is just as much of a temptation after we are saved as before we are saved, as Paul will point out in chapter 7. Paul also says that a saved person still has a "vile body" (Philippians 3:21), even after he is saved. This means that a saved person has the same ability to sin after he is saved than before he was saved. Granted, a saved person can walk in the Spirit, but he can also, just as easily, fulfill the lusts of his flesh.

We also need to note that there is no such thing as a "big" sin. God says that all sins are "deadly" (6:23). He says that, "Whosoever shall keep the whole law, and yet offend in one point, he is guilty of all" (James 2:10). Moreover, you "offend in one point," not when you physically commit the sin, but once you like the idea of committing that sin. Jesus said, "Whosoever looketh on a woman to lust after her hath committed adultery with her already in his heart" (Matthew 5:28). Therefore, if your salvation is contingent upon your works after you are saved, you will lose your salvation with one, bad thought. For example, if I like the idea of telling a lie, even if I later change my mind and do not tell the lie, I am just as guilty of breaking God's law and just as deserving of hell fire as if I were a mass murderer. Therefore, if my salvation is conditional upon my performance of the law IN ANY WAY WHATSOEVER, I will go to hell, guaranteed! This means that Christ's blood is absolutely worthless, because His death on the cross saves no one! This is why salvation MUST be a free gift (6:23), and it cannot be based upon my works, even in the slightest way, after I am saved. That is why David, a man after God's own heart (Acts 13:22), committed adultery (II Samuel 11:3-4) and murder (II Samuel 11:14-17), after he was saved, and he could correctly say about himself afterward, "Blessed is the man to whom the Lord will not impute sin" (4:8). It is pure, unadulterated, human pride that cleverly tries to sneak in works as part of salvation by saying, "You are eternal secure, unless you commit one of the 'deadly' sins."

Sadly, nearly all Christian churches fall into one of two categories when it comes to your salvation. The first category is that they believe that any sin, after you are saved, will cause you to lose your salvation, and you will have to get re-saved. The second category is that they proclaim that you are eternally secure. However, if you commit a "big sin" (We have already proven there is no such thing.), or you go against their rules, such as you stop paying your tithes or coming to church, that this lack of desire to serve the Lord shows that you never had saving faith. Therefore, you were never saved in the first place. Really, these two categories are the same. It is just that the latter category uses the term "eternal security" so that they do not have to change Bible verses to fit their doctrine, and the latter category lets you commit the "minor sins" (Again, there is no such thing.) without losing your salvation.

The reason that it is rare to find people, who truly believe they cannot lose their salvation, is that Satan has blinded the minds of unbelievers through his ministers (II Corinthians 11:13-15) to keep "the light of the glorious gospel of Christ" (II Corinthians 4:3-4) from saving people. Therefore, they say that the gift of eternal life is really a license to do evil things (3:8). This is a slanderous accusation of the gospel of grace. Those, who slander God's gospel of grace, provided that they never believe this gospel themselves, receive a greater punishment in the lake of fire than "evil" people, because they have kept people from being saved. That is why Paul says that their "damnation is just" (3:8). That is why the hottest and worst part of the lake of fire is reserved for false Christians, proclaiming a false gospel.

Their accusation, that God's gospel of grace is a license to sin, is actually the opposite of the truth. Before we were saved, the only thing we could do was sin (7:15-18). We had no ability to serve God. After we are saved, we have the opportunity to serve God by allowing Christ to live through us (Galatians 2:19-20). Therefore, the free gift of eternal life actually gives us license to walk in the Spirit, not to do evil things (8:1-4)! Paul will go into detail regarding this in Romans 6-8.

3:9 The next argument used against the gospel of grace is that they will say that Paul is saying that the Gentiles are better than the Jews. In other words, opponents of the gospel claim that all religions say they are the only way to eternal life, but everyone is really just saying the same thing. As long as you are a good person, you will have eternal life. So, if you are a good

Jew, you are saved. If you are a good Muslim, you are saved, etc. In other words, this argument is that Paul says that "his religion" is somehow better than the Jewish religion, and Paul's religion should be dismissed since every religion claims the same thing.

Paul says, "No, this is not a religion. No, the Gentiles are not better than the Jews." Rather, "we have before proved both Jews and Gentiles, that they are all under sin" (3:9). In other words, Paul is not promoting his religion over the Jewish religion. Rather, he is saying that ALL religions are wrong. They need to recognize "that they are all under sin" (3:9). Then, they can get the answer to their sin from God, and not from religion.

In 1:18 – 2:16, God showed that all Gentiles were concluded under sin at the Tower of Babel in Genesis 11. God then gave the Jews a favored position with Him, as seen in giving them the oracles of God (3:2). However, because they rested and made their boast in that law (2:17), God concluded the Jews under sin, as well. Therefore, it is not that the Gentiles are better than the Jews. It is that God has declared that the Jews are in the same wretched status as the Gentiles have been in all along. Therefore, the result is not that the Gentile is better than the Jew. Rather, the result is that all are under sin, and, because of this, all have the opportunity to believe the gospel and be saved. This is not a religious message, but it is God's message!

3:10-18 Of course, the self-moralizing Jew does not believe he is in the same, wretched category as the Gentile is, because he thinks he is righteous because he has the law. Therefore, Paul now gives a string of quotes from the Old Testament to show that the very law that he rests in and boasts in (2:17) is the very law that judges him, concluding him to be under sin, just like the Gentile. The funny thing is that the Jews were so self righteous that they took these Old-Testament passages to refer to the lawless Gentiles, not to themselves. Paul shows that they apply to "both Jews and Gentiles;" "they are all under sin" (3:9).

By the way, there are 7 passages from the Old Testament that are quoted here, and 6 of them come from the Psalms. Most Christians think the Psalms are for feel-good devotionals, but these quotes show that the Psalms are for communicating sound doctrine, just like the rest of the Bible.

Paul uses these quotes to show the progression of unbelieving man. 3:10-12 says that unbelievers are fools who are unrighteous. 3:13 says that they use their tongues to lead people astray with false doctrine. 3:14 says that they curse and are bitter towards believers. 3:15-17 says that they are swift to kill believers, trying to silence them. Since they are unrighteous, lead people astray, and persecute and kill believers, the conclusion, in 3:18, is that "there is no fear of God before their eyes."

3:10-12 This is a quote of Psalm 14:1-3 and 53:1-3. Both of these passages start by saying that, "the fool hath said in his heart, There is no God." God has given all men the wisdom that there is a God (1:19-20), and all men have a sin nature that rejects this truth. This is why the passage goes on to say that there is none that does good. To keep the Jews from not applying these passages to themselves, God goes on by saying, "God looked down from heaven upon the children of men, to see if there were any that did understand, that did seek God. Every one of them is gone back" (Psalm 14:2-3 and 53:2-3). Since God found no one among the children of men who did good, this must mean that not a single Jew was righteous on his own. This shows that, although the Jews had the law, they did not do the law. Therefore, apart from God's imputed righteousness, none is righteous and no one doeth good, not even the Jew.

3:9-12 is the conclusion of everything in Romans up to this point. No one is ever saved until he agrees with this conclusion. Otherwise, he will say, "Well, Christianity is a nice crutch for the people who cannot cope with life, but I am a good, law-abiding citizen. I get along just fine without all of this Bible stuff." By contrast, the believer says, "Yes, I have sinned and come short of the glory of God (3:23). What must I do to be saved?" (Acts 16:30).

Sadly, very few people, even among Christian churches, ever reach this conclusion. That is because such a conclusion eliminates religion. Christianity, Islam, Judaism, Buddhism, Hinduism, and all other religions crumble when man realizes, "There is none righteous, no, not one" (3:10). That is because all of man's efforts are utterly pointless, so, why bother with religion? Man can then hear the gospel, believe it (10:17), buy a King James Version Bible, and let the Holy Ghost teach it to him (I Corinthians 2:12-15)—no religion needed. Since man's ability to gain power and money and Satan's ability to lead people into hell are destroyed by that one, little statement, man and Satan will fight God to keep this truth from penetrating through man's pride and Satan's lie program. That is why, even among Bible readers, only a minority truly believe that "there is none righteous, no, not one" (3:10).

3:13 This is a composite quote of Psalm 5:9 and 140:3. The Jews would have read these Psalms and thought they applied to Gentiles. However, remember from Psalm 14:1-3 and 53:1-3 that all people are fools, due to their sin nature. Psalm 5:9 says that "THEIR throat is an open sepulchre," and Psalm 5:5 says that "THEIR" refers to fools. The subject of Psalm 140:3 is "the evil man" (Psalm 140:1), and we also learned from Psalm 14:1-3 and 53:1-3 that none do good, which means they are evil. Therefore, the "bad" people in the Psalms are not just Gentiles, but they are all who do not trust God, including those of the Jewish religion.

Jesus must have had Psalm 5:9 in mind when He told the Jewish religious leaders, "Ye are like unto whited sepulchres, which indeed appear beautiful outward, but are within full of dead men's bones, and of all uncleanness." "The poison of asps...under their lips" is the religion that the Jews spewed.

They were of the devil, being "serpents" and the "generation of vipers" (Matthew 23:33). The words that they spewed to the Jews were really poison, because they caused the common Jews to die spiritually as well, trusting in the traditions of the fathers, rather than in God's law covenant with them (Mark 7:7-9).

Thus, the religious Jews read these passages and said that they referred to the Gentiles, when Jesus said that they really referred to the religious Jews. Similarly, Christianity reads the warnings against religion that are found in Paul's epistles, and think that those warnings apply to other people, when they really apply to themselves. This shows that man's pride will always take the bad things about themselves found in God's Word and say that God is talking to someone else, not to them.

3:14 This verse is a quote of Psalm 10:7. In its context, it is talking about a wicked man. His mouth is full of cursing and bitterness when he confronts his enemies (Psalm 10:5), who would be believers. Therefore, wicked men use their mouths both to spew false doctrine and to curse those who believe sound doctrine. Lest you think this applies only to a few people, remember that the context is referring to ALL unbelievers (3:10-12). Everyone has beliefs that they hold to, and their beliefs come out of their mouths. If they are unbelievers in God's Word, then they believe lies. The only way a lie can triumph over the truth is if a lie is seen as the truth and vice versa. Therefore, in order to justify themselves, all unbelievers speak lies and seek to add credibility to their lies by speaking against the truth. They may not go on a crusade, but they will at least seek to justify themselves in their everyday lives.

3:15-17 These three verses are a quote of Isaiah 59:7-8. In Isaiah, it is clear that God is speaking to the Jews. He says that "YOUR iniquities have separated between you and your God, and YOUR sins have hid His face from you....YOUR hands are defiled with blood, and YOUR fingers with iniquity; YOUR lips have spoken lies, YOUR tongue hath muttered perverseness" (Isaiah 59:2-3). Here, Paul is showing the progression of their faulty teaching. They taught religion, which got people apart from God and His law. The result, then, was that their actions became evil, and the Jews, who had the law, ended up doing the same, wicked things that the Gentiles did in 1:29-31.

Also, as mentioned in the previous verse, these verses refer to all unbelievers, not just Jews. Most unbelievers do not follow this physically, as apostate Israel will do during the Great Tribulation. However, spiritually speaking, all unbelievers are murderers. Look at Satan. Jesus said that, "he was a murderer from the beginning" (John 8:44), yet there is no record of Satan killing people physically. Rather, he murdered people spiritually by getting them to believe his lies (John 8:44). Similarly, most unbelievers would never physically kill people. However, they all speak lies and speak against the truth. When people believe them over God's Word, then they have been murdered by those unbelievers.

For example, let us say you have a co-worker who believes that all religions lead to heaven (A majority of people today, who say they are Christians, believe this!). This co-worker hears of a terrorist attack and makes the comment that we should not be hating Muslims, because most of them are good people. If you believe this, over the truth that "there is none that doeth good, no, not one" (3:12), that co-worker has just murdered you spiritually. Therefore, when we are told that "their feet are swift to shed blood" (3:15), we should think of how they murder people spiritually with the false doctrine that they say. That is why God says that the tongue "is an unruly evil, full of deadly poison" (James 3:8); "and it is set on fire of hell" (James 3:6).

3:18 Now, for the summation of 3:10-17. The reason unbelievers say there is no God, do no good, speak lies, speak against the truth, and spiritually murder people through their words is because they have "no fear of God before their eyes" (a quote of Psalm 36:1). That is why Psalm 111:10 says, "The fear of the Lord is the beginning of wisdom." When you fear the Lord, you recognize there is a God, that you are unrighteous, and that God will judge you for your sins. You will then believe the gospel God has given you and receive the gift of eternal life. All of this starts with fearing the Lord. But, when you do not fear the Lord, you will do the things of 3:13-17. Therefore, where a person spends eternity all centers around whether or not he fears the Lord.

3:19 The law says that whoever breaks the law is worthy of death (6:23). But, you have to be under the law in order for the law to condemn you to death. Gentiles have "the work of the law written in their hearts" (2:15), which means they are under the law. The Jews have the Mosaic law (3:2), which means they are under the law. The only ones not under the law are believers (6:14) and children before they obtain the conscience (7:9). Everyone else is under the law, and everyone has not obeyed the law (3:10-12). This means that all people with a conscience are worthy of death, before they believe the gospel.

The reason for this is so "every mouth may be stopped, and all the world may become guilty before God." No one can stand before God and say, "I should have eternal life because I did this and that." Every argument by man to get into God's kingdom is stopped by every man's violation of the law. Therefore, no one can boast before God. In this way, the only thing we can glory in is "the cross of our Lord Jesus Christ" (Galatians 6:14). We cannot glory in religion, i.e., our own efforts. In this way, God gets the glory for all eternity, because God Himself redeemed man.

"For the Lord hath redeemed Jacob, and ransomed him from the hand of him that was stronger than he" (Jeremiah 31:11). Therefore, the Jews' resting in the law (2:17) does not save them. Rather, the Jews have "become guilty before God" under the law. The Gentiles, having the law in their hearts (2:15), are also guilty under the law before God. The result, then, is that "all the world," both Jew and Gentile, are guilty before God. Therefore, no one is righteous (3:10) on his own. The law has condemned the whole world to death.

3:20 Paul will later explain that the sin nature works with the conscience to make every person exceeding sinful (7:8-13). That is because "by the law is the knowledge of sin," meaning that we learn that we have a sin nature through our disobedience of the law. (In Romans, the word "sin" refers to the sin nature, while "sins" refers to sins that you commit as a result of your sin nature.) Sinning is just as natural to humans as breathing is. You breathe without thinking about it, except when you have trouble breathing. Then, you think about it a lot. The same goes for sin. Because sin is in your nature, if God did not try to block your sin with the law, you would do it without thinking about it. You would then go to hell and not know why. So, God gave everyone the conscience so that they would try not to sin, thereby recognizing that they cannot stop sin. That way, honest people will seek to be justified by grace through faith. Therefore, no one is justified by the deeds of the law. Rather, the law shows us our sin so that we will believe the answer to sin that God has given us, i.e., the gospel.

The only reason Jesus Christ was able to obey the law perfectly was because He had no sin nature. (Jesus was "in the LIKENESS of sinful flesh" (8:3), but He did not actually have sinful flesh.) That is not to say that it was easy for Jesus Christ not to sin. The temptation not to go to the cross was so strong that Jesus only overcame it by sweating "as it were great drops of blood" (Luke 22:44). Adam, who was also created without a sin nature, sinned. Therefore, even with the absence of a sin nature, it was still difficult for Jesus Christ to live a perfect life. This shows the impossibility of not sinning for everyone else, since we all have a sin nature.

3:21 The conclusion of time past is that all are guilty before God. However, there is good news, and it starts with "but now." The "but now" dispensation of the grace of God started in Acts 9. The whole point of time past, in which God brought the whole world guilty under the law, was so that God could give His righteousness to man apart from the law.

Now, when this verse says that the law and the prophets witnessed God's righteousness, it does not mean that the gospel of grace was given in the Old Testament, because it was a mystery until revealed to Paul (Ephesians 3:2-5). Rather, the Old Testament witnessed that the righteousness of God would come through the Messiah's coming to offer the sacrifice for sins that makes possible the righteousness of God being given to man. The Old Testament says that the Messiah would be wounded for Israel's transgressions and bruised for their iniquities, and He would heal believing Israel with His stripes (Isaiah 53:5). However, the gospel of trusting in Jesus' death, burial, and resurrection as atonement for sin was not given to man until revealed to Paul (Luke 18:34; Galatians 1:11-12; I Corinthians 15:3-4). God used time past to show that no man could receive eternal life, unless God gave it to him as a free gift, which came by Jesus' shed blood on the cross, even though the people in time past were not given that gospel for salvation; they had a different gospel (Mark 1:14-15).

3:22 All modern translations change this verse from "faith OF Jesus Christ" to "faith IN Jesus Christ." However, it is the faith OF Jesus Christ that made Him "obedient unto death, even the death of the cross" (Philippians 2:8). Jesus Christ said to His Father, "not My will, but Thine, be done" (Luke 22:42). This shows that Jesus Christ had faith in the Father's plan for Him to go to the cross. Without this faith, Jesus Christ never would have gone to the cross, and no one would have the opportunity to have eternal life with God. Therefore, it is vitally important that Jesus Christ's faith NOT be removed from this verse. Also, whenever Jesus Christ's faith is mentioned in the Bible, our trust in that faith for salvation is also mentioned. Therefore, it is also not necessary to remove Christ's faith. In this case, we see our faith mentioned shortly thereafter by saying that God's righteousness is "upon all them that believe" (3:22).

It took Jesus Christ's faith to manifest God's righteousness to man. It took man's faith in Christ in order for man to be saved in the current dispensation. This is what is meant by the righteousness of God being "revealed from faith [Christ's faith] to faith [our faith]" (1:17). Thus, the modern translations are in error when they change 3:22 from the faith OF Jesus Christ to faith IN Jesus Christ for there is no salvation for anyone without Jesus Christ's faith. This is especially true down in 3:25, where Paul addresses the righteous of God remitting the sins of those who lived in time past, because they had faith in the gospel they were given, which was to believe God's promise and follow the law covenant. It was not to have faith in Jesus Christ's death, burial, and resurrection for salvation.

Note also in this verse that the offer of God's righteousness is "unto all," but it is only "upon all them that believe." In other words, God has made the offer of eternal life to every single human being, but only those, who take Him up on His offer, will actually be saved. This shows that the doctrine of universal salvation is incorrect. This is the flip side of 3:5-6. There, we were told that God is not unrighteous in taking vengeance upon unbelievers. Now, in 3:22, we are told that God's righteousness goes only to those who believe.

Why does God's righteousness come upon ALL believers? Because "there is no difference" (3:22) between Jew and Gentile. Why is there no difference? Because "both Jews and Gentiles ... are all under sin" (3:9). At the Tower of Babel in Genesis 11, God concluded the Gentiles under sin, since they did not believe God's message to them to repent or else He would scatter them abroad on the face of the earth (Genesis 11:4 and Romans 1:28). In Acts 7 with the stoning of Stephen, God concluded the Jews under sin, since they did not believe God's message to them to repent and be water baptized (Acts 2:38). Therefore, "God hath concluded them all in unbelief, that He might have mercy upon all" (11:32). This is one of the reasons why God did not reveal the gospel of trusting in Jesus' death, burial, and resurrection as atonement for sin until He told it to Paul in Acts 9, because He waited until Acts 7 to conclude the Jews in unbelief. (The other reason God did not reveal the gospel of grace until after the cross is because, if Satan's forces knew that gospel beforehand, "they would not have crucified the Lord of glory" (I Corinthians 2:8).

It is important to note that salvation does not come by the things that Christianity says that it comes by. Turning from your sins, inviting Jesus into your heart, living a good life, saying the sinner's prayer, walking an aisle, making a confession of faith, and being water baptized are all works that man adds to faith. Since God's righteousness is "upon all them that believe" (3:22), the only thing you do, in order to be saved, is believe the gospel. Belief is not a work, because "faith cometh by hearing, and hearing by the word of God" (10:17). Therefore, salvation stems from the word of God, and not from anything that man says or does.

3:23 This verse concludes everything that Paul has said up to this point. First, he proved that Gentiles have sinned. Then, he proved that Jews have sinned. Therefore, "all have sinned." And, because "all have sinned," no one will be saved by trusting in his own righteousness, as Paul showed in 3:19. Now, Paul can focus on God's righteousness being imputed unto believing man.

3:24 Justification, then, must be a free gift. This verse does not say that it is by the redemption of Christ Jesus plus our living a good life. Redemption is by Christ Jesus ALONE. Thus, it is "the gift of God...through Jesus Christ our Lord" (6:23). Justification is free, and it is by grace, which means that we receive it based on nothing we have done or said. Our only part is believing the word of God, which is God's work in us, not our work (Ephesians 2:8-10).

3:25 The word "propitiation" means a fully satisfying sacrifice. The Lord Jesus Christ's sacrifice on the cross fully satisfied the wrath of God against sin. This is explicitly stated for us in Isaiah 53:11: "He shall see of the travail of His soul, and shall be satisfied." Since God is satisfied, we do not have to do anything ourselves in order to be saved. This is a very good thing, since we cannot do anything to be saved, since "in me (that is, in my flesh,) dwelleth no good thing" (7:18). This also shows that Christ's blood is invaluable. Only Christ's blood can atone for a person's sin, and nothing can be added to it to help in that atonement. That is why all things, both in heaven and in earth, will be gathered together in Christ (Ephesians 1:10). Therefore, those, with "faith in His blood" (3:25), are declared righteous by God.

When this verse talks about "the remission of sins that are past," it is referring to those in time past. They believed the gospel given to them, but God could not remit their sins until Jesus' fully satisfying sacrifice upon the cross. Therefore, for the first 4,000 years of mankind's history, God practiced a great deal of "forbearance," meaning that He withheld the punishment of believers for that entire time until He could remit their sins. Therefore, if you think of someone like Abel, God declared that he was righteous (Matthew 23:35), but he did not actually receive God's righteousness until his sins were remitted 4,000 years later when Jesus became a propitiation for his sins. This is what is meant by "the remission of sins that are past, through the forbearance of God."

This is why, when Old-Testament saints died, they did not go to heaven, because God's wrath would have destroyed them, since God's wrath was not fully satisfied until Jesus died on the cross. Rather, they went to "Abraham's bosom" (Luke 16:22), which was a place of peace apart from God (Genesis 15:15). Then, after Jesus' death on the cross, He "led captivity captive" (Psalm 68:18 and Ephesians 4:8), bringing paradise into heaven, where God is.

3:26 "To declare, I say, at this time His righteousness" (3:26). This is God's way of emphasizing that His righteousness was not available until after the cross. First, God's righteousness being available now makes Him "just" (3:26). "The wages of sin is death" (6:23), yet, for all of mankind's history before the cross, God had forborne death for all believers. They deserved death because they had sinned, and no one had paid for that sin. A continuance in that status would make God unjust. But, once Jesus Christ paid for believers' sin, they could receive God's righteousness, and God would be just in giving them His righteousness. This makes God "just." Of course, this also makes God "the justifier of him which believeth in Jesus" (3:26).

We should not confuse "believeth in Jesus" with the gospel of grace. All people, who believe what God has told them, have believed in Jesus, but only those in the dispensation of grace have believed in Jesus' death, burial, and resurrection as atonement for their sin. "Believeth in Jesus" means that they have believed in what Jesus has told them. John 1:1 says that Jesus is "the Word." As such, He is "the true Light, which lighteth every man that cometh into the world" (John 1:9). Therefore, those, who only have the witness of God mentioned in 1:19-20, have believed in Jesus, because Jesus, as "the Word" has given them that light. Similarly, those, in Israel's program, who believed God's Word to them, also believed in Jesus. That is why John 3:16 says that, "whosoever believeth in Him should not perish, but have everlasting life." Thus, "believeth in Jesus" is a term that is synonymous with believing God's Word, since Jesus IS God's Word. Therefore, Paul can use the term "believeth in Jesus" to refer to all believers in all dispensations, and it does not mean that those, in Israel's program, believed in Jesus' death, burial, and resurrection for their salvation.

3:27 Because man does absolutely nothing to be saved, regardless of dispensation, man cannot boast in his salvation. Ephesians 2:9 says that salvation is "not of works, lest any man should boast."

The verse goes on to say that boasting is excluded, not by the law of works, but by the law of faith. Where some Christians get confused is that they think that "law" always means the Mosaic law or the Ten Commandments, but "law" can refer to other things. That is because God's spirit realm also operates by its own set of laws. For example, 8:2 says that "the law of the Spirit of life in Christ Jesus hath made me free from the law of sin and death." In other words, when we are saved, the law of the Spirit of life replaces the law of sin and death in our lives. We are now under a faith law, rather than a works law. In 3:27, the law of works is that you receive a just payment according to your work, and that payment is death. The law of faith says that you receive a just payment according to your faith, and that payment is life. If salvation were by works, then you could boast in your work, because you earned it. But, because salvation is by faith, you can only boast in faith. Thus, boasting is excluded by the law of faith. The faith, about which Paul is talking, is "the faith of Jesus Christ" (3:22). Therefore, salvation by the faith of Jesus Christ means that you can only boast "in the cross of our Lord Jesus Christ" (Galatians 6:14), which is a boast of faith, whereby boasting by works is excluded. This gives God all the glory.

3:28 Justification, in this dispensation, is by faith alone in Christ's shed blood on the cross. Works have nothing to do with it. However, in the prophecy program, justification is by faith plus works. Compare James 2:24 ("By works a man is justified, and not by faith only") with 3:28 ("A man is justified by faith without the deeds of the law"). These statements are contradictory, yet they both must be true. The only way for both of them to be true is for them to be true at different times. People, who do not rightly divide the word of truth (II Timothy 2:15), make God out to be a liar, by saying that both of these statements apply today, but that one needs to be changed. Some Christians change Romans, while others change James. Whichever one they change, they, unknowingly or not, change the truth of God's Word into a lie, in some form or fashion. Only when we rightly divide the Word of truth do we understand that Romans is written to us today in the dispensation of grace, since Paul is the apostle of the Gentiles (11:13), while James is written to the Jews in the tribulation period (James 1:1), which is part of the prophecy dispensation. Thus, 3:28 can be left the way it is and can be applied to us today, and James 2:24 can be left the way it is and can be applied to Israel when they are going through the tribulation period after the Body of Christ has been raptured up to fill the heavenly places that Christ has for us.

By the way, the James 2:24 passage does not mean that, in Israel's program, they must perform works of the law in order to be justified. We know this because we just read that "by the deeds of the law there shall NO flesh be justified in His sight" (3:20). If they had to do works of the law, they would have the same problem that the Gentiles have, and that is that the law causes people to sin more. The context of James 2:24 shows that people, in the prophecy program, are justified by faith plus works of faith. So, it is all faith, regardless of dispensation, because, "without faith it is impossible to please" God (Hebrews 11:6). Still, they have to have the works of faith to be justified, when we do not have to have those works today, which shows that salvation is accomplished differently in different dispensations, showing that we must rightly divide the Word of truth (II Timothy 2:15) in order to keep from changing God's Word to fit our doctrine.

(The difference in salvation plans has to do with the fact that the body of Christ receives the atonement when they believe (5:11), but Israel does not receive the atonement until the second coming (Acts 3:19-21). That is because God treats Israel as servants by putting them under the Mosaic law (Leviticus 25:55), while He treats the body of Christ as full-grown sons (Galatians 4:5-7).)

3:30 It is interesting that Paul says that the circumcision are justified "BY" faith, while the uncircumcision are justified "THROUGH" faith. In general, "by" means being near to something, while "through" means from one end to the other, although "by" can also mean "through." However, there must be some significance to different words being used. Perhaps "by" is used for Israel, because they have to have faith plus works of faith in order to be saved, while "through" is used for the body of Christ, because faith alone saves them. So, Israel is justified by faith, because faith is used, along with works of faith, while the body of Christ is justified through faith because only faith is used in the justification process.

However, today, the Jews are not saved by faith plus works, as James 2:24 says. Today, the middle wall of partition between Jew and Gentile is down (Ephesians 2:14), such that there is no difference between Jew and Gentile, meaning that all, in the dispensation of grace, are justified by the faith of the Lord Jesus Christ through the faith that they place in Christ's death as atonement for their sins.

3:31 How do we establish the law through faith, when we are no longer under the law but under grace when we are saved (6:14)? The answer is in 3:24 with Christ being our propitiation. God's perfect standard of obeying the law perfectly had to be completed, or else God would not be just in giving eternal life to someone who does not meet the standard for eternal life (2:7). Therefore, the Lord Jesus Christ came and fulfilled the law perfectly (Hebrews 4:15 and I Peter 2:22), meeting the standard for eternal life. He was then "made...sin" (II Corinthians 5:21) so that He could become the curse of sin for us (Galatians 3:13), and that curse is death (6:23). This makes His death on the cross the sacrifice that fully satisfies God's wrath against sin (Isaiah 53:11). When we have faith in Christ's death as atonement for our sins, we establish the law in that God applies the perfect standard of the law to us, and we pass because Jesus perfectly fulfilled the law, and our lives are now "hid with Christ in God" (Colossians 3:3). Therefore, the law is established as the way to have eternal life, through Christ's fulfillment of the law, when we have faith in Christ's blood shed for our sins. In other words, the law is established in faith.

4 3:28 and 5:1 both say that we are justified by faith. Since chapter 4 is sandwiched between these two statements, this chapter shows how our performance, or lack of performance, of the law cannot interfere with our justification. The key verse is that "Abraham believed God, and it was counted unto him for righteousness" (v. 3). A man also cannot lose his salvation, since David committed adultery and murder and proclaimed afterward, "Blessed is the man to whom the Lord will not impute sin" (v. 8). Verses 9-22 go back to Abraham, showing that he was justified by God before he received the law, which means that he was saved by faith alone. Since Abraham is the father of all who believe God (v. 16), we know that God's righteousness is imputed to us by faith alone, also (vs. 23-25).

4:1-8 Christians use these verses to try to prove that justification by faith without works was always the method of salvation. This cannot be true because James says that justification is by faith plus works (James 2:24), while Paul says that justification is by faith alone (3:28). The point of confusion is that Christians automatically equate "works" with "law." However, the "works," that James is talking about, are not the deeds of the law, because "by the deeds of the law there shall NO FLESH be justified in His sight" (3:20). James is talking about works of faith. We know this to be true because the two examples of being justified by works that James gives are actually violations of the Mosaic law. Abraham was "justified by works, when he had offered Isaac his son upon the altar" (James 2:21), which breaks the commandment of "Thou shalt not kill" (Exodus 20:13). Rahab was "justified by works, when she had received the messengers, and had sent them out another way" (James 2:25), which breaks the commandment of "Thou shalt not bear false witness against thy neighbour" (Exodus 20:16).

The reason for the difference in justification methods is that, as we have already seen, God has treated people differently in the prophecy program than in the mystery program. All people have the law of the conscience, but only Israel in the prophecy program also has the Mosaic law. When a person has faith in the gospel that God has given him, regardless of dispensation, the law of the conscience is taken away from him. For the mystery dispensation, this statement is supported by 6:14, which says that "ye are not under the law, but under grace." Since we do not have the Mosaic law, God gives us our justification and atonement right now (Romans 5:9,11), as a present, eternal possession. For the prophecy dispensation, the law of the conscience is also purged. Hebrews 9:14 (written to the prophecy dispensation) says that, when a person believes the gospel, "the blood of Christ" shall "purge your conscience from dead works to serve the living God." However, they are still under the Mosaic law, because the Mosaic covenant, that God gave with Israel, "IS READY to vanish away" (8:13). It will not vanish away until Jesus' second coming. That is when Israel, in their program, receives the atonement (Acts 3:19-21), and they are placed under the new covenant (Jeremiah 31:31-34). It is only then that God "WILL forgive their iniquity" and "WILL remember their sin no more" (Jeremiah 31:34). Until then, they are called the "children of Israel" (This phrase is found over 600 times in the Bible.) and "servants" (Leviticus 25:55). That is why God says of saved Israel at Jesus' second coming that, "I WILL be his God, and he SHALL be my son" (Revelation 21:7). While, in the mystery program, God says that "thou ART no more a servant, but a son" (Galatians 4:7).

In summary, believing Israel, in the prophecy program, is still under the Mosaic law, while believers in the mystery program are under grace. Now, we already know that the law causes people to sin more, not to obey the law (7:11-13), because the law gives us the knowledge of sin (3:20). Therefore, the works, that God looks for from believing Israel in the prophecy program, are works that come from faith, not works that come from the law. Abraham broke the law of "Thou shall not kill" because he had faith that God would raise Isaac from the dead (Hebrews 11:19). Rahab broke the law of "Thou shalt not bear false witness against thy neighbour," because she had faith that God would destroy Jericho through Israel, as God said that He would (Joshua 2:9-11). Therefore, even in Israel's program, God is only looking for faith, because, "without faith it is impossible to please" God (Hebrews 11:6).

At the same time, it is impossible for someone with faith to displease God by sinning under the law, even in Israel's program. That is why, Paul gives the example of David, who committed both adultery and murder, two crimes punishable by death under the law (Leviticus 20:10 and Numbers 35:16-21), and God would not impute his sin unto him (4:7-8). Therefore, 4:1-8 is not talking about the gospel. Rather, these verses build upon the closing statement of 3:31 that, by believing, "we establish the law." What these verses build are that: 1) Justification is by faith (4:1-3), not by obeying the law, and 2) Justification is kept by faith, not by disobeying the law (4:5-8). In other words, the law is established in faith, not in how we perform under the law.

4:1-3 4:2 says that Abraham was not justified by works, but James 2:21 says that Abraham was "justified by works when he had offered Isaac his son upon the altar" (James 2:21). Do we have a contradiction? Of course not! The context of Paul's question is that "as pertaining to the flesh" (4:1), Abraham found that he was not justified by works. The context of James' question is that children, because they are "under tutors and governors" (Galatians 4:2), need to have works of faith, coupled with faith, in order to make their faith perfect (James 2:22). Therefore, as pertaining to the soul, Abraham found that he needed faith, plus works of faith, in order to be justified.

Does this mean that Abraham was justified twice? Yes, it does! Initially, God justified Abraham by faith without works in Genesis 15:6. Abraham did not believe in Jesus' death as atonement for his sins, like we do today (I Corinthians 15:3-4), neither did he repent and be water baptized like Israel does in the at-hand phase of the kingdom in their program (Acts 2:38). Abraham believed what God told him, which was that God would make his seed as the stars in heaven (Genesis 15:5-6). Since all Abraham had to do was believe, it is an unconditional covenant, as seen by the fact that Abraham did not pass between the animal pieces—only God did (Genesis 15:17), as a sign that God had given him the heaven as an inheritance (Genesis 15:7-8).

God then made a second covenant with Abraham that He would give him the land of Canaan as an inheritance (Genesis 15:18-21). For this second covenant, God said that Abraham must keep this covenant with God, and the token of that covenant is the law of circumcision (Genesis 17:9-14). Therefore, this second covenant is conditional upon having works of faith, which circumcision is a token of (Genesis 17:11), since it symbolizes the cutting off of the flesh and walking in the Spirit.

Now, I realize that no one would ever see that God made two, different covenants with Abraham by reading Genesis 15-17. But, that is to be expected, since the details of the first covenant were kept secret until revealed to Paul (Romans 16:26 and Ephesians 3:2-5). The way we see that God made two, different covenants with Abraham is by the eyes of faith. Paul says that Abraham was justified by faith alone (4:1-3), and James says that Abraham was justified by faith plus works (James 2:21-22). Since God cannot lie (Titus 1:2), He must have made two, different covenants with Abraham. The first one, in Genesis 15, is the promise that his seed will be as the stars in heaven (the Body of Christ in heavenly places) (Genesis 15:5). The second one is the promise that his seed will be "as the sand which is upon the sea shore" (saved Israel in God's kingdom on earth) (Genesis 22:17).

This makes Abraham and Paul (Paul's dual justification is explained in my commentary on Acts 9:18.) the only two men in history to be saved under both programs, meaning they have positions both in the heavenly and in the earthly realms of God's eternal kingdom. Since Jesus is the leader in both realms, why can't Abraham and Paul be in both realms as well? This is why Paul can call Abraham the father of the Gentiles (4:1), and James can call Abraham the father of the Jews (James 2:21). This makes Abraham the father of all believers (4:16). Since Paul is giving Abraham as an example of justification by faith for the dispensation of grace, Paul focuses on the Genesis 15 justification. Since James gives Abraham as an example of justification by faith plus works for the kingdom dispensation, James focuses on the Genesis 22 justification.

Getting back to the context of Romans 4, Paul's point is that Abraham's flesh did not bring him justification, and that is true, because, regardless of the dispensation, it is faith in what God says that brings justification (Hebrews 11:6). The difference between dispensations is that God has given different instructions for man to have faith in, depending on the dispensation. By using Abraham as an example, Paul is being consistent with what he said in 2:6-7. What Abraham found as pertaining to the flesh, then, was that he was not able to continue patiently in well doing all his life (2:7). Therefore, he had to have faith in what God told him.

4:3 "What saith the scripture?" (4:3 and Galatians 4:30) is the question we should always ask so that we have the mind of Christ (I Corinthians 2:16) on every issue we face. Since different portions of God's Word give different instructions to different people, the only way we will understand what the scripture says to us is by "rightly dividing the Word of truth" (II Timothy 2:15). This means that we recognize that Romans through Philemon is the only portion of scripture written directly to us, although all of God's Word is profitable for us (II Timothy 3:16-17). Therefore, our doctrine should ALWAYS be based on God's Word rightly divided, regardless of if other people, including other Christians, believe it or not. Our teacher is the Holy Spirit (I Corinthians 2:10-13), not a church denomination, a pastor, or even the writer of this commentary.

4:4-5 Man's flesh sins (7:18), and the wages of sin is death (6:23); therefore, man's wage is death, not justification. This is why having faith in God, i.e., believing what God says, is the ONLY way to eternal life, regardless of the dispensation. Therefore, Abraham was saved by faith in God. It was nothing that he did to earn his salvation. We can use Abraham's justification in Genesis 15, then, as an example that demonstrates how we are saved by faith alone today in the blood of Christ (3:28 and I Corinthians 15:3-4).

These verses also help explain why Paul said that, if Abraham were justified by the works of his flesh, he could boast, but not before God (4:2). If he were justified by his own works, then eternal life would be a debt owed to him by God. He could boast before other men, because other men did not do the work to earn eternal life, but he still could not boast before God, because all he would have done would have been a good job. He would still be under God. This is important in light of the fact that Jesus Christ was a man, Who did earn eternal life by His own works. Yet, He said, "I do nothing of myself; but as My Father hath taught Me" (John 8:28). As such, Jesus merely did what it was His duty to do (Luke 17:10), and Jesus Christ will always be under God the Father (I Corinthians 15:28). How much more, then, is every mouth stopped, and all the world is guilty before God (3:19)!

4:6-8 Paul quotes Psalm 32:1-2, where David praises God for forgiving him of his sins of adultery with Bathsheba and the murder of her husband, Uriah. Leviticus 20:10 says that an adulterer is to be put to death. Numbers 35:31 says that a murderer is to be put to death. Therefore, according to the Mosaic law, David had two death sentences upon him that could not be forgiven with animal sacrifices. However, God forgave him, restored him as king, and David will rule in God's kingdom forever (Ezekiel 37:24). God did this because of David's faith in God's imputed righteousness to save him. The point that Paul is making is that David was worthy of death under the law, but God saw his faith and gave him eternal life instead, even though David was under the law. How much more, then, in the dispensation of grace, when "all have sinned, and come short of the glory of God" (3:23), will God forgive the sins of those who believe the gospel (3:22) and "are not under the law, but under grace" (6:14).

Note also that God's forgiveness is for both past and future sins. David's past iniquities are forgiven (4:7), and the Lord will not impute sin to his account for future sins (4:8). Therefore, even the "deadly" sins, committed by someone who has already believed the gospel, do not cause the person to lose his salvation. The blood of Christ is strong enough to forgive even those bad, future sins, as well.

4:9-10 God's gift of eternal life to all those who believe is the best news you could ever receive. Yet, very few people believe it. That is because the heart is so "desperately wicked" (Jeremiah 17:9) that it will come up with every excuse under the sun to say that it is not true. The excuse of 4:9 is that, since Paul used the examples of Abraham and David, justification by faith must only be available in Israel's program, not today. At first, this seems like a valid argument, because God started the nation of Israel with Abraham (Genesis 12:1-3). However, as Paul points out, here, Abraham was actually justified in Genesis 15:4-6 as a Gentile. The covenant that started the nation of Israel was circumcision (Genesis 17:14 and John 7:22), but Abraham was justified before God gave him the covenant of circumcision. This means that he was justified in uncircumcision. Therefore, justification by faith must be available to all Gentiles. It is also available to all Jews, since David received justification while being circumcised. Thus, this argument of the flesh is incorrect.

4:11 This verse says that circumcision is a sign. When someone believes the gospel that God has given him, he has recognized that in his flesh dwells no good thing (7:18). Therefore, he has reckoned his flesh to be dead, meaning that he has "cut off" or circumcised his flesh, spiritually speaking. Thus, physical circumcision is merely a sign of what has happened spiritually in his heart (Compare Deuteronomy 10:16 with Acts 7:51). Therefore, Abraham experienced spiritual circumcision in Genesis 15:6, and God gave him physical circumcision in Genesis 17:9-14 as a sign of what had already taken place in his heart. Because the spiritual circumcision occurred first, Abraham is the father of all those who believe today in the dispensation of grace, where it does not matter if you are physically circumcised or not (Galatians 5:6 and 6:15).

4:11 goes on to say that circumcision is also "a seal of the righteousness of the faith which he had yet being uncircumcised." This means that Abraham was already saved in Genesis 15, but his circumcision, in Genesis 17, guaranteed that he would stay saved. Today, in the dispensation of grace, when we believe the gospel, we are told that we are "sealed with that holy Spirit of promise" (Ephesians 1:13), which is why we do not need to be physically circumcised today in order to have eternal life. Because Christ's death for sin was future to Abraham, God gave him a different seal than what He gives us today. The Jews often had physical circumcision without having spiritual circumcision, due to their unbelief. Today, Christians often have the spiritual seal of the Holy Spirit without the physical evidence of it, because they do not walk in the Spirit.

It is interesting that 4:11 says that God gave Abraham the sign of circumcision so that he would be the father of the uncircumcision. It seems like the sign would qualify him to be the father of the circumcision instead. This may tell us a little more about how circumcision is a seal of righteousness for Abraham. All those justified by faith without works of faith are justified now and receive the atonement now (5:9,11). They do not have to wait until Jesus' second coming, as Israel does (Acts 3:19-20). Since we still have vile bodies (Philippians 3:21), we still sin after we are saved. Therefore, God gives us the seal of the Holy Spirit "which is the earnest of our inheritance until the redemption of the purchased possession" (Ephesians 1:14). In other words, God seals us with the Holy Spirit to guarantee that we will be redeemed, in spite of the sin that we commit afterward.

Because Jesus Christ had not yet provided the sacrifice for sin in the heavenly tabernacle at the time that Abraham was on earth, Abraham could not receive the Holy Spirit (John 16:7). Therefore, he could not be sealed with the Holy Spirit. Therefore, God gave him the seal of circumcision so that he was guaranteed to have eternal life, in spite of the sins he would commit afterward. This means that he was justified and received the atonement right then, making him the father of believers today. In other words, circumcision sealed Abraham's salvation so that it was secure. Since the body of Christ also has a seal to make their salvation secure, this makes Abraham the father of believers today. Therefore, God gave Abraham "the sign of circumcision, a seal of the righteousness of the faith which he had yet being uncircumcised" (4:11).

4:12 Physical circumcision saves no one. Male Jews were required to be physically circumcised (Leviticus 12:2-3). This was supposed to be a faith response to God's commandment. In other words, Jews would have faith in God and circumcise their male children in response to that faith. However, in Jesus' day, religious Israel had made physical circumcision into the way someone was saved. As such, they were judging after the flesh (John 8:15). That is why Paul makes the distinction that, in order to be saved, the circumcision must also walk in faith, as Abraham did (4:12). If they are circumcised but do not walk in faith, then they are just following a tradition, they have no faith, and they are children of the devil (John 8:44).

4:11-12 The two, distinct gospels of Israel's prophecy program and the body of Christ's mystery program are clearly seen here. The reason God justified Abraham in Genesis 15 and gave Abraham the law of circumcision afterward in Genesis 17 was so "that he might be the father of all them that believe, though they be not circumcised" (4:11). In other words, Abraham is the father of those saved today in the mystery program, because salvation is by faith alone in the mystery program. Abraham is also "the father of circumcision" because, in Israel's prophecy program, they had to "walk in the steps of that faith of our father Abraham" because they were justified by faith plus works (James 2:24), as Abraham was when he acted on his faith by sacrificing Isaac on the altar in Genesis 22. These two, distinct gospels are seen in that Paul does not say that the body of Christ has to "walk in the steps of that faith," nor does he say that Israel was saved by faith alone. Abraham is "the father of all them that believe" (4:11) in the body of Christ, and he is the father of all those who believe and "walk in the steps of that faith" (4:12) in Israel's program. This makes him "the father of us all" (4:16).

4:13 Galatians 3:16 explains that Abraham's seed, to whom the promise was made to be "heir of the world," is Christ. The meaning of this is that it is not all those who are natural descendants of Abraham who will be saved, as this would be inheritance "through the law" (4:13). Rather, the inheritance is "through the righteousness of faith" (4:13). If it were by the law, Ishmael and Esau would have received the inheritance, because they were the firstborn sons of Abraham and Isaac, respectively. Instead, Isaac and Jacob, the secondborn sons of Abraham and Isaac, respectively, received the inheritance because they were begotten by faith.

Similarly, God's firstborn son was Adam (Luke 3:38), but he did not receive the inheritance. Instead, it went to God's secondborn son, Jesus (Psalm 2:7-8), because He had faith in His Father's plan (Matthew 26:39). (I realize that God the Son has always existed. But, Jesus, as a man "in the likeness of sinful flesh" (8:3), was not begotten by God until His resurrection (Acts 13:33). This refers to a spiritual birth, making Him God's "only begotten Son" (John 3:16), while, in the flesh, He was God's secondborn son.) Then, all those, who have faith in the gospel God has given them, are taken out of Adam and placed into Christ so that they may also receive the inheritance (I Corinthians 15:21-22 and Romans 8:17). Therefore, the reason that all physically circumcised Jews do not receive eternal life is because that is the way the law works. It is not how faith works.

Therefore, this verse is saying that the promise to reign in God's eternal, earthly kingdom is to all those in Israel's program with faith in what God told them. Similarly, today, in the dispensation of grace, the promise of eternal life in heavenly places comes only to those who have faith in what God has told them, which is to trust in Jesus' death, burial, and resurrection for atonement of sin (I Corinthians 15:3-4). In either case, eternal life is by faith, not by the law.

4:14-15 The promise of being heir of the world is based upon having faith in God. God cannot give the world to those under the law, "because the law worketh wrath," which means that God would have to punish them, making the promise "of none effect." In other words, if God's promise of being heir of the world is based upon the law, the Jews would not become heirs of the world because they would continue in sin. But, since the promise is by faith, they can become heirs of the world because "where no law is, there is no transgression." Paul will later explain that "sin is not imputed when there is no law" (5:13). We just learned that David sinned, but God would not impute his sin to his account (4:8). That is because God declared him righteous by faith.

In summary, God put the Jews under the law. Then, God only gave His righteousness to those who had faith in what God told them. He then removed them from being under the law. (Granted, they were still supposed to observe the Mosaic law (Matthew 23:2-3), but as a work of faith, not as a means of salvation.) Therefore, if the Jews boast in the law (2:17), they will not receive God's promise. Instead, they need to have faith in God to give them His righteousness, removing them from the requirements of the law so that, when they sin, they have life with God because sin is not imputed unto them.

4:16 By basing the promise on faith, we do not receive eternal life by any works that we do. This makes it based upon grace. This is important because our works make us unrighteous (3:9-12), and grace and works do not mix (11:6). Therefore, God had to get rid of our works in order for us to be saved by grace through faith (Ephesians 2:8). Because eternal life is a gift from God (6:23), the promise of inheriting the world is "sure to all the seed"—both Jews and Gentiles (4:16)—instead of being "made of none effect" (4:14) by the law.

The way the Jews received the promise was by having faith in God and then acting on that faith by placing themselves under God's law covenant with them so that others would see the work of faith in them so that others might be saved. Since the promise is of faith, and not of the law, their transgression of the law is forgiven by God's grace, just like He forgave David who committed adultery and murder. The Lord would not impute sin unto him because he was saved by faith in God (4:6-8). Therefore, although Israel had the law and was required to put themselves under that law, even after having faith in God's imputed righteousness to bring them into the kingdom, God would not impute sin to their account when they transgressed the law because they are of faith; therefore, there is no transgression imputed (4:15) to these Jews under the Mosaic law. As such, the promise is not to all of Israel under the law, but it is to all of Israel under the law who also have faith in God like Abraham did. Today, in the dispensation of grace, we are under the law of the conscience (2:14-15) until we have faith. Then, we are no longer under that law (Galatians 3:24-25).

This means that we are of faith only.

Abraham was justified by faith only in Genesis 15:6 (see 4:2-3), as we are today in the mystery program. Abraham was also justified by faith plus works of faith in Genesis 22 (James 2:21-24), as those in the prophecy program are. This makes him "the father of us all" (4:16). It is extremely important that Abraham is the father of us all, because the promises were made "to Abraham and his seed," and that seed is Christ (Galatians 3:16). Therefore, mystery-program people can inherit the portion of the world in heavenly places (Ephesians 1:3), because they have faith in what God told them, as Abraham did, making them part of Christ's seed as the stars in heaven (Genesis 15:5). Also, prophecy-program people can inherit the portion of the world on the earth (Matthew 5:5), because they have faith plus works of faith, as Abraham did, making them part of Christ's seed as the sand on the seashore (Genesis 22:17). If God did not set up this dual-justification plan through "Abraham and his seed" (Galatians 3:16), God only would have reconciled one realm—earth or heaven—back to Himself through Christ, and not both. Granted, Christ's death still would have counted for both realms, but no one would have been placed into Christ in the one realm without a justification plan.

Said another way, in order for God to reconcile the world back to Himself, He needed the sacrifice for sins, and the people who would trust God to save them. If God never set up justification by faith alone in Genesis 15, Christ still would have spoiled principalities and powers and triumphed over them in heavenly places (Colossians 2:14-15), but there would have been no people to place in those positions of authority, since all those with faith would have been justified in the prophecy program, not in the mystery program. In other words, because the promise to inherit the world is specifically to "Abraham and his seed" (Galatians 3:16), Abraham's inheritance must include both earthly and heavenly places in order for all things in heaven and earth to be gathered together into Christ "in the dispensation of the fulness of times" (Ephesians 1:10). That is why Abraham was justified twice.

4:17 Understanding this helps us to understand why God told Abram that He would make of him a great nation (Genesis 12:2). Then, later, He changed his name to "Abraham," which meant that God would make him "a father of MANY nations" (Genesis 17:4). Christians think that Genesis 17:4 is a just a restatement of the Genesis 12:2 promise, because Genesis 12:3 says that "all families of the earth" will be blessed in Abram. However, if this were the same promise as Genesis 17:4, God would have changed his name to Abraham in Genesis 12, not in Genesis 17. The promise, of Genesis 12, is that Abram will be the father of the nation of Israel, and all Gentiles, who bless Israel during the prophecy program, will also be part of God's earthly kingdom. The promise, of Genesis 17, is that Abraham will be the father of many nations, which are all believers during the mystery program, and they will be part of God's heavenly kingdom.

Ephesians 2:1 says that we "were dead in trespasses and sins." But, because we believed the gospel of grace, God has resurrected us from the dead, spiritually speaking, and He will do this for us physically, as well, at the rapture. Calling us "alive" when we were dead is how God "calleth those things which be not as though they were." This is how God could tell Abraham that, "a father of many nations HAVE I made thee" (Genesis 17:5), when he would not be a father to anyone under that promise until the dispensation of grace began with Paul over 2,000 years later.

This phrase also explains many other things in the Bible, such as how "the Lamb" could be "slain from the foundation of the world" (Revelation 13:8), when Jesus did not die on a cross for at least 4,000 years after the world was created. Another example is of martyred believers receiving white robes and being with God in heaven before the tribulation period is over (Revelation 6:9-11), when they do not receive the atonement for their sins until Jesus' second coming (Acts 3:19-20), which is still future during the tribulation period. An example for the mystery dispensation is of us being seated together with Christ in heavenly places today (Ephesians 2:6), looking down on our vile bodies on this earth, longing for Christ to come and give us glorified bodies, even though God says we are in heavenly places right now (Philippians 3:20-21)! These examples show that, since God is outside of time, He can declare "the end from the beginning" (Isaiah 46:10), which means that He can call things as they will be in their final state, rather than as they are right now (4:17).

4:18-20 "Who against hope believed in hope." What this means is that Abraham, in his flesh, had no hope of ever having a great nation come out of his bowels, because he was dead reproductively, as was Sarah. Yet, God told him that he would have seed as innumerable as the stars in heaven and that his seed would come forth out of his own bowels (Genesis 15:4-5). It was this promise that Abraham believed, and God counted it to him for righteousness (Genesis 15:6). In other words, Abraham saw that his body and Sarah's body were dead reproductively (4:19), and so a belief that he would have seed was "against hope." However, since God knows everything and God said that his seed would be as the stars in heaven, Abraham "believed in hope."

Similarly for us, there is no profit from our labour on this earth (Ecclesiastes 1:3). Man's days are full of sorrow and grief with no rest (Ecclesiastes 2:23). Yet, God has given us the gift of eternal life and an inheritance, and, because God declared the end from the beginning (Isaiah 46:10), we can trust the Lord, as Abraham did, believing in the hope of God by going against the hope of this world.

The point is that Abraham's righteousness had nothing whatsoever to do with his ability to perform, because he was incapable of producing seed through Sarah. Abraham only received righteousness because he believed

God (Genesis 15:6). This means that our own works have nothing whatsoever to do with the righteousness we receive from God.

Note how 4:20 says that Abraham "staggered not at the promise of God through unbelief." Because no one does good, no one is righteous based upon his own works (3:10-12). Therefore, we all have sinned (3:23), or we have all "staggered" like a drunk man on the path to earning our own righteousness. The only area in which we are able not to stagger is in belief. We can believe what God has said to us "nothing wavering" (James 1:6), and then God gives us eternal life. Unfortunately, most people never believe, they stagger along through life like drunken men, and so God has had to have hell enlarged to accommodate them (Isaiah 5:14), when hell was only "prepared for the devil and his angels" (Matthew 25:41).

4:20 also tells us how we give glory to God. We do so by being "strong in faith." Every man has "a measure of faith" (12:3), according to how much of God's word he has believed. That measure is increased as we read and believe more of God's word. Therefore, the more of God's word we read and believe, the stronger our faith is, and the more glory we bring to God. Thus, glorifying God comes by reading and believing His word, and not just by closing your eyes, raising your hands, and "feeling" the words to a "worship" song that you sing in church. God is glorified in truth (John 4:24), not in feelings (James 3:15).

4:21-22 These verses say that the way Abraham received God's imputed righteousness was by "being fully persuaded." God is the One Who spoke to him (Genesis 15:4-5). "Faith cometh by hearing, and hearing by the word of God" (10:17). Therefore, faith is hearing God's reasoning and believing it. This is important to note, because, just like worship, many people think that faith is based on a feeling or emotion. An unbeliever might say, "Faith is okay for you Christians who need a crutch, but I base my beliefs on logic and reason." However, God's word says that faith is when someone hears God's argument and is fully persuaded that it is true. In other words, faith is based on reason. Without hearing God's word and reasoning it to be true, there is no faith. In Abraham's case, he thought about what God said and recognized that, as God, He could do it. Therefore, Abraham was fully persuaded that God would do what He said He would do.

4:23-24 The implication of "it was not written for his sake alone" is that writing down Genesis 15:6 did help Abraham. However, the book of Genesis was written by Moses, about 400 years after Abraham died. Therefore, the only way writing down Genesis 15:6 could help Abraham is if it is used in the future. This must mean that God will use the Bible to judge man. Therefore, when Abraham stands before God to be judged, God can open the Bible to Genesis 15:6 and show that God has already declared Abraham righteous. This is important to recognize because Paul goes on to say that Genesis 15:6 was also written for our sakes. This means that God will use this same scripture to show that God has also declared the body of Christ to be righteous.

This also helps us understand why the future tense is used when it comes to God's righteousness being imputed unto us. After all, 5:9 says that we are "NOW justified by His blood," and 5:11 says that "we have NOW received the atonement." So, how can we NOW have justification and atonement when God's righteousness "SHALL be imputed" (4:24) unto us? And, "IF we believe on Him" (4:24) makes it sound like we can lose our salvation if we stop believing on Him in the future.

4:24 is not saying that our salvation can be lost or that we have not received salvation yet, because losing our salvation contradicts the statements of 5:9 and 5:11. Rather, 4:23-24 is saying that there is a future time when "the Lord...shall judge the world with righteousness, and the people with His truth" (Psalm 96:13). The Lord will open books, and judge people out of those books (Revelation 20:12). Unbelievers will be judged based upon their works (Revelation 20:12). That is the Lord judging the world with righteousness. All believers will be judged "with His truth" (Psalm 96:13), which means that they are judged by the Bible, specifically Genesis 15:6. In other words, all believers receive God's imputed righteousness because they believed what the Lord told them, and that is established as truth by Genesis 15:6, since "Thy word is truth" (John 17:17). Therefore, the moment we believe the gospel, we are justified and our sins are atoned for, as 5:9 and 5:11 say. Then, one day, we will stand before the Lord, and He will officially impute His righteousness to us at that time. So, how can we have justification and the atonement right now if He has not imputed His righteousness to us yet? Because "God...calleth those things which be not as though they were" (4:17).

The phrase "book of life" is found eight times in scripture. Revelation 20:15 says that all those, whose names are not written in the book of life, are cast into the lake of fire. Christians usually think of the book of life as a list of all saved people. However, God will use Genesis 15:6 to substantiate both Abraham and the body of Christ receiving eternal life. Jesus said that "the words that I speak unto you, they are spirit, and they are life" (John 6:63). Given this, it makes sense that "the book of life" would really be the Bible. After all, there is no life apart from God's word. If the Bible is the book of life, the way that our names are written in the book of life is that we are included with Abraham in Genesis 15:6. This makes Genesis 15:6 the most important verse in the Bible to saved people. (This also would take away man's pride in saying that he was someone special by having his name in God's book.)

Believing "on Him that raised up Jesus our Lord from the dead" (4:24) means that we believe the gospel that God has given us. Paul does not specify the gospel of grace, because Abraham believed a different gospel. Abraham was saved by believing that his seed would be as the stars in heaven (Genesis 15:5-6), while, today, we are saved by believing in Jesus' death, burial, and resurrection as atonement for our sin (I Corinthians 15:3-4). The reason we should believe what God has told us is because He alone has the power over death (I Corinthians 15:54-57), as demonstrated by the fact that He "raised up Jesus our Lord from the dead" (4:24).

4:25 In fact, 4:25 says that our justification is made possible by Jesus' resurrection. That is why Paul says in I Corinthians 15:17, "And if Christ be not raised, your faith is vain; ye are yet in your sins."

5 Now that we know that we have been justified by faith (v. 1), Paul will show how we cannot lose our salvation. First, he tells us to expect tribulations (vs. 3-5), because tribulations in our flesh bring glory to God (v. 2). Lest we get prideful about this glory, Paul reminds us that we were ungodly (v. 6), and that Christ died for sinners (v. 8), not for those who cleaned up their act in order to be glorified. Then, he tells us that we were justified by God (v. 9), and this took place by God changing our identity, taking us out of Adam and placing us into Christ. Because we did nothing to earn this justification, we also can do nothing to lose it (vs. 13-17). Thus, God says we are righteous (v. 19), not because of anything we did, but because God's grace abounded to us through the Lord Jesus Christ (vs. 20-21). Therefore, we can stop worrying about losing our salvation, and we can start allowing God to work glory in us through trials.

5:1 "Therefore, being justified by faith" (5:1). These first, five words of this verse show that the issue of our justification has been settled by the end of Romans 4. Therefore, we now know that we are justified by faith. This means that we have God's righteousness, or a right standing with God. This right standing means that the wrath of God is not upon us (1:18), meaning that we have peace with God. Since this peace comes only through the shed blood of our Lord Jesus Christ, there is nothing we can do to lose this peace. Once we recognize we are sinners and trust in Jesus' death, burial, and resurrection to save us, we have peace with God for all eternity, regardless of how badly we behave! (We will learn more about our behavior in Romans 6-8).

This means that Romans 5 – Philemon does not talk about how we are justified, which means that NO verse in that section of scripture can be twisted to say that we can lose our salvation. Since we have been justified by faith, none of the following verses speak about losing our salvation:

- "There is therefore now no condemnation to them which are in Christ Jesus, who walk not after the flesh, but after the Spirit" (Romans 8:1)

- "If thou continue in His goodness: otherwise thou also shalt be cut off" (Romans 11:22)

- "Nor drunkards, nor revilers, nor extortioners, shall inherit the kingdom of God" (I Corinthians 6:9)

- "By which also ye are saved, if ye keep in memory what I preached unto you, unless ye have believed in vain" (I Corinthians 15:2)

- "Ye are fallen from grace" (Galatians 5:4)

- "They which do such things shall not inherit the kingdom of God" (Galatians 5:21)

- "Nor unclean person, nor covetous man, who is an idolater, hath any inheritance in the kingdom of Christ and of God" (Ephesians 5:5)

- "Work out your own salvation with fear and trembling" (Philippians 2:12)

- "If ye continue in the faith grounded and settled, and be not moved away from the hope of the gospel" (Colossians 1:23)

- "If we deny Him, He also will deny us" (II Timothy 2:12)

In other words, because God's word is true (John 17:17), He cannot lie (Titus 1:2), and Paul's epistles are God's word (I Corinthians 14:37 and II Peter 3:15-16). Therefore, the fact, that the first four chapters of Romans have led to the conclusion that we are justified by faith (5:1), means that we do not have to worry about our salvation from here on out. Therefore, when we come across the aforementioned passages, even if we do not know what they are talking about, we at least know that they are not saying that we can lose your salvation, because that would make God a liar in Romans 1-4. (We will discuss what each passage means as we come to them in this commentary series.) The fact, that much of Christianity wants our salvation to be dependent upon our performance, shows how desperately wicked the flesh really is (Jeremiah 17:9).

5:2 Because Jesus is the "propitiation" or fully satisfying sacrifice for our sins (3:25), we are "accepted" by God "in the Beloved" (Ephesians 1:6), Who is Christ (Matthew 3:17). This means that "your life is hid with Christ in God" (Colossians 3:3). Therefore, not only do you have peace with God, but you also have access to God through our Lord Jesus Christ. Therefore, when we place our faith in Jesus Christ, we now stand in grace, as 6:14 says, "Ye are not under the law, but under grace."

Paul says in I Thessalonians 5:16 to "rejoice evermore." 5:2 tells us the reason to "rejoice evermore" is because we have eternal life. That is our hope and giving eternal life to us brings God glory because it exalts His Son in that He has brought another son to glory (Hebrews 2:10). Therefore, we can "rejoice in [the] hope" of eternal life, which gives God glory.

5:3-5 "We glory in tribulations also" (5:3). Are you crazy, Paul? How many people actually glory in tribulations? The answer is that all who stand in the grace of God by faith should glory in tribulations (5:2). In order to receive justification, we must have faith in Jesus' shed blood as atonement for our sins (5:1). The common misperception among Christians is that that is the end of our faith. They think that, once we are justified, we suddenly become superhumans, who can now work for God in our flesh. That is not true. Rather, our flesh is still vile. The flesh is not changed until the rapture (Philippians 3:20-21).

However, when we are saved, the Holy Spirit baptizes us into one body (I Corinthians 12:13). That baptism is into Christ's death (6:4), which means that we are freed from having to allow our sin nature to control us (6:7) if we walk in the Spirit (Galatians 5:16). Therefore, although we still have our vile flesh, we can now choose to walk in the Spirit and not fulfill the lusts of the flesh. If we have the attitude that our flesh is dead (6:11), it shows we are living by faith, which is what the just are supposed to do (1:17). This means, instead of standing in our flesh, we stand in the grace of God to work through us in spite of our flesh.

With that attitude, any tribulations in the flesh should not bother us because the flesh is dead anyway. The flesh is like a headless chicken. Without its head, the chicken will soon die, but its flesh can run around for a few minutes before it actually dies. No one is worried that the chicken will get away, because it will soon be dead. Similarly, God says that, when you are saved, your flesh is dead. Functionally, your flesh can still act for the rest of your life, which is not a long time when compared with eternity. However, God is not worried about your flesh, because He knows that, once you physically die, your vile flesh will never do anything again.

After you are saved and before you physically die, you have an incredibly unique opportunity that will never come up again. That opportunity is that you can "reckon...also yourselves to be dead indeed unto sin, but alive unto God through Jesus Christ our Lord" (6:11). In other words, you can recognize what God has done for you and choose not to live in sin any longer. This choice will make you different to others so that they may be saved and come unto the knowledge of the truth (I Timothy 2:4).

In other words, when you recognize the weakness of the flesh, God can be strong through you. The easiest time to recognize the weakness of your flesh is when you go through tribulations. That is why Paul says that we "glory in tribulations," because "tribulation worketh patience" (5:3). Once we are saved, God begins doing a work in us to change us into the image of Christ (II Corinthians 3:18). God, Who began "a good work in you will perform it until the day of Jesus Christ" (Philippians 1:6). Therefore, when we go through tribulation, God is working patience in us to be content in all situations (Philippians 4:11), knowing that, by the tribulations we face, God is slowly changing us into the image of Christ. It is not that we enjoy tribulation, but it is that we have faith in the result that the tribulation will produce in us. "For our light affliction, which is but for a moment, worketh for us a far more exceeding and eternal weight of glory" (II Corinthians 4:17). Thus, we "glory in tribulations" (5:3).

Although God has reckoned our flesh to be dead, and we should, too, we will not see the reality of our vile flesh being done away with until we receive our glorified bodies at the rapture. Tribulations, then, help us, because they cause us to see how worthless our flesh is so that we will develop the patience to deny the flesh's lusts until the flesh is done away with at the rapture. Therefore, we can actually glory in tribulations!

The patience, produced by the tribulations, gives us the experience to see that what God says about our flesh is really true, i.e., our flesh is dead. This then produces hope, which is the confident waiting for our glorified bodies. Therefore, when we reach the hope stage, we do not care one bit about our fleshly bodies. However, this does not make us ashamed of our flesh, because the flesh can still be used by the Holy Ghost to manifest God's love to the world. In other words, at the hope stage, we are allowing the Holy Ghost to spread God's love to others, and He does so through our flesh. He does this by the love of Christ constraining us to judge everyone according to who they are spiritually, rather than who they are physically (II Corinthians 5:14-16). They are either in Christ and need to come more unto the knowledge of the truth, or they are in Adam and need to believe the gospel. In either case, our goal is to share truth with them to help them spiritually, it is NOT to change people's behavior or make them "better" people. Thus, we show God's love to them and shed the labels of being uppity, judgmental, and hypocritical, as most unbelievers have labeled Christians.

Paul's point, in 5:3-5, is that, now that we are justified by faith, we can be guided by the Spirit and love, instead of being guided by the flesh and lust, and this transformation starts with tribulation. Knowing this, we "glory in tribulations" (5:3). Christians normally think of tribulation as physical suffering for Christ, and it can include this. However, we also need to keep in mind that our "flesh lusteth against the Spirit" (Galatians 5:17), which means that the primary source of tribulation that we face is within ourselves. Thus, tribulation occurs, not just if we are put in prison for believing the gospel, but also when we make the daily decision to die to the flesh so that Christ may live through us (I Corinthians 15:31). "For he that hath suffered in the flesh hath ceased from sin" (I Peter 4:1). If we die to the flesh, then we have allowed God to take the flesh, which is a huge negative, and actually turn it into a positive. This allows God to get the glory for any good thing the Holy Ghost does through us, as II Corinthians 4:7 says, "But we have this treasure in earthen vessels, that the excellency of the power may be of God, and not of us." This tells us why God does not give us glorified flesh the moment we are saved. God is performing a work in our vile flesh to conform us to the image of Christ so that: 1) Others will see God in us and want God in them, and 2) We will not get prideful and think we are something in ourselves.

Also, note that 5:5 tells us that the Holy Ghost has been given unto us. Since we are sealed with the Holy Spirit until (Ephesians 1:13-14) and unto (Ephesians 4:30) the day we receive our glorified bodies, He indwells us permanently. This is in stark contrast to what Old-Testament saints experienced. Very few of those saints ever received the Holy Spirit. And, of those who did receive the Holy Spirit, He was only given to them for a specific task they were to do. The Holy Ghost could not be given to all believers on a permanent basis until after Jesus ascended to the Father after His resurrection (John 16:7). The Holy Ghost teaches us the things of God (I Corinthians 2:9-13), so that we may walk after the Spirit, rather than after the flesh (8:1). Therefore, we should not take lightly the fact that all believers today receive the indwelling Holy Ghost so that Christ may live in us through His word (Galatians 2:20).

5:6 The "gospel," that most churches preach, includes some form of the following: Invite Jesus into your heart, turn from your sins, make a commitment to serve the Lord, and make Jesus the Lord of your life. These are all things that I do, which means they have made salvation about me. If I could do these things, why did Christ die for me? The answer is that I cannot do these things, because 5:6 says that when Christ died for us, "we were yet without strength." Therefore, the gospel preached by most of Christianity is a false gospel, and Paul says that we should let the person preaching that gospel be accursed (Galatians 1:8-9). That is how serious this is! Why would they preach a false gospel? Because the cross of Christ alone as atonement for my sins is offensive to the flesh (Galatians 5:11).

5:6 goes on to say that "Christ died for the ungodly." Again, if I could do the things of the false gospel preached by Christianity, I am godly, because I just turned myself from being a bad person to being a good person. Yet, Paul does not mention godliness as an attribute of the body of Christ until I Timothy 2:2. That is because it takes all of the sound doctrine of Romans through II Thessalonians to produce a godly life. But, I cannot learn any sound doctrine until I am saved, because I do not have the Holy Ghost until I am saved and the Holy Ghost is the One Who teaches me the things of God (I Corinthians 2:9-14). Therefore, I am "yet without strength" (5:6) to live a godly life before I am saved. That is why Paul said, "There is none righteous, no, not one" (3:10).

Christianity will argue: "Oh, but you have to recognize what Jesus Christ did for you before you can change." While the power to change is found only in the crosswork of Christ, the fact remains that I cannot change. Christ must change me AFTER I am saved. If I am the one doing the changing, then Christ's death is of no effect (Galatians 5:4), as Paul just said: "For if they which are of the law be heirs, faith is made void, and the promise made of none effect" (4:14). Even if I recognize Christ's death for my sins, a commitment to change as part of the gospel is of the flesh, because I am dead in my trespasses and sins until God saves me (Ephesians 2:1). Therefore, I do not have the spiritual capacity to make a commitment to allow God to change me until after I am saved. Since no good thing dwells in my flesh (7:18), such a promise is not of faith, making it a sin (14:23). Thus, it is the pride of man that delivers a false gospel to the masses in saying that I must do something before Christ will save me, and it is "the slight of men, and cunning craftiness" to deceive people (Ephesians 4:14) into thinking they are saved by including Christ as part of their gospel, when God has made Christ the entirety of the gospel.

Also note that 5:6 says that Christ died "in due time." In His wisdom, God knew that the right time for Christ to die would be 4,000 years after the fall of man in Genesis 3. Thus, Christ's death was completely according to God's plan, as Galatians 4:4 says that "the fulness of the time was come."

5:7 This verse says that, because we are ungodly, no man would die for us, even if they had the capacity to do so.

5:8 Many people feel like they have to "clean up their act" or be "good enough" before they will attend church. While this may be true before most churches will accept you, it is not true with God. Christ died for us "while we were yet sinners." Man would never do this; therefore, God had to do this. If God had not died for us "while we were yet sinners," no one would have eternal life, because we cannot clean up our own act, as we just learned (5:6). This again proves that the "gospel" that is often taught today of having to turn from your sins in order to be saved is a FALSE gospel.

Also, note that 5:8 says that "God COMMENDETH His love toward us." This means that He gave us His love. Most modern translations say that He "showed," "demonstrated," or "proved" His love for us. These are all incorrect. God actually gave us His love, as we just learned in 5:5. It is God's love that constrains us to judge as God judges people (II Corinthians 5:14). Without His love, we would seek to please God through our performance, rather than through Christ living in us (Galatians 2:20). Therefore, God commended His love toward us so that we could walk in the Spirit, but you would never learn this by reading a modern translation!

5:9 Under Israel's prophecy program, their sins will not be blotted out until Jesus' second coming, as Acts 3:19b-20a says, "Your sins may be blotted out, WHEN the times of refreshing shall come from the presence of the Lord; And he shall send Jesus Christ." (All modern translations omit the word "when" so that you do not understand that salvation is still future in Israel's program.) Under today's mystery program for the body of Christ, our sins are remitted the split second we believe in Jesus' death, burial, and resurrection as atonement for our sins, because we are "NOW justified by His blood." This shows that the doctrine of eternal security is true for us today, but it is not true for those going through the tribulation period because they can lose their salvation, as seen in Jesus' statement in Matthew 10:33 that "whosoever shall deny Me before men, him will I also deny before My Father which is in heaven." The conditional salvation of Israel is seen even more clearly in Revelation 14:9-11, which says that "if any man worship the beast and his image, and receive his mark in his forehead, or in his hand, the same shall drink of the wine of the wrath of God...and he shall be tormented with fire and brimstone...for ever and ever." If you do not rightly divide the word of truth (II Timothy 2:15), you will not notice the difference between the two programs, leading to the belief of false doctrine.

Also note that we are "justified BY HIS BLOOD" (5:9). This confirms that our own works have nothing to do with our salvation. It is Christ's blood ALONE that justifies us. If we add any requirement to our justification, we cheapen the blood of Christ by saying that it alone is not enough to save us. We say that we must do something ourselves. This is akin to treading under foot the Son of God, counting the blood of the covenant an unholy thing, and despising the "Spirit of grace" (Hebrews 11:29), which means that the person, who believes such a false gospel, is not saved and will go to hell. Therefore, it is absolutely essential that we believe in Jesus' death, burial, and resurrection alone to atone for our sin (I Corinthians 15:3-4).

Romans 5:9 is also a good proof text of a pre-tribulation rapture, because it says that "we shall be saved from wrath through Him." This is confirmed by another 5:9 passage in I Thessalonians which says, "God hath not appointed us to wrath, but to obtain salvation by our Lord Jesus Christ." In other words, we do not have to go through the wrath of the tribulation period because God has given us His righteousness right now.

5:10 Paul continues to talk about the rapture in which our flesh will be changed into a glorified body (Philippians 3:21). Since God was able to change us from being His enemies to being reconciled to God, then we can rest assured that He will also save our flesh through His life, as Paul says in I Corinthians 15:22-23, "In Christ shall all be made alive. But every man in his own order: Christ the firstfruits; afterward they that are Christ's at His coming."

As such, Paul is saying that it is easier to believe in a pre-tribulation rapture than it is to believe that Jesus died for your sins. After all, if you can believe that God could change you from being His enemy to being His heir (8:16-17), certainly you can believe that He will save His children from the wrath that He will pour on His enemies! Sadly, many still do not believe in a pre-tribulation rapture.

This also shows God's great love for us. We were His enemies. You usually try to destroy your enemies or at least separate yourself from them. Instead, God reconciled us to Himself by giving up His most precious possession, His

Son, to die in our place. This is a fact that is incomprehensible to our fleshly minds.

5:11 If you did not get the message in 5:9 of eternal security and the contrast between Israel's prophecy program and today's mystery program with regard to the timing of the forgiveness of sins, it is given even more clearly here. Since "we have NOW received the atonement," we NOW have eternal life in Christ. Therefore, when we sin after we are saved, our sin is already forgiven because it has already been atoned for by the blood of our Lord Jesus Christ.

But, that is not the point of this verse, because we already knew that. Rather, this is a transition verse to explain why "we also joy in God through our Lord Jesus Christ" (5:11). In other words, just because we still have our vile flesh after we are saved does not mean that we live in misery until the rapture takes place. In other words, when God saved us, He did not just give us forgiveness of sins, but He also placed us into Christ, as Paul will explain in 5:12-21 and then go into detail about what that means in chapters 6 – 8. Because we are in Christ, we can "rejoice evermore" (I Thessalonians 5:16), by allowing Christ to live through us (Galatians 2:20). Otherwise, we would have no joy, because we would continue to live in sin with no power to overcome sin until the rapture takes place.

5:12 "Sin" refers to the old, sin nature, while "sins" refer to the actual sins committed as a result of the sin nature. Paul will now explain how Christ's death overcame the sin nature for us, which sets up Romans 6-8, which talks about how a believer can walk in the Spirit and allow Christ to live in them. It is critical that we recognize the difference between the words "sin" and "sins," because Christianity does not. They focus on "sins" and how they, in their flesh, can overcome them. Of course, they cannot overcome them in their flesh, so they have to re-define what sin is. They refuse to recognize the sin nature, or, if they do recognize it, they will say that God gives you power in your flesh to overcome the sin nature. By ignoring the sin nature or by saying that you can overcome it in yourself, they make the Christian life all about how good you make yourself to be. (Christianity's cure for sin is like an alcoholic trying to cure his liver problem by painting his yellow skin white.)

By contrast, Paul says that the problem is not "sins," but "sin." In other words, your problem is that, even after you are saved, you will do nothing but sin in the energies of your flesh, because the problem is not overcoming your "sins," but it is allowing Christ, in your new identity of who you are in Christ, to overcome the sin nature within you so that you do not commit sins. This means that you cannot brag about how good you are or look like a super Christian to others, because it is Christ Who overcomes for you, not yourself. ("But we have this treasure in earthen vessels, that the excellency of the power may be of God, and not of us" (II Corinthians 4:7).) All you do is let Christ do the overcoming for you. "LET this mind be in you, which was also in Christ Jesus" (Philippians 2:5), not "overcome sin by trying really hard not to sin, and, when you mess up, promise not to sin again, except mean it this time."

With this in mind, let's look at 5:12. We just learned that we have "joy in God through our Lord Jesus Christ" (5:11) because we are in Christ, and so what Christ did counts for us. "Wherefore" (5:12), then, tells us that the reason one man's (Christ's) obedience counts for us is because one man's (Adam's) disobedience also counts for us. "Sin" entered into the world by one man. This means that, thanks to Adam, all men have the sin nature (not that you or I would have done any better than Adam did). Since the wages of sin is death (6:23), the sin nature also brought death into the world. Since we all have the sin nature, it is impossible for unsaved man not to sin (7:18). Everything unsaved man does is sin (6:19-21), because his sin nature rules over him (6:14). Therefore, all have sinned (3:23) and are worthy of death.

5:13-17 These verses are a parenthetical reference, explaining 5:12. 5:12 says that, because of Adam's sin, 1) The sin nature "entered into the world," 2) Death came as a result of sin, and 3) All men die because "all have sinned" by sin being imputed to all men through Adam's sin. The latter is the key point that Paul explains in 5:13-17. Man dies because of Adam's sin being imputed to man's account. By making the sin nature the issue, the solution cannot be man making himself righteous by trying not to sin. The solution must be overcoming the sin nature by something greater, which is faith in the blood of Christ. Thus, man's efforts are eliminated, and God receives all the glory through Christ.

5:13-14 Based upon the reference to Moses in 5:14, we can determine that "until the law" is a reference to the Mosaic law. The point in bringing up the law is to show that, when it comes to our sin nature, the law is not the issue. The law makes our sin nature "exceeding sinful" (7:13). In other words, the law makes it easier for us to see that we have a sin nature, but we still have a sin nature, whether or not the Mosaic law was given. By recognizing that sin was in the world even before the Mosaic law was given, the reader is not able to make an excuse for his sin. He cannot say that he would be righteous if God never gave the law to Israel. Granted, there is no imputation of sin when there is no law, but death still reigned from the fall of man (Adam) to the giving of the law (Moses) (5:14), because man still had the sin nature. We cannot say that God was not fair during that time, because God did tell man about Himself (1:19-20), and God would have granted forgiveness of sin to man if he believed what God told him.

However, the point of 5:13-14 is not salvation. The point is that all have sinned because all have the sin nature because all are children of Adam. Paul is establishing that we have received an inheritance of sin that brings us death, even if there is no law to tell us that we are sinners and worthy of death. (Actually, even before the law, man knew that his sin made him worthy of death, according to 1:32.)

The reason that Paul establishes how sin and death by sin work by Adam is because Adam "is the figure of Him [Jesus Christ] that was to come" (5:14). Adam is a figure of Jesus Christ because they are the only two men in history who had a choice with regard to sin. This is so because they are the only two men in history ever born without a sin nature. The first Adam chose to sin, which means that he chose death. Since all of us are born into Adam, because we are all born with a sin nature, we are born into death. This may seem unfair, but remember that God told everyone about Himself (1:19-20), and He gave man the law of the conscience (2:14-15) so he would recognize that he is a sinner and needs God to save him. Since "sin is not imputed when there is no law" (5:13), those, who die before receiving the law of the conscience, will receive eternal life (7:9), even though they are born into death. Now that we have taken care of the supposed unfairness of the imputation of sin, we can see the great benefit of this imputation.

How sin and death works with Adam is actually a great thing, because he is a figure of Jesus Christ. Jesus Christ, the second Adam, chose life. He chose not to sin. Therefore, just like all those in Adam have Adam's choice count for them, all those in Christ have Christ's choice count for them. In other words, the principle of faith and life works just like the principle of sin and death. Just like death comes upon all men because of their sin nature, even if they do not commit the same sin that Adam did, life comes upon all men who believe what God has told them, even though they have not made the choice to earn life. The reason this is a great principle is that, because of our sin nature, we cannot choose to earn eternal life. Therefore, Christ's choice for life is the only way that eternal life is possible for us, which means that, without the imputation principle, no one would have eternal life with God except for Christ. Therefore, instead of complaining about sin and death, we should rejoice over faith and life in the Lord Jesus Christ.

In other words, without imputation of sin through Adam, there would be no imputation of life through Christ. If every person was born without the sin nature but with the choice to sin or not like Adam had, there would be no rest, because everyone would be striving against sin, until they finally yielded to sin, and then they died eternally. What a blessing that sin is imputed to us so that Christ's life can also be imputed to us when we believe, so that there is eternal rest in God for believers.

Therefore, 5:13 also speaks of our eternal security. Once we believe the gospel today, we are no longer under the law, but under grace (6:14). Since "sin is not imputed when there is no law" (5:13), our salvation is eternally secured, because, when we sin, our sin is not imputed to our account, because we are not under the law. Therefore, we can rest in who we are in Christ.

5:15 We have just learned that life in Christ is imputed to believers in the same way that death in Adam is imputed to all who are born. Therefore, it may be a little confusing that 5:15 says, "but NOT as the offence" (5:15). The way that the free gift of life in Christ is not as the offence of death in Adam is that life abounds over death. That is why this verse says, "MUCH MORE the grace of God...hath abounded" (5:15). In other words, if the free gift was equal to the offence, there would still be no life in Christ for believers, because that life would be cancelled out by the death in Adam, giving us a clean slate, similar to the situation that Adam was in before the fall. We would then have to choose not to sin in order to have life. But, since life in Christ abounds over death in Adam, once we believe the gospel we are "quickened...together with Christ" (Ephesians 2:5). In other words, Christ's death did not just cancel out the death we would receive by the sin of Adam, but His resurrection from the dead also gives us resurrection life to live in Christ for all eternity. This is only possible by Christ's life abounding over Adam's death.

"Many be dead" (5:15) through Adam's offence of the law not to eat of the tree of the knowledge of good and evil. However, Jesus Christ, as the second Adam, made the choice not to commit an offence. He chose life by never sinning (I Peter 2:22). Through His death, burial, and resurrection, God makes possible the free gift of eternal life (6:23). The point is that, since all die because of Adam's sin, all can choose to live forever because of Jesus Christ's obedience. Some may argue that Jesus Christ's death cannot atone for everyone's sins. However, since Adam's death counts for all mankind, Jesus Christ's death can also cancel out Adam's death and His resurrection can give life to all mankind for those who accept "the gift by grace" (v. 15). Thus, Adam's offence causes many to be dead, but Christ's obedience causes many to be alive over Adam's death. (By the way, this offer is also extended to Adam.)

5:16 In 5:15, Paul said that one way that God's gift of life is different from Adam's death is that it is stronger, such that it abounds over death. Now, in 5:16, we are told another way that God's gift of life is different from Adam's death. That is that Adam brought universal death with just one sin, but Christ's death and resurrection bring victory over all sins, not just one sin. In other words, Adam sinned and brought about the sin nature. Christ died and took care of all of the sins of the sin nature, not just Adam's one sin. This means that the blood of Christ alone is powerful enough to atone for all sins. Therefore, the gift of eternal life is available to all people (3:22), not just the ones who are "better" than others. In other words, the cold-blooded killer can have his sins forgiven and receive the gift of eternal life, even though he has committed many sins, just like the child who tells a "little, white lie" can have his sin forgiven and also receive the gift of eternal life. This also means that we do not have to be sorry for our sins, go to church, and attempt to do good deeds in order to become worthy of God's forgiveness. God came to us, "while we were yet sinners" (5:8), and gives us eternal life once we believe in Jesus' death, burial, and resurrection as atonement for our sins, because Christ's blood atones for all of our sins, even the "really bad" ones. Thus, Adam's one sin brought condemnation, but God's gift overcomes "many offences unto justification" (5:16). Therefore, not only does Christ's life abound over Adam's death (5:15), but it also abounds over all sins, not just the sin of Adam (5:16).

5:17 The ability of sin to bring death (6:23) is so great that death reigned over all men for thousands of years by just one sin that Adam committed. This shows the great strength of death. Then, Christ came along and conquered death. "Death is swallowed up in victory...through our Lord Jesus Christ" (I Corinthians 15:54,57). Since death was destroyed by Christ, life in Christ must be stronger than death in Adam. Since death ruled by one sin and Christ's death overcame "many offences" (5:16), the free gift of eternal life must be much stronger than death. Therefore, since Adam's death was secure in that there was nothing we could do to overcome death in Adam, Christ's life must be way more secure than Adam's death, which means that it is absolutely impossible for us to do anything to lose our salvation. That is why Paul says that we have received an "ABUNDANCE of grace" (5:17); it is God's grace abounding over sin and death.

The contrast, then, is that anyone, who says that you can lose your salvation, is really saying that sin is stronger than God, because God was not able to destroy sin's effects, much less sin itself! However, because righteousness is a gift to those who believe, and Christ's life abounds over Adam's death, righteousness cannot be taken away, because it is not conditioned on anything we do, since we are so much more powerless to stop our life in Christ than we are to stop Adam's death. Therefore, if someone is saved by grace through faith in Jesus' death, burial, and resurrection, and that person sins many times over, he still has eternal life because life is conditioned upon God's grace, not upon man's work. 11:6 says, "And if by grace, then is it no more of works: otherwise grace is no more grace. But if it be of works, then is it no more grace: otherwise work is no more work."

Verse 17 concludes the parenthetical reference by showing that two men sprouted two kings. Adam, by his sin, caused King Death to reign. Christ, by His life apart from sin, caused King Life to reign. The question then is, "Who are you in? Are you in Adam, or are you in Christ?" If you have not believed the gospel, you are in Adam, and death reigns in your life. If you have believed the gospel, you are in Christ, and life reigns in you through the gift of righteousness by Jesus Christ. But, you may say, I believed the gospel at one time, but then I stopped believing, stopped going to church, and starting living my old again, so, I lost my salvation. However, since you could not stop death from reigning in your life by doing "good" deeds and life is more powerful than death, it is even more impossible that you could do "evil" deeds to stop Christ's work of life in you.

Paul is confronting the pride of man. Man says he can work his way to heaven. Then, he is confronted with the gospel and must confess that he is not righteous on his own. Then, pride comes back in and says that, with God's help, I am righteous enough to maintain my salvation, if not by doing good deeds then by at least avoiding the really evil deeds. Therefore, Paul must squash that pride by showing that, because life is more powerful than death, you are even less powerful to stop the good work that Christ started in you (Philippians 1:6) than you are to stop the bad work that Adam did in you. Since Paul is talking to believers by this point, his audience all knows that they could not stop Adam's work of death in them. Now that they know that Christ's life is greater than Adam's death, they must also admit that no sins, no matter how evil and frequent they are, can stop Christ's work of eternal life in them.

5:18 This verse may be used by some to say that universal salvation is true, i.e., the idea that all will be saved, regardless of if they believe the gospel or not. The reason is because the verse says that the free gift is "upon all men unto justification." However, the verse also says that judgment is "upon all men to condemnation." People are either condemned, or they are justified. They cannot be both. Therefore, this verse cannot be saying that universal salvation is true, just like it cannot be saying that universal condemnation is true.

The verse is saying that Adam brought men "TO condemnation," meaning that he brought men to the place where they would be condemned for sin. Similarly, Christ brought all men "UNTO justification," meaning that He brought all men to the place to be justified for Christ's life. In other words, all people have the opportunity to be justified, but they are only justified if they believe the gospel. If they do not believe, they have walked away from the place of justification to be condemned for their sin. This is similar language to what we find in 3:22, where we are told that "the righteousness of God…is…UNTO all," but it is only "UPON all them that believe." So, "the free gift came upon all men" to bring them UNTO justification (5:18), but justification is only "UPON all them that believe" (3:22). Similarly, "the offence of" Adam brought judgment "upon all men TO condemnation" (5:18), but condemnation is only UPON all them that do not believe the gospel God has given them. If you are in Adam, having not believed the gospel, you have been brought to condemnation, and you receive condemnation. If you are in Christ, having believed the gospel, you have been brought to justification, and you receive justification.

5:19 "All have sinned" (3:23), yet this verse says that only "many were made sinners" (5:19). That is because only those who are in Adam are "sinners." As far as God is concerned, all those in Christ are "saints" (1:7, 8:27, etc.). Sure, all have sinned, but our identity is that we are "saints" if we are in Christ and we are "sinners" if we are in Adam. That is why "many were made sinners" by Adam, and many shall be made righteous by Christ. Thus, the two men—Adam and Christ—are shown, again, to be in contrast to each other.

5:20 "The offence" is Adam's violation of the law, which brought about the sin nature. God does not want sin to abound in a person's life. However, because of man's pride, man will usually compare himself with others in order to accuse others and excuse himself of his own sin (2:15). Therefore, God brought in the "holy, and just, and good" (7:12) standard of the law. The law works with the sin nature to make it "exceeding sinful" (7:13), so that we recognize that we are sinners and need to believe what God has told us in order to have righteousness and the gift of eternal life. Therefore, God brought the law in so that the offence might abound so that we see our need for the Saviour. Then, when we see that need, we believe the gospel God has given us, and God's grace abounds over our sin nature to give us the gift of eternal life. Therefore, when someone chooses life, by God's grace King Death is defeated, and King Life now reigns in that person. But, without the law, we would not recognize King Death for who he is, and we would go to "hell in a handbasket."

5:21 Because Jesus conquered sin for us, sin's reign unto death is over in our lives. Now, grace can reign through God's righteousness, producing eternal life in us.

6 In 3:28, we learned that we have been justified by faith alone. In chapter 4, we learned that we cannot lose our salvation, since David committed adultery and murder after he was saved and God did not impute those sins to his account (4:6-8). This means that we are eternally secure (5:9,11). We then learned that the reason we are eternally secure is because we have been taken out of Adam and placed into Christ (5:12-21). Now, in chapter 6, we learn the details of our new identity in Christ. Because we are in Christ, we are dead to sin (v. 2). The way that took place was by the Holy Spirit baptizing us into Christ's death (v. 3). Since we are identified with Christ's death, we are also identified with Christ's resurrection life (vs. 4-5). This means that God has reckoned us to be dead to sin and alive unto God, and we should reckon this to be true, also (v. 11). If we reckon this to be true, we will yield our flesh to God so that Christ can live in us (v. 13). Then, sin no longer has dominion over us (v. 14). The resulting fruit of Christ living in us will be holiness and an everlasting reward in heavenly places (vs. 22-23). Thus, the main point of Romans 6 is that we learn who we are in Christ after we are saved so that we embrace our new identity, which results in Christ living in us, instead of us trying to control our flesh ourselves which would only result in sin.

6:1 At every point along the way of the sound-doctrine edification process, your flesh lusts against the Spirit (Galatians 5:17) and will come up with every argument possible to keep your spirit from correctly applying new doctrine so that you do not walk in the Spirit. Justification by faith was settled by the end of chapter 4. Your flesh then tried to make your salvation contingent upon you working after you are saved. That is, it tried to get you into human good. Your eternal security was settled by the end of chapter 5. (By the way, very few Christians ever suppress their flesh long enough to get this far in the edification process.) So, now the flesh will try to get you into human evil. Your flesh will say, since "grace did much more abound" over sin (5:20) (I hate it when my flesh quotes scripture to advance its own agenda.) and I cannot lose my salvation, I should devote my life to sinning as much as possible so that I receive more grace. If your flesh has never objected to grace by saying that it is a license to sin, then you have not advanced as far as Romans 5, because you have never believed in your eternal security. Therefore, you need to stop and go back to Romans 5.

6:2 The Spirit's answer to your flesh's attack is "God forbid." Before you were saved, your flesh was alive and your spirit was dead in trespasses and sins (Ephesians 2:1). Since no good thing dwells in your flesh, all you could do was sin (7:18). After you are saved, God reckons your flesh to be dead to sin (6:2), and your spirit is alive so that Christ can live through you (6:11 and Galatians 2:19-20). Although God did cause grace to much more abound over your sin so that He could give you the gift of eternal life, eternal life is just the first step in God's grace toward you. God then begins to work in your life so that you mature to the point that He can bless you with a high position in heavenly places (Ephesians 1:3,21-23). In other words, God wants to spend "the ages to come" shewing us "the exceeding riches of His grace in His kindness toward us" (Ephesians 2:7).

If you allow your flesh to overcome this goal by seeing grace as a license to sin, you are quenching the Spirit's (I Thessalonians 5:19) work in revealing the things that God hath prepared for you (I Corinthians 2:9-13), which are "the treasures of wisdom and knowledge" (Colossians 2:3) found in His Word rightly divided (II Timothy 2:15). The result will be that, even though your soul will be saved, you will lose your reward in heavenly places (I Corinthians 3:13-15). Therefore, all those, who allow their flesh to trick them into thinking that grace is a license to sin, have esteemed the treasures of this world and the pleasures of sin for a season to be greater than the eternal riches found in the reproach of Christ (Hebrews 11:25-26). Instead, we should set our "affection on things above, not on things on the earth" (Colossians 3:2). We will then agree with God that we should not live any longer in sin (6:2). "Reckon ye also yourselves to be dead indeed unto sin, but alive unto God through Jesus Christ our Lord" (6:11).

6:3-4 Paul now explains that the way we were made dead to sin was by being baptized into Christ's death. When Christians see the word "baptized," they immediately think of water baptism. However, baptism just means to be identified with. For example, I Corinthians 10:2 says that Israel was "baptized unto Moses in the cloud and in the sea." The cloud was how the Lord went with Israel (Exodus 13:21), and the sea was the Red Sea, in which Pharaoh's army drowned, while Israel walked across on dry land (Exodus 14:28-29). Therefore, the ones who were water baptized were Pharaoh's army, who were killed. Israel's baptism unto Moses was a dry one.

With that in mind, let us look at what kind of baptism our baptism into

Christ's death is. I Corinthians 12:13 says we were baptized into the body of Christ by the Holy Spirit. When we are justified by faith, the Holy Spirit is given unto us (I Thessalonians 4:8). The Holy Spirit then baptizes us into the death of Jesus Christ. This makes us dead to sin, because our sin is buried with Christ in the grave. This means that our being baptized into Christ's death gives us eternal life. In other words, we must be baptized by the Holy Spirit into Christ's death in order to have eternal life; otherwise, our sin would still be on us.

Therefore, the baptism, of 6:3-4, is part of our salvation process. If burying our sin with Christ in the grave were accomplished with water baptism, Paul would have made sure he water baptized every single convert. Otherwise, those not water baptized would still be lost and would still be servants of sin. Yet, Paul said that "Christ sent me not to baptize, but to preach the gospel" (I Corinthians 1:17). In other words, water baptism is not part of the gospel, even though our being baptized into Christ's death is essential for us to have our sins paid for by Christ's death. Therefore, our baptism into Christ's death must not be accomplished by water. This is confirmed by the fact that Paul also thanked God that he baptized only a few of the Corinthians (I Corinthians 1:13-16). If water baptism causes us to be dead to sin, it would have been to Paul's shame that he did not baptized all of the Corinthians, because those not baptized would not be saved. He would then be thanking God that some of the Corinthians were not saved! Furthermore, I Corinthians 12:13 says that the Spirit baptized ALL of them into Christ's body. If He baptized ALL of the Corinthians into one body and not all of the Corinthians were water baptized, then water baptism must not be how the Spirit baptized them into Christ's death.

Also, note that 6:4 says that we are "BURIED with Him by baptism into death." You can dunk, sprinkle, spray, submerge, immerse, dip, or plunge someone into water, but you cannot bury someone in water. That is called drowning. Also, note the parallel passage in Colossians 2:12, which also says that we are "buried with Him in baptism." This is significant because the preceding verse says that, when we are saved, we "are circumcised with the circumcision made without hands" (Colossians 2:11). Since circumcision is not physical and the baptism of Colossians 2:12 is part of that spiritual circumcision, our baptism must also be spiritual. Both take place spiritually without us knowing about them, which makes sense since it is the Spirit who baptizes us into Christ. Colossians 2:17 goes on to say that the things under the law, such as circumcision, "are a shadow of things to come; but the body is of Christ." Therefore, physical circumcision and water baptism are physical figures under the law of what God does spiritually for all believers today.

Therefore, with the dispensation of grace comes the elimination of water baptism, because the Holy Spirit accomplishes the spirit baptism of all believers into Christ's death so that they are free from sin. Or, in terms of Colossians 2:17, since the body has come (spirit baptism), the shadow has passed away (water baptism). In fact, water baptism is not even recognized as a valid baptism of today's dispensation, because Ephesians 4:5 says that there is only "one baptism." Therefore, water baptism accomplishes nothing and is merely a tradition of religion that is not to be observed.

Yet, water baptism is the sacred cow of fundamental Christianity. You can go to church and read your Bible, but if you are never water baptized, you are viewed as being less of a Christian than others, who have been water baptized. They say that water baptism is an outward manifestation of an inward work of grace. Therefore, you must be ashamed of the gospel if you are never water baptized. However, this idea is never found in scripture. In fact, when God did have people water baptized, it was necessary for their salvation. The following verses apply to Israel during the at-hand phase of the kingdom:

- "He that believeth and is baptized shall be saved" (Mark 16:16)
- "Repent, and be baptized every one of you in the name of Jesus Christ for the remission of sins" (Acts 2:38)
- "Even baptism doth also now save us" (I Peter 3:21)

Therefore, a Biblical view of water baptism is either that it saves us, which was true during the at-hand phase of the kingdom for Israel, or that it has been replaced by spirit baptism into Christ's death, which is true for us today. The view of fundamental Christianity is not based on any scripture, making it a false doctrine.

The reason that Christianity believes this false doctrine is because they all have rejected eternal security, as we discussed in chapter 5. Since baptism into Christ's death (6:3-4) is built upon the doctrine of eternal security (Romans 5), they do not see our dry baptism by the Spirit into Christ's death, because they lack the proper "measure of faith" (12:3) due to their unbelief in Romans 5 doctrine.

Today's false doctrine of water baptism is a top priority of Satan's for Christianity to keep because it prevents them from seeing who they are in Christ. After all, if the baptism is water, then it is a fleshly baptism, rather than a spirit baptism. The first thing most churches do once you believe their gospel is that they baptize you. This gives the new convert a visual and emotional experience to make them think that God is concerned with the flesh, not with the spirit. They then build upon this flesh foundation so that they view their Christian lives as lives that are lived out in the flesh, rather than Christ living through them. This keeps them from obtaining their reward in heavenly places, because nothing good has ever come out of my flesh (7:18).

Satan and his forces occupy positions of authority in heaven. God has promised to fill these positions of authority with the body of Christ

(Ephesians 1:20-23). The more sound doctrine a person has built up in his inner man, the more qualified that person is to take one of those positions. Once "the fulness of the Gentiles be come in" (11:25), meaning once God has qualified people for all of these positions, the rapture will take place and Satan and his forces will be kicked out of heavenly places (Revelation 12:7-9). Therefore, if Satan can keep the body of Christ from obtaining the knowledge to take the higher positions in heavenly places, then "the fulness of the Gentiles [cannot] be come in" (Romans 11:25), which means that Satan and his forces will continue to occupy their positions, and Satan will continue to be "the god of this world" (II Corinthians 4:4).

Since water baptism starts most new converts down the path of changing the truth of God's Word into a lie and looking at the things of God from a fleshly perspective, Satan is very much interested in keeping alive the false doctrine of water baptism. (This is also why Christianity is focused on "soul winning," but it does not care about edification from God's Word.) (The fact, that mankind is so spiritually ignorant, is probably why Satan believes he will continue to occupy his positions in the heaven and the earth, as evidenced by his interactions with God regarding Job (Job 1:9-11 and 2:4-5).)

Since our sin is buried with Christ by baptism into death, this means that we have also been raised with Christ. Ephesians 2:1,5 "And you hath He quickened, who were dead in trespasses and sins....Even when we were dead in sins, hath quickened us together with Christ." Colossians 2:13 "And you, being dead in your sins and the uncircumcision of your flesh, hath He quickened together with Him, having forgiven you all trespasses." Since we have been made dead to sin and alive unto Christ (6:11), "we also should walk in newness of life" (6:4). Note the word "should." Although we are dead to sin, we have the choice to go back to living in sin or walking in newness of life. However, Paul's point, in 6:2, is that it is crazy to live in sin now that we are dead to sin. God has a position for you in heavenly places. All you have to do is "let the word of Christ dwell in you richly in all wisdom" (Colossians 3:16). Then, you will rule with Christ forever. Why squander that away to enjoy the pleasures of sin for a season?

6:5 5:8 taught us that "Christ died for us." But, that is not the end of the story. It is only the beginning. Christ did not die for us so that we could continue in our sin and still be saved. John 10:10 says, "I am come that they might have life, and that they might have it more abundantly." In referring to His Own crucifixion, Jesus said, "Except a corn of wheat fall into the ground and die, it abideth alone, but if it die, it bringeth forth much fruit." (John 12:24). When we believed the gospel, we were planted together with Christ in the likeness of His death, but we were also raised up with Him in the likeness of His resurrection so that we may bring forth much fruit by His living through us. Ephesians 2:10 says that "God hath before ordained that we should WALK IN" good works (Ephesians 2:10). It does not say that we are to do the works ourselves, but we are to walk in them. That is why 6:4 tells us to "walk in newness of life." Therefore, Christ died, and we died with Him. Then, He rose from the dead, but we did not rise from the dead. Rather, "ye ARE dead, and your life is hid with Christ in God" (Colossians 3:3). Therefore, we are to present our bodies as living sacrifices unto God (12:1). Then, it is not I that liveth, "but Christ liveth in me" (Galatians 2:20).

6:6 Since we have been buried with Christ by baptism into His death, we do not have to serve sin any more because the body of sin has been destroyed with Christ in the grave. The importance of this occurrence cannot be overemphasized. We can see why, then, that Satan has convinced all of Christianity that baptism is only by water, and most believe it is just an outward manifestation of an inward work of grace. Satan has succeeded in masking the body of sin being destroyed and not having to serve sin by saying that it is really just a neat ceremony to show your family and friends what a great person you are now that you have decided to become a Christian. The problem is that Christianity teaches that Christ died for you, and then they water baptize you. So, you must be a new creature by yourself, which means that you can serve God on your own. But, this verse teaches that my old man was crucified with Christ, and that was the end of him. Sure, I am a new creature, but God did nothing with my flesh. Instead, "all things are of God" (II Corinthians 5:17-18). My new identity is Christ. Therefore, it takes Christ living through me to serve God. I cannot do it myself.

6:7 When a woman's husband dies, she is freed from the law of that husband. Similarly, "ye also are become dead to the law by the body of Christ; that ye should be married" to Christ (7:2-4). Since "our old man is crucified with" Christ (6:6), we are dead. Since we are dead, we are freed from sin (6:7). Why, then, would we "be...entangled again with the yoke of bondage" (Galatians 5:1)? Instead, we should "stand fast therefore in the liberty wherewith Christ hath made us free" (Galatians 5:1), and "rejoice in hope" (5:2), knowing that we are finally free!

6:8 While it is true that we will be raised from the grave at the rapture, the context of this verse is living in the here and now. As Ephesians 2:1,5, and Colossians 2:13 say, God has ALREADY made us alive in Christ so that we may serve Christ and not sin. In other words, our identity is Christ. This means that, whatever life Christ is capable of, we can allow Him to live that life through us. We do this by reading God's Word, allowing the Holy Spirit to teach it to us, and believing the doctrine. We are then "strengthened with might by His Spirit in the inner man" (Ephesians 3:16), such that we make decisions as Christ would make them, because "we have the mind of Christ" (I Corinthians 2:16).

Now, we often do not see the results of this, because it is a spiritual battle. "We wrestle not against flesh and blood, but against principalities, against powers, against the rulers of the darkness of this world, against spiritual wickedness in high places" (Ephesians 6:12). "The weapons of our warfare are not carnal, but are mighty through God to the pulling down of strong holds" (II Corinthians 10:4). The reason that strong holds are pulled down is because it is Christ doing the work. "Yet not I, but Christ liveth in me" (Galatians 2:20). "The excellency of the power [is] of God, and not of us" (II Corinthians 4:7). Since God is omnipotent or all powerful (Revelation 19:6), the only limit to the havoc you allow Christ to wreck in Satan's kingdom is your unbelief. ("Your faith should not stand in the wisdom of men, but in the power of God" (I Corinthians 2:5).) That is why Paul will later tell the Romans that "the God of peace shall bruise Satan under your feet shortly" (16:20). We should now be able to see why "God forbid" (6:2) that I continue to live in sin after I am saved (6:1).

6:9-10 When Christians see the word "Christ," they think of Him as God. While He is God, by just calling Him "Christ," Paul is referring to His humanity. As God, Jesus had the power to raise Himself from the dead (John 10:18). As man, God raised Christ from the dead (Ephesians 1:20). The reason that Paul keeps referring to Christ's humanity is that we are human, too. The fact, that both we and Christ are human, is how Christ can live through us. Thus, since we have already been raised to live with Christ and death has no more dominion over Christ, death has no more dominion over us either. We are free from sin and alive unto Christ, just like Christ is free from sin and alive unto God.

Note that "He died unto sin ONCE" (6:10). This means that sin never revived. This is important because it means that we do not have to get re-saved when we sin. Because Christ died unto sin once, sin is dead to us, even if we sin after we are saved. Sinning after we are saved is just "the motions of sins" working in our flesh (7:5). Just like a headless chicken is dead even though it runs around, our flesh is dead, even though the motions of sins still work in it. That is because sin died with Christ's death. That is why 6:10 says that "He died" and now "He liveth." Death is in the past; life is in the present and future. So, too, for us, sin is dead, and we can "walk in newness of life" in Christ (6:4).

6:11 All saved people need to obey this verse. If they have learned and believed the doctrine in Romans up to this point, they will obey this verse. Sadly, very few Christians believe enough sound doctrine to come to this conclusion. This verse says to "reckon ye ALSO yourselves to be dead indeed unto sin, but alive unto God." The word "also" tells us that God has already reckoned us to be dead to sin. God is "the only wise God" (I Timothy 1:17). Therefore, we should believe what He believes. If we have allowed the Holy Spirit to teach us the doctrine found in Romans so far, then we will reckon ourselves to be dead unto sin and alive unto God, also.

Our sin nature works with the conscience to sin more (7:8-13). "God through Jesus Christ our Lord" (8:1) has delivered us from having to allow the sin nature to cause us to sin. Because Jesus Christ blotted out the law for us by obeying it perfectly (Colossians 2:14), "I through the law am dead to the law, that I might live unto God" (Galatians 2:19). Stated another way, when Christ died and you believed the gospel, God purged "your conscience from dead works to serve the living God" (Hebrews 9:14). Therefore, when God saved you, He gave you a clean conscience by purging it from dead works, i.e., religion. Once you are saved, He seeks to give you a "good conscience" (I Timothy 1:5,19), which is one founded on sound doctrine. In that way, you will understand who you are in Christ, and you will allow Christ to live in you.

However, there are multiple obstacles in your way. First, your flesh is jealous of what you have by the Spirit (Galatians 5:17), and so it will try to deceive you into following its wickedness (Jeremiah 17:9). For the Christian, this usually happens by the second obstacle, which is the Christian religion. Religion comes along and teaches you false doctrine, which is "having [your] conscience seared with a hot iron" (I Timothy 4:2). As recently mentioned, this happens very quickly, as most churches try to water baptize you once you are saved, putting you back under the law. Galatians 5:3 says, "For I testify again to every man that is circumcised, that he is a debtor to do the whole law." Paul mentions circumcision, because that was the issue in his day. If Paul were writing today, he would probably use water baptism instead. Third, Satan, the tempter (I Thessalonians 3:5), has his forces, enticing Christians to follow their flesh. Fourth, Satan has all unbelievers and many believers following "the course of this world" (Ephesians 2:2-3). Since Satan is not omnipresent, like God is, he has come up with a course of sin and unbelief, as "the god of this world" (II Corinthians 4:4), for the world to follow. These four obstacles remain in your way, even after you are saved.

In order to overcome these obstacles, you need to believe what God has believed about you, which is that you are "dead indeed unto sin, but alive unto God" (6:11). Moreover, because these obstacles are in your way at all times, you must make this choice to believe God day by day, hour by hour, and minute by minute. That is why Paul said, "I die daily" (I Corinthians 15:31). God wants to build sound doctrine in your inner man, have you talk it over with Him in your mind as you go about your life (This is what "pray without ceasing" (I Thessalonians 5:17) means.), and have you make the decision that you are dead to sin and alive unto God. Therefore, you can choose to walk in newness of life (6:4), rather than continuing in the motions of sin, but it all starts by believing what God has said is true about you—"ye are dead, and your life is hid with Christ in God" (Colossians 3:3).

6:12-13 Before you were saved, the only thing you could do was sin (Ephesians 2:3). Once we believed the gospel, we were taken out of the grip of Satan, because God "purchased [us] with His Own blood" (Acts 20:28). Before we were saved, God did not force us to believe the gospel. Similarly, after we are saved, God does not force us to allow Christ to walk in us. We can let sin reign in our mortal bodies (6:12), or we can "let the word of

Christ dwell in [us] richly" (Colossians 3:16). The choice is ours.

Given the doctrine we have already learned in Romans, Paul makes the plea for us not to let sin reign in our bodies, but to yield our flesh over to God so that He can work His good works through us. "Ye are bought with a price: therefore glorify God in your body, and in your spirit, which are God's" (I Corinthians 6:20). If we make this choice, we will yield our flesh to be used by God "as instruments of righteousness" (6:13). Note that WE do not use OUR flesh to serve God, because our flesh is still vile (Philippians 3:21). Therefore, it does not have the capacity to serve God. We MUST recognize this, because Christianity is stuck trying to use their flesh to serve God. Rather, you are to "yield yourselves unto God" so that God may use your flesh "as instruments of righteousness unto God." "The excellency of the power [is] of God, and not of us" (II Corinthians 4:7). We just say, "Okay, God. I believe what you have said about me that my flesh is dead and alive unto God. So, here is my flesh to use for your glory." Practically speaking, the way this is accomplished is by reading and believing sound doctrine found in God's Word rightly divided (II Timothy 2:15). Then, God does good works through you, as you use "the mind of Christ" (I Corinthians 2:16) to make decisions based upon the sound doctrine built up in your inner man.

6:14 Because the body of sin has been destroyed with Christ, being buried by baptism into His death, we are no longer under the law. Galatians 3:24-25 says that "the law was our schoolmaster to bring us unto Christ, that we might be justified by faith. But after that faith is come, we are no longer under a schoolmaster." Therefore, we are not under the law, but under grace, meaning that "all things are lawful unto me" (I Corinthians 6:12). Most Christians will emphatically deny that I can do whatever I want and still be saved. If they do admit that all things are lawful, they will be sure to quote the last part of that verse that "all things are not expedient" (I Corinthians 6:12). "Therefore," they will say, "I should do everything I can to serve God. That is the least I can do to pay back God for all He has done for me." However, this is nothing more than pride, which gets people back under the flesh, which means you are not serving God any more. Paul will address this in Romans 7. Instead, we need to read 6:14 in its context and realize that we serve God by yielding ourselves to God (6:13), rather than trying to serve God in the flesh. The way we do this is by reading God's Word rightly divided, which allows the Holy Spirit to teach us sound doctrine so that the Holy Spirit can work through us, having yielded our "members as instruments of righteousness unto God" (6:13).

Note that this verse says that "sin shall not have dominion over you." Once you are saved, your new identity is Christ. Even if you choose to continue to live in Adam all of your life, God will still give you a glorified body at the rapture (Philippians 3:21). This new body will not have the sin nature, and so you will not sin for all eternity. Therefore, "sin shall not have dominion over you." Basically, before you were saved, all you could do was sin. In eternity, all you can do is have Christ live through you. In the interim, you have a choice. Paul is saying that you should choose to allow Christ to live through you, because that is who you are now—you are in Christ. "Sin shall not have dominion over you," so, get rid of sin right now.

6:15 The number one argument against eternal security is this one. People say it gives you a license to sin. As we saw in 6:1-2, that is not true. Eternal security gives us the license for Christ to live through us. Under the law, all we could do was sin. Under grace, we can still sin, but we also have the opportunity to live for Christ, which we could never do before we were saved.

A good analogy to use is that, when you were a child, you were under the law of your parents. For example, let's say that your parents made you go to bed by 10 PM each night. If you did not obey this law, you were punished. Then, you become an adult, and you have a job. You are no longer under the law of a nightly bed time, but are under grace. However, it would not be smart to stay up all night, because you would be too sleepy to perform your job the next day. The law was required when you were a child because you did not have the maturity to decide on an early bed time. Once you became an adult, you still went to bed at the same time, not because you had to, but because you used your liberty to determine that was the best time to go to bed.

Similarly, before you were saved, you had no spiritual maturity. Once you are saved, you have believed what God told you. This faith shows that you have some spiritual maturity, and so God entrusts you with making your own choice about what to do. ("The law was our schoolmaster to bring us unto Christ, that we might be justified by faith. But after that faith is come, we are no longer under a schoolmaster" (Galatians 3:24-25).) God will not send you to hell for disobeying the law, because you are not under the law. However, many of the things contained in the law should still be followed, not because you have to, but because that is what someone with spiritual maturity would choose to do so that Christ can live in them. Thus, "God forbid" (6:15) that we sin when we are under grace, because God is glorified through us when we do not sin.

6:16 Paul speaks of our choice again. We are freed from sin (6:7), but we still have the choice to sin. The difference is that we can now choose to serve Christ. If you really want to pay God back for all He has done for you, you will serve Christ by reading God's Word rightly divided, allowing the Holy Spirit to teach you sound doctrine which will allow Christ to live out that sound doctrine through your life. You do NOT pay God back by trying to do a whole bunch of good things in the flesh. That is pride, and that brings you back under the law, making you a servant of sin.

According to this verse, you are either the servant of sin or the servant of obedience. Being the servant of obedience makes it sound like you obey the law. However, 6:17-18 says that they "obeyed from the heart that form of doctrine," and that doctrine made them "free from sin." Since you have to believe the gospel in order to be made free from sin, being the servant of obedience means that the way they obeyed was by believing the gospel. In other words, they had "the obedience of faith" (16:26).

6:17-18 When we get to 8:2, we will find out that, when we are saved we are taken out from being under "the law of sin and death," and we are placed into "the law of the Spirit of life in Christ Jesus." This is the new law that God wants us to obey after we are saved. (This does not contradict 6:14, since this new law is in grace.) Thus, we WERE servants of sin. Then, we became the servant of obedience by believing the gospel. Then, obedience brought us unto righteousness (6:16), so now we can be servants of righteousness by continuing in the faith of Jesus Christ, which will result in us yielding our flesh to God.

The "spiritual gift," that Paul wants to impart to the Romans in this epistle "to the end [they] may be established" (1:11), is recognizing the transformation God has done in their lives to place them under "the law of the Spirit of life in Christ Jesus" (8:2) so that they will obey their new master, righteousness, instead of their old master, sin.

6:19 This verse shows that the Romans did not possess the "spiritual gift" of how to live in grace after you are saved. Although their faith for salvation was "spoken of throughout the whole world" (1:8), they were not living their lives by faith because they were yielding their "members servants to uncleanness and to iniquity unto iniquity."

Note how "iniquity" progresses "unto iniquity," but "righteousness" progresses "unto holiness." When we have our new bodies, we will live righteously without sin, which will result in holiness. We have already been declared by God to be holy (Colossians 3:12) because we are in Christ, but we can actually live holy lives right now by allowing sound doctrine to work through our lives. Christianity would say to us that "much learning doth make thee mad" (Acts 26:24). They would have us spend time raising our hands, singing worship songs, and "feeling the spirit," instead of being edified by God's Word. However, we just learned that sound doctrine results in our obeying righteousness, which leads unto holiness. Therefore, there is nothing more practical to do in church than to learn sound doctrine from God's Word, because doctrine changes your life, while emotionalism does not.

Paul says that he spoke "after the manner of men because of the infirmity of [their] flesh" (6:19). In other words, if not for the flesh, the sound doctrine in Romans would be obvious to us. Instead, the flesh comes up with every argument possible not to believe the sound doctrine that is in Christ, and so Paul has to spend several chapters refuting each one of these arguments so that they will believe God, even though Paul is writing to Christians! It should not be surprising, then, that many Christians think we are crazy when we believe what God has revealed to us through the apostle Paul. They have "itching ears" (II Timothy 4:3), not wanting to hear the truth of God's Word because it discerns that "the thoughts and intents of the heart" (Hebrews 4:12) are "only evil continually" (Genesis 6:5). That is a reality that Christianity refuses to face. Therefore, they turn their ears unto fables (II Timothy 4:4). In fact, the reason why most people attend church is because they have recognized that they are sinners, but they do not want to believe the gospel in order to be saved, because doing so means admitting that they are completely evil. Therefore, they go to a church that teaches a false gospel, and their guilty consciences are appeased without having to admit what a bad person they are. That is why Christians are such sticklers for their own moral codes, because it is the following of those codes that makes them feel like they will go to heaven.

Since Paul spoke after the manner of men, it is reasonable to assume that God speaks after the manner of men throughout scripture. We probably cannot grasp how much more is in scripture for us to learn once "the infirmity of [our] flesh" (6:19) is removed! I guess that is why we will be studying the Bible and learning more information for all eternity.

6:20 When they were servants of sin, they were free from righteousness. Now, that they have righteousness, they should be free from sin.

6:21 The "fruit" of sin is death, as Paul will state in 6:23. It makes no sense to continue to follow death, when God has freed you from death and given you eternal life (6:23).

Note that this verse says that Christians are ashamed of sin. They will still sin, due to the flesh, but they are ashamed of their sin. Religion, however, is bold about their sin when that sin is according to their religion. A great example of the contrast is Saul and David. When the prophet told Saul that he had sinned, Saul justified his actions by saying that he had really made a supplication unto the Lord (I Samuel 13:11-12). When the prophet told David that he had sinned, David said, "I have sinned against the Lord" (II Samuel 12:13). Similarly, Christianity excuses their sin. They say things like, "Oh, I didn't really sin with that thought, because I did not entertain the thought," "That was not a sin; it was an error," "The Bible never says that gambling is a sin, so it is okay if I go to the casino," or "I keep a short account with God, so, I am okay." However, those, who have believed the gospel, have already recognized that they are sinners, and they are ashamed of their sin, which is why they believed the gospel in the first place.

6:22 The end of the fruit is "everlasting life." This does not refer to the gift of eternal life (6:23) that comes by believing the gospel. Rather, Paul is saying that, when you serve God, the fruit of that service lasts forever. In other words, you receive a higher position in heavenly places for being a servant to God. By contrast, the fruit of being a servant of sin is death (6:21), meaning the loss of a reward in heavenly places (I Corinthians 3:15). Therefore, a servant of God receives a reward that is everlasting, which is beneficial, because he also has the gift of eternal life (6:23) for having believed the gospel.

6:23 This is a popular verse used by Christians in giving a presentation of the gospel to an unbeliever. And, it is a good verse to use for this purpose because, in one verse, you are told that man earns death by his sin, but God gives eternal life to those who believe the gospel. However, man's sin (3:9-12) and God's gift of righteousness (3:21-28) were dealt with by the end of Romans 3.

In Romans 6, Paul has been dealing with the sanctification of the believer as a result of being dead to sin and alive unto God (6:11). Therefore, in its context, this verse refers to Christ living in the believer, rather than being a verse to show unbelievers that they are lost. The believing Romans were sinning, and Paul says that "the end of those things is death" (6:21). God has made them "free from sin" and "servants to God." Therefore, they can serve God, instead of sin, and that service of God results in a reward that is everlasting (6:22). The reason, then, that the Romans should stop sinning and start serving God is because "the wages of sin is death; but the gift of God is eternal life through Jesus Christ our Lord" (6:23). Therefore, they should do things (serving God) that will last forever, rather than doing things (serving sin) that will die. In other words, 6:23's intent is to motivate the believer to live as who they are in Christ, because anything done in sin will die, while anything done in Christ will last forever (see I Corinthians 3:12-15). This tells us that even our service to God is a gift from God, since it is Christ living is us that results in our reward in heavenly places, rather than us serving God ourselves in the energy of our flesh. Yet, Christianity never sees this, because they only use this verse for salvation, rather than for sanctification.

7 When a marriage is broken by death, the surviving spouse is free to marry again (vs. 2-3). Similarly, the believer has had his spouse of sin die on him so that he can marry Christ (v. 4). This means that "we are delivered from the law" (v. 6) and are now under grace (6:14). That is not to say that the law is sin (v. 7). The law actually worked with our sin nature to show us that we needed to believe the gospel (vs. 8-13). If we continue under the law after we are saved, we will continue to do the works of sin, because there is nothing good in our flesh (vs. 14-21). Thus, we need a deliverer from the flesh, and that deliverer is "God through Jesus Christ our Lord" (v. 25). Therefore, the lesson of Romans 7 is that, now that you have been delivered from sin (Romans 6), stop letting the flesh run your life. Instead, walk in the Spirit, which Paul will tell us how to do in Romans 8.

7:1 6:6 says "that our old man is crucified with" Christ. Since we have been crucified with Christ, we are dead (6:7). A dead person cannot be judged by the law. For example, if I committed murder and the judge sentenced me to death, but I was killed before the sentence was carried out, the law could not revive me and kill me again. Since I am dead, the law has no power over me. Similarly, "all have sinned" (3:23), and "the wages of sin is death" (6:23). So, the law says that we are worthy of death due to our sin. However, all believers have already died because they have been crucified with Christ (6:6-7). Therefore, the law has no control over believers. It is our death in Christ's crucifixion that means that, "ye are not under the law, but under grace" (6:14). As such, this shows how Christ released us from the power of the law of sin and death (8:2).

7:2-3 Paul now uses an illustration of marriage to prove his point from 7:1 that the law has dominion only as long as a person lives. Marriage is a lifelong contract that is binding as long as both parties are alive. However, if one of the parties dies, the remaining living person is loosed from the law of marriage. Therefore, the law has dominion until death. That person can then marry someone else, being free from the law of marriage with the first spouse. This shows that God set up marriage in the way that He did so that we can better understand that we must die before we can have eternal life in Christ.

Today, the majority of Christian marriages end in divorce. So, you may ask, does God allow divorce today? If that is your question, then you have not learned the lesson of Romans 6. The issue is not what God allows, because, as someone who is dead, the law has no control over me. Therefore, as far as the law is concerned, "all things are lawful for me" (I Corinthians 6:12 and 10:23). Rather, the issue is, "How can Christ live through me with regard to divorce and remarriage?" Jesus said that "Moses because of the hardness of your hearts suffered you to put away your wives: but from the beginning it was not so. And I say unto you, Whosoever shall put away his wife, except it be for fornication, and shall marry another, commiteth adultery: and whoso marrieth her which is put away doth commit adultery" (Matthew 19:8-9).

Therefore, marriage is for life, and you have committed sin if you divorce someone unless your spouse has already divorced you by committing adultery. Also, based on Matthew 19:8-9, a man, who marries a divorced woman, has committed adultery, even if he is a virgin himself and she did not commit adultery herself. Perhaps the best way to understand this is to get the Biblical definition of marriage, which is much different from the world's definition of marriage. I Corinthians 6:16 tells us that marriage is sex between two people; it is not the marriage ceremony. Even sex between a person and a prostitute is called marriage by God. Therefore, spouses, who commit adultery, are actually marrying the people with whom they are committing adultery, which means that the original marriage can be broken off by the spouse who has been cheated on.

Since we should be yielding our members to God as servants of righteousness, rather than as servants of sin (6:18-19), we should not be doing these things. Rather, we should stay married for life in all circumstances. You may say, "Yes, but my spouse is very abusive. Yes, but my spouse does not love me. Yes, but, etc." Granted, it is much more difficult to stay married to a person in these circumstances, but it is still a sin to divorce someone for ANY reason other than infidelity. Therefore, all other reasons are sinful and are just excuses to follow the hardness of your heart. That is not my opinion, but that is the clear Word of God on the matter. If Christians obeyed God's Word, the divorce and re-marriage rate would be essentially zero among Christians. Based on this fact alone, many unbelievers would become believers. Isn't getting more people saved worth doing your best to avoid a divorce, even in difficult situations? Why not give up your happiness so that others may receive eternal life because they see your example of staying married when everyone else in your situation would get a divorce? This is the idea behind Paul's statement that a believing spouse should not divorce an unbelieving spouse (I Corinthians 7:12-16), even though a believer should not marry an unbeliever (I Corinthians 7:39).

7:4 Just like the law binds a woman to her husband, before we were saved, we were married to the law. Jesus Christ obeyed the law perfectly, "blotting out the handwriting of ordinance that was against us,…nailing it to His cross" (Colossians 2:14). When we believe in Jesus' death, burial, and resurrection as atonement for our sins, Christ's perfect obedience of the law is counted for us such that we have "become dead to the law by the body of Christ" (7:4). Since we are "dead to the law," the marriage that we had with the law has been broken. We then become "married" to Jesus Christ. This is not an adulterous relationship because our first spouse, the law, is dead to us. We are joined to Christ, making us free from the law, which is now dead to us, and we are now under grace by our "marriage" to the Lord Jesus Christ.

When two people are married, the two become one flesh (Genesis 2:24). As such, they only have one identity. That is why I Corinthians 7:4 says that "the wife hath not power of her own body, but the husband." Therefore, because we are married to Christ, our "life is hid with Christ in God" (Colossians 3:3). When God looks at us, He does not see us, but He sees Christ. We are "accepted in the beloved" (Ephesians 1:6).

Now, that is not to say that we are the bride of Christ. We are never called that. Rather, we are called the "body of Christ" (I Corinthians 12:27). Believers in Israel's program are Christ's bride (Revelation 21:2,9). Therefore, we are married to Christ in the sense that His body is married to Himself. He is the head, and the body is to obey what the head tells it to do (Ephesians 1:22-23, 4:15-16, and 5:23-24).

In fact, this verse tells us why we are called the "body of Christ." It is because we have "become dead to the law by the body of Christ" (7:4). Christ's body died, which means He is not married to His body any more. By giving up His body, we become dead to the law, which means we are not married to the law any more. Therefore, we can now become His body. This makes the marriage analogy fit even better. If a man's wife dies and the two are one flesh, you could say that his body died. Then, if a different woman's

93

husband died, the law of the husband died with him. Then, she could marry the guy whose wife died, and she would become his body, just like we became Christ's body after His body died and the law died to us.

7:5 Notice carefully the terminology used here, because it clues us in as to how the law, sin, and the flesh work together. In Matthew 5:21-48, the Lord Jesus Christ clarified that sinning against the law occurs in the heart. Thus, sin is committed before the physical act that breaks the law is committed. For example, Jesus said in Matthew 5:28 "That whosoever looketh on a woman to lust after her hath committed adultery with her already in his heart." Not only is sin committed before the physical act that breaks the law, but the law actually increases a person's violation of the law. Paul says in 7:8-9 that the sin nature takes "occasion by the commandment" such that "when the commandment came, sin revived." This background information helps us to understand what 7:5 means when it says that "the motions of sins, which were by the law, did work in our members."

Before we were saved, we had the law, the flesh, and the sin nature. Being under the law, our sin nature rebelled against the law we were under, and we committed sins in our heart. Then, our flesh acted out those sins. That is why they are "the MOTIONS of sins," since the sins had already been committed. "The motions of sins," then, are not what kill you. They are just the fruit of the sin nature and the law working together like a machine. Therefore, the law and the sin nature are a deadly combination, literally. Our sin nature wants us to sin, and the law causes the sin nature to commit sin in our flesh. Therefore, we were in a doomed state. We did not have the power to overcome sin.

The good news, though, is that "we WERE in the flesh" (7:5). Granted, we still have flesh after we are saved, but we are not IN the flesh any more. Instead, we are IN Christ. This means that the sin machine of the sin nature and the law is stopped from running when we yield our "members as instruments of righteousness unto God" (6:13). Now, our flesh can be run by a new machine, which is the machine of "life in Christ Jesus" (8:2). The point is that, either way, someone is running our lives. Either the devil runs our lives by using "the course of this world" (Ephesians 2:2 and James 3:15) to control our flesh, or God runs our lives by using His word to control our spirit (8:12-14 and I Corinthians 2:10-16).

7:6 "But now" that we have been justified by faith, "we are delivered from the law." The sin nature is still in us, but it has no power where there is no law. Therefore, we now have the ability to "serve in newness of spirit."

When we were under the law, we were powerless to obey the law, because in our flesh dwelleth no good thing (7:18). Now that we are saved, Christ can obey the law through us, but that is not why Christ saved us. All the law does is hold up the perfect standard to follow. If we obey that perfect standard, then we have earned eternal life (2:7). However, we have already obtained "the gift of...eternal life through Jesus Christ our Lord" (6:23). Therefore, there is no point in spending our time trying to obey the law, when, through Jesus' death on the cross, we have already received the best that the law can give us.

Now, instead of trying to meet the perfect standard of the law, we can walk in the Spirit, which means we can go on to "love, joy, peace, longsuffering, gentleness, goodness, faith, meekness, temperance: against such there is no law" (Galatians 5:22-23). That is why "the oldness of the letter" (7:6) is "a shadow of things to come; but the body is of Christ" (Colossians 2:17). In other words, receiving eternal life is just a shadow of walking in eternal life. For example, winning the lottery is great, but it does no good unless you actually use the money that you won. Similarly, receiving eternal life is great, but it does not help anyone else out unless you walk in that eternal life. Jesus Christ brought about eternal life through His fulfillment of the law, and now we can allow Him to walk in that eternal life for us to produce the fruit of the Spirit. That is why Galatians 2:19 says, "For I through the law am dead to the law, that I might live unto God." Thus, eternal life comes by fulfilling the law, which Jesus Christ did for us, and living that eternal life comes by walking in who we are in Christ. Walking in that life is how we serve "in newness of spirit, and not in the oldness of the letter" (7:6).

7:7 Since the sin nature has no power without the law, the question comes up: "Is the law sin?" The answer is "God forbid." Now, the law does combine with the sin nature to cause us to sin. Without the law, Paul says that he was alive (7:9), meaning that he had life in God before the conscience comes, because "sin is not imputed when there is no law" (5:13). Then, when he got the law, he started sinning. So, the law may seem like a bad thing, but it is not.

"By the law is the knowledge of sin" (3:20). The law gives us a holy standard to meet (7:12). We then know that we have a sin nature when we do not meet that holy standard. God has already given every human being the knowledge that the Godhead exists and that God has eternal power (1:20). Because of this, everyone knows that, because they have failed to meet God's holy standard, they are subject to God's judgment of them, which is death (1:32). Man now has two options: 1) Deny the truth that he knows, or 2) Look to God for a solution. Because "the heart is deceitful above all things, and desperately wicked" (Jeremiah 17:9), man, as a whole, chooses to deny the truth, as 1:21 says: "Because that, when they knew God, they glorified Him not as God, neither were thankful; but became vain in their imaginations, and their foolish heart was darkened." However, for those, who look to God for a solution, they believe the gospel that God has revealed to them. They then have faith, receive the gift of eternal life, and can be edified in the truth.

Paul says that the law is not sin (7:7), but the law brings the knowledge of sin (3:20). Since most people deny the truth, they end up going to hell. If they died before the conscience came, they would have received eternal life, as Paul says: "For I was alive without the law once" (7:9). Therefore, the knowledge of sin works out for the bad for most people, because of their unbelief of the gospel. If they never received the knowledge of sin, sin would not have been imputed to them, because sin is not imputed when there is no law (5:13), and they would have received eternal life. Therefore, although the law is not sin, it appears that the law is bad, but that is not the case. What is bad is man's response to the law.

So, why did God even give the law if it means more people in hell, as a result? The reason is that God's will is not just to save people. His will is to save people AND have them come unto the knowledge of the truth (I Timothy 2:4). Why is that?

In the past, Satan and one-third of the angels rebelled against God (Revelation 12:4). Halfway through the tribulation period, God will cast them out of heaven (Revelation 12:7-12) and will replace them with the body of Christ (Ephesians 1:23 and Colossians 1:19). God has a governmental structure in heavenly places that includes thrones, principalities, powers, mights, and dominions (Ephesians 1:21 and Colossians 1:16). The higher the position, the more knowledge a person needs in order to be qualified to fill that position. If an infant dies, he receives eternal life because sin is not imputed unto his account since the law had not come upon him yet. That certainly is better than going to hell, but the infant does not have any knowledge to fill a position in heavenly places. Therefore, God wants believers to come unto the knowledge of the truth (I Timothy 2:4) so that they will be qualified to fill the heavenly positions currently occupied by Satan and his forces. If all God does is fill the heavenly places with infants, Satan and his forces cannot be kicked out, because the heavenly government would be left without qualified people to rule them.

Christianity is ignorant of this aspect of God's plan. That is because, for the last three hundred years or so, the church has been focused on getting people saved, and not much else. They want people to believe the gospel so they have eternal life, but they do not learn much sound doctrine after they are saved. So, you come to church, get saved, and then make yourself happy with worship songs and uplifting speakers. The problem with that model is that no one learns sound doctrine. They are not coming into the knowledge of the truth. Satan's kingdom cannot be overthrown until God has qualified people to fill the positions of Satan's forces in heavenly places. Therefore, while ignorance of sin may sound good, since the justice of God requires Him to give eternal life to ignorant people, the law is absolutely necessary.

The law brings the knowledge of sin, which causes believers to have faith. God is pleased with the faith (Hebrews 11:6), because He can then build sound doctrine on that faith so that Satan's forces can be overthrown and knowledgeable members of the body of Christ can take their place. If not for the law, Satan and his forces would continue to rule in heavenly places.

Thus, the law is not sin. "God forbid" (7:7). Rather, the law is part of the process to reconcile both the earth and the heaven back to God. Therefore, the law is good (7:12), even though we sin because we have the law.

7:8 In this verse, Paul shows that the "bad guy" is the sin nature, not the law. "The law is holy, and the commandment holy, and just, and good" (7:12), but the sin nature takes advantage of the commandment by using it to cause you to lust after things. I would not break the commandment of "Thou shalt not covet" if not for the law, because I would not know that lust exists without that law (7:7). For example, tell a kid not to touch the stove or an adult not to touch a dinner plate because it is hot, and almost the first thing the person will do is touch the stove or the dinner plate. The kid was not even thinking of touching the stove, but the law said, "Don't touch the stove." So, the sin nature within him says, "Hey, I never thought of touching the stove. If I am forbidden to touch the stove, it must be a good thing to touch. I think I will touch the stove." This is how the sin nature takes occasion by the commandment to bring about all manner of concupiscence or lust within you.

So, we have a sin nature in us that would sit dormant without the law. Thus, the sin nature "was dead" (7:8). The law was given to us to point us to Christ (Galatians 3:24), but the side effect of this is that our sin nature flourishes under the law, causing us to break the law.

7:9 This verse answers the question of what happens to a child who dies before reaching "the age of accountability." Does he go to heaven or hell? All people are born with a sin nature, but "sin is not imputed when there is no law" (5:13). Paul says that he "was alive without the law once," which means that, as a newborn child, he would have eternal life because he was not under the law. At some point, "the commandment came," which would be the time when he received the conscience. That is when "sin revived, and I died." So, until a child receives his conscience, he has eternal life if he dies. Once his conscience comes in, he falls in the category of having sinned and fallen short of the glory of God (3:23). Therefore, he is now spiritually dead. He then has to believe whatever gospel he knows in order to receive eternal life. Initially, this would be the internal gospel of acknowledging God as the Creator with the eternal power to judge him to hell for his sin (1:19-20,32). Later, he would be judged by the gospel of trusting in Jesus' death, burial, and resurrection as atonement for his sin (I Corinthians 15:3-4).

Since the initial gospel is God as the Creator, we can see why Satan is very much interested in destroying this gospel. Therefore, he has gotten many schools all over the world to teach evolution. The sooner Satan can get a lie taught that combats the truth, the sooner he can get a child not to believe God. Then, if he dies, he will go to hell. If he lives, at least he has started down the path of changing the truth of God into a lie very early in life (1:25), such that he will likely continue to believe a lie. "Train up a child in the way he should go: and when he is old, he will not depart from it" (Proverbs

22:6). Conversely, you can train up a child in lies, and he will probably believe lies all of his life. Therefore, Satan corrupts children with the theory of evolution. Those children become adults who quickly squash their own children's belief in the Creator so that lies are passed down from generation to generation. Thus, they change "the glory of the uncorruptible God into an image made like to corruptible man, and to birds, and fourfooted beasts, and creeping things" (1:23).

However, all of this is not Paul's point. Paul's point is that the law works with the sin nature to cause us to commit sins against God.

7:10 The commandment "was ordained to life" in the sense that those, who keep the law perfectly, receive eternal life (2:6-7). The problem is that, since the sin nature works with the commandment to produce a bunch of lust within me (7:8), I end up sinning. Since "the wages of sin is death" (6:23), the commandment of how to receive life ends up producing death in me.

7:11 Jeremiah 17:9 says, "The heart is deceitful above all things, and desperately wicked: who can know it?" The heart is another way of saying, "the sin nature." So, our sin nature is desperately wicked, but, "above all things," it is deceitful. So, when the conscience comes into us, our sin nature tricks us so that it can do its wickedness. We see this in the various vices that people have. For example, let's say that you have trouble with drunkenness. The pride of your sin nature will work with the commandment and say, "I will not get drunk ever again," which is a human-good statement. Since you are now thinking about drinking, you start thinking how good it would be to have a drink. Your sin nature tells you, "There is no harm in having just one drink. I can handle my liquor," which is a human-evil statement. The next thing you know, you are drunker than Cooter Brown. As such, your sin nature played both the good and the evil sides of your conscience to cause you to sin. Therefore, your sin nature is a murderer.

Since the sin nature is still with us after we are saved, we should expect it to continue to try to trick us to do the wicked things it wants us to do by using both the knowledge of good and the knowledge of evil against us. Before you were saved, your sin nature worked "all uncleanness with greediness" (Ephesians 4:19). Since you have been saved, the Holy Spirit has taken up residence inside you (5:5), and He is contrary to the flesh (Galatians 5:17). Therefore, the sin nature will try even harder to cause you to sin. That is why it is absolutely essential that you recognize that you are complete in Christ (Colossians 2:10) so that you will allow Christ to live through you, rather than the sin nature. That is why 7:24-25 says that "God through Jesus Christ our Lord" is the only One able to deliver us "from the body of this death."

7:12 Sin slays us; the law does not slay us (7:11). We were just told that "the wages of sin is death" (6:23). In other words, it is the sin nature that works in you, causing you to sin. The law does not cause you to sin. Rather, the law is "holy" in that it is sinless. Anyone, who obeys the law perfectly, will receive eternal life (2:6-7), because he will be holy and can then live in the presence of a holy God. Of course, no one has ever met that perfect standard except the Lord Jesus Christ. The law is "just" in that it is fair. It only condemns those who disobey the law. The law is "good" in that it points us to Christ. "The law was our schoolmaster to bring us unto Christ" (Galatians 3:24), and "there is none good but one, that is, God" (Matthew 19:17). So, the law shows our guilt before God, bringing us to Christ, which makes the law good.

By the way, we should now see how the Lord Jesus Christ lived a perfect life. He "did no sin" (I Peter 2:22), because He "knew no sin" (II Corinthians 5:21). In other words, because He did not have the sin nature, He was not slain by it when the law came unto Him. That is not to say that any of us would have accomplished the same thing, because Adam also had no sin nature, and he still made the choice to sin. However, we have learned that the sin nature makes it impossible for us to live without sin. In other words, it takes away our choice.

This is actually a good thing because all of us would make a choice to sin at some point, which would make us worthy of hell. But, if we lived without sinning for even part of the time, we probably would never believe the gospel. After all, most people, who are told the gospel, reject it by saying that they are good and will go to heaven based upon their own merits. Since the pride of most men keeps them from seeing that they are sinners, even though they sin 100% of the time, the pride of man would probably keep all men from seeing that they are sinners if they had the choice and chose not to sin at least some of the time. An example of this is Lucifer. He served God until his pride caused him to say that he would be like God (Isaiah 14:12-14). Thus, he sinned, and there has not been one good thing found in him ever since. He still thinks he will be like God!

7:13 The law does not bring about death. Paul has already shown that all men have a death sentence upon them because of the sin nature that they have within them that was imputed to them through Adam's sin (5:12-14). Therefore, death comes to us from our sin nature, not from the law. What the law does, though, is that it makes the sin nature active. "For without the law, [the] sin [nature] was dead" (7:8). When the law comes, the sin nature uses the law to have you commit sins.

This is the best thing that could happen to us because "sin by the commandment [becomes] exceeding sinful" (7:13). In other words, the sin nature works with the law to cause us to commit more sins, which makes it easier for us to recognize that we are sinners so that we will believe the gospel and receive the gift of eternal life. For example, an alcoholic will never admit that he has a problem unless he hits "rock bottom." In other words, alcoholism has to get so bad that even the person enslaved by it recognizes that he has a problem. That is what is meant by "sin, that it might appear sin" (7:13).

"Might become exceeding sinful" (7:13) means that, the more we sin, the more obvious it becomes to us that our flesh's response, that we are okay just the way we are, is wrong. In other words, sin needs to become sinful enough to exceed our prideful flesh. Thus, overcoming our flesh is why God gave us the law, because we can then have faith that pleases God (Hebrews 11:6). If the sin nature did not work "death in me by that which is good" (7:13), i.e., by the law, how would I know that I am dead? Therefore, the sin nature is to blame for my death, and the law is good because it works with the sin nature to teach me to come to Christ in order to be justified by faith (Galatians 3:24). This means that, if I believe the gospel, the law is life to me, which is the exact opposite of the question: "Was then that which is good made death unto me?" (7:13). Therefore, Paul's answer to this question is: "God forbid" (7:13).

7:14-25 Most Christians view this passage as what Paul was like before he was saved. That is because they do not understand what he taught us in Romans 6. In Romans 6, he said that "our old man is crucified with Christ" (6:6), our flesh is "buried with Him by baptism into death" (6:4), "the body of sin" is destroyed (6:6), and we are "freed from sin" (6:7). Christians interpret these four statements to mean, "God crucified the old man and made me a better person," "I was water baptized to show the world that I am a better person now," "I sin less now," and "I have replaced sin with going to church and doing good deeds," respectively. Thus, God's statements, about what He has done for us so that Christ can live in us, are all changed into what I can supposedly do for God now that I have been saved. The attitude is that God is blessed to have such great servants like us! Thus, pride has kept Christianity from believing what Paul taught in Romans 6.

Really, this all starts with churches not teaching a clear gospel. The gospel, that gives eternal life, is not believed by most people because it is all about Christ's sacrifice. People, in their pride, want to think they have at least some, small part in their eternal life. Even those, who do believe the gospel, end up thinking they can serve God in their flesh, because, in their pride, they think that God has made them a better person once they are saved. They refuse to believe that their flesh is just as vile after being saved as it was before they were saved (Philippians 3:20-21). Therefore, they try to serve God in the energy of their flesh without allowing the Holy Spirit to work through them.

It is to these Christians that Paul writes 7:14-25. It is as if Paul is saying, "For those who refuse to believe what God told you in Romans 6, here is what will happen if you try serving God in the flesh. Maybe after you see this play out, you will believe Romans 6." Sadly, Christianity looks at these verses and says, "That's who I used to be, but not anymore. I no longer struggle like this because I serve Christ." Thus, they explain away God's Word to them due to their unbelief.

7:14 Right away, those trying to serve God with their flesh have a problem. The law is spiritual, and they are carnal. Because our flesh and the law are two, different things, there is no way we can use the flesh to obey the law.

"I AM carnal" (7:14) is in the present tense, which means that Paul, AFTER he was saved, was still carnal. After he counted all things loss for Christ, he was still carnal (Philippians 3:7-8). Yes, he made the right choice after he was saved, but that choice was based upon who he was in Christ. His flesh's carnality had not changed. Paul is carnal, in spite of allowing Christ to live in him, just as much as the Corinthians are carnal (I Corinthians 3:3). The difference is only that Paul chose to allow Christ to live through him, while the Corinthians were acting out their carnality.

You may say, "But, I am a good Christian. I go to church; I pay tithes. I don't smoke or chew or go with girls who do." A woman may put makeup on to make herself appear younger, but, underneath that makeup, her flesh is still the same. Similarly, Christians may put on a big smile and refrain from cursing, but their flesh is still the same. We need to understand that Adam did not eat of the tree of the knowledge of evil; he ate of the tree of the knowledge of good and evil. This means that saved man can use his conscience to try to do good works for God, and such work is still of the flesh. The question is, "What is your motivation?" If you decide to do something based upon the sound doctrine built up in your inner man, that good work is of faith and is done through you by Christ. If you decide to do something to make yourself look good to others, it is not of faith in God, which means it is sin (14:23). Thus, it is just as sinful for me to be water baptized to impress the people at church (knowledge of good), as it is for me to rob a bank (knowledge of evil). In other words, human good is just as much a sin as human evil is. Why? Because "I am carnal" (7:14), even after I am saved. Therefore, your actions should be based upon who you are in Christ, rather than trying to do good deeds out of your carnal flesh.

7:15 My flesh is "sold under sin" (7:14). Do NOT confuse this with your soul and spirit. Your soul was "dead in trespasses and sins" (Ephesians 2:1), but it is now "quickened...together with Christ" (Ephesians 2:5). Therefore, the Holy Spirit can work with your spirit to teach you the things of God (I Corinthians 2:13). Your flesh, however, is still vile, still under sin, and will not be changed until the rapture (Philippians 3:20-21).

Therefore, there are two "I"s, warring against each other in this verse. There is the "I" of the flesh, and the "I" of the spirit. Caught in the middle is your soul. If you make the decision in your soul to follow the spirit, you will obey the law, because the law is spiritual. Paul will talk about this in Romans 8. Right now, he is dealing with someone who decides in his soul to let his flesh control him. Since his flesh is carnal, sold under sin, he will do the opposite of what the law tells him to do. Therefore, he does what his spirit says he should not do, and he does not do what his spirit says he should do.

101

In fact, he does what his spirit hates to do. In other words, if you try to serve God in the flesh, you end up only doing things that are contrary to God, because your carnal flesh cannot serve God.

7:16 The flesh's disobedience of the law proves that the law is good, and it also proves that the flesh cannot serve God.

7:17 "Now then it is no more I that do it" (7:17). Why? Because I am "dead with Christ" (6:8), making me "freed from sin" (6:7). After I am saved, I am no longer attached to my sin nature, but I am attached to Christ. Granted, I still have my sin nature, but my identity is Christ, not my sin nature. Therefore, Christ's death on the cross has separated me from being identified with my sin nature.

We have learned that the sin nature works with the law, i.e., the conscience, to sin even more (7:13). After we are saved, we still have the conscience, and we still have the sin nature. Yet, Paul says that "ye are not under the law" (6:14), and that ye are "freed from sin" (6:7). The only way we can still have the conscience and the sin nature and be free from both is that our identity is now Christ. We have been married to Christ (7:4). Therefore, Paul can "NOW" say that, when he sins after he is saved, he is not really doing the sinning, because he is freed from sin and he is in Christ. Rather, it is his sin nature within him that does the sinning now. In other words, his identification with his sin nature has been severed because he is now joined to Christ.

7:18 The saved person wants to serve God but has no power in the flesh to do any good thing. Before we were saved, "we were yet without strength" (5:6) to serve God. After we are saved, we are still without strength to serve God in our flesh, because no good thing dwells in the flesh. Note that Paul adds the parenthetical reference of "(that is, in my flesh)," because there is power within us to serve God. That power is the Holy Ghost working through us. Therefore, Paul has to qualify that when he says "in me dwelleth no good thing," he is referring to his flesh. The will to obey the law is there in the inward man (7:22), but the ability to obey the law is not there in the flesh. It is there in the Holy Spirit instead.

7:19-21 To recap, after being saved, the inward man wants to serve God. The problem is that the flesh cannot serve God. Therefore, we cannot please God when we try in our flesh to serve Him. Paul says that the law is "that, when I would do good, evil is present with me." This means that, even if we want to do good IN OUR FLESH, we cannot do good, because only evil is in our flesh.

We must clarify, as we have said before, that the good, that Paul wants to do, are the good works of God that we should walk in (Ephesians 2:10). God's good works are only things done in faith, which means that they are things done through the Holy Spirit and the mind of Christ. Therefore, "good" is not defined by the action, but it is defined by the heart motivation. For example, let us say that you decide to serve God by volunteering at a soup kitchen. If you decided to volunteer because you read God's Word rightly divided and allowed the Holy Spirit to teach you to be kind to others so that they may see the love of God shed through you and desire to have that same love, that is a good work. Now, let us say that I decide to do the same volunteer work because I want to show people at church than I serve God just as much as you do. The result will be that I will feel good about myself for being a good Christian and for helping out less fortunate people. This is the sin of pride. Therefore, I do a good work, but evil is with me in pride, such that the good I did is now corrupted by the evil, meaning that I really did not do any good thing at all.

God gives an illustration of this in the Old Testament. He says, "if one that is unclean by a dead body touch" "bread, or pottage, or wine, or oil, or any meat," "shall it be unclean?" "So is this people, and so is this nation before Me, saith the Lord; and so is every work of their hands; and that which they offer there is unclean" (Haggai 2:12-14). In other words, because Israel uses their flesh and are in unbelief, everything they do for God is unclean or evil in His sight, regardless of how "good" the work may be. This serves as an illustration for us today. Since no good thing dwells in my flesh (7:18), every good work that I try to do in my flesh is turned into an evil work by the flesh. Thus, "when I would do good, evil is present with me" (7:21).

Therefore, no one can make a list of good works and evil works. Everything, that Christ does through decisions you make based upon sound doctrine, is a good work. Everything, that you do based upon your feelings, is an evil work. Therefore, I can present the gospel to someone in an effort to look good to my fellow church members, and that is considered an evil work, even though the result may be good. Conversely, I can tell the pastor at church that he should be fired, because he teaches a false gospel and I am offended by that, and God will consider that a good work, even though the result may be a division in the church. Therefore, we must stop focusing on the actual work, and start focusing on the motivation behind the work in order to view things the way that God does.

7:22 This verse is another proof that Paul is talking about himself AFTER he was saved. If you are not saved, then your inner man is dead in trespasses and sins (Ephesians 2:1). Only after you are saved, does God make your soul alive, such that you "delight in the law of God after the inward man" (7:22).

7:23 "The law in my members" (7:23) is "the law of sin and death" (8:2). "The law of my mind" (7:23) is "the law of the Spirit of life in Christ Jesus" (8:2). These two laws war against each other, if we try to serve God in our flesh. Before we were saved, we spent our entire lives making decisions based upon an emotional flesh (James 3:15) and a carnal mind (8:6), because that was all we could do, since our inner man was dead in sin

(Ephesians 2:1). When we get saved, our inward man delights in serving God. However, since we have always operated in our flesh, we try to serve God with our flesh, especially since that is what Christianity tells us to do. Thus, we allow the flesh to overcome the spirit, bringing us "into captivity to the law of sin" (7:23), even though we are trying to serve God. Paul says that this kind of service causes us to be "vainly puffed up by [our] fleshly mind" (Colossians 2:18).

7:24-25 The result of this inner turmoil should be the exclamation, "O wretched man that I am! Who shall deliver me from the body of this death?" Most Christians never make this internal exclamation. Instead, in their pride, they convince themselves they are doing just fine, and then put on a good front at church and around other Christians to convince them of the same. They say, "O good man that I am!" instead of declaring themselves to be wretched. However, the Christian, who takes an honest look at himself, will realize that he cannot serve God in the strength of his own flesh and will look for deliverance from the flesh. Since God gave Him eternal life, he will look to God's Word for his deliverance.

When he reads God's Word, the Holy Spirit will teach him that "our old man is crucified with Him, that the body of sin might be destroyed, that henceforth we should not serve sin. For he that is dead is freed from sin" (6:6-7). He will then "thank God through Jesus Christ our Lord" (7:25) that Christ has delivered him from the body of sin so that he can walk in the Spirit, as Paul talks about in Romans 8. He will then believe those five, little words in Galatians 2:20 that are the key to the Christian life: "Yet not I, but Christ." Sadly, though, most Christians never get out of Romans 7, because their pride keeps them from ever believing the truths of Romans 6.

8 Paul starts Romans 8 with walking after the Spirit, so that we do not fulfill the lusts of the flesh (v. 1). He then says that we should live by the "law of the Spirit of life in Christ Jesus" so that we will be "free from the law of sin and death" (v. 2). The rest of the chapter is about how walking in the Spirit works. Because those in the flesh cannot please God (v. 8), God sent His Son to condemn sin in the flesh (v. 3). By believing the gospel, we are in the Spirit (v. 9), and Christ is in us (v. 10). Therefore, we should "mortify the deeds of the body" (v. 13) and be led by the Spirit (v. 14), which will result in serving God, because the Spirit has a special relationship with the Father (v. 15). By being children of God, we are heirs of God with Christ (v. 17). Since Christ suffered, we suffer, too (v. 17). However, we should not worry about that because the suffering pales in comparison with the eternal glory that it creates (v. 18). We are also not alone in our suffering, because God's whole creation suffers, being under the curse of sin (vs. 19-22). Suffering produces patience in us (vs. 24-25). It also helps us learn sound doctrine, which is why the Spirit intercedes for us with the Father (vs. 26-28). Suffering is part of the plan that God had in mind before the foundation of the world (Ephesians 1:4). Therefore, we can trust that it will lead to our glorification (vs. 29-30). This means that God is for us, even in our suffering (v. 31).

Therefore, no one, including ourselves (v. 34), can separate us from the love of God in Christ (vs. 35-39), which means that, if we believe Romans 8 doctrine, we will do God's will. If you do not believe and understand the doctrine given in Romans 8, you will not walk in the Spirit. **This is why Romans 8 is the most important chapter in the Bible for the believer to understand.**

8:1 This verse is often pulled right out of its context to make salvation conditional by saying that the only way God will not condemn you is if you "walk not after the flesh, but after the Spirit." However, Paul spent the first four chapters of Romans settling the issue that works have nothing to do with our justification, concluding in 5:1: "Therefore, being justified by faith, we have peace with God through our Lord Jesus Christ." How could Paul say in 5:1 that we have peace with God right now, in 5:9 that we are "now justified by His blood," and in 5:11 that "we have now received the atonement," then turn around and say, "you had better walk after the Spirit or God will condemn you?"

Also, the words of 8:1 themselves tell you that your salvation is not conditional. It says there is "no condemnation to them which are IN CHRIST JESUS" (8:1). If you are "in Christ Jesus," you must be saved, because being in Christ Jesus means that "your life is hid with Christ in God" (Colossians 3:3). This means you are "accepted in the beloved" (Ephesians 1:6). If God condemned someone in Christ Jesus, then He would be condemning Himself. II Timothy 2:13 says that those, who choose not to suffer with Christ in this life, will still receive eternal life because Christ Jesus "abideth faithful: He cannot deny Himself" of eternal life. Therefore, the very fact that you are in Christ Jesus means that you have eternal life, regardless of what you do, which automatically rules out the possibility of God condemning you.

Also, the context of 8:1 makes it clear that Paul is not talking about eternal life. The verse says, "there is THEREFORE now," which tells us that 8:1 is a conclusion based on what has just been said in chapter 7. What has just been said was that God will deliver us from the body of sin when we, by faith, learn that our flesh is wretched (7:24-25). In other words, God said that our old man is crucified with Christ, the body of sin is destroyed, and we are freed from sin (6:6-7), but our flesh does not give up that easily. It battles the spirit, trying to gain back the control of the soul that it lost when we were saved. Therefore, we struggle with sin by trying to serve God in our flesh, as Paul mentioned in Romans 7. Finally, we read God's Word and reckon ourselves "also...to be dead indeed unto sin, but alive unto God through Jesus Christ our Lord" (6:11). When we make this reckoning, then our struggle with sin is over, being delivered by God from the body of sin that we had been serving. Therefore, the condemnation that we no longer have in 8:1 is not of God condemning us to hell. God says, "it is appointed unto men once to die, but after this the judgment" (Hebrews 9:27). Since we are "dead to sin" (6:2), God has judged that sin, "nailing it to His cross"

(Colossians 2:14), so that we are "freed from sin" (6:7). Therefore, Paul is not bringing up God's condemnation of us, because we have already been judged to receive eternal life.

Rather, the condemnation in 8:1 is SELF condemnation. We no longer condemn ourselves by saying, "O wretched man that I am!" (7:24), because we have been delivered from our wretchedness by God. Therefore, we stop condemning ourselves and our guilt is gone when we stop walking after the flesh and start walking after the Spirit, because Christ's blood purges our "conscience from dead works to serve the living God" (Hebrews 9:14). In other words, God has freed us from trying to obey the law through our flesh so that Christ can live in us, relieving us of condemning ourselves for failing to serve God in the flesh.

In summary, the moment we are saved, God declares us dead to sin (6:2). But, we follow the sin nature by trying to serve God in our flesh. Then, we learn the sound doctrine of Romans 7 that we cannot serve God through our flesh. We then do what God told us to do along, which is to reckon ourselves to be dead to sin (6:11). Once we make this reckoning, we stop condemning ourselves, and we start serving God by allowing Christ to live in us (Galatians 2:20). (This is a decision that we must make every day of our lives (I Corinthians 15:31).) Now that we have learned this lesson, Paul will use chapter 8 to give us the details of what life in Christ Jesus is all about. Therefore, instead of starting this chapter questioning our salvation, which is the defeatist attitude of Christianity, Paul is really starting this chapter with a praise report and moving on to sound doctrine of how we walk in the Spirit now that we are dead to sin and alive unto God.

As if this verse is not hard enough to understand as is, due to not understanding the first seven chapters of Romans, modern translations come along and completely remove the phrase out of 8:1 that says, "who walk not after the flesh, but after the Spirit." This removal makes it harder to see that 8:1 is talking about self-condemnation. Christianity, as mentioned previously, wants this verse to be talking about your salvation. Therefore, they eliminate the last phrase as a supposed copyist error. That way, they can then talk about how you will live the Christian life if you are truly "in Christ Jesus" because of what Paul says in verse 2 and following. In other words, they eliminate your choice to walk in the Spirit by saying that "true" believers WILL walk in the Spirit. The implication is that, if you do not walk in the Spirit, you are not saved. Therefore, they take this phrase out to make salvation about your performance so that they can put you under the law, which translates into more money in the offering for them.

They say, "Oh, some copyist got tired and accidentally wrote down the same words in 8:1 that are in 8:4. So, we have rightfully taken the words out." Really? So, I am supposed to believe that ONE copyist accidentally made his eyes wander down to 8:4, wrote a phrase from there, and then went back to 8:2 and never caught his error. Then, in spite of the hundreds of manuscripts to the contrary, the King James Version translators never caught the error, even though they checked and cross-checked their work with individuals and committees over a period of years. It then took another 300 years before someone finally caught the error. I am sorry, but that argument is way too far-fetched to believe. What makes it even more far-fetched is that God promised to preserve His Word forever (Psalm 12:6-7), down to the last "jot and tittle" (Matthew 5:18), such that "heaven and earth shall pass away, but My words shall not pass away" (Matthew 24:35). Because of these promises, modern versions call God a liar, when they say His Word was wrong for nearly 2,000 years! So, I am supposed to believe that God is strong enough to overcome death for me (6:23) by condemning my sin (8:3), but He is too powerless to keep someone from corrupting His Word! If that is the case, why study God's Word in the first place? Of course, we know the answer to that question. Christianity studies God's Word to find verses to substantiate their false teachings. Therefore, they change God's Word when they do not like it, instead of changing their beliefs to match God's Word.

8:2 This verse is a great summary of Romans 6-7. Christians will admit that they did bad things before they were saved. However, once God saves them, they think that their flesh is suddenly capable of serving God, but that is not true. (By the way, Christians' focus on the flesh is also why they have a standard you must uphold in your flesh in order to "stay" saved, whether that is just refraining from the "really bad" sins like murder or a more strict code such as going to church, paying tithes, and doing good deeds.) The reason they think their flesh is good is because they have not read and believed their Bibles. Instead, their focus is on this world, even if it is focused on what the pastor says. The wisdom of this world is "sensual [and] devilish" (James 3:15), which means that it uses the senses. That is why most churchgoers will say that a service was good because they "felt" the presence of the Lord. They sing songs and close their eyes so that they will feel the Spirit. They pray for the Holy Spirit to fall upon them. In summary, Christians think that God is with them when they feel good, which means that they concentrate on the flesh or their senses, even after they are saved.

However, Christ did not die on the cross to make us feel good. He died to save us from ourselves. God's salvation of us does not take our bad flesh and make it good. Rather, it leaves our vile bodies unchanged (Philippians 3:21). Instead, God takes our dead spirits and makes them alive in Christ (Ephesians 2:1). Thus, the change is in the spirit, not in the flesh. Now, the soul is caught in the middle of the flesh and the spirit. That is where doctrine is stored. If you have sound doctrine in your soul, that means that the Holy Ghost has taught your spirit the things of God (I Corinthians 2:10-13) through His Word, such that you are now "strengthened with might by His Spirit in the inner man" (Ephesians 3:16). However, if you have not read and believed God's Word, the only input your soul will have will be from "the god of this world" (II Corinthians 4:4) teaching you "the course of this world"

(Ephesians 2:2). You may say, "But, I go to church and the pastor uses scripture, so I am following God." However, when Satan came to Jesus, he also used scripture, and he used it to tempt Jesus to disobey God (see Matthew 4:6). We must allow the Holy Ghost to teach us the truth of God's Word, rather than listening to man twist scripture to satisfy the flesh. If you have not done this, the only input your soul has is from the flesh. Therefore, you will continue to follow "the law of sin and death." The only way to be freed from that law is by using sound doctrine to make decisions so that you walk after "the law of the Spirit of life in Christ Jesus."

In summary, Christianity says, "I am basically good. I just need God to bring out the good in me. Then, I will live for God." However, God says that "I am carnal, sold under sin" (7:14). I have a law of sin and death operating in me. When I was saved, God said that I did not have to follow that law of sin and death any more. He gave me His Holy Ghost (5:5) to teach me the things of God (I Corinthians 2:10-13). He strengthens my soul through His Word not to listen to my nasty flesh any more (7:18), which means I can now operate under "the law of the Spirit of life in Christ Jesus." Those, operating under the law of the Spirit, "have suffered the loss of all things [of the flesh], and do count them but dung, that [they] may win Christ" (Philippians 3:8). Unfortunately, most Christians do not read and believe their Bibles, which means that their soul's only input comes from the devil, even if they go to church, which is why Paul calls these false-doctrine preachers, ministers of Satan (II Corinthians 11:13-15).

Therefore, the typical Christian has not abandoned his fleshly mind (Colossians 2:18) for the mind of Christ (I Corinthians 2:16), but he has continued to think the same after he was saved as before he was saved. In other words, he is still in bondage to "the law of sin and death" (8:2). The only difference is that the Christian now has more pride, thinking that he can serve God out of his flesh. Therefore, he starts acting and talking differently to match his pride, instead of counting his flesh as dung and letting God live through him. In short, he is still living by the law of sin and death, but he has slapped some lipstick on it to make his flesh look like it is now of God. The lesson of Romans 6-7 is that God has made us free from the law of sin and death so that we can now follow the law of the Spirit of life in Christ Jesus. However, most Christians never recognize this because they are focused on their flesh.

8:3 The law is holy, just, and good (7:12), but it does not give a man power to overcome sin. In fact, we learned that the law works with our sin nature to make us "exceeding sinful" (7:13). So, the law was "weak through the flesh" (8:3). In other words, law + flesh = sin, because there is no power in the flesh to perform the law. However, "the Lord God [is] omnipotent" (Revelation 19:6). Therefore, God could use His power to fulfill the law.

However, if God just came and fulfilled the law, it would do us no good, because we would still have the flesh problem. God needed to take our flesh out of the way, which means that He had to become flesh. Therefore, God sent "His Own Son in the LIKENESS of sinful flesh" (8:3). He did not put His Own Son IN sinful flesh, because then His holiness would have been corrupted. Rather, God prepared Jesus a fleshly body (Hebrews 10:5), so that He could be our kinsmen redeemer, since the law states that trespasses may be recompensed to a kinsman in order to bear his sin (Numbers 5:8). Hebrews 2:16-17 is clear that Jesus Christ did not take "on Him the nature of angels; but He took on Him the seed of Abraham. Wherefore in all things it behoved Him to be made LIKE UNTO His brethren...to make reconciliation for the sins of the people." He had a corruptible body just like us, but He did not have a sin nature. Therefore, Christ did not have the problem that we have of trying to obey the law through the flesh, which Paul has shown is an impossibility (7:14-21). This means that the power of God was in Christ's flesh to make Him capable of obeying the law perfectly, because He did not have the sin nature. That does not mean that it was easy for Him to live a perfect life. He had to learn "obedience by the things which He suffered" (Hebrews 5:8).

Because Jesus Christ was in flesh, He had the capacity to suffer by being "in all points tempted like as we are, yet without sin" (Hebrews 4:15). Since Jesus Christ "did no sin" (I Peter 2:22), He could then be "made...sin for us;...that we might be made the righteousness of God in Him" (II Corinthians 5:21). He "redeemed us from the curse of the law, being made a curse for us" (Galatians 3:13). In other words, He became the "propitiation" or sacrifice that fully satisfies the wrath of God (3:25). That is why Isaiah 53:11 says that God "shall see of the travail of His soul, and shall be satisfied." Because Jesus' blood is pure in that He did no sin and it is human blood, He fully satisfies the payment for sin which is death (6:23) such that He "condemned sin in the flesh" (8:3). Thus, He was fully man, tempted, overcame every temptation, took our sin upon Him, and defeated sin for us.

By condemning the sin nature for us, we can now live without self-condemnation (8:1). Note that sin is condemned IN THE FLESH, which means that the sin nature has been put to death for us. That is not to say that we do not have the ability to sin any more, but Paul's point is that God won the victory over our sin nature for us. Therefore, we will not sin when we choose to walk "after the Spirit" (8:4). Thus, unsaved man's equation is law + flesh = sin. The Lord Jesus Christ's equation is God + law + flesh = death of sin. The law provided the holy standard, and God provided the holiness to meet that holy standard (I Peter 1:16).

8:4 Most people today, who believe in eternal security, do so as an excuse to sin. Legalistic Christians call this "easybelievism." In other words, they answer the question of: "Shall we continue in sin, that grace may abound?" (6:1) with "Absolutely!" rather than with "God forbid" (6:2). Now, Paul gives us the reason why Jesus Christ condemned sin in the flesh. It was not so you could keep sinning, but it was so "the righteousness of the law might be fulfilled in us" (8:4). Note that it does not say that we will do the righteousness of the law, but it says that the righteousness of the law "might be fulfilled in us." This means that God through Jesus Christ condemned your sin nature to death, but kept you in your vile flesh (Philippians 3:21) so that Christ could live in you. If you allow this to happen, people will look at you and see "that the excellency of the power [is] of God, and not of us" (II Corinthians 4:7). Then, they are more likely to have faith in the gospel so that God can make the same transformation in them.

Therefore, God does not zap you into heaven when you are saved, because He wants to live through you. You have a unique opportunity to let Christ live in you, because this can only happen with saved people. Thus, saved man's equation should be grace + Christ = life of Christ in us, so that others are saved and come unto the knowledge of the truth (I Timothy 2:4). Instead, Christianity has made it: grace + flesh = hypocritical sin, so that others remain unsaved and reject the truth. Your decision on what to do with Christ after you are saved has eternal consequences for yourself and for those in your life. Therefore, you should walk after the Spirit, rather than after the flesh.

8:5 Paul says that the reason the righteousness of the law is fulfilled in us when we walk after the Spirit is because we end up minding the things of the Spirit. Since "the law is spiritual" (7:14) and the Spirit is obviously spiritual, we are able to fulfill the righteousness of the law by yielding our flesh to God (6:13).

8:6-7 All people are born with a carnal mind. Once you are saved, God gives you "the mind of Christ" (I Corinthians 2:16). Your soul now has to choose which mind to use. Christians think that this means that they were bad people before they were saved, and now they are good people after they are saved. They think that they will now make good choices. However, choices between good and evil are rooted in the fleshly mind, NOT in the mind of Christ. After all, the eyes of Adam and Eve were opened to discern between good and evil (Genesis 3:22), which means that all people have the ability to choose the good and shun the evil if they want to. Getting saved does not change that ability one iota.

For example, some people make the choice to become alcoholics. Later on, they may see how messed up alcohol made their lives, and they then make the choice to stop drinking alcohol. That is a choice out of the fleshly mind. They used the fleshly mind both to choose to drink alcohol and to choose later not to drink alcohol. Christians will say, "No, the Lord delivered me from alcohol." If the choice to stop drinking alcohol was made out of sound doctrine in the inner man, knowing that being an alcoholic will damage the ability to do God's will, then, yes, the Lord delivered that person from alcohol. However, in almost all cases, Christians give up alcohol for societal reasons. They "clean up their acts" and "get right with God," because their spouses will leave them if they do not. (Johnny Cash is a great example. He said that the Lord delivered him from drugs, but he really stopped taking drugs in order to be with June Carter.) Or, they stop drinking to fit in with their new found, Christian friends, so that others think they are changed now.

People will say, "but Alcoholics Anonymous requires a belief in a higher power. So, it is God Who helps them overcome alcohol." This is incorrect thinking, because it makes the "god" of every religion equal, which is why Christianity now thinks that all religions lead to heaven. However, Jesus said, "I am the way, the truth, and the life: no man cometh unto the Father, but by Me" (John 14:6). God also said, "I am the Lord, and there is none else, there is no God beside Me" (Isaiah 45:5). Therefore, if God really did deliver someone from alcoholism, it can only be the God of the Bible Who did it, because all other religions have powerless gods. Yet, the lowest alcohol-consumption rates in the world are found among Muslim countries, who do not believe in the God of the Bible. Why? Because the societal pressures in Muslim countries not to drink are greater than they are in Christian countries—not because of a belief in a higher power—because the Muslim god is powerless.

The result of the idea that Christians are suddenly better people now that they are saved is that New Age philosophy has crept into Christianity. New Agers believe that you are your own god, because you can will yourself to do things. If you want to stop drinking alcohol, you can make the choice to do so. You do not need God. This thinking is correct, in the sense that everyone, apart from God, can use their fleshly minds to choose the good, instead of the evil. But, they attach God to their thinking and give Him the credit, which causes people to follow the New Age philosophies, rather than God's Word. Thus, "the power of positive thinking" is the god of Christianity now, instead of the Lord Jesus Christ. However, even when Christians change for the better with positive thinking, the "good" that they are now doing is human good. It is NOT godliness, and that is the problem here.

For example, once Adam and Eve ate of the fruit of the knowledge of good and evil, their "eyes...were opened," such that they now knew good and evil (Genesis 3:5,7,22). When that happened, the first thing they noticed was that they were naked. They did not use that knowledge to choose evil, but they used it to choose good. That is, they made the choice to cover up their nakedness by making aprons out of fig leaves (Genesis 3:7). However, this did not solve their problem. Their problem was sin. They had a clothing of light before they sinned (Psalm 104:2 and Genesis 1:26-27), and now that clothing was gone. Instead of asking God how they could get that clothing back, they made their own clothes, choosing human good over godliness, or human clothing over godly clothing. The point is that, while they chose the good, they still had a sin problem that did not go away when they chose to do good. In other words, they chose to try to solve the sin problem themselves, instead of allowing God to solve the sin problem for them.

111

Similarly, people can use their fleshly minds to choose to do good all the time, and they will still have a sin problem. Sure, they volunteered at the hospital, they fed the poor, they took care of their families, they did not curse, they went to church, they paid tithes, they smiled at everyone they met, and they did anything and everything they could for others, but they still have sinned and fallen short of the glory of God (3:23). Therefore, they are still worthy of death (6:23). All of their own "righteousnesses are as filthy rags" (Isaiah 64:6). In other words, when it comes to the eternal, choices made out of a carnal mind do not help you achieve anything, no matter how "good" those choices are.

That is what Paul is trying to tell the Romans. Regardless of what choices they make in their carnal minds, those choices result in death (8:6). The reason is because whatever is not of faith is sin (14:23), which means that all choices, even the "good" ones, are subject to "the law of sin and death" (8:2). Therefore, they are never "subject to the law of God, neither indeed can [they] be" (8:7).

The problem is that, because Christians think that their flesh has changed, they now use their same carnal minds to try to serve God. Then, all of the good things they do out of that mind are attributed to God, causing them to be "vainly puffed up by [their] fleshly mind" (Colossians 2:18). The result is that they blaspheme God's name by "having a form of godliness, but denying the power thereof" (II Timothy 3:2,5). (That power is God and His Word.) You then have no way of reaching them with the truth, because they think they are serving God, when they are really serving their own flesh.

The solution to all of this is to recognize who you are in Christ. When you recognize that "the carnal mind is enmity against God" (8:7), you will be capable of judging all things (I Corinthians 2:15). That is, you will allow the love of Christ to constrain you to judge "that if one died for all, then were all dead" (II Corinthians 5:14). In other words, you will reckon yourself "to be dead indeed unto sin, but alive unto God through Jesus Christ our Lord" (6:11). You will reckon all unbelievers to be dead. Therefore, you will not brag about what a good Christian you are or that God delivered you from alcoholism. You will not tell people that they need to clean up their acts. Instead of glorying in your vain flesh, you will glory in the Lord (I Corinthians 1:29,31).

But, this all starts with recognizing who you are in Christ. If you choose to go down the path of making good decisions in your flesh, your service to God is only "enmity against God" (8:7), and that service will die at the judgment seat of Christ (I Corinthians 3:15), because "to be carnally minded is death" (8:6). However, if you choose to be led by the Spirit (8:14) by allowing Him to teach you the deep things of God (I Corinthians 2:10-13) and then using the mind of Christ (I Corinthians 2:16) to make decisions, the result will be eternal life of that service (I Corinthians 3:14). You may say, "But I am not doing anything that way. All I am doing is reading my

Bible." That is right. That is exactly what you need to do is to do nothing! That is because "Christ liveth in me" (Galatians 2:20), and He is "the Word" (John 1:1). When I read the Bible, I behold the face of Jesus Christ (II Corinthians 3:18 and 4:6). But, if I try to serve God in my flesh, I am not beholding Christ. So, how can God, Who is a Spirit (John 4:24), live through me if I am focused on the carnal, rather than the spiritual, and the spiritual is only found in God's Word? Therefore, the only way I can serve God is by reading my Bible. Doing good works only serves my flesh, because it obeys the law of sin and death (8:2). Allowing God to do the works through me (Ephesians 2:10) serves God, because it obeys the law of life and peace (8:6).

But, you may say, "God's Word says, 'Knowledge puffeth up, but charity edifieth' (I Corinthians 8:1), so I should be doing charitable work, instead of keeping my nose in a book." However, God's Word says that the process of "the love of God [being] shed abroad in our hearts by the Holy Ghost" (5:5) starts with tribulations (5:3). Tribulations come from living godly in Christ Jesus (II Timothy 3:12). Living godly in Christ Jesus comes only by using the mind of Christ (I Corinthians 2:16), which comes by the Holy Ghost teaching you the things of God (I Corinthians 2:10-13). Therefore, the only way to have charity coming through your life is by having sound doctrine built up in your hearts by reading God's Word. Otherwise, your "charity" is really your own pride coming out of a fleshly mind. Thus, your good works are not godly unless you first have the knowledge of sound doctrine in the inner man. That is why that sound doctrine is referred to as "the TREASURES of wisdom and knowledge" (Colossians 2:3). Only by mining those treasures in God's Word can charity come through you to edify others. Charity, which is a synonym for the love of God, is not you doing good deeds in the flesh; it is God doing His work through you.

8:8 Note how 8:7 says that the carnal mind cannot be subject to the law of God. This leads to the conclusion that you "cannot please God" (8:8) in your flesh. So, forget about doing good deeds and just let the love of God come through you. When you do that, people will notice. The reason is because only Christians have the ability to let the love of God come through them, and very few Christians actually allow this to happen. All unbelievers are "in the flesh" (8:8). Because of this, their flesh, including the flesh of most Christians, will cause them to invent ulterior motives from you, such that your good works will be evil spoken of (I Peter 2:12). Still, they WILL notice the love of God, because it is something that they probably have never experienced before. They will then have to make the choice to either have faith in God or continue in their flesh, but at least you would have forced them to make a choice.

So many Christians think that God transforms their flesh once they are saved to enable them to serve God. They then start praying to know God's will of what He would want them to do. They do not hear a voice from God telling them what God wants them to do, but, if they admit this, they will look like they are not in fellowship with God and are not saved. Therefore, they make something up. Just like the carnal Corinthians, who chose tongue talking as the gift they wanted because it impressed others, these carnal Christians will make up something that looks good to others, such as becoming a missionary or a worship leader. The problem is that, because they are doing their "calling" in the flesh, it will not please God. Oh how important it is to understand the doctrine of Romans 6-8, lest a life of service to God go to waste because it is done purely in the flesh!

8:9 Physically, we still have flesh, but God says that "our old man is crucified with" Christ (6:6). Therefore, functionally speaking, God says that we are no longer in the flesh. Christ made us alive unto God (6:11), and God gave us the Holy Ghost (5:5). Therefore, functionally speaking, we are "in the Spirit" (8:9). However, we can still make the choice to "walk AFTER the flesh" or "AFTER the Spirit" (8:1).

For example, when a man and a woman are married, the two become one flesh (I Corinthians 6:16). Since they are one flesh, the woman is now "in the man." Paul mentioned that a married woman, if she marries another man, is considered an adulteress (7:3). That is because she was in her husband, but then she walked after another husband. Similarly speaking, the body of Christ is "in the Spirit," but we can still walk after the flesh, even though we are in the Spirit. This makes us adulteresses. Of course, that is not God's plan for us.

"If so be" and "if any man" (8:9) are not put in this verse to make you think you can lose your salvation. Remember, that issue was already settled by Romans 5. You have been "justified freely by His grace" (3:24). This took place "NOW" in the present (5:9). God also gave you the Holy Ghost (5:5). Then, in chapter 6, Paul explained what happened to your sin nature when you were justified. Then, in chapter 7, Paul explained how the flesh still battles you. Now, in chapter 8, Paul describes what happens when you allow God to give you the victory over your flesh by His Spirit.

8:1 is the first verse where Paul mentions the "Spirit" with a capital "S." He mentions the "Spirit" with a capital "S" 21 times in Romans, and 19 of those times are in chapter 8 alone. This tells you that this chapter is the primary section in Romans about the Spirit working in you. There is no uncertainty regarding the Spirit indwelling you by this point. If you have believed the gospel, then the Spirit of God and the Spirit of Christ both dwell in you. In other words, Paul established, through the first seven chapters of Romans, that all believers have the Spirit. This means that all believers can allow God to gain the victory over the flesh for them because the Spirit dwells in them.

For example, let's say that a police officer pulls you over The first thing he asks you is, "Do you have a driver's license?" If your answer to that is, "Yes," he does not have to ask to see your written test results, because you must have passed the written test since you have a driver's license. Similarly, Paul has written seven chapters to the Romans. If they have believed those seven chapters, they are saved, which means they have the Spirit within them. Therefore, Paul can say "if so be that the Spirit of God dwell in you" (8:9), as a way of checking to make sure they have believed the gospel, because the Spirit being in them is proof that they have believed the gospel, just like having a driver's license is proof that I passed the state's driving tests. Therefore, instead of going backward and explaining the gospel that they have already believed, Paul moves forward with a simple reminder that they have the Spirit of God and the Spirit of Christ within them because they have already believed the gospel. Since that is the case, they can "please God" (8:8), because they are now "in the Spirit" and not "in the flesh" (8:9). Thus, he can move on with the details of how they please God in the Spirit.

By the way, the term "Holy Ghost" is mentioned 89 times in the King James Version, and only 14 of those times are found in Paul's epistles. Since Paul uses "Spirit" so many more times, all Bible versions, except the King James Version, change all 89 references to the "Holy Ghost" to the "Holy Spirit." The reason that the King James translators used the term "Holy Ghost" 89 times is because those 89 references were to the third member of the Godhead.

John 4:24 says that "God is a Spirit." We know that Jesus Christ is the only member of the Godhead with a body (II Corinthians 4:4), but He also has a Spirit. Of course, the Holy Ghost is also a Spirit. Thus, all three members of the Godhead are spirit. The reason that "Spirit" is used so many times by Paul is because all three members of the Godhead are involved in us walking in the Spirit. This verse says that we are "in the Spirit," which is probably the Holy Ghost. But, we also have "the Spirit of God" and "the Spirit of Christ" (8:9) in us. Now, primarily, God the Father came up with a glorification plan, Christ executed that plan, and the Holy Ghost dwells in us to work that plan through us. However, all three of Their Spirits are within us, and the Three are One (I John 5:7). So, when "the Spirit" works through us, which One of the Three works? The answer is that They all do. Because of this, Paul uses the term "Spirit," instead of "Holy Ghost." This shows how intimately involved all of the Godhead are in our lives. However, if you read a modern version, the term "Spirit" is synonymous with the "Holy Spirit," and you will miss the fact that all three members of the Godhead are working through you to accomplish God's plan. But, if you have a KJV and ask the question, "Why does Paul say 'Spirit' rather than 'Holy Ghost?'", you may learn this very important point of the whole Godhead working through you.

The work of the Godhead through you is mind boggling when you consider that, when God appeared to Israel, "the whole mount quaked greatly" (Exodus 19:18), such that Moses himself exceedingly feared and quaked (Hebrews 12:21). That happened when God gave the law to man. Yet, when God gave Himself to us, a much scarier prospect, all of the fear was removed. Moses had to put a vail over his face after he received the law from

God (II Corinthians 3:13), even though the law is just a shadow of things to come (Colossians 2:16-17). Yet, today, we can behold Christ's glory with open face, and God can change us into Christ's glorious image (II Corinthians 3:18). Why? Because Christ made us holy (Colossians 3:12) by His blood sacrifice. The power of God is just as real in us today as it was on Mount Sinai, but the fear is gone, which means that God can now work through us, meaning that His power is demonstrated to a lost world so that they might be saved. Yet, Christianity comes along and wants to "feel the presence of God" or "move in the Holy Ghost." In light of the difference between the law covenant and the grace of God in the body of Christ today, we should all be exceeding grateful that God can work through us today without us "feeling" Him! Otherwise, we would literally and physically die, when Christ lived through us the first time.

8:10 Again, "IF Christ" is not being mentioned to make you doubt your salvation. Rather, Paul is building on the facts that the Romans have already learned that Christ lives in them and that they have been made dead to sin. Based on these facts, "the Spirit is life because of righteousness" (8:10).

Regarding the Word, John says, "In Him was life; and the life was the light of men" (John 1:4). John is talking about spiritual life. Because God has imputed His righteousness to you (3:22), He has raised you from the dead. However, He did not just raise you from the dead, bound like Lazarus was (John 11:44). No! He gave you His Spirit which has enlightened or empowered you to allow God to work through you.

As we mentioned in the commentary on 7:9, you were alive before the conscience came. However, that life just meant you would spend eternity in heaven if you physically died. There was no power in that life. Then, the conscience came, and you died, spiritually speaking (7:9). Then, you believed the gospel, and you were declared righteous by God. Because God declared you righteous, He gave you His Spirit, and you now have a spiritual life with power. That life is much better than the life you had before the conscience came, because it is God's life through you, rather than the life of an ignorant infant. Jesus calls this life in the Spirit, abundant life (John 10:10).

A great illustration of the difference in your spiritual life as a baby versus your spiritual life as a believer is seen in the caterpillar. The caterpillar is alive at first, but it can barely crawl along the ground. It does not experience much at all. Then, it goes into a cocoon and dies. It emerges as a butterfly that can fly all over the place. Thus, the butterfly's life is much more abundant than the caterpillar's life, just like the believer's life in the Spirit is much more abundant than his life as an infant before the conscience came on him.

8:11 Paul just told us about our new, spiritual lives as believers, but we may not feel like we are any different, because "man looketh on the outward appearance" (I Samuel 16:7) and our physical bodies are not changed when we are saved. We were in vile bodies before we were saved, and we are in vile bodies after we are saved (Philippians 3:21). However, this is not a permanent situation. Paul says that "this mortal must put on immortality" (I Corinthians 15:53). How is it that people, who die physically, can become alive to live forever? It is because God's Spirit dwells in us. God's Spirit raised Jesus' mortal body from the dead, and He could do things in His new body that He could not do in His old body, such as disappear (Luke 24:31), travel to heaven and back (Compare John 20:17 with John 20:27), and go through walls (John 20:19).

Since God's Spirit raised Jesus from the dead and we have that same Spirit within us, God's Spirit will also raise us from the dead and give us bodies that are like Jesus' glorious body (Philippians 3:21). For the time being, we have the Spirit within our mortal bodies so people can see that the power is of God, and not of us (II Corinthians 4:7). But, when the time of salvation for this dispensation of grace passes for the world, there will no longer be a need to conceal God's power in our mortal bodies, and God will give us immortal bodies instead.

Note that this verse says that the Spirit "SHALL also quicken your mortal bodies." Ephesians 2:5 says that "when we were dead in sins [God] HATH QUICKENED us together with Christ." The quickening, in 8:11, is in the future, while the quickening, in Ephesians 2:5, is in the past. This is further proof that, when Paul says that we are "dead indeed unto sin, but alive unto God" (6:11), he is saying that, at the moment we are saved, God makes our souls alive in Christ, and that our flesh does not become alive in Christ until the rapture. That is why Paul just said that "the body is dead because of sin" (8:10). In other words, before you are saved, your flesh is alive and your soul is dead. Once you are saved, your soul is alive, and God renders your flesh dead. If He did not render your flesh dead, Christ could not live in you because your sin nature would work with your flesh to become exceeding sinful (7:13). But, at the rapture, "death is swallowed up in victory" (I Corinthians 15:54), which means that the sin nature cannot work death in you. Therefore, God makes your flesh alive in Christ, resulting in a glorified body.

Therefore, while most Christians think that God makes their bodies better so that they do not sin as much after they are saved, the truth is actually quite the opposite. God has to make the flesh dead so that Christ can work in you so that you do not commit sins. If God made your body better, He would actually be creating a greater capacity within your flesh to sin. Just like a blood sucking parasite sucks more blood when it is given more life, so too, your flesh would sin more if it was given more power, since no good thing dwells in your flesh (7:18). Therefore, you would only use your more powerful flesh to sin more. That is why it was absolutely necessary for God to kill your flesh so that Christ could live in you. Therefore, the Christian, who understands Romans 6-8 doctrine, would say: "God can live through me now that I am saved," instead of saying, "I can live for God now that I am saved."

Since more power in your flesh means you would sin more, being weaker in your flesh means you will sin less. This means that suffering is actually a good thing, which Paul will begin to address in 8:17.

8:12 This is the point that almost all Christians miss. They say, "Christ died for me. The least I can do is live for Him." By saying this, they say that they are a debtor to the flesh. Paul does say that "we are debtors" (8:12). I Corinthians 6:20 says that, "ye are bought with a price: therefore glorify God in your body, and in your spirit, which are God's." Thus, we are debtors to God to bring glory to Him. We are not debtors to live after the flesh, because "if ye live after the flesh, ye shall die" (8:13). If I die, I cannot glorify God, which means that I have not paid my debt to God. Therefore, the Christian, who understands Romans 6-8 doctrine, would say: "Christ died for me. Now, I am indebted to God to allow Christ to live in me" (Galatians 2:20). This is walking "by faith, not by sight" (II Corinthians 5:7).

8:13 "My thoughts are not your thoughts, neither are your ways My ways, saith the Lord. For as the heavens are higher than the earth, so are My ways higher than your ways, and My thoughts than your thoughts" (Isaiah 55:8-9). My way of thinking is that I know good and evil, and so I can decide to choose the good over the evil. Then, I will be okay. But God says, "there is none that doeth good, no, not one" (3:12). Once I believe God's thought on the matter, I then need to believe God's way (the gospel) so that I am saved. God's way is Jesus' death, burial, and resurrection as atonement for my sin (I Corinthians 15:3-4). Once I believe this gospel, I have eternal life (6:23). This is the sound doctrine that Paul covered in Romans 1:1-5:11. Now, my "life is hid with Christ in God" (Colossians 3:3), and "Christ...IS our life" (Colossians 3:4). We now have the mind of Christ (I Corinthians 2:16).

The mind of Christ was that, even though He is equal to God, He became obedient to God the Father, even to the point of death (Philippians 2:5-8). Why did He do this? Because He recognized that God's thoughts and ways are higher than man's thoughts and ways. Therefore, He spoke only what His Father taught Him to speak (John 8:28), and He did only what His Father told Him to do (John 15:10). Because Christ was fully man and fully God and He did everything perfectly, God has given us Christ's mind to use ourselves. We access Christ's mind when we read the Bible rightly divided, believe it, and allow the Spirit to teach it to us.

With all of this in mind, 8:13 says, "if ye live after the flesh, ye shall die: but if ye through the Spirit do mortify the deeds of the body, ye shall live." The problem is that Christianity does not keep all of the aforementioned doctrine in mind. Instead, they come to this verse and say, "You can lose your salvation if you live after the flesh." But, wait a minute! We have been "justified by faith" (5:1), we have been "now justified by His blood" (5:9), and "we have now received the atonement" (5:11). Rather than building upon the doctrine already given by Paul in Romans, Christians try to tear down that doctrine using verses that are on a completely different topic. The topic we are on in Romans 8 is walking after the Spirit (8:1); it is not justification. Thus, when 8:13 talks about dying, it is saying that if I live after the flesh, my walk after the Spirit will die—not my soul. Similarly, if I kill the deeds of the body through the Spirit, my walk after the Spirit will live.

This verse cannot be talking about your salvation, because that has already been settled, as previously mentioned. I Corinthians 3:15 says that "if any man's WORK shall be burned, he shall suffer loss: but he HIMSELF shall be saved; yet so as by fire." This verse builds on Romans 1-8 doctrine to say that a man's soul is eternal secure in Christ, but that His walk will live or die based upon using the mind of Christ or not. Similarly, Galatians 6:8 says that "he that soweth to his flesh shall of the flesh reap corruption." In other words, his work is corrupted by the fire. "But he that soweth to the Spirit shall of the Spirit reap life everlasting" (Galatians 6:8). In other words, his work lasts forever.

The reason you are saved, regardless of what you do, is because you are "in Christ" (12:5). If you believe the gospel, you are placed into Christ. Because Christ lives forever, you live forever. If you choose not to believe the Bible any more after that, you still live forever. II Timothy 2:13 tells us this very thing: "If we believe not, yet He abideth faithful: He cannot deny Himself" (II Timothy 2:13). In other words, if you have believed the gospel and you choose to live a more sinful life after you are saved than before you were saved, Christ would have to throw Himself into the eternal lake of fire in order to throw you into the eternal lake of fire.

Here is why God does things this way: "I through the law am dead to the law, that I might live unto God" (Galatians 2:19). God does not want you to worry about the law any more after you are saved. That is why He killed it for you, "nailing it to His cross" (Colossians 2:14). Instead of reading Romans 8 in your flesh, looking for ways you can lose your salvation so you can put yourself back under the law, read Romans 8 in light of the doctrine learned in Romans 1-7. Read it to find out how you can walk after the Spirit. Since God's ways and thoughts are higher than our ways and thoughts and God has given us the mind of Christ in order to learn and obey the things of God, our focus needs to be on "the treasures of wisdom and knowledge" (Colossians 2:3) that are hid in Christ in His Word, and not on looking for ways to twist God's word to exalt my flesh above Christ. When we have the attitude of believing the Bible, then the Holy Ghost will teach it to us, and we can use that mind of Christ to make the same decisions that He would make every day in life. If we make those decisions, then we will live (8:13). If we do not make those decisions, then we will die (8:13)—not our souls, but our walks, because they are not after the Spirit.

Note also how this verse says that mortifying the deeds of the body, in itself, does not cause you to live. Rather, you have to mortify the deeds of the body "through the Spirit" (8:13). This speaks to the fact that we have the power in the flesh to put to death certain things of the flesh. For example, an unsaved person can choose to stop alcoholism, drug abuse, fornication, murder, etc. all on his own without God's help. But, he will just replace those things with other things of the flesh, and he will still be sinning. Similarly, Christians often use willpower in using their flesh to neglect certain sinful pleasures. Such "will worship" actually satisfies the flesh, because you can then brag to others what a good Christian you are (Colossians 2:23). Therefore, mortifying the deeds of the body in this manner is still walking after the flesh, which means that your walk is dead. However, if you use the method of allowing the Holy Ghost to teach you the things of God and using the mind of Christ to make decisions, then you are using God's ways and thoughts to make decisions. But, it is not you who does it, but Christ does it through you (Galatians 2:20), so that sinful pride is not an issue. Then, you have mortified the deeds of the body "through the Spirit," and "ye shall live" (8:13), meaning that your walk in Christ will thrive.

In Christ: Before moving on to 8:14, we need to understand what being "in Christ" actually means. All major religions view Jesus as a man only, except for Christianity, which views Him as God in a human body. Both views are incorrect. Jesus is both 100% God and 100% man. Granted, Christianity says that they believe that Jesus is fully God and fully man, but, in practice, most Christians' doctrine is based upon Him only being God. For example, Jesus said that "the Son of MAN hath power on earth to forgive sins" (Matthew 9:6), yet most all Christians will tell you that Christ forgave sins in His power as God. Moreover, Acts 2:22 says that "Jesus of Nazareth, [was] a MAN approved of God among you by miracles, and wonders, and signs, which GOD did by Him in the midst of you." Yet, most all Christians will tell you that Christ performed miracles as God, rather than God doing miracles through the man, "Jesus of Nazareth." Therefore, Christianity teaches that Jesus God in a human body.

This teaching leads to incorrect thinking regarding what "in Christ" means. In other words, if I think that Christ is 100% God and not 100% man, then, for me to live in Christ, I would expect to perform miracles, cast out devils, and do no sin. Therefore, I must not be in Christ, because He is God, and I am not. Therefore, Christians create this idea that Christ, as God only, indwells me. This view leads to the idea that there will be times when God will, sort of, magically take over what happens. He will guide me into the right circumstances, He will lead me to think a certain way, and I will "feel" His presence at times. If I overcome alcoholism, it was all God. If I say the right thing in a certain situation, God must have taken over my vocal cords and gave me the words to say. In other words, Christianity has interpreted "in Christ" to be the spontaneous, supernatural, and miraculous workings of God through me from time to time.

The reason for such an interpretation is that it means that I do not have to do anything. I just go to church and pray, and God takes over when He feels like it. However, that is NOT how Christ operated. Christ is both fully God AND fully man. He "thought it not robbery to be equal with God" (Philippians 2:6), because He IS God. But, He is also man, and so He became obedient unto the Father "unto death, even the death of the cross" (Philippians 2:8). Therefore, He had daily Bible studies with His Father (Isaiah 50:4-6). He "learned...obedience by the things which He suffered" (Hebrews 5:8). He was tempted "in all points as we are..., yet without sin" (Hebrews 4:15). He even set aside His own will as a man to stay alive and said, "nevertheless not My will, but Thine, be done" (Luke 22:42).

That is what being "in Christ" is all about, which means it eliminates my flesh's excuse. I can no longer say, "God, take over whenever You feel like it. In the meantime, I will use my flesh to do the best I can." NO! We are told: "Let this mind be in you, which was also in Christ Jesus" (Philippians 2:5). This means I need to have daily Bible studies with God; I need to learn to obey God by suffering; I need to be tempted; and I need to set aside my will for God's will. And, I do not want to do that, because that is a whole lot of work, and my flesh will not like it!

8:14 Using the typical interpretation of what it means to be "in Christ" leads to a false interpretation of what it means to be "led by the Spirit." Pentecostals say that it means that you start feeling the Holy Ghost moving, and so you start speaking in tongues and move right along with Him. Baptists and non-denominationals take a less overtly emotional approach. They pray for a burning in the bosom or an internal feeling that God's Spirit is leading them to do whatever it is. They will say, "the Lord led me to take this job," "the Lord put me and my spouse together," "the Lord impressed it upon my heart to tell you such and such," etc.

However, being led by the Spirit involves none of these things! Since we are to have the mind of Christ, we need to study God's Word as Christ did. When we do that, the Spirit of God will lead us (I Corinthians 2:10) into "the things which God hath prepared for them that love Him". These would be the spiritual things of God that are revealed to us in His Word by the Spirit (I Corinthians 2:12-13). Once we receive these spiritual things, we have the mind of Christ and act accordingly based on having Christ's mind (I Corinthians 2:16). Therefore, being led by the Spirit means that we read God's Word so that the Holy Ghost can lead us into God's truth and work out the practical application of that truth in us. It is NOT some extra-Biblical revelation that is sensed in the spirit when we pray, a feeling of God's moving, or a thought placed there supernaturally by God for us to do something.

Since all believers are sealed by "the holy Spirit of God" (Ephesians 4:30), all believers are led by the Spirit of God. However, just because we are all led by the Spirit, it does not mean that we will all follow the Spirit.. If we do not follow, we have quenched the Spirit (I Thessalonians 5:19), but we are still led by Him to read and believe God's Word, pray, and use the mind of Christ within us to make decisions. Therefore, this verse is NOT saying that if we disobey the Spirit, we are not sons of God. Rather, this goes back to the discussion we had in 8:9. If you have believed the gospel, then you are led by the Spirit of God to say "no" to your flesh and "yes" to God. You then use your soul to make the decision of who you will listen to.

Paul is saying that this leading by the Spirit is a proof that we are sons of God. That is not to say that we must follow that leading. Christians will use this verse to say that, if you are a Christian, you will do God's will. They say this as a justification to disassociate themselves from people who do not agree with them, or who make them look bad through their bad behavior. For example, Christians will say that a murderer is not a Christian, because he was not led by the Spirit to do that. Therefore, he is not a son of God. However, James says that if you break the law in one point, you have broken the entire law (James 2:10). Therefore, if I tell a little, white lie, I am just as guilty of sinning as if I murdered someone. The Spirit of God never leads someone to sin, which means that I was not led by the Spirit to lie. Therefore, by Christianity's own logic, no one today is a son of God, because all of us sin, even after we are saved. Thus, we must conclude that being "led by the Spirit of God" (8:14) and actually following the Spirit of God are two, different things. Paul is just saying that all saved people have the Spirit of God indwelling them, and so they can walk after the Spirit, which means that Christ can live in them.

Another point to note from this verse is that we are the sons of God. The phrase "children of Israel" occurs 647 times in the Bible. The term "sons of Israel" only occurs 4 times in the Bible. The reason that Israel is called "children" is because they were given the law covenant. Thus, they were under the law. As such, they were children, differing nothing from a servant (Galatians 4:1-3). Once God started the dispensation of grace, we were saved by grace through faith in Jesus Christ (Ephesians 2:8-9), which means that we "are not under the law, but under grace" (6:14). Not being under the law means that we have received the adoption of sons of God (Galatians 4:5). Therefore, we "art no more a servant, but a son" (Galatians 4:7). That is why we have the Spirit of God within us, as that Spirit is God's down payment on us that He will redeem us at the rapture (Ephesians 1:13-14). Therefore, because we have believed the gospel, we are God's sons and are led by the Spirit to live as He would want His sons to live.

8:15 This verse is another proof of our eternal security. "Abba, Father" is found only three times in scripture, and it means "Dear, Father," as only a child in close relationship with his father can cry. Therefore, we must be God's sons. The first reference comes from Jesus Christ, praying to the Father, just before the cross (Mark 14:36). The last two references are here and in Galatians 4:6. Here, it is the body of Christ crying "Abba, Father" by "the Spirit of adoption." In Galatians 4:6, it is "the Spirit of [God's] Son" crying "Abba, Father" through the body of Christ. These two references show that our connection with Christ is so close that both Christ and us can be said to be crying to God as "Abba, Father." This shows how our identity, after we are saved, is completely in Christ.

In Mark 14:36, Christ's cry of "Abba, Father" was in response to His battle with the flesh. He said, "Abba, Father, all things are possible unto Thee; take away this cup from Me: nevertheless not what I will, but what Thou wilt." In other words, in crying "Abba, Father," Christ asked for the Father's help in His battle with the flesh, and the result was that He chose the spirit over the flesh. The context of "Abba, Father," in 8:15, is the same for us. We can live after the flesh and die, or we can mortify the deeds of the flesh through the Spirit and live (8:13). How do we overcome in this battle? We cry "Abba, Father."

How can we cry "Abba, Father?" Because we "have received the Spirit of adoption" (8:15). Christ is God's "only begotten Son" (John 3:16). However, because we are "accepted in the Beloved" (Ephesians 1:6), Who is Christ, we are God's sons, too. But, we are God's adopted sons. Since we are God's sons, we have the Spirit of His Son within us. Therefore, in spite of our sin nature and our flesh, we can still be in the same, close, intimate relationship that Christ had with the Father, such that, when we have a battle between the flesh and the spirit, which is all the time, we can also cry "Abba, Father." When Christ cried "Abba, Father," God gave Him the victory over the flesh. Similarly, when we cry "Abba, Father," we get the victory. This means that we can live above sin.

Paul says that "we have not received the spirit of bondage again to fear" (8:15). "Again" tells us that, before we were saved, we only had the spirit of bondage. In other words, we were bound to sin, because we found no ability within our flesh to perform that which is good (7:18). This caused us to fear God's punishment of us, because we knew we were guilty under the law, and there was nothing we could do about it. Now, however, we have "the Spirit of adoption" (8:15). Therefore, we are no longer in bondage to the law, but we are free to allow Christ to live through us by His Spirit. "Stand fast therefore in the liberty wherewith Christ hath made us free, and be not entangled again with the yoke of bondage" (Galatians 5:1). In other words, why worry about your old master (Satan) by trying to do good works in your flesh, when you have the Spirit of Christ living in you so that He can serve your new Master (God) through you by walking after the Spirit? After all, Christ overcame the cross, and whatever you face is less difficult than the cross. Therefore, Christ will overcome every one of your trials that you let Him overcome for you. "There hath no temptation taken you but such as is common to man: but God is faithful, Who will not suffer you to be tempted above that ye are able; but will with the temptation also make a way to escape, that ye may be able to bear it" (I Corinthians 10:13). God does not remove the temptation, but He makes you able to bear it. How do you bear it? By crying "Abba, Father."

8:16 The Spirit bears witness with our spirit, not by some good, inner feeling we have when we pray, but He does so through His Word. As we read God's Word, the Holy Ghost teaches our spirit the spiritual things found in God's Word (I Corinthians 2:12-13), and that is how we know that we are the children of God.

If we are not saved, our spirit is functionally dead (Ephesians 2:1). We can read God's Word, but we will not understand the things of God, because the natural man cannot receive those things (I Corinthians 2:14). That is why Hollywood can produce "Christian" movies, but no spiritual truths are conveyed in those stories. For example, many years ago, there was a movie called "The Ten Commandments." When you compare the movie with the book of Exodus, you will find that the movie was Biblically accurate for the most part. However, God did not give us the book of Exodus as a nice biography of Israel. Rather, He gave us that book as examples and ensamples of what not to do (I Corinthians 10:1-11). It also teaches us things like the miracles in Egypt are a type of God's deliverance of the little flock during the tribulation period, and that Pharaoh's army drowning is a type of unbelievers drowning in the lake of fire. None of these lessons were brought out by the movie. That is because Hollywood did not learn any spiritual truths from the movie because their spirits are functionally dead.

Sadly, this is also why most Biblical commentaries are void of truth. Instead of conveying spiritual truths, the commentators argue over definitions of words and differences of opinions among scholars. Similarly, seminaries argue over who wrote certain books of the Bible, which manuscripts are the most reliable, and differences of opinion regarding theological concepts. They do these things because, if they are unsaved, that is all they can do, because they are spiritually dead. All of these are examples of "ever learning, and never able to come to the knowledge of the truth" (II Timothy 3:7). Meanwhile, a twelve year-old kid can believe the gospel, read God's Word, and instantly know more than the scholars and commentators know. We have an example of this very thing in Jesus Christ, Who, at age 12, asked the scholars questions and then answered those questions Himself, when the religious leaders had no answers (Luke 2:46-47). The reason for this is that the religious experts use their natural minds, which cannot discern the things of God (I Corinthians 2:14). But, when saved people read and believe God's Word, the Holy Ghost teaches them the deep things of God; thereby, bearing "witness with our spirit, that we are the children of God" (8:16).

8:17 Since we have been adopted as sons of God, that makes us heirs of God. Since we were buried with Christ, raised to life with Him, and are Christ's body, we are "joint-heirs with Christ," meaning that we receive every spiritual blessing that Christ receives as a son of God. Thus, we are "blessed...with all spiritual blessings in heavenly places in Christ" (Ephesians 1:3), we are "accepted in the beloved" (Ephesians 1:6), we have an inheritance (Ephesians 1:11), and we are sealed with the Holy Spirit

(Ephesians 1:13), among other things. These things are all related to our salvation, which is by faith in Jesus Christ. It has nothing to do with our performance.

Then, why does our heirship seem to be conditional upon us suffering? Well, it is, because 8:17 says so. However, we are guaranteed to suffer in this world if we are sons of God. Philippians 1:29 says that "it is given" that we will "suffer for His sake." Suffering is God's gift to you! That may not mean that you are beheaded for believing in Christ or that you are thrown in jail. It just means that suffering is the natural result for someone whose "conversation is in heaven" (Philippians 3:20) but is living where Satan, "the god of this world" is in control (II Corinthians 4:4). The suffering, then, entails having the mind of Christ, the Spirit of God, and the inner man within us as sons of God and seeing a world filled with deceitfulness and wickedness. Even if we do not serve God, we still suffer inwardly just from living in enemy territory.

Remember what we have already learned in Romans. "Our old man is crucified with Him" (6:6). Crucifixion involves suffering. Therefore, we suffer for believing the gospel, even if we never yield our members to God as instruments of righteousness (6:13). The Corinthians were known for their carnality (I Corinthians 3:3), yet Paul says that the Lord Jesus Christ will confirm them "unto the end that [they] may be blameless in the day of our Lord Jesus Christ. God is faithful, by whom ye were called unto the fellowship of His Son Jesus Christ our Lord" (I Corinthians 1:7-9). In other words, although the Corinthians were carnal, they would still be saved because God is faithful. He called them unto the fellowship of Jesus, which means they have been called into suffering.

This is not a physical suffering, although it can include that, but it is an internal suffering. Once we are saved, God indwells us (5:5). Since no good thing dwells in our flesh (7:18), "the flesh lusteth against the Spirit" (Galatians 5:17). If we yield to the flesh, we still suffer, because the flesh never gains the things of the Spirit. If we yield to the Spirit, we still suffer, because the flesh battles against us. Therefore, after we are saved, regardless of if we obey God or not, we suffer. Why? Because God is good, and He indwells us, and our flesh is not good. Therefore, there is always conflict within us between God and our flesh. This is "the fellowship of His Son" in that we suffer internally. As proof that Paul is talking about internal suffering, Paul gives us the details of this suffering in 8:23. There, he says "we ourselves groan WITHIN OURSELVES, waiting for the adoption, to wit, the redemption of our body." If you are groaning within yourself, then you are suffering within yourself. Why are you groaning? Because your body is contrary to God. So, you wait for God to redeem your "vile body, that it may be fashioned like unto His glorious body" (Philippians 3:21).

You may ask, "Why does Paul say 'IF so be that we suffer with Him?'" (8:17). He says it for the same reason he used "if" in verses 9-11. That is, he states a fact, that they know to be true, to show them something else that they do not know to be true. The Roman believers know that God's Spirit dwells in them, because Paul has already told them that they have God's Spirit (5:5). Therefore, when he says, "If so be that the Spirit of God dwell in you" (8:9), the believer's reaction is, "Of course, the Spirit of God dwells in me." Therefore, he learns the condition of the "if" is true, which is that he is "in the Spirit" (8:9). Then, Paul says, "if Christ be in you" (8:10). The believer's reaction is, "Of course, Christ is in me, because I have been 'baptized into Jesus Christ'" (6:3). Therefore, he learns the condition of the "if" is true, which is that "the body is dead" and "the Spirit is life" (8:10). Then, Paul says, "if the Spirit...dwell in you" (8:11). The believer's reaction is, "Of course, the Spirit dwells in me." Therefore, he learns the condition of the "if" is true, which is that God will quicken his mortal body (8:11).

Now, Paul says, "if children" (8:17). The believer's reaction is, "Of course, I am God's child, because the Spirit has borne witness to my spirit of this fact" (8:16). Therefore, he learns the condition of the "if" is true, which is that he is an heir of God and a joint-heir with Christ (8:17). Then, Paul says, "if so be that we suffer with Him" (8:17). The believer's reaction is, "Of course, I suffer with Him because I am a wretched man, who cannot do the things that I want to do (7:24). That is why God gave me His Spirit so I could get help by crying 'Abba, Father' (8:15)." Therefore, he learns the condition of the "if" is true, which is that he will be glorified together with Christ (8:17). Thus, the "if," with regard to suffering, is known to be true by the believer, because he has learned the lesson of Romans 7, even if he does not walk after the Spirit (8:1).

We should also note that Galatians 4:7 says that all believers are heirs of God, not just the ones who obey God while on earth. Why? Because heirship is based on faith, not on performance. Romans 4:14,16 says, "For if they which are of the law be heirs, faith is made void, and the promise made of none effect....Therefore it is of faith, that it might be by grace." Therefore, if I come along and say that you must choose to suffer for Christ in order to be joint-heirs with Christ, then I have made heirship based upon my performance, which makes it of the law. Then, faith is made void, and the promise of heirship is made of none effect.

You may say, "what about the term 'joint-heirs'? This term is only found here. Sure, we are heirs of God by faith, but we are only 'joint-heirs' with Christ by performance." No, that is not true. We have already established that we are in Christ. Since we are in Christ, we receive whatever He receives, making us "joint-heirs" with Him. We were placed into Christ based on our faith in His faith. We did no works to be placed into Christ. If works are involved in us being joint-heirs with Christ, then works are involved in our salvation. In other words, God ties our heirship to faith, not to performance.

Now, having said that, I Corinthians 3:12-15 does say that our reward within that heirship is based upon how much sound doctrine we build up in our inner man. Nevertheless, we are still heirs with Christ, even if we built up nothing, because "He cannot deny Himself" (II Timothy 2:13). In other words, once we are saved, our identity is so connected with Christ that, even if we do not allow Christ to work through us at all, God still cannot deny us from being heirs with Christ, because, in doing so, God would be denying Christ from being an heir. The justice of God will not allow that to happen, because Christ was faithful. Therefore, all believers are joint-heirs with Christ, no matter how hard they may try to get out of it. And, because everything is dependent on Christ, and not ourselves, Christ will "present…to Himself a glorious church, not having spot, or wrinkle, or any such thing" (Ephesians 5:27), not because of our performance, but because of His faithfulness: "He which hath begun a good work in you will perform it until the day of Jesus Christ" (Philippians 1:6). In other words, you may allow your flesh to control completely your life after you are saved to the point that you have done absolutely nothing that will last for eternity. Yet, because God is faithful, He will take away all of those impurities, and present you holy to the Father. As a holy son of God, because you are in Christ, you will receive the inheritance with Christ. Then, as a joint-heir with Christ, Christ will determine the position you will have in heavenly places for all eternity. You could be the next level under Him or you could be the lowest level under Him. Either way, you are a joint-heir with Christ.

8:18 In 8:17, Paul mentioned that all believers suffer. We learned that this mostly entails internal suffering because our spirits are alive in Christ but our flesh is dead in sin.

"No man ever yet hated his own flesh; but nourisheth and cherisheth it" (Ephesians 5:29). Because of this, very few Christians are willing to believe what the Bible says their identity in Christ is all about. They usually neglect the spirit in favor of the flesh. Since this is contrary to the mind of Christ, they must use their fleshly mind to make decisions. Today, this usually means continuing to do the evil things of the flesh just like they did before they were saved. In other words, if they gambled, smoke, and drank before they were saved, they continue to do these things after they are saved. A couple of generations ago in America, most Christians went the other way with the flesh, using their fleshly mind to do the good things of the flesh. They went to church, prayed, read their Bibles, gave money to the church, and tried to refrain from the evil things. But, they did all of this in the energy of their own flesh. Therefore, they neglected their bodies to the satisfying of their flesh (Colossians 2:23). Both the human-evil Christians and the human-good Christians suffer internally, because their spirits groan within them, waiting for their bodies to be redeemed, which will end the suffering (8:23). However, because their suffering comes from denying the spirit and satisfying the flesh, they will receive a loss of reward in heavenly places, but they will still receive eternal life (I Corinthians 3:15). Therefore, even in this worst-case scenario, the suffering of Christ, living in a fleshly body, will STILL produce glory that so exceeds the suffering that the two "are not worthy to be compared" (8:18). That is because Christ will give the believer eternal life. Therefore, your reward for believing the gospel far exceeds the internal suffering that takes place after you are saved, even when you do not walk after the Spirit. That is why Paul will say later in this chapter that, "we are more than conquerors through Him that loved us" (8:37). Stated another way, when we were saved, Christ's blood overcame all of our sins, no matter how bad they were. The same holds true after we are saved. Christ's blood is so strong that, even after He has given us victory over sin, we can still sin and it does not change our eternal dwelling place at all.

However, God's will for us is not to continue in sin after we are saved. Rather, He wants Christ to live in us (Galatians 2:20). If we choose to walk after the Spirit by reading and believing God's Word and making decisions using the mind of Christ, we will experience even more suffering. II Timothy 3:12 says that "all THAT WILL LIVE GODLY in Christ Jesus shall suffer persecution." Primarily, this suffering is internal, as well, and it is of the flesh lusting after the things that we gain in Christ from believing God's Word (Galatians 5:17). The more we believe God's Word, the more treasures of wisdom and knowledge we mine out of it (Colossians 2:3), and the more the Spirit strengthens us with might in the inner man (Ephesians 3:16). This strength enables us to take a greater beating from the flesh, which means that we suffer more.

This process is not unlike bodybuilding. When a bodybuilder lifts weights, he tears down the muscles in his body. Because they are torn down, he experiences pain from injuring himself. The muscles then respond by building up bigger and stronger, in preparation for another beating. If the bodybuilder continues to lift weights, he continues to suffer pain after every workout, and his muscles continue to grow larger. Once he stops lifting weights, his muscles gradually get smaller, as the muscles know they do not need to be strong any more, since they are not being torn down with weights. The former bodybuilder no longer experiences pain, because he is no longer tearing down his muscles, but he also is not strong anymore, because his muscles have shrunk.

Applied to scripture, if you quit reading and believing God's Word, your internal suffering diminishes. (The pain does not completely go away because the Lord does not leave you, and your flesh is still vile.) But, you are no longer strong in the inner man, because Christ is not working in you. Just like most people do not exercise because they do not like to suffer, most Christians will not read and believe God's Word because it discerns the thoughts and intents of your heart as evil (Hebrews 4:12 and Jeremiah 17:9), causing your flesh to suffer. Just like most people in a gym's weight room do not push themselves to pain, most Christians, who read their Bibles, do not believe their Bibles, because they do not want their flesh to suffer. That is why preachers skirt sound doctrine by saying things like: "The original Greek really means this," or "a better translation is such and such."

By contrast, Christians, who actually read and believe God's Word, are beating down their flesh. Paul says, "I keep under my body, and bring it into subjection" (I Corinthians 9:27). Your flesh suffers pain and fights back, getting stronger for the next attack with your inner man being strengthened by the Spirit (Ephesians 3:16), much like a bodybuilder's muscles get stronger after an intense workout. That is why the Lord said that, "My strength is made perfect in weakness" (II Corinthians 12:9), and why Paul responded with: "When I am weak, then am I strong" (II Corinthians 12:10).

Paul calls this: "The fellowship of His sufferings, being made conformable unto His death" (Philippians 3:10). When we are made conformable unto His death, then we are "always bearing about in the body the dying of the Lord Jesus, that the life also of Jesus might be made manifest in our body. For we which live are alway delivered unto death for Jesus' sake" (II Corinthians 4:10-11). Therefore, Paul said that he "now rejoice[s] in [his] sufferings for you and fill[s] up that which is behind of the afflictions of Christ in [his] flesh for His body's sake" (Colossians 1:24). Christ suffered on the cross, but then He also suffers today through your flesh when you choose to believe God's Word and allow the Spirit to work it out through your life. Therefore, "the afflictions of Christ" continue in your flesh when you believe God's Word. Paul calls this a "light affliction, which is but for a moment." It "worketh for us a far more exceeding and eternal weight of glory" (II Corinthians 4:16-17). Therefore, while you experience suffering, which will work glory for you, just by being saved, there is another level of suffering that God wants to work through you, which will produce even more glory than what is generated by just being saved.

Now, you may think it is mean of God to want you to suffer, but you are not alone in the suffering. Christ suffered when He lived a perfect life and then died on a cross. Moreover, because "Christ liveth in me" (Galatians 2:20), when you suffer for Christ, it is actually Christ doing the suffering in you, as Paul says: "The sufferings of Christ abound in us" (II Corinthians 1:5). So, your suffering for believing God's Word is also Christ's suffering.

On top of that, God Himself suffers. To better understand this, we will use an example. Let's say that you are a clean freak. If you must have everything clean in order to feel at ease, you suffer when you allow something to be dirty. God is holy (Leviticus 11:44-45). Therefore, He suffers whenever there is sin or uncleanness. God's justice demands that He execute wrath upon sin. 1:18 says that "the wrath of God is revealed from heaven against all ungodliness and unrighteousness of men." There are billions of people on earth right now who deserve God's wrath, and yet He suffers with ungodliness and unrighteousness being prevalent in the world today, because He knows that, if He is willing to suffer ungodliness, some of those people will be saved and He can spend eternity with them. 9:22 says that "God...endured with much longsuffering the vessels of wrath fitted to destruction" (9:22). In fact, I Peter 3:20 says that God suffered for 100 years, while Noah built an ark, just so seven more people could be saved! II Peter 3:9 says that "the Lord...is longsuffering to us-ward, not willing that any should perish, but that all should come to repentance."

Therefore, God suffers with Satan being "the god of this world" (II Corinthians 4:4) and "the prince of the power of the air" (Ephesians 2:2). He has suffered with the heavens not being clean in His sight (Job 15:15). He has suffered with billions of people on earth being unrighteous. You may not think this constitutes suffering, but it does when you consider that Habakkuk 1:13 says about God: "Thou art of purer eyes than to behold evil, and canst not look on iniquity" (Habakkuk 1:13). God is so holy that He cannot behold iniquity, and yet He has suffered with rampant iniquity for more than 6,000 years, just because He knows that people will eventually believe Him and be saved if He keeps suffering. This world is to God what the filthiest house imaginable is to a clean freak, and yet God continues to put up with it without cleaning it up via His wrath so that people will be saved.

We have seen that suffering for God works glory for Him and suffering for Christ works glory for Christ. Therefore, it should not surprise us that, when Ephesians 1:17 calls God "the Father of glory," God has also developed a glorification plan for us that is linked to our sufferings. Therefore, the more we suffer for Christ, the more glory we will receive eternally. The more we read God's Word rightly divided, the more the Holy Ghost teaches us the things of God. As a result, we use the mind of Christ more and our inner man is strengthened more (Ephesians 3:16). The more this happens, the more we walk after the Spirit, which is contrary to the world around us, which means we will suffer more. Therefore, the more we do what God wants us to do, the more we will suffer. To keep us focused on God's glorification plan for us, we need to set our "affection on things above, not on things on the earth" (Colossians 3:2). Then, we will read our Bible rightly divided more so that we can suffer more so that we can have more glory for all eternity, as Galatians 6:8 says, "he that soweth to the Spirit shall of the Spirit reap life everlasting."

Not only is suffering linked to our glorification for all eternity, but it also helps us persevere in this life. Romans 5:3-5 says that tribulation gives us hope, which is the confidence to wait for God to give us our glorified bodies at the rapture. Moreover, the end result of tribulation is that "the love of God is shed abroad in our hearts by the Holy Ghost," which means that more people will be saved and come to the knowledge of the truth, which is God's will (I Timothy 2:4), as a result of sufferings we endure. Therefore, the popular idea in Christianity that God wants you to be happy, healthy, and wealthy is completely contrary to scripture. Rather, God wants you to "glory in tribulations" (5:3) and suffer (II Corinthians 4:17) so that Christ can be strong in you (II Corinthians 12:10). You will then "reckon that the sufferings of this present time are not worthy to be compared with the glory which shall be revealed in us" (8:18).

8:19 A creature is something that God created. Usually, we think of it as an animal, as in Genesis 1:20, 21, and 24. However, Jesus told the 11 apostles in Mark 16:15 to "preach the gospel to every creature." Colossians 1:15 says that Christ is "the firstborn of every creature." II Corinthians 5:17 and Galatians 6:15 say that the believer in the body of Christ is "a new creature." Therefore, a creature can also be a human.

Given the context around 8:19, "the creature" is probably a reference to all of God's creation except humans. The reason is because 8:22 says that "the whole creation groaneth and travaileth in pain." Then, 8:23 says that "we ourselves groan within ourselves," but the groaners are qualified as being only those "which have the firstfruits of the Spirit." In other words, if "the creature" referred to humans, Paul would not have to say that believers groan within themselves. Also, it appears that unbelievers do not groan, because they are spiritually dead (Ephesians 2:1). In other words, all of creation is in "the bondage of corruption" (8:21) with the exception of saved man, because we have already been set free from sin, and unsaved man does not recognize his fallen state, since he is spiritually dead. All of creation, except all men, will be saved from this bondage of corruption, and so they groan, waiting for this to happen. Saved men also groan, although we have already been saved from corruption, because we are waiting to be delivered from sinful flesh (8:23).

The reason Paul brings this up is so believers know that they are not the only ones in pain because of their flesh, but creation is groaning right along with them. The reason that the creature is waiting for the sons of God to be manifested (8:19) is because, when they are manifested, it means that the creature stops suffering, because the curse of sin will be lifted.

8:20 The creature being made subject to vanity means that the creation could not do what God had designed it to do. The ground was supposed to feed man. Instead, it started producing thorns and thistles (Genesis 3:18), and there are many desolate and desert places on the earth that do not produce anything useful. The mountains and the hills are supposed to sing praises to the Lord, while the trees keep the rhythm by clapping (Isaiah 55:12). The hills are supposed to rejoice, while the pastures and valleys are to shout for joy and sing (Psalm 65:12-13). Instead, these things sit in silence, not able to worship the Lord.

Man was supposed to have dominion over all the animals (Genesis 1:26). Instead, under the curse of sin, animals run away from man, being afraid of him (Genesis 9:2). Man and animals were supposed to only eat fruits and vegetables (Genesis 1:29-30), but now they kill and eat each other. Thus, animals are not able to serve man as God created them to do. However, when the curse of sin is lifted, animals will dwell with each other and with man in perfect harmony, such that they will not hurt nor destroy (Isaiah

131

11:6-9). Therefore, "the creature was made subject to vanity" (8:20), not being able to serve the Lord as God had created them to do. However, they are now subjected in hope. In other words, the creation knows that, once the sons of God are manifest, God will lift the curse, and the whole creation can do what God created them to do, which is to worship God.

8:21 As children of God today, the body of Christ already has liberty in Christ (Galatians 5:1). However, believing Israel does not receive the atonement until Jesus' second coming (Acts 3:19-20). Until that time, unbelievers have the opportunity to believe the gospel and be saved, which means that the earth must continue under the curse of sin until then. Therefore, the creation must also remain under the "bondage of corruption" until that time.

8:22 Therefore, the whole creation has groaned and travailed in pain since Genesis 3, and it will continue to do so until Jesus' second coming. Putting together everything we have learned, all of creation, except for unsaved man, groans in pain, waiting for salvation from the rule of Satan over this sin-cursed world. Meanwhile, unsaved man is only spared this pain while he is on the earth. Once he dies, he suffers in the flames of hell (Luke 16:23-24), where he will be in such utter agony for all eternity that his torment will literally be seen as a smoke coming from him (Revelation 14:10-11). Plus, unsaved man still suffers on this earth because everything he does is sin (14:23). That is why he turns to drugs, alcohol, and many other things to try to make him forget the pain of sin in his life. As such, unsaved man is in more pain than saved man is, even if he does not groan about his depraved state, because he is dead while he liveth (I Timothy 5:6). Thus, the suffering body of Christ should not get depressed over our suffering, because it is temporal, while our joy will be eternal (II Corinthians 4:17-18).

8:23 This verse is a great explanation of the suffering to which Paul referred in 8:17. The moment we are saved, God quickens us together with Christ, raises us up, and makes us sit together in heavenly places with Christ Jesus (Ephesians 2:5-6). The only thing He does not change about us is our flesh. Philippians 3:20-21 says that it is from our position in heavenly places that we look down on earth for "the Saviour, the Lord Jesus Christ" to "change our vile body, that it may be fashioned like unto His glorious body." What this means is that, while our spirits are alive in Christ, our flesh is not any better now that we are saved. We can either choose to allow the Holy Ghost to teach our spirits the things of God and then allow the Spirit of God to control our lives by making decisions based upon sound doctrine (I Corinthians 2:9-16), or we can choose to live as we did before we were saved, which means we can allow our sin nature to work with our flesh to produce sins (7:18-20). This ability of the flesh to control our lives causes our spirits to groan within ourselves, waiting for the Lord Jesus Christ to redeem our bodies (8:23). If we choose to walk after the Spirit, our spirits groan within us due to the opposition that the flesh puts up against us. If we choose to obey the lusts of the flesh, our spirits still "delight in the law of

God after the inward man" (7:22), causing our spirits to groan at not accomplishing God's will. Therefore, regardless of what we do after we are saved, our spirits groan within us, waiting for the Lord Jesus Christ to redeem our bodies.

We should not skip over the fact that this verse tells us that we "have the firstfruits of the Spirit" (8:23). I Corinthians 15:20 says that Christ has "become the firstfruits of them that slept," which means that Christ was the first man to receive His glorified body. Therefore, when we are told that we "have the firstfruits of the Spirit," this tells us that the body of Christ are the first believers in history to receive the permanent, indwelling Holy Spirit. We are told that we are "sealed with that holy Spirit of promise,…until the redemption of the purchased possession" (Ephesians 1:13-14). In other words, we are guaranteed that the Lord Jesus Christ will redeem our bodies because God has given us His Holy Spirit, and He will not take Him away.

Contrast this with David, in Psalm 51:11, when He said, "Take not Thy Holy Spirit from me." That is because, in the Old Testament, the Holy Spirit was not given to all believers. God only gave the Holy Spirit to certain individuals and only for them to perform certain tasks. For example, once God said that He would make Saul king "the Spirit of God came upon him, and he prophesied" (I Samuel 10:10). Once God had David anointed as king, "the Spirit of the Lord came upon David from that day forward" (I Samuel 16:13). Then "the Spirit of the Lord departed from Saul, and an evil spirit from the Lord troubled him" (I Samuel 16:14).

After the cross, God told Israel that He would pour out His Spirit upon all flesh, meaning that all of saved Israel would receive the Holy Spirit, not just certain people, as in the Old Testament (Acts 2:16-17). Yet, even this was not a permanent indwelling, as seen by the fact that Acts 4:31 says that there was a group of believers praying, "and they were all filled with the Holy Ghost." In other words, if they already had the permanent, indwelling Holy Ghost, they would not have been filled with the Holy Ghost, here, because they already had Him. Ezekiel 36:24-28 says that it is not until God takes believing Israel from among the heathen, water baptizes, and places them into their land that they will finally receive the permanent, indwelling Holy Spirit, like the body of Christ has today. This takes place at Jesus' second coming when He puts them under the new covenant (Jeremiah 31:31-34).

Because mainstream Christianity believes God changed things for us today at Acts 2, rather than at Acts 9, they will debate this point with you. However, if believing Israel in Acts 2 had the permanent, indwelling Holy Spirit, then God would not say through Paul that the body of Christ today has "the FIRSTFRUITS of the Spirit" (8:23) Just like Jesus' receiving the new body first is called "the firstfruits of them that slept," so, too, the body of Christ today must be the first ones to receive the permanent, indwelling Holy Spirit, or else the term "firstfruits of the Spirit" could not be applied to the body of Christ. Therefore, those saved in the dispensation of grace are the first to receive the permanent, indwelling Holy Spirit, enabling us to "walk in the Spirit" (Galatians 5:16).

8:24-25 Today, the word "hope" is usually used as a wish, as in "I hope I win the lottery." However, the dictionary definition of hope is that you reasonably expect that thing to happen. Therefore, when Paul says, "we are saved by hope" (8:24), he means that we are saved from being depressed over the battle we have with our flesh, because we reasonably expect that battle to be temporary, because we know that the Lord Jesus Christ will redeem our bodies.

Since our hope is "the redemption of our body" (8:23) and "hope that is seen is not hope" (8:24), this is another proof that God did not change our flesh one bit when we were saved. In other words, Paul says that, if God changed our bodies when we were saved, we would have no hope because God would have already redeemed us completely. Yet, I Corinthians 13:13 says that the three things that abide for us right now are "faith, hope, charity." Thus, Christianity's common belief, that our flesh is somehow strengthened to serve God once we are saved, is a false belief.

These verses also tell us why God does not change our flesh once we are saved. They tell us that, by hoping for our bodies to be redeemed, "then do we with patience wait for it" (8:25). In other words, God could have changed our flesh the moment we were saved. That would have been what we would have done if we were God. However, God's ways are higher than our ways (Isaiah 55:8-9). God sees that, in our eternal positions in heavenly places, we need to have the quality of patience. As we learned in 5:3-5, tribulations work patience, experience, hope, and God's love. If God glorified our flesh the moment we were saved, we would not suffer tribulations, because our sin nature would be taken away, such that we would obey God perfectly. If that happened, we would not have patience. Therefore, God gives us His Word to tell us that the Lord Jesus Christ will redeem our bodies at the rapture. Because we have faith in God's Word, we have the hope, or the confident expectation, that He will redeem our bodies. We then wait all of our lives for that to happen, and the result is that it builds patience in us.

This also affirms the dictionary definition that hope is not a wish, but it is a confident expectation that our bodies will be redeemed in the future, since, if it were a wish, we would have no patience. For example, if we wished that we would win the lottery, we would not learn patience, because we would keep buying tickets and keep wishing that we would win. However, if we actually won, we would know that the lottery check is coming, and so we would stop buying lottery tickets and wait for the check to come. Similarly, when we believe Romans 1-8 doctrine, we have the confident expectation that God will redeem our bodies. Therefore, we will not try to work our way to heaven, try to follow man's philosophies, or worry about our eternal dwelling place. Instead, we will rest in the sound doctrine of Romans 1-8, knowing that it is true. This will stop our striving and develop patience in us, because we know that our redemption is coming. Therefore, there is no need to worry. All we have to do is wait.

8:26-27 Very, very few Christians can even begin to understand what in the world these verses are talking about, because they have not believed the sound doctrine that has been revealed so far in Romans. Christians tend to think that the Spirit's interceding "for us with groanings which cannot be uttered" is some mystical spiritual language that only the Trinity understands. In this view, we have no idea what to pray for, but that is okay, because the Spirit will magically translate our words into what we should have prayed so that God gives us what we need, rather than what we desire. (This view is expressed in The Message's translation, which reads, "If we don't know how or what to pray, it doesn't matter.") So, if I pray to win the lottery, the Spirit will groan out a prayer to God that what I really meant to say, if I knew how to pray, was that I wanted more opportunities to help others. In this view, it does not really matter what we pray. If this were true, when the disciples asked Jesus to teach them how to pray (Luke 11:1), Jesus would have said, "Don't worry about what you say. Just give it your best shot, and the Spirit will take care of the rest."

However, this is NOT even close to what these verses mean. First, 8:26 begins with: "Likewise the Spirit also helpeth our infirmities." Since the verse starts with "likewise," we know that the process of the Spirit helping our infirmities is similar to the process of 8:24-25. In 8:24-25, we learned that God did not change our flesh when we were saved because God wants us to have the hope that He will change our flesh at the rapture, and that hope builds patience in us. Therefore, just like our flesh was not glorified at the time of our salvation, the Spirit does not heal our flesh as part of the sanctification process, because He wants us to learn how to pray. Not only does the Spirit not heal our flesh, but He actually makes our flesh worse because He "HELPETH our infirmities." He does not heal, relieve, or eliminate our infirmities, but He helps them. If He helps our infirmities, then He makes our infirmities stronger. Just like God did not glorify our flesh because He wanted us to learn patience, the Spirit makes our infirmities worse so that we learn to concentrate on the spiritual, rather than the physical.

You only need to look at what Christianity does today to see how necessary the Spirit's work is. Christians spend most of their "prayer life," if you want to call it that, asking God for physical healing for people. Then, they spend most of their "praise life," thanking God for physical healing. Their focus is on the physical, while God's focus is on the spiritual. Since Christians focus on the physical when God does not, if God DID focus on the physical, Christians would never even open their Bibles. Instead, they would gather for physical healings and miracles, much like the thousands in Israel, who followed Jesus for His physical healings.

Therefore, since God wants Christians to focus on the spiritual, rather than the physical, He has to do the opposite of physical healings. In other words, He has to help our infirmities. We have already seen that, the more affliction we have, the more glory is produced in us (II Corinthians 4:17). Why? Because suffering in the flesh causes us to focus on what is important.

We have an example with Paul. He had "a thorn in the flesh, the messenger of Satan to buffet me, lest I should be exalted above measure" (II Corinthians 12:7). In other words, because Paul had received an "abundance of...revelations" from God (II Corinthians 12:7), there was the danger that he would become prideful in himself. So, God allowed a messenger of Satan to hurt him physically to keep him humble. In other words, the Spirit helped his infirmities increase so that his prayers would be proper. As most Christians do, Paul prayed for physical healing (II Corinthians 12:8). The Lord's answer to Paul was that "My grace is sufficient for thee: for My strength is made perfect in weakness" (II Corinthians 12:9). Grace is God giving you something good that you do not deserve. In this case, God's grace was a thorn in the flesh. Why would hurting Paul be God's grace? Because the Lord's "strength is made perfect in [man's] weakness." God's strength is in the inner man, not in the flesh (Ephesians 3:16). (This is easily seen in the Lord Jesus Christ winning the victory over death by dying on a cross.) Therefore, what the Lord told Paul was that Paul needed to have trouble in the flesh so that he would recognize that "the excellency of the power" is "of God, and not of" Paul (II Corinthians 4:7).

Once God gave Paul that answer, Paul concluded: "Most gladly therefore will I rather glory in my infirmities, that the power of Christ may rest upon me....For when I am weak, then am I strong" (II Corinthians 12:9-10). In other words, Paul thought, "I get it now. God wants me to be strong spiritually. He knows that, if I am strong physically, I will concentrate on the flesh. So, God made me weak physically so that I would be strong spiritually. Therefore, I will stop praying for physical healing, and thank God that He loves my soul enough to increase the infirmities of my flesh."

Now, let us apply this to what is going on in 8:26-27. In 8:24-25, we learned that God does not glorify our flesh the moment we are saved because we need to learn patience. Now, in 8:26, we learn that, not only does God not glorify our flesh, but He also actually makes us more physically weak. Why? Because "we know not what we should pray for as we ought" (8:26).

In order to understand this, let us briefly define what prayer is. God commands us to "pray without ceasing" (I Thessalonians 5:17). Since we cannot always have our heads bowed and our eyes closed, prayer must be a thought process, rather than a posture. Ephesians 6:17-18 tells us that the way we defeat Satan is by taking the Word of God and pray "always with all prayer and supplication in the Spirit." Therefore, prayer is not always getting down on your knees and pouring out your heart to God, although it can be that. Mainly, prayer should be a constant communication in your mind between you and God in order to determine how to apply what the

Word of God says regarding each decision/situation that you face.

Therefore, if "we know not what we should pray for as we ought" (8:26), it means that we do not have enough sound doctrine built up in the inner man to pray correctly. Why is that? Because we have not been reading and believing God's Word and allowing the Holy Ghost to teach it to us. Why is that? Because we have valued the flesh over the spirit. The way God gets us to devalue the flesh is by making the flesh weak. "When I am weak, then am I strong" (II Corinthians 12:10). In other words, when my flesh is weak, then Christ is strong through me. Therefore, the Spirit intentionally "helpeth" or increaseth our physical infirmities, because we have not been reading and believing God's Word to learn the sound doctrine to walk after the Spirit (8:1-5). So, He increases our physical infirmities so that we may learn the same lesson that Paul learned, which is that it is the spirit that matters, not the flesh.

In the comments on 8:9, I said that, because modern translations have changed "Holy Ghost" to "Holy Spirit" in all instances, Christianity makes the assumption that, whenever "Spirit" is used, it refers to the Holy Ghost. However, as we saw in 8:9, all three members of the Godhead have a Spirit. Therefore, when we see "Spirit," here in 8:26, we should not automatically assume that it is a reference to the Holy Ghost. As always, the context will give us the understanding. According to Hebrews 7:25 and Isaiah 53:12, it is the Lord Jesus Christ, Who intercedes to God for believers. In fact, Paul specifically says, in 8:34, that it is Christ, "Who ... maketh intercession for us." Therefore, the Spirit, in 8:26, is the Spirit of Christ, not the Holy Ghost.

What are these "groanings which cannot be uttered" (8:26)? We have already given the example of Paul having a thorn in the flesh in II Corinthians 12, as something similar to what is going on here. It is no coincidence, then, that, in II Corinthians 12:4, Paul says that, when he was caught up into the third heaven, he "heard unspeakable words, which it is not lawful for a man to utter." Since God dwells in the third heaven, He would not allow unlawful words to be spoken there, since God cannot behold iniquity. Yet, because Paul "HEARD" these words, someone must have uttered them, even though they are "unspeakable." Therefore, it is reasonable to conclude that, while the words are not lawful FOR A MAN to utter, they ARE lawful for God to utter. If they are "unspeakable" for man, they must be speakable for God. Therefore, Paul must have heard the Spirit speak these words. To man, these are probably "groanings which cannot be uttered" (8:26). These would be spiritual words that the Spirit of Christ speaks to the Spirit of God the Father, since "God is a Spirit" (John 4:24) and Christ intercedes to God the Father on our behalf (8:34).

Of the three members of the Godhead, only God the Son has a body (Colossians 1:15 and Hebrews 10:5) and only Christ was tempted to sin (Hebrews 4:15). Of man, only Christ "did no sin" (I Peter 2:22). As such, the Lord Jesus Christ is the only member of the Godhead Who is "touched with the feeling of our infirmities" (Hebrews 4:15). This means that, while God the Father would do everything to our flesh, short of killing us, to get us to read and believe God's Word, Christ is a more compassionate judge of what to do to us, having lived among mankind and their infirmities. Therefore, when Christ sees that we are not praying as we ought, He increases our physical infirmities so that we will read and believe God's Word so that we will begin to pray as we ought. Yet, He does not go that far in afflicting us, because He is "touched with the feeling of our infirmities" (Hebrews 4:15).

Since the Son is subject to the Father, He speaks to the Father about what infirmities are appropriate to inflict upon us. Since the Father is Spirit only, the Spirit of Christ speaks to the Father "with groanings which cannot be uttered" (8:26), which would be words that only a Spirit can say to another Spirit. In other words, man cannot utter these words, because they are Spirit words. The reason it is important for us to know that they are words we cannot utter is because it shows that, as the God-man, only the Lord Jesus Christ can intercede between us and the Father to help us in our spiritual growth.

Note that 8:27 says that "He maketh intercession for the saints according to the will of God." I Timothy 2:4 tells us that God's will is for "all men to be saved, and to come unto the knowledge of the truth." Since we are already saints, we are already saved, which means that the Spirit of Christ makes intercession to God the Father so that we may come unto the knowledge of the truth. Since Christ is the God-man, He knows best how to afflict man to accomplish God's will.

8:27 starts off by saying that "He...searcheth the hearts." Who is the He? Jeremiah 17:9-10 says that "the heart is deceitful above all things, and desperately wicked: who can know it? I the Lord search the heart, I try the reins" (Jeremiah 17:9-10). Therefore, "He that searcheth the hearts" (8:27) is the Lord. Philippians 2:11 tells us that "Jesus Christ is Lord," which means that Jesus Christ, as man, knows the heart. The next part of 8:27 says that He "knoweth what is the mind of the Spirit." We have already concluded that the "Spirit," in this context, is Christ. Since "Spirit" has a capital "S", we know that the "mind of the Spirit" refers to Jesus Christ as God. Thus, the man, Jesus Christ, knows the mind of God, because He is God, which means that only Jesus Christ can search the heart to understand what man is going through and then give the Father advice on how to help man spiritually, since He also has the mind of God. This means that only the Lord Jesus Christ, being both fully God and fully man, has the wisdom to bring about the infirmities that we need in order to get us to come unto the knowledge of the truth so that Christ can live in us (Galatians 2:20).

Based on this interpretation, the logical conclusion is that Christians would have more physical infirmities than unbelievers. However, we also have to consider that the vast majority of Christians today are so hardened against God's sanctification process for them and are so spiritually ignorant of the truths of Romans 1-8 that, regardless of the physical infirmities that come their way, they still would not recognize those physical infirmities as a sign that they need to read and believe God's Word more. Note II Timothy 2:25-26, which says that those believing false doctrine are in "the snare of the devil...,taken captive by him at his will." This passage also says that, if we instruct them with sound doctrine, they will believe that doctrine "if God peradventure will give them repentance to the acknowledging of the truth." Obviously, God's will is for them to acknowledge the truth, but He will not override man's free will. Since Christ searcheth the hearts, He knows if helping their physical infirmities will cause them to believe the truth or not. Since most will not believe, there is no need for Christ to increase their infirmities. Therefore, we do not see Christians, as a whole, physically suffering more than unbelievers. Also, most people, who attend Christian churches, are not really Christians anyway, because they have never heard and believed the gospel alone for their salvation.

With that being said, we do know that Christ is sanctifying and cleansing the church with the Word so that He can present us to the Father as "holy and without blemish" (Ephesians 5:26-27). We also know that He will perform this "good work" in us until the rapture takes place (Philippians 1:6). Therefore, due to the stubbornness of most members of the body of Christ, His work of helping our infirmities is probably a more subtle work that takes place over thousands of years before He can finally fill all heavenly positions with the body of Christ. (This is why the dispensation of grace has gone on for about 2,000 years and counting.)

Another thing to consider is that, when Paul said, "we know not what we should pray for," the full revelation of the mystery had not been given yet when Paul wrote Romans. Therefore, one could argue that, once all mystery doctrine is revealed, they will know what to pray for. However, Paul says that "we know not what we should pray for AS WE OUGHT." By adding "as we ought," Paul is showing that, although all mystery doctrine has not been written down yet, the Romans are not even using the mystery doctrine that they do have to pray to God. Therefore, the Spirit of Christ intercedes for them to God the Father to help them learn that doctrine. In fact, the reason Paul wrote the epistle to the Romans was to "impart unto you some spiritual gift, to the end ye may be established" (1:11). Thus, Christ is also interceding for the Romans, and for us, by having Paul write this epistle. And, Christ continues to intercede for the body of Christ to the Father today so that we can occupy the positions in heavenly places that Christ has for us to fill.

In summary, the common view of these verses in Christianity is that the Holy Spirit turns our prayer into an appropriate prayer for us. We have learned that this is incorrect. What is actually going on, according to these verses, is that Christ hears our prayer, notes that it is not an appropriate prayer, and then discusses with the Father about how to weaken our flesh so that we will grow in sound doctrine so that our prayers are appropriate in the future. Appropriate prayers mean that we walk after the Spirit, because our decisions will be based upon talking out sound doctrine to God in order to make decisions based upon the Spirit, rather than upon our flesh.

8:28 Christianity teaches that we should look to circumstances and learn from them. So, if I get married and I get divorced later on, I should ask God what He wanted me to learn from that experience. Then, I can marry someone else and be a better spouse to that person, because God taught me, through my painful experience with my first spouse, how to be a better person. After all, Christianity will say, this must be true because "all things work together for good to them that love God" (8:28). First, this is a sneaky way of saying that God wants you to be wealthy and happy in your flesh, and that He had to get you to a place where you would accept and appreciate all the material blessings that God wants to give you by letting you make poor decisions at first. This is not unlike the Mormons telling people that God wanted Adam to sin because he had to sin in order to know joy later. If that is the case, then God must not have joy, because He has never sinned!

Second, when Christianity misuses this verse, it is really Christianity following the lusts of their flesh and trying to make their sins look good by cloaking them in the name of God. How do I know this? Because God says to the married: "Let not the wife depart from her husband" (I Corinthians 7:10). Even if the husband is a believer and the wife is an unbeliever, the husband should not put away his wife (I Corinthians 7:12). The point is that 8:28 is not in the Bible for Christians to run to to justify their sinful decisions. We should believe God's Word over man's philosophies.

Thus, 8:28 should not be ripped out of its context to say that God allowed you to make sinful decisions so that you would go through pain so that you would become a better person. We learned, in 8:24-25, that we are not better people after we are saved, because our flesh will not be changed until the rapture. Then, in 8:26-27, we learned that God increases our suffering so that we concentrate on the spiritual, rather than on the physical. Therefore, when 8:28 tells us that "we know that all things work together for good to them that love God," we know that this means that we should not be upset with God about our suffering. Granted, no one wants to suffer, because suffering is not pleasant. However, all of our physical suffering works together for our SPIRITUAL good. If we use the mind of Christ (I Corinthians 2:16), we will realize that suffering is good for us because it helps us reckon ourselves "to be dead indeed unto sin, but alive unto God" (6:11) so that we may do God's will, by coming into the knowledge of the truth by reading God's Word rightly divided and then praying that sound doctrine to make the right decisions. Therefore, 8:28 is not in the Bible to say that God will make you happy in this life. God never promised that. Rather, 8:28, in its context, is saying that physical suffering is part of God's overall plan to bring eternal glory to His Son and, by extension, to us, since we are in His Son (Ephesians 1:6 and Colossians 3:3).

This verse says that all things work together for good to them that LOVE GOD. Does this refer to all Christians, or does it only refer to those Christians who love God? And, how do we determine that we love God or not? If we obeyed God perfectly, we would love God, but no one does that, even after they are saved. Therefore, loving God cannot be based on some standard of obedience, because any such standard would be arbitrary. In other words, which sins are okay for me to do and still love God, and which ones are a sign that I no longer love God? Fortunately, Paul gives us the answer. He says that those who love God are "the called according to His purpose" (8:28). Since the verse says "THE called," rather than just "called," we know that Paul is referring to a group of people.

In 1:6-7, we learned that all members of the body of Christ are "the called." Therefore, by cross-referencing 1:6-7 with 8:28, we learn that all Christians love God. This is confirmed by the immediate context which says that "whom He called, them He also justified" (8:30). Since all "the called" are also justified, we know that "the called" refers to all saved people. Therefore, those, who love God, are all saved people. You may say, "But, I know plenty of Christian people who do not love God, because they curse, smoke, rarely go to church, and are engaged in much immoral behavior." However, that statement is based upon their works, and justification is based upon faith alone (3:28) and we just learned that all saved people love God. Therefore, loving God must be something that is internal, which may or may not be shown externally. That is because the Christian may choose to follow the lusts of his flesh, rather than walking after the Spirit.

Note also that they are not "the called" based upon their performance, but they are "the called according to His purpose" (8:28). That purpose is "not of works, but of Him that calleth" (9:11). God's purpose is to use His wisdom to gather all things in heaven and earth in Christ (Ephesians 1:9-11). This is done "in Christ Jesus our Lord...by the faith of Him" (Ephesians 3:10-12). This is entirely God's work, as seen in 8:29-32. Those verses show that God foreknew us, predestinated us, called us, justified us, and glorified us. He then freely gives us all things, because He spared not His Own Son.

Therefore, we need not wonder if we love God enough to be "the called" so that He works all things for good. We just trust the verses that that is what is happening. Therefore, when we suffer, we should not think that God is punishing us for bad behavior, that God does not love us, or that we are going to hell. Rather, we should look at the big picture. God purposed to glorify His Son in both heaven and earth for all eternity, and He used wisdom to bring "many sons unto glory" (Hebrews 2:10) with Him so "that God may be all in all" (I Corinthians 15:28). And, since God "spared not His Own Son" (8:32) but made Him "perfect through sufferings" (Hebrews 2:10), we should trust that the "good work," that Christ does in us (Philippians 1:6), also involves sufferings (Philippians 1:6). Therefore, we should rest in knowing that, in spite of the suffering we go through, in the end, it all works for good in that Christ will be eternally glorified in God and we will be eternally glorified in Christ. That is why Paul says: "Now thanks be unto God, which ALWAYS causeth us to triumph in Christ, and maketh manifest the savour of His knowledge by us in EVERY place" (II Corinthians 2:14). You may say, "but I don't feel savoury." Well, no, you are not, but God's knowledge is savoury through you, even when you let the flesh control you. That is because the power of God, through the cross work of Christ, is infinitely stronger than your flesh. You cannot keep Christ coming through your flesh, even if you try to stop Him. But, if you walk after the Spirit, then Christ does even greater work through you, bruising "Satan under your feet" (16:20).

In summary, the main points to learn from 8:28 are: 1) Your suffering on this earth is used by Christ to create eternal good in heavenly places, 2) You love God in your spirit, because God saved you by giving you the gift of eternal life because you believed the gospel. Therefore, you love God, regardless of what you do in your flesh, and 3) Because you believed the gospel, you are part of "the called," who will fulfill God's purpose in heavenly places for all eternity.

8:29-30 Calvinists say that predestination means that God selected certain individuals to be saved and others to go to hell. Arminians say that God predestinated those individuals who chose to believe the gospel. Therefore, Calvinists believe in God's sovereignty, while Arminians believe in man's free will. If a person asks you if you are a Calvinist or an Arminian, that person is a theologian, because he wants to put a label on you. While the Arminian position is the correct one in this case, your answer to the question should be that you are not either one, but that you are a Bible believer. That way, you tell him that the Bible is your final authority, rather than a theological system. Also, Arminians believe false doctrine, and you do not want others to assume you believe in false doctrine. The person, who wants to put a theological label on you, is probably studying theological systems, rather than studying God's Word. Therefore, this person is probably "ever learning, and never able to come to the knowledge of the truth" (II Timothy 3:7). God says regarding these people: "from such turn away" (II Timothy 3:5). The reason is because they are "doting about questions and strifes of words" (I Timothy 6:4), rather than simply believing what the Bible says. Therefore, in order to keep away from being trapped in the yoke of theological bondage, just state that you are a Bible believer and turn away from him.

Because of this guidance from God's Word, I am not going to get into the five points of Calvinism and the Arminian response to those, because all theological discussions are a waste of time. Instead, we are just going to read and believe what the Bible says.

What does "foreknow" mean?

The first thing we are told is that God foreknew that we would be saved. In this context, foreknowledge means that we made the choice to believe the gospel, and God knew in advance that we would do so.

A great example of what God's foreknowledge means comes from Acts 2:22-23. There, we are told that "Jesus of Nazareth" was delivered "by the determinate counsel and foreknowledge of God" to Israel, Who they "have taken, and by wicked hands have crucified and slain." Note that Israel was wicked. Because they were wicked, they were children of the devil (John 8:44). Because they were children of the devil, they chose to do what the devil wanted them to do. Therefore, God kept His plan, regarding the Messiah, a secret. God told Israel that their faith response to their Messiah should be to "bind the sacrifice [Jesus] with cords" (Psalm 118:27) on the altar in the temple. Satan thought that, if he got Israel to crucify Jesus on a cross, Satan would be the god of heaven and earth. However, dying on a cross was God's plan for Jesus all along. That was the only way, God could reconcile both the earth and the heaven back to Himself in Christ (Ephesians 1:10). Yet, if God had revealed that plan, Satan's forces would not have had Him crucified (I Corinthians 2:7-8).

In other words, God planned all along to have Jesus crucified on a cross. God revealed to Israel that they should sacrifice Him on the altar in the temple. Because Israel was wicked, they followed what Satan wanted them to do, which was to kill Jesus on a cross. In so doing, Israel followed God's plan without even knowing it. This is the ultimate example of God disappointing "the devices of the crafty, so that their hands cannot perform their enterprise. He taketh the wise in their own craftiness" (Job 5:12-13 and I Corinthians 3:19).

Now, you may ask, what does all of this have to do with Romans 8:29? The answer is that, according to Acts 2:23, all of this took place "according to the determinate counsel and FOREKNOWLEDGE of God." In other words, God's foreknowledge, with regard to the cross, meant that He knew, in advance, that Israel would disobey Him. Therefore, He did not tell Israel His plan so that Israel would, by disobeying Him, end up actually doing what God wanted them to do.

The point is that man still has free will to make his own decisions. If God's sovereignty overrides man's free will, God would have told Israel, in Psalm 118:27, that the Messiah would be crucified on a cross, because man could not stop it. But, because man has free will, he can choose to disobey God. Therefore, God kept His plan a secret and used His foreknowledge to figure out how to get man to fulfill His plan, even though man thought that they were thwarting God's plan. Therefore, God's foreknowledge does NOT mean that He overrides man's free will. Rather, it means that God knows man's response to whatever He says, and so He can alter what He says so that man's free-will responses align with His plan. Applied to our salvation, God foreknew that we would choose to be saved and be part of the body of Christ, but He did not force us to be saved.

143

What does "predestinate" mean?

I Peter 1:2 says that the believing remnant of Israel are the "elect according to the foreknowledge of God the Father." Based on what we just learned about God's foreknowledge, we know that this means that God elected to save this group of people who would believe the gospel. Similarly, God predestinated the body of Christ to have eternal life with Him.

Therefore, predestination means that, in time past, God formulated a plan by which He would reconcile all things in heaven and earth back to Himself (Ephesians 1:10). This plan includes two group of believers—Israel and the body of Christ—that He foreknew would believe the gospel presented to them. For us, this means that He foreknew a group of people, called the body of Christ, which would believe the gospel presented to them, and He "pre-determined the destiny" or predestinated that group of believers to occupy heavenly places with Him for all eternity.

Again, the foreknowledge of God does not override man's free will. That is why God says, "WHOSOEVER WILL, let him take the water of life freely" (Revelation 22:17). Moreover, if God were completely sovereign, such that man has no free will, all people would be saved. We know this because God's will is for "ALL men to be saved" (I Timothy 2:4), and "the Lord is...not willing that any should perish, but that ALL should come to repentance" (II Peter 3:9). Therefore, predestination means that, in time past, God foreknew that a group of people, known as the body of Christ, would each individually believe the gospel God gave them, and He predestinated that group to have eternal life with Him in heavenly places. It does not mean that He forced certain people to be saved and others to go to hell, because, if God forced man, all would be saved, since hell was "prepared for the devil and his angels" (Matthew 25:41), not for man.

What does "called" mean?

We have already discussed this briefly in the commentary on 8:28. 1:6-7 says that the Romans are "the called of Jesus Christ...,called to be saints." This means that all members of the body of Christ have been called. We also see this in 8:30, because this verse says that all the called are justified.

However, this call goes way beyond justification. According to Galatians 1:6, we are called "into the grace of Christ." "In the ages to come, God will shew us "the exceeding riches of His grace" (Ephesians 2:6). Ephesians 4:1 beseeches us to "walk worthy of the vocation wherewith [we were] called." I Thessalonians 2:12 says that "God...hath called [us] unto His kingdom and glory." By putting all of these verses together, we can determine that "called" means that God has called us to work for Him in heavenly places for all eternity. Faith pleases God (Hebrews 11:6), and, because we have had faith in God, God wants us to work for Him. The more we believe God's Word, the more qualified we will be to take a higher position in heavenly places. Either way, God will glorify us for having faith in Him, and He will pour out the riches of His grace upon us for all eternity.

Usually, when we think of eternal life, we think of just being with God in heaven. While it does include that, there is so much more involved than just bowing down to God in heaven. Jesus promised ABUNDANT life to those who believe in Him (John 10:10). I Timothy 6:12 is a good summary of this. It says: "Fight the good fight of faith, lay hold on eternal life, whereunto thou art also called." In other words, if you will just learn the sound doctrine of Romans 1-8, then you will understand your calling. You will "LAY HOLD on eternal life," which means that you will recognize that God has called you to serve Him in heavenly places, and so you will "fight the good fight of faith," and Christ will reward you with a high position in heavenly places.

Thus, being "the called" starts with our justification and ends with our glory, as seen in 8:30, and it involves us walking after the Spirit, because we have laid hold on our eternal lives in heavenly places.

Summary

Now that we have defined terms using the Bible, not man's philosophies, we can understand what 8:29-30 is saying.

First, we need to recognize that the context of these verses is suffering. Earthly suffering produces heavenly glory, which far exceeds the suffering (8:18). Our spirits groan within us, waiting to be delivered from our vile bodies (8:23 and Philippians 3:21). But, we should not be discouraged, because we know that "all things work together for good to them that love God, to them who are the called according to His purpose" (8:28).

Why do we know this? Because God is taking us through a process that leads to our glorification. First, He foreknew that we would believe the gospel. Second, He predestinated us to be in heavenly places with Christ for all eternity. Third, He called us to live abundant lives in which Christ would live through us from our justification to our glorification.

Since our calling takes us from death in hell to abundant living in Christ and God's grace for all eternity, Paul must add a footnote as to how such a radical transformation could take place. Therefore, between our predestination and our calling, he mentions that we are predestinated "to be conformed to the image of His Son, that He might be the firstborn among many brethren" (8:29).

Colossians 1:18-19 says that Christ is "the head of...the church: Who is the beginning, the firstborn from the dead....For it pleased the Father that in Him should all fulness dwell." That fulness is the fulness of the heavenly places (see Ephesians 1:20-23). Applied to 8:29, we learn that the way God

145

takes us from death to abundant living with God for all eternity is that He had to have a "new creature" (II Corinthians 5:17) born, because our flesh is vile (Philippians 3:21). This "new creature" is a glorified body like the body of the Lord Jesus Christ. It is incapable of committing sin, as we are told that "whosoever is born of God doth not commit sin; for His seed remaineth in him: and he cannot sin, because he is born of God" (I John 3:9).

Note that Acts 13:33 says that the day in which Jesus Christ was begotten of the Father was the day of His resurrection. Thus, He was born of God that day, and, at the rapture, our bodies will "be fashioned like unto His glorious body" (Philippians 3:21), which means we will also be born of God. In the context of 8:29, all of this means that, the reason God waited until Jesus' resurrection to make Him born of God, is because God's plan is for us to rule with Him in heavenly places for all eternity. Since there is no good thing dwelling in our flesh (7:18), God will have to give us new flesh that will live perfectly in heavenly places. He does not give all of mankind that flesh, because the only way to please God is to have faith in Him (Hebrews 11:6).

Therefore, all of us are born with flesh that cannot please God. If we have faith in the gospel, God is pleased with us and will conform us to the image of His Son. To accomplish this, Jesus had to come "in the likeness of sinful flesh" (Romans 8:3), "did no sin" (I Peter 2:22), and was "made...sin for us" (II Corinthians 5:21) on the cross. Because He did no sin, He rose from the dead with a glorified body that can be used to serve God for all eternity. When we have faith in the gospel, Jesus becomes the "propitiation" or fully satisfying sacrifice for our sin (3:25). We are identified with His death so that we can receive a glorified body like His (6:3-4). And, the reason God did things this way with Christ is so He could separate out believers from unbelievers. The unbelievers rot in hell for all eternity, while the believers are "conformed to the image of His Son," which is possible because He is the "firstborn among many brethren" (8:29).

Therefore, the Lord Jesus Christ's perfect life in mortal flesh, his death and burial of that mortal flesh, and His resurrection into glorified flesh were all done so that we would receive glorified flesh which empowers us to serve God forever in heavenly places for all eternity. In other words, the power to serve God is only given to those who want to serve God, which keeps unbelieving man from using the power of God for evil purposes, since they will never receive His power. In other words, unbelieving man has not recognized that he is weak and needs God's power. Therefore, if God gave him His power, he would abuse it. Believing man, on the other hand, has recognized his inability to obtain righteousness on his own. Therefore, God gives him eternal life. And, the more that believing man reads and believes God's Word, the more he realizes his weakness to serve God after he is saved. Therefore, God gives him even more power to serve God in a greater capacity in heavenly places, because he will use that power for God, rather than becoming prideful and trying to become his own god, as Lucifer did with his power (Isaiah 14:12-14).

8:31 8:31-39 is a conclusion of what should have been learned in the first 30 verses of the chapter. He says, "what shall we then say to these things?" If we have the sound doctrine of 8:1-30 built up in our inner man, then we will say what Paul says in 8:31-39 being "persuaded" (8:38) that no one or no thing can keep us from allowing God to work through us (8:38-39).

8:29-30 has proven that God is for us. Therefore, "if God be for us" (8:31) is a statement of fact, not a hypothetical situation. With regard to who is against us, since the devil is called our adversary (I Peter 5:8), he is certainly against us, as are his ministers (II Corinthians 11:13-15), and everyone else on his side. That is why we are "troubled on every side...,perplexed..., persecuted...,cast down" (II Corinthians 4:8-9). Therefore, the question of: "Who can be against us?" (8:31) is not asking for a list, but it is really saying that, in spite of everything we suffer, no one can stop God from fulfilling His purpose in us, because "the Lord God [is] omnipotent" or all powerful (Revelation 19:6). In fact, Paul will soon give us a list of things that come against us (8:35) and state that "we are more than conquerors through Him that loved us" (8:37).

Therefore, Paul's point, in 8:31, is that because God's plan is to give us eternal glory and God is all powerful, it really does not matter what we suffer through, we will be conquerors of those attacks through God. Therefore, "be careful for nothing" (Philippians 4:6).

8:32 God is all powerful, and yet He "spared not His Own Son" (8:32). Why? Because the more God gives, the more He can bless His Son in return. And, because we are "in Christ" (8:1), we receive what He receives. Look at just the things listed in Ephesians 1 that we "FREELY" (8:32) receive because God gave up His Own Son:

1) "All spiritual blessings in heavenly places" (v. 3)
2) Holiness, blamelessness, and His love (v. 4)
3) Adopted as God's children (v. 5)
4) Accepted in Christ (v. 6)
5) Redemption, forgiveness of sins, and grace (v. 7)
6) "All wisdom and prudence" (v. 8)
7) Knowledge of God's will (v. 9)
8) An inheritance in Christ (vs. 10-11)
9) The Holy Spirit (v. 13)
10) God's great power (v. 19)

Also notice that we are told that God delivered up Christ "for us ALL" (8:32). This is a new revelation as part of the mystery program. In Israel's program, we were only told that Christ would die for Israel. Isaiah 53:8 says, "for the transgression of MY PEOPLE was He stricken," and Jesus said in Matthew 26:28 that He shed His blood "for MANY for the remission of sins." It is not until the mystery was revealed to Paul that we find out that Jesus' blood was shed for the Gentiles as well, "to be testified in due time" (I Timothy 2:6).

8:33 There are plenty of people who WANT to lay things to the charge of God's elect. Satan will try to persecute us to keep us from growing in grace by receiving edification in God's Word rightly divided. He does so by using his ministers (II Corinthians 11:13-15) to preach false doctrine to make us think we can lose our salvation, and Satan has done a bang-up job to that end, as only part of Christianity ascents to eternal security and then only according to their rules, which means that they really do not believe in eternal security. However, if we choose to believe God and His Word about who we are in Christ, Satan's forces cannot stop us from allowing Christ to live in us. And, even if we do not believe God's Word, if we have believed the gospel, God has justified us, which means that there is nothing we can do to become unjustified, because it is a done deal.

What does "elect" mean?

As mentioned under our definition of predestination in 8:29-30, election just means that God decided that He would bless a group of people with eternal life and everything that entails. I Peter 1:2 says that the believing remnant of Israel are the "elect according to the foreknowledge of God the Father," meaning that God elected Israel to be saved based on His foreknowledge that they would believe the gospel. Similarly, the body of Christ is elected by God to be saved, not because God in His overriding sovereign will forced us to have eternal life, but because He knew we would use our free will to believe the gospel. Once we do that, we are justified and receive the atonement right now (5:9,11). We are then sealed with the Holy Spirit (Ephesians 1:13-14), such that we cannot lose our status of being part of God's elect.

8:34 While 8:33 is concerned with our salvation, 8:34 is concerned with our sanctification. In Romans 7, Paul went over the self-condemnation that we experience when we try to serve God in the energies of our flesh. Since no good thing dwells in our flesh (7:18), we need deliverance "from the body of this death" (7:24). "God through Jesus Christ our Lord" (7:25) has given us this deliverance, such that "there is therefore now no condemnation to them which are in Christ Jesus, who walk not after the flesh, but after the Spirit" (8:1). With this in mind, we already know that the one who condemns you is your flesh. Therefore the question of: "Who is he that condemneth?" (8:34) is not asking "who" in terms of "who is that person," but it is asking "who" in terms of "what power does the condemner have?" In modern terms, it might be stated: "Who does your flesh think he is, coming in here condemning you?"

Therefore, Paul's answer has to do with the power of your flesh. He says that "Christ...died, yea rather,...is risen again" (8:34). Since you were identified with His death and His resurrection life (6:3-4), your flesh is dead, having been crucified with Christ (6:6-7 and Galatians 2:20). Therefore, the answer to the question of "who is he that condemneth" (8:34) is "no one. He is some dead guy that is hanging around. But, he cannot do anything because he is dead."

However, I can still choose to allow my flesh to control me, which is why Paul goes on to say that Christ is "at the right hand of God," and He "maketh intercession for us" (8:34). Now, we learned the details of that intercession in 8:26. There, we learned that, when we do not believe sound doctrine, we do not pray as we ought, meaning that we do not make decisions based on sound doctrine. In that case, the Spirit of Christ speaks to the Father in "Spirit talk" to make our flesh weak so that we learn to read and believe sound doctrine, instead of listening to our flesh.

Therefore, what Paul is saying, in 8:34, is that your flesh will condemn you, but your flesh has no power over you because you are dead. And, even if you do listen to your flesh, Christ is interceding to the Father on your behalf to keep you from making that mistake of flesh control in the future, culminating in the redemption of your bodies at the rapture so that you will never sin again (8:23). There are so many Christians who want to "enjoy" the things of this life, such that they do everything they can to live long lives. While there is nothing wrong with living a long life, the desire to do so represents hanging on to the things of the flesh. The Christian, who knows sound doctrine, is all too familiar with the sufferings of this present time and says with Paul: "For to me to live is Christ, and to die is gain" (Philippians 1:21).

Christ's death, burial, and resurrection allow God both to justify you (8:33) and to sanctify you (8:34), ending with glorified bodies that He will present to Himself (because we are His body) as "holy and without blemish" (Ephesians 5:27).

8:35 Although the list in this verse is a list of things, the question is "who" shall separate us, not "what" shall separate us from the love of Christ. Therefore, the "who" of this verse would be the one behind the list of things. Satan is "the god of this world" (II Corinthians 4:4), and "the prince of the power of the air" (Ephesians 2:2). As such, he has all unbelievers and many believers following "the course of this world" (Ephesians 2:2). We also know that the whole creation is under the curse of sin (8:20-22). Therefore, the "who" behind this list is Satan and his forces, which is why Paul lists angels, principalities, powers, height, depth, and any other creature as those who are trying to separate us from the love of Christ (8:38-39). That is why Paul says in another place that "we wrestle...against principalities, against powers, against the rulers of the darkness of this world, against spiritual wickedness in high places" (Ephesians 6:12). The good news is that we have "the whole armour of God" which enables us "to stand against the wiles of the devil" (Ephesians 6:11). Therefore, the devil's forces are really powerless to keep us from the love of Christ.

In 8:35, Paul lists seven of the devil's tactics to try to separate us from the love of Christ. These things can happen to anyone, but, because the context is separating us from the love of Christ, Paul is referring to Satan's forces inflicting these things upon believers to try to get us to get back to following the course of this world. The first three tactics are physical things that happen to you to get your focus off of the spirit and onto the flesh.

Tribulation is external suffering. The way this works is that Christians begin suffering, and they start asking why. This causes them to focus on the circumstances around them, which gets their focus off of God's Word. The ironic thing is that, while Satan uses tribulation to try to get your focus off of God, if you believe God and His Word, rather than looking at circumstances for the answer, the tribulation will get you to focus more on God's Word. The tribulation's end result will be the love of God being shed abroad in our hearts (Romans 5:3-5). Therefore, for the believer, what Satan means for evil, God works it out for good (Genesis 50:20), as we just learned in 8:28.

Distress is internal suffering, as we see the word "stress" in it. When we are under stress, it is very easy to make decisions based upon our emotions, rather than upon God's Word. Again, the result is that, if you concentrate on circumstances you may make a bad decision, but, if the Bible is your final authority, you will look at the big picture in God's Word, which alleviates the stress so that you make a good decision based upon God's Word.

Persecution is suffering from allowing Christ to live in us. II Timothy 3:12 says that "all that will live godly in Christ Jesus shall suffer persecution." This is a result of you living godly in a world that is living in sin. Hebrews 11:35-39 lists some of these persecutions with the note that the world was not worthy of the people they were persecuting. Paul says that "our conversation is in heaven" (Philippians 3:20). If we allow Christ to live through us in an ungodly world, we will suffer persecution.

The next four tactics—famine, nakedness, peril, and sword—may seem like things that naturally take place in a fallen world. While these things can happen to unbelievers, again, Paul's focus is on the adversary's tactics to separate us from the love of Christ. Therefore, he is referring to things that happen to believers who live godly lives. All four of these tactics are really threats to you for godly living. If you believe God and His Word over the course of this world, you will not be part of any club or any organization that will take care of you. For example, famine and nakedness may not seem like problems in a modern world. However, if you lose your job because of godly living, they suddenly become an issue. If you go along with the course of this world, your employer will usually take care of you, but, if you are living godly, you may lose your job just because Christ is living in you. In fact, in the culture we are in right now, you may get a job with an employer, because your boss is a Christian. Then, you may lose your job because you have Christ living in you, while your boss is a Christian in name only.

Perils are dangers that you may face. In just one verse, Paul mentions eight categories of perils that he faced (II Corinthians 11:26). The last category he mentions is "in perils among false brethren." This one is certainly applicable today, since most people, who claim to be Christians, have never believed today's gospel of grace, because their church does not teach it. There are great dangers to your Christian walk when you are around them, because they are deceived by false doctrine, making it easier for you to become deceived.

Note that the last tactic is "sword," not "death." In 13:4, in referring to governmental authority, Paul says that the leader "beareth not the sword in vain" (13:4). Therefore, "sword" is probably a reference to the threat of being killed or harmed by the government for godly living, because it is that threat that can cause you to change your thinking.

In summary, the last four of the seven tactics are threats of things that could happen to you as a result of godly living. Then, when they do happen, they become one of the first three things. Therefore, the last four wear on you mentally, while the first three wear on you both physically and mentally. Regardless, the goal of all tactics is to get your focus off of God and His Word and onto the things of this world.

If you have made the Bible your final authority, you will "stand against the wiles of the devil" (Ephesians 6:11). If your final authority is anything else, you will find answers elsewhere, and those answers will cause you to fall in the battle. For example, if you turn to preachers and doctrines of mainstream Christianity, you will be "tossed to and fro, and carried about with every wind of doctrine, by the sleight of men and cunning craftiness" (Ephesians 4:14). If your final authority is the world, you will run to philosophies. Either way, if your final authority is NOT the Word of God, you will use your fleshly mind to make decisions, and you will not allow Christ to live in you. However, if the Bible is your final authority, these tactics of the devil will actually turn against him, as you will read and believe more of God's Word and use the mind of Christ to respond to these situations.

Regardless of which path you choose, remember that Paul says that these tactics cannot separate us from the love of Christ. Therefore, even if Satan's tactics work, they only work temporarily. Why? Because of who we are in Christ. Remember that God saved you, and Christ is the one working to make you "holy and without blemish" (Ephesians 5:27). "He which hath begun a good work in you will perform it until the day of Jesus Christ" (Philippians 1:6). Therefore, the love of Christ dwelling with you is predicated upon Christ's ability, rather than your performance. Since your flesh's performance leads to death (6:23) and Christ destroyed all sin and death in you (6:6-8), there is nothing you can do to overcome the love of Christ in you. If you think that you can be separated from the love of Christ, then you think that you are more powerful than Christ is. Moreover, God cannot lie (Titus 1:2). He has promised to make you holy and without blemish and He has promised to perform His work in you until Jesus Christ comes back. If you could stop Christ's work in you, then God is a liar, He has very little power, and His love is not great. Therefore, even if you refuse to believe God's Word after you are saved, the worst Satan can do is delay Christ's work being done in you until the rapture.

Job is a great example of the staying power of the love of Christ. He lost his possessions, his family, and his health (Job 1:15-19 and 2:7). When his wife told him to "curse God, and die," Job said, "Thou speakest as one of the foolish women speaketh" (Job 2:10). In the end, God restored everything to him, giving him twice as much as he had before (Job 42:10). Similarly for us, we may suffer all seven tactics from the devil, but nothing can separate us from the love of Christ, because "your life is hid with Christ in God" (Colossians 3:3). This means that Satan cannot touch the things that will last forever, which are "the deep things of God" (I Corinthians 2:10). They are too deep and you are too deep in Christ for Satan to remove them from you.

Therefore, we are free to walk after the Spirit for our entire lives and experience tremendous spiritual growth and blessing. If circumstances are against us, that is even better, because the Lord's "strength is made perfect in weakness" (II Corinthians 12:9). This is the perspective that Paul has been leading up to for the first half of Romans. Once you look at things this way, Satan's kingdom will suffer major damage, because there is absolutely nothing Satan can do to stop Christ's love from working through you!

8:36 Satan's tactics are not new, as Psalm 44:22 says that, for God's sake, "are we killed all the day long." Psalms is referring to saved Israel going through the tribulation period, but the Holy Ghost, through the pen of the apostle Paul, applies it to us today in the dispensation of grace, as well.

When your focus is on the things of God, it is not on the things of this world. Since all unbelievers and most believers focus on the things of this world, their perspective is much different from the believer, who is allowing Christ to live in him. The former is focused on getting a good paying job, getting rich, having a good family, and enjoying all the lusts of the flesh. The latter is focused on what he has in Christ, which is all spiritual blessings. Since all unbelievers are dead spiritually, they cannot understand the things of God (I Corinthians 2:14). We have the mind of Christ (I Corinthians 2:16), and they have reprobate minds (1:28). Because of this and the fact that nothing can separate us from the love of Christ, unbelievers' attacks against us are all on the flesh level. Since we are concerned only with the spiritual level, we do not defend the removal of those fleshly things. Therefore, "we are accounted as sheep for the slaughter." In other words, Satan's forces, including all people who are children of the devil, think that we are nincompoops. And, because they are evil and we are not trying to stop them, they will do everything they can against us. That is why "we are killed all the day long." But, that is okay, because I am dead, and my "life is hid with Christ in God" (Colossians 3:3). So, they keep killing our flesh, which is just a wasted effort, because our flesh is already dead. Meanwhile, Christ is strong through us, living abundantly, and there is nothing they can do to stop it.

8:37 That is why this verse says that "in all these things we are more than conquerors." We have conquered Satan's forces, stopping them from doing anything to us, but that is not all. On top of that, Christ is living in us, which means that God's kingdom is growing through us. This makes us "MORE than conquerors!" Furthermore, God's kingdom will never stop growing. Isaiah 9:7 says regarding the Lord Jesus Christ: "Of the increase of His government and peace there shall be no end." This speaks of the abundant life that we have been talking about. God did not save you for you to lounge around eating grapes for all eternity. He saved you to work in Christ. His kingdom will increase for all eternity because Christ will live in us, but we can get started on that now by believing the sound doctrine found in Paul's epistles.

Note that this verse does not say that God delivers us from the sufferings that Satan sends our way. Rather, it says that "IN all these things we are more than conquerors." We have to go through suffering so that we can have God's will accomplished in us, which is for us to come into the knowledge of the truth (8:27 and I Timothy 2:4).

Note also that the way we are more than conquerors is "through Him that loved us" (8:37). This is in keeping with our identity being in Christ. "Christ liveth in me" (Galatians 2:20) to make me more than a conqueror. This keeps us from becoming prideful and gives the glory to God, so that others may be saved and come unto the knowledge of the truth.

8:38-39 Paul says that he is "persuaded." Of the 10 things listed, he only has firsthand experience with life and things present. The remaining things listed can only be known by someone in the spirit realm, and that someone must be God, or else Paul would not have believed what was told to him. Therefore, the reason he is persuaded about these things is because the Holy Ghost has communicated these things to his spirit (I Corinthians 2:13). By contrast, the reason, that all unbelievers and most Christians are not persuaded that nothing can separate them from the love of Christ, is because they have not read and believed Romans 8. If they were persuaded, they would want to walk after the Spirit, and Christ would live through them.

1) Death cannot separate us from God's love because Christ defeated death on the cross (I Corinthians 15:55-57).

2) Life cannot separate us from God's love because Christ lives in us (Galatians 2:20).

3) Angels cannot separate us from God's love because they are ministering spirits for saved people (Hebrews 1:14). If they sin, God can put them in chains to keep them from hurting us (II Peter 2:4).

4&5) Principalities and powers cannot separate us from God's love because Christ triumphed over the ones on Satan's side through the cross (Colossians 2:14-15).

6&7) Things present and things to come cannot separate us from God's love because the things that are not of God are temporal (II Corinthians 4:18), since the Lord Jesus Christ will destroy those things at His coming (II Peter 3:7-12).

8) Height cannot separate us from God's love, because no one is higher than God, since He dwells on "the sides of the north" (Psalm 48:2).

9) Depth cannot separate us from God's love because His wisdom and knowledge are so deep that no one can find them (11:33). Moreover, God created the deep (Psalm 104:5-6 and 135:6).

10) Any other creature cannot separate us from God's love because the Lord Jesus Christ is "King of kings and Lord of lords" (I Timothy 6:15 and Revelation 19:16). Therefore, no one can override His authority.

Note how I used scripture to prove every one of these points. This shows that God is the One Who persuaded Paul that nothing can separate us from the love of God.

Since God gave up His Own Son for us and gave us justification and glorification, no one can separate us from God's love. In 8:35, we were told of things the adversary does to try to separate us from God's love. Now, in 8:38-39, we are told of spiritual powers, such as Satan's devils, which will try to separate us from God's love, and all fall short. Therefore, we should glory in our sufferings, because they will produce an eternal weight of glory in us (II Corinthians 4:17). Therefore, we can be confident that, not only do our sufferings not take away our eternal life and spiritual blessings, but they actually enhance them.

How appropriate that the last thing we are told in Romans 8 is that the love of God "is in Christ Jesus our Lord" (8:39), because the whole chapter has been about us living in the Spirit as a result of who we are in Christ. Therefore, since we are in Christ and the love of God is in Christ, we cannot be separated from God's love.

9-11 Romans 9-11 are a parenthetical reference to Paul's letter to the Romans (Interesting how the dispensation of grace is a parenthetical dispensation in Israel's program, and Israel is a parenthetical reference within Romans, which is the foundational doctrinal book in the dispensation of grace.). Paul's goal in writing Romans is to "impart unto you some spiritual gift, to the end ye may be established" (1:11). For the most part, this gift is to know that they are dead to sin and alive unto Christ (6:11), and that they should live by faith (Romans 1:17) now that they have been saved by faith.

In Romans 6-8, Paul described this walk in faith for the believer. However, "the just shall live by faith" was a promise originally given to Israel under their program (Habakkuk 2:4). Israel's program involves God ruling the world with Israel (Revelation 5:10). In Acts 9, that program was set aside for the dispensation of grace. Therefore, doubt, with regard to God fulfilling His promises to us today, may arise, because Israel has yet to receive God's promises to them. After all, why should we suffer with Christ (8:17-18), believing God will make up for it in eternity, if God's promises to Israel will never be fulfilled?

Therefore, Paul spends three chapters with the Romans, showing that God was not unfaithful in not fulfilling His promises to Israel because God WILL fulfill them later. His promises to Israel are just delayed in being fulfilled, not because of God's failure, but because of the unbelief of Israel (Hebrews 3:19 and 4:11). Therefore, if we live by faith in the grace dispensation today, we can be certain that God will be faithful to give us the things He has promised in eternity.

Paul also writes these chapters to instill a sense of urgency into the body of Christ. God cut unbelieving Israel out of His olive tree (11:17), graffed the Gentiles into His tree (11:17), and will cut the unbelieving Gentiles out of the tree when He graffs Israel back in (11:22-26). Therefore, we should take advantage of God's mercies toward us today (11:30) by reading and believing God's Word so that others may be saved and come unto the knowledge of the truth through us (I Timothy 2:4), before the dispensation of grace ends.

9 The body of Christ is not a continuation of what Jesus started with Israel. God will still give Israel all of the things that He promised in the Old Testament to give them (vs. 4-5). The reason they have not received the promises yet is because of their unbelief. Thus, God's Israel is Israel in the spirit, rather than Israel in the flesh (vs. 7-13). For the most part, Israel in the flesh has not believed God. As such, they are subject to God's wrath. Yet, God's foreknowledge told Him that, if He showed mercy to Israel, the Gentiles would fear God (v. 22). Then, when He hardened Israel at Acts 7 and started the dispensation of grace, the Gentiles would believe God's gospel to them (vs. 25-26). Then, the Gentiles' belief will cause Israel to believe God after the rapture (vs. 27-28). The lesson to learn in all of this is that salvation is by faith, not by works, because Israel worked for righteousness and did not attain it, while the Gentiles had faith and received God's imputed righteousness (vs. 30-33). Therefore, God did not fail in keeping His promises, but Israel failed to believe God to give them those promises freely. This means that we can have faith in God to keep His promises to us today in the dispensation of grace.

9:1-4 Paul wrote Romans around the time of Acts 20:1-3. Paul had a great desire for Israel to be saved, such that he would soon go to Jerusalem, knowing full well that he would suffer and perhaps die there for preaching the gospel to the Jews. We know this because the Holy Ghost told Paul that, if he went to Jerusalem, the Jews would bind him and deliver him to the Gentiles (Acts 21:11). Paul responded to this by saying, "I am ready not to be bound only, but also to die at Jerusalem for the name of the Lord Jesus" (Acts 21:13). Therefore, Paul is not exaggerating when he says that he has "great heaviness and continual sorrow" (9:2) for the Jews. Of course, we do not need Acts 21:13 to show that Paul is telling the truth because we have the "witness in the Holy Ghost" (9:1) that what he is saying is true.

Sound doctrine for today is found in Paul's epistles. Your flesh does not want you to be strengthened with might in the inner man (Ephesians 3:16). Therefore, out of all scripture, your flesh fights the most against studying and believing Paul's epistles (Galatians 5:17). This is the main reason why Christianity regards Paul's epistles as being less authoritative than the rest of the New Testament. They view what he says more as his opinion, rather than as sound doctrine to be followed. Another reason for this view comes from the nature of today's dispensation. God says we are His adult sons (Galatians 4:3,6), while He tells Israel, even in the New Testament, that they are still servants to Him (Revelation 1:1, 2:20, 7:3, and 19:2,5). Because of this, Paul will "beseech" his audience to do something (12:1, 15:30, and 16:17), instead of "commanding" (I John 2:3-8) them to do it, just like you would beseech an adult to do something, but command a child to do it.

Because of these reasons and others, when Paul's epistles differ from Matthew – John, Christians believe the red letters of the gospels over the black letters of Paul's epistles. However, Paul says that what he writes comes from the Lord (I Corinthians 14:37). Peter also affirms that Paul's epistles are scripture (II Peter 3:15-16). Since all scripture is true (John 17:17), we can have the same confidence in Paul's epistles being true as we have in the rest of scripture. Therefore, Paul should not have to say that he has "witness in the Holy Ghost" (9:1) that what he is saying is true. We have this same "witness in the Holy Ghost" for all of Paul's epistles, because II Peter 1:20-21 tells us that all scripture are the very words of the Holy Ghost.

When Paul says that he could wish that he "were accursed from Christ" for Israel (9:3), he means that he is willing to give up his eternal life if it means that Israel would receive eternal life. Christians will say, "No, that's not true. He is not willing to give up his eternal life." However, being accursed from Christ means to be separated from Him. Since Paul's life is hid with Christ in God (Colossians 3:3), being separated from Christ means he would no longer be in God, which means he would not have eternal life. This conclusion can also be reached by examining Paul's other uses of the word "accursed" in his epistles (See I Corinthians 12:3 and Galatians 1:8-9).

Note that Paul says that he "could wish" (9:3). First, this tells us that this is not possible. After all, Paul just said that nothing can separate us from the love of Christ (8:35-39). Therefore, not even Paul's own desire to lose his salvation for Israel's salvation could cause him to go to hell. This also speaks to the eternal security of the believer. After all, if someone, who wants to give up his salvation, cannot do so, then someone, who commits the most heinous sins, also cannot lose his salvation. Second, this tells us that "hope," in Paul's epistles, is different from "wish," as we mentioned in 8:24-25. "Hope" is the confident expectation that something will happen based upon sound doctrine, while "wish" is something that he wants to happen, but it will not happen. Third, since Paul wants to go to hell so that Israel will be saved, this "wish" is something found in his spirit, because his flesh only wants to save itself (Ephesians 5:29). All of this put together shows the power of the love of Christ, such that it can overcome even your own flesh to the point of being willing to go to hell just so others will be saved! This should not surprise us because that is exactly what Christ did. "God commendeth His love toward us, in that, while we were yet sinners, Christ died for us" (5:8). He became "a curse for us" (Galatians 3:13), taking on our sin "that we might be made the righteousness of God in Him" (II Corinthians 5:21). Therefore, instead of changing the wording of this verse to make it sound like Paul really would not give up His eternal life, we should believe what the verse says, because it is probably the greatest example of the love of Christ, coming through a man other than Christ, that is recorded in scripture.

Thus, we see Paul's great love for Israel, and his actions back it up, as seen in Acts 21-28. Christians will talk about how Paul preached "easy-believism" and grace. However, as we have already learned, the purpose of grace is not that you can sin more, but it is so you can live for God (6:1-4). IN GRACE, Paul took a Nazarite vow (Acts 18:18), took four men with similar vows into the Jerusalem temple (Acts 21:23-24), and was arrested and almost killed (Acts 21:30-32). He probably remained a prisoner the rest of his life, as a result. Paul did this, even though he knew these things would happen to him (Acts 21:11). Thus, Paul allowed the love of Christ to come through him to such an extent that he used God's grace upon him to perform purification rites under the Mosaic law, knowing full well that he would be arrested, all in hopes that such a display would cause Israel to be saved. And, Biblical scholars, in their fancy homes and Armani suits, dare to accuse Paul of trying to get out of serving God by preaching easy-believism!

Paul says, here, that Israel has six things. 1) The Adoption: Paul has just finished saying that we, in the dispensation of grace, have been adopted as sons of God (see 8:14-17). Originally, however, the promise of adoption as sons was given to Israel. Israel will not receive the adoption until Jesus Christ's second coming (Revelation 21:7), because they do not receive the atonement until then (Acts 3:19-20). Therefore, "the adoption" refers to the national day of atonement for the nation of Israel at Jesus' second coming.

2) The Glory: Israel will receive glory in God's kingdom on earth, because they had faith in what God told them.

3) The Covenants: Under Moses, God told Israel that they were to obey His voice and keep His covenant. "These are the words which thou shalt speak unto the children of ISRAEL" (Exodus 19:5-6), not Gentiles. Israel "rejected His statutes, and His covenant that He made with their fathers" (II Kings 17:15), such that they became Satan's "lawful captive" (Isaiah 49:24). Because God is faithful, He "redeemed Jacob, and ransomed him from the hand of him that was stronger than he" (Jeremiah 31:11). God then said, "Behold, the days come, saith the Lord, that I will make a new covenant with the house of Israel, and with the house of Judah" (Jeremiah 31:31). Under this new covenant, God will "forgive their iniquity, and...remember their sin no more" (Jeremiah 31:34). These verses are clear that God made the old and new covenants with Israel. He did NOT make these covenants with us today. Christians will say, "Oh, but we are spiritual Israel, because of Israel's unbelief. Therefore, the covenants pertain to us today." There are several problems with this line of thinking. First, if God was going to remove His covenants from Israel due to their unbelief, He never would have made the new covenant with them, since God's Word is clear that Israel has been in unbelief throughout its whole history ("Which of the prophets have not your fathers persecuted?" (Acts 7:52)). The second problem is that Paul specifically says here that the covenants pertain to Israel. They do not pertain to us today. The revelation that the Lord Jesus Christ gave to Paul fulfills the Word of God (Colossians 1:25). Therefore, God has the final say so on the matter through Paul, and God still says that the covenants pertain to Israel. The third problem is that we cannot be under the new covenant today, because those under that covenant will never sin again. God says that, under the new covenant, He will "cause [Israel] to walk in My statutes, and [they] shall keep My judgments, and do them" (Ezekiel 36:27). That is why I John 3:9 says that "whosoever is born of God doth not commit sin...; He cannot sin." Therefore, regardless of where you are in scripture, the Bible is clear that the old and new covenants pertain to Israel in their program. They do NOT apply to us today.

4) The Giving of the Law: The law was given to Moses for all of Israel, as we saw in Exodus 19:5-6. Paul even mentioned this in 3:1-2 by saying that, to the Jews, "were committed the oracles of God." Therefore, Christianity should not promote obeying the ten commandments. Rather, we should give unbelievers the gospel and give believers sound doctrine from Paul's epistles so that they may come unto the knowledge of the truth (I Timothy 2:4). Christians will say, "How dare you speak against the ten commandments! They came directly from God. Are you saying that we should kill, steal,

commit adultery, etc.?" Of course I am not saying that! We SHOULD obey the ten commandments, but we should do so under grace, and not under the framework of the law (6:14).

5) The Service of God: Granted, we can serve God in the dispensation of grace, but this does not say "the SERVING of God." It says "the SERVICE of God," meaning a particular service, which involves Israel in the service of God in the temple. God gave them the book of Leviticus so that they would know the proper way to serve God in the temple. Today, the body of Christ as a whole is "the temple of God," because the Spirit of God dwells in us (I Corinthians 3:16). Therefore, we serve God by presenting our bodies as living sacrifices to God (12:1), allowing Christ to live in us (Galatians 2:20), as opposed to an outward formality of service. The Levitical laws "are a shadow of things to come; but the body is of Christ" (Colossians 2:17).

6) The Promises: This is everything that God will give Israel for all eternity, such as reigning with Him on earth as kings and priests of God (Revelation 5:10), ruling over all the Gentiles on earth (Deuteronomy 32:8), and enjoying the riches of God's new earth (Isaiah 61:6).

These six things mentioned are specifically for Israel. We should not be so selfish as to try to claim them for ourselves. After all, God has already "blessed us with all spiritual blessings in heavenly places in Christ" (Ephesians 1:3), and He will use the ages to come to shew unto us "the exceeding riches of His grace" (Ephesians 2:7). What more could you want? Therefore, we should not try to steal Israel's blessings away from them, too!

A final point to make about these verses is that Paul says that he has "great heaviness and continual sorrow in [his] heart" (9:2) for Israel. I have often heard Christianity say that Christians should be the happiest people on the earth. While it is true that we are told to "rejoice evermore" (I Thessalonians 5:16) because of everything we have in Christ, Christians, who are allowing Christ to live through them, should actually be unhappy. Joy comes from within, while HAPPI-ness is based upon HAPPEN-stance—things that happen to someone. But, the Christian's "conversation is in heaven" (Philippians 3:20). Since Satan is "the god of this world" (II Corinthians 4:4), and he has the world following his lie program (Ephesians 2:2), we should, for the most part, be unhappy with circumstances, because the world is filled with unbelief. That is why Paul was continually sorry and why "Jesus wept" (John 11:35). Since we have noted that Paul's sorrow came from the love of Christ coming through him to the Jews, we can conclude that, if Christians are happy with the things that are happening around them in this world of unbelief, they must not have much of the love of Christ demonstrated in their lives.

9:5 All of these promises to Israel could not be fulfilled when Israel was Satan's lawful captive due to their sins (Isaiah 49:24-25). Therefore, Christ came. "Of whom" (9:5) tells us that Christ was a Jew. This does not mean that He only came to save Jews, because Paul says that He gave His life a ransom for all (I Timothy 2:6). In order to save us, Jesus Christ had to be our kinsman. So, how can He save Gentiles when He is a Jew? He does so because Jesus was only a Jew "as concerning the flesh." As concerning our soul, which is what Jesus saves for us, Jesus was of the human race, which means that He can be the kinsmen redeemer of both Jew and Gentile, even though His flesh was of the Jews. However, Paul's point is that, because God made promises to Israel, Jesus Christ was born a Jew. In fact, Paul will later "say that Jesus Christ was a minister of the circumcision for the truth of God, to confirm the promises made unto the fathers: And that the Gentiles might glorify God for His mercy" (15:8-9). Therefore, Jesus' sacrifice saves both Jews and Gentiles.

9:6 "Not as though the word of God hath taken none effect" (9:6) means that the word of God DID take effect. The promises, in 9:4, took effect upon the believing remnant of Israel. Israel, as a whole, rejected their Messiah (John 12:37). That is why Jesus told them that the kingdom of God would be taken from them and be given to a nation bringing forth the fruits thereof (Matthew 21:43). According to Luke 12:32, this "nation" is the little flock. They need to be "a kingdom of priests" (Exodus 19:6) to reach the rest of the world with the gospel. Not enough people in Israel believed the gospel for God to send them out to the Gentiles. Therefore, God put Israel's program on hold and began the dispensation of grace with Paul in Acts 9. The word of God still took effect upon the little flock in that they will still be part of God's eternal kingdom on earth, but that kingdom has yet to come to fruition due to the unbelief of Israel as a whole. This is all succinctly summed up in Paul's statement: "They are not all Israel, which are of Israel" (9:6). In other words, just because man CALLS them Israel, it does not mean that they ARE Israel. God's nation is "the Israel of God" (Galatians 6:16), not the Israel of man.

Man says that the nation of Israel was re-established in 1948. God says, "that's not Israel. My Israel is the one that has faith in Me in that program." That is what Paul is telling his audience. They need to understand that God set aside His earthly program, due to the unbelief of Israel, and that God's Israel is the one that has faith in Him. Therefore, when Israel did not receive the six things mentioned in 9:4, it was not because God's word did not take effect. Rather, it was because there was not a large enough spiritual nation of Israel for God's word to take effect on, such that God put that program on hold until there would be a large enough group of believers to be a kingdom of priests to the world. If Paul's audience does not understand this, they may think that God did not hold up His end of the bargain. If they think that, they will think that God will not give them eternal life. If that is the case, "let us eat and drink; for to morrow we die" (I Corinthians 15:32), which means living after the lusts of the flesh rather than walking after the Spirit. Therefore, the body of Christ's effectiveness is predicated upon us properly understanding what happened to Israel. Since most Christians do not have this understanding, they live after the flesh, rather than after the

Spirit.

9:7-8 Now, Paul gives an explanation of the statement he made to close 9:6. Abraham had a son named Ishmael. As such, he is a child of Abraham, but God said, "in Isaac shall thy seed be called" (9:7). Therefore, although Ishmael was a child of Abraham, he was not counted as Abraham's seed. This means that the seed is not physical Israel, but it is spiritual Israel. Jesus explained this to the Jewish religious leaders of His day. They said, "we be Abraham's seed" (John 8:33). Jesus said, "I know that ye are Abraham's seed," meaning that Jesus knows that they are physical Jews, "but ye seek to kill Me" (John 8:37), meaning that they are not children of promise. He further said, "If ye were Abraham's children, ye would do the works of Abraham" (John 8:39). In other words, God does not look for "children of the flesh;" He looks for "children of the promise" (9:8). In other words, God's children are the ones who please Him, and the ones who please Him are the ones who have faith in what God has told them (Hebrews 11:6). If they have faith, they receive the promise. Because Jesus Christ had faith in what God told Him, God said, "This is my beloved Son, in Whom I am well pleased" (Matthew 3:17). By contrast, God looked at the Jewish religious leaders and saw that they did not have faith. Therefore, although they were Jews, according to the flesh, they were not Jews, according to the spirit, making them children of the devil (John 8:44).

What this tells us is that, when God looked on the earth in Acts 7, He did not see 2 million Jews, even though there were probably that many physical Jews on earth at the time. He only saw several thousand Jews, because that was all who had believed the gospel of the kingdom. God said, "I need another 144,000 saved Jews (based on Revelation 7:4 and 14:1) before I have a kingdom of priests. Therefore, I will set Israel aside for the time being and start dispensing grace, irrespective of physical status, through the ministry of Paul." Now, God explains to the body of Christ through Paul that "the children of the flesh...are not the children of God: but the children of the promise are counted for the seed" (9:8) so that we do not worry that God will abandon us. Remember, the word of God did take effect upon the believing remnant of Israel. Therefore, even though the body of Christ may be in the minority, we can still have faith that God will give us the promises that He has made to us, because we are counted as the seed because we have faith in the gospel given to us.

9:9 God Himself promised to come and give Sarah a son. Thus, it was a promise of God, and it was a miraculous birth. Abraham did not work to receive that promise. It was Abraham's faith in this promise of God that justified him (Genesis 15:4-6), as Paul pointed out earlier (4:3). So, too, those, who "are of Israel" (9:6), are those who have faith in God's promises to Israel (9:4). In other words, Abraham believed God's offer, and God turned that offer into a promise. Similarly for us today, we believe God's offer of eternal life, and God turns that offer into a promise. But, the point is that all saved people, from all dispensations, are children of promise, not children of flesh. Therefore, when unbelieving, physical Jews appear before God to be judged, God will say, "I never knew you" (Matthew 7:23), because "man looketh on the outward appearance, but the Lord looketh on the heart" (I Samuel 16:7). Because they are not Jews inwardly, they are not real Jews (2:29).

9:10-12 Ishmael and Isaac were sons of Abraham, but they had different mothers. If you were to think after the flesh, you may think that that was why Isaac was the seed, when Ishmael was not. Therefore, in the case of Jacob and Esau, God had them born of the same parents and at the same time. Moreover, he had Esau born first. The law says that the firstborn receives the greater inheritance. Therefore, if only one was to receive the promise, the flesh would say that Esau would receive the promise. However, God was not going by the flesh; He was going by promise. Therefore, the seed line goes through Jacob (the secondborn), not Esau (the firstborn).

Now, since Isaac and Jacob were both the secondborn, you may think that God is still going by the flesh, but just in a different way than man does. Therefore, Paul inserts the parenthetical reference of 9:11 to explain that this is not the case. Note that God told Isaac that "the elder shall serve the younger" before Jacob and Esau were even born (Genesis 25:23-26). This makes it clear that God did not call Jacob the seed based upon any works that he had done. Rather, Jacob was called by God by election to be the seed (9:11).

Immediately, the Calvinist jumps up and says that God, in His sovereignty, overrode man's free will by condemning Esau to hell and giving Jacob eternal life with God. However, let us not forget that Paul has already mentioned election and calling. 8:29-30 says that those, that God foreknew, He predestinated and called. This shows that God's calling starts with His foreknowledge. Before Esau and Jacob were born, God knew that Esau would not believe Him, and Jacob would believe Him. Based on that foreknowledge, He called Jacob, and not Esau. Genesis shows this to be true, since Esau despised his birthright (Genesis 25:31-34 and Hebrews 12:16), while Jacob valued it. Therefore, God extended the Abrahamic covenant to Jacob (Genesis 28:13-15).

Election was mentioned in 8:33. Based upon what we learned in 8:29-30, we concluded that the elect are a group of people, who God will bless, because of their faith in Him. I Peter 1:2 says that believing Israel are the "elect according to the foreknowledge of God the Father." This makes it clear that election, like being called, is based upon God's foreknowledge. Therefore, God's calling to elect Jacob to be saved and Esau to be unsaved is not based upon His sovereignty. Rather, it is based upon His foreknowledge of the free-will decisions that Jacob would make to believe God and that Esau would make not to believe God.

Now that we have gotten through the smoke and mirrors of the Calvinist, we can look at what the passage is really talking about. 9:9-12 says that God made Isaac and Jacob the children of promise because His foreknowledge told Him that they would have faith in God, while Ishmael and Esau were children only of the flesh because His foreknowledge told Him that they would not have faith in God. Therefore, God chose the people that He did entirely based on spiritual considerations, not on fleshly considerations.

The application to the context of Romans 9 is that the flesh would say that the Jewish religious leaders are the seed line and the promises of 9:4 pertain to them. Therefore, when they did not receive the promises, God must have failed. However, because God judges based upon the spiritual, rather than the carnal, He looked at the Jewish religious leaders' unbelief and took the kingdom away from them because of their unbelief, not because God failed. By the way, this taking away of the kingdom from the religious leaders was also based upon God's foreknowledge, as He prophesied, in Deuteronomy 32:21, that this would happen. Thus, the true Israel of God started with promise with Isaac then Jacob, and it continued through the believing remnant of Israel (the foolish nation of Deuteronomy 32:21), rather than through the people who man said were Israel, because God called only those, who would believe Him, to be part of His Israel. Thus, "they are not all Israel [of God], which are of Israel [of man]" (9:6).

9:13 This is a quote of Malachi 1:2-3. By reading Malachi 1:1-5, we learn that loving Jacob means loving the nation of Israel and hating Esau means hating the nation of Edom. There, God says that He will "throw down" Edom's building, while He will magnify Israel (Malachi 1:4-5). John 3:16 says that "God so loved the world." Romans 5:8 says that God commendeth His love toward us by having Christ die for us. II Peter 3:9 says that God is "not willing that any should perish, but that all should come to repentance." Therefore, when we are told that God hates Esau and loves Jacob, we cannot conclude that God forces Israel to be saved, while He forces Edom to be lost, because it is against God's will and love that some people be lost.

Instead of taking this verse out of context, we must build upon what we just learned in 9:10-12, which is that God elected Israel to be saved and Edom to be lost, because His foreknowledge allowed Him to see the free-will decisions of these groups and determine that Israel would make the free-will decision to believe God, while Edom would make the free-will decision not to believe God. Perhaps a little background of Israel will make this clearer.

In Genesis 11:1, "the whole earth was of one language, and of one speech." Man rebelled against God, and God saw that He needed to create nations to keep man from being lost from Him forever (Genesis 11:6). According to Genesis 10:25, God divided the world into nations during the days of Peleg. God started the nation of Israel with Abram (Genesis 12:1-3), through whom God promises to reconcile the earth back to Himself (Exodus 19:5-6). According to Genesis 11:16-26, Peleg was Abram's great-great-great grandfather, being born 191 years before Abram. If we assume the

Calvinists are correct in saying that God uses His sovereignty to force people to believe, then God would have started His nation of people with Peleg at the same time that He divided the world into nations, since God wants all people to be saved (I Timothy 2:4). In other words, if God forces people to be saved or lost, He would have at least forced some of the people over the next 200 years and five generations to receive eternal life. Why wait 200 years before starting Israel? Thus, this 200-year gap between Babel and Abram shows that God's foreknowledge told Him that He needed to divide the world into nations in the days of Peleg so that, 200 years later, there would be born a man, named Abram, who would make the free-will decision to believe the gospel God would give to him (Genesis 15:4-6). In other words, God created nations at Babel so that someone, 200 years later, would choose to believe God's Word to him. Then, there would be believers, who would come out of Israel, over the next 2,000 years. Then, at least 2,000 years afterward (allowing for the body of Christ), there would be at least 144,000 more believers that would come out of Israel during the first half of the tribulation period after the rapture of the body of Christ (Revelation 7:4). Then, it will take another 1,000 years for that believing nation of Israel to reach the Gentiles with the gospel during Jesus' millennial reign. Thus, the fact, that it takes over 5,000 years for God to reconcile the earth back to Himself, shows that God does not force people to believe the gospel. What this tells us is that, the reason God hated the nation of Edom, was because it is an unbelieving nation, while God loved the nation of Israel, because, eventually, it will be a believing nation.

A great example of this, individually speaking, is seen in Saul and David. God removed Saul from being king because he did not slaughter animals in a battle, but saved them to sacrifice to the Lord (I Samuel 15:9-23). God then set up David to be king (I Samuel 16:12-13). David proceeded to commit adultery (II Samuel 11:3-4) and murder (II Samuel 11:14-17). Not only did God not remove David from being king, but He also forgave him of his sin (4:7-8). Obviously, David's sin is greater than Saul's sin. Therefore, it can be said that God hated Saul by removing him as king, but loved David by continuing to bless him. The reason is because God judged both men according to the heart (I Samuel 16:7) and found that David was a man after God's Own heart (Acts 13:22), while Saul was not.

Thus, God's election and calling (7:11) are based upon His foreknowledge of man's free-will decisions. Applied to Romans 9, the reason Paul brings up God hating Esau and loving Jacob is because, when those two nations were in Rebecca's womb, God knew that the end result of the nation of Esau would be unbelief, and the end result of the nation of Israel would be belief.

Why is this important? Because God has now changed dispensations without fulfilling His promises to Israel. However, the example of Jacob and Esau shows that God's plan with Israel was not an educated guess. After the cross, God did not say, "Oh well. I thought Israel would believe, but they did not. Let me try something else with the Gentiles. Maybe this body-of-Christ idea of Mine will work instead." No! When God chose Jacob before he was born, God knew that Jacob would believe. Similarly, God used His foreknowledge about the body of Christ to know that we would, eventually, believe Him. In other words, at the beginning of Acts 9, the Lord Jesus Christ declared, "The body of Christ I love, and the rest of the world I hate, because I see that only the body of Christ will believe. And, because they will believe, I am calling Paul to give the gospel to them." In other words, Jacob and Esau serve as an example to the fact that God called Paul and started the body of Christ because He knew that the body of Christ would believe. As such, we can have full confidence that God will fulfill His promises to us and to Israel, based on how God handled Jacob and Esau.

9:14 Isaac is Abraham's seed, not Ishmael (9:7). Similarly, God loved Jacob and hated Esau before they were even born (9:10-13). This may seem unfair, which is why Paul asks the question: "Is there unrighteousness with God?" (9:14). The answer is "God forbid."

First, we need to understand that man has earned death, not life. In 3:10, we learned that "there is none righteous." 3:23 says that "all have sinned, and come short of the glory of God." Since all are deserving of eternal damnation in the lake of fire, God is not unrighteous in giving man what he deserves. In fact, it is only by God's grace that Jacob received the gift of eternal life. As we have already learned, the reason God favored Jacob over Esau is because His foreknowledge allowed Him to see that Jacob would believe God, while Esau would not. Therefore, God's pronouncement of "the elder shall serve the younger" (9:12) is really a prophecy based on their free-will decisions, rather than being a case of God's unrighteousness.

9:15,17-18 Now that we understand that God acts based upon man's future free-will decisions, we can begin to understand why God treats some unbelievers better than others. In 9:15, we have the example of Israel under Moses. They had disobeyed God by serving other gods (Exodus 32:2-6). They deserved to be consumed by God (Exodus 32:10). However, God's name was attached to them, due to the miracles He had done through them in Egypt (Exodus 32:12-13). Therefore, instead of consuming them, God goes with them into the Promised Land. God says that He will make His goodness pass before them and will proclaim His name before them. In doing so, He will shew mercy on whom He will shew mercy (Exodus 33:19). So, basically God is saying that apostate Israel should have been consumed under Moses, but He shewed mercy to them. Why? Because it caused the Gentile nations that they encountered to see God's mercy so that they may believe that He is the only God.

9:17 gives an example of God hardening an unbeliever. Exodus 9:16 is quoted here. The context is that God raised up Pharaoh and hardened his heart so that he would mistreat Israel even more so that God could cut Pharaoh off with plagues so that the whole earth would know that God is the only God and His name would be declared among all the earth (Exodus

9:12-16). Therefore, in this case, God hardened an unbeliever so that the Gentiles may believe He is the only God. This was not unrighteous because Egypt deserved God's wrath anyway, due to their unbelief.

In the first case, God shewed mercy to Israel, and His name was proclaimed before them. In the second case, God hardened Pharaoh, and His name was proclaimed to the whole earth. Either way, God's name was proclaimed. God's foreknowledge means that God knows man's response to all possible scenarios. He shewed mercy to Israel, because His foreknowledge told Him that His name would be proclaimed in doing so. He hardened Pharaoh's heart, because His foreknowledge told Him that His name would be proclaimed in doing so.

In summary, because "all have sinned, and come short of the glory of God" (3:23), all of us are subject to the wrath of God. Yet, because God loves us, He provided a way for us to be saved. If we have faith in what God tells us, He is pleased with us (Hebrews 11:6) and gives us the gift of eternal life (6:23). If we do not have faith, we get the just punishment of our sin which is death in the lake of fire (Revelation 20:11-15). God's foreknowledge tells Him who will never believe the gospel no matter what happens, and it tells Him those who will believe under specific scenarios. Therefore, God can create the scenarios necessary so that all, who would believe the gospel, will believe the gospel.

For example, God knew that Pharaoh would never believe, regardless of the circumstances, but He knew that sending plagues upon Egypt would cause the earth to fear the God of Israel. ("The fear of the Lord is the beginning of knowledge" (Proverbs 1:7).) Therefore, He hardened Pharaoh's heart so that He could send the plagues so that others may believe. Then, when Israel sinned against Him, He knew that showing mercy by bringing them unto the Promised Land would lead others to believe. (They would hear the word of God (10:17) now that they feared the Lord.) Therefore, He did not consume Israel.

Now, we apply what we have learned to the situation in Romans 9. The whole world united against God in Genesis 11. So, God chose Abram and started the nation of Israel so that they might be saved and then they can go out with the gospel to save the Gentiles. Because of the unbelief of Israel, in Matthew - John, God chose "a foolish nation" (saved Israel) to provoke the rest of Israel to jealousy (10:19 and Deuteronomy 32:21). In early Acts, apostate Israel still did not have faith in God. Therefore, at the end of Acts 7, God set aside the nation of Israel as His people, and He called Gentiles His people so that they may provoke Israel to jealousy, which is the point that Paul will make in 11:11.

Israel was in unbelief in Exodus 33, and God showed them mercy so that Gentiles might be saved. Israel was in unbelief in Acts 7, and God hardened them so that Gentiles might be saved. Neither action is unrighteous because unbelievers still go to hell either way. God acts based upon His foreknowledge of what will cause people to be saved. Therefore, God demonstrates His graciousness, regardless of how He treats unbelievers on this earth, rather than unrighteousness, because His actions lead people to be saved.

If we look at the whole picture, we can see that jealousy is a motivating factor for people to believe the gospel. After Adam sinned, God treated everyone the same. The result was that, in Noah's day, "the wickedness of man was great in the earth, and that every imagination of the thoughts of his heart was only evil continually" (Genesis 6:5). Then, at the Tower of Babel, the whole world was united against God. 2,000 years went by during the first 11 chapters of Genesis, and the world had twice ended up being unbelievers. Therefore, God started playing favorites. He started the nation of Israel and placed them "above all people that are upon the face of the earth" (Deuteronomy 7:6). Even though Israel was in unbelief, God showed mercy to them in Exodus 33 so the Gentiles would get jealous and have faith in God. In early Acts, God did miracles through believing Israel so that unbelieving Israel would be jealous (10:19). However, unbelieving Israel was so hardened against God that they would not believe. Therefore, God hardened Israel some more by setting them aside at the stoning of Stephen. He then gave the miracles to the Gentiles to provoke Israel to jealousy (11:11) so that they will believe after the rapture of the body of Christ (11:25-26). Therefore, when God hated Esau but loved Jacob, He was not being unrighteous. Rather, He recognized the lusts of the flesh and used those lusts (jealousy) so that people might be saved.

This explains why God started reconciling the earth back to Himself in Genesis 12 through Israel, set aside that program in Acts 7, started reconciling the heaven back to Himself in Acts 9 through the body of Christ, and will reconcile the earth back to Himself through Israel after the rapture of the body of Christ. God knew that He had to make Israel His chosen people, and then set them aside in their unbelief, before the Gentiles, as a whole would believe. God also knew that Israel would not believe until the Gentiles believe. Therefore, God started Israel's program, put it on hold, is saving the Gentiles now, and will save Israel once the Gentiles are saved. "O the depth of the riches both of the wisdom and knowledge of God!" (11:33).

See how convoluted things have to be in order for man to be saved? How, then, could anyone believe the Calvinists regarding predestination!?

9:16 "Him that willeth," in this context, is Moses. Moses asked for mercy from God for Israel and they received it, but they received mercy because God wanted to show them mercy, not because Moses willed it to happen. "Him that runneth" (9:16) would be someone who tries to earn God's mercy. We see this today in the legalism of Christianity. What this verse shows is that man is powerless to change his condition. He cannot will himself to have eternal life, nor can he work his way into heaven. Instead, he needs to recognize God's plan and get in line with that. Since God has revealed today that we have eternal life when we trust in Jesus' death, burial, and resurrection as atonement for our sin (I Corinthians 15:3-4), we need to believe that gospel to receive eternal life. Since God has revealed that His treasures are found in Christ (Colossians 3:2-3), we need to read and believe God's Word so that we realize those treasures.

By contrast, most people have it in their will that they will earn heaven themselves, and then they run to do so. If they do this, they are unbelievers. God will show them mercy or harden them so that others will be saved, but they will not be saved themselves, because they have not aligned themselves with God's plan.

9:19 The context of this verse is unbelievers. Because they have sinned and refuse to believe the gospel, they will go to hell. That is why God found fault with them. Granted, they cannot resist God's will in terms of being shown mercy or being hardened, but that does not matter, because they still made the free-will choice not to believe the gospel. Since they made that choice, they will suffer eternal torment in the lake of fire. Temporary mercy or hardening on this earth does not matter in the view of eternity, just like the temporary suffering of the body of Christ for living godly does not matter (8:18 and II Timothy 3:12).

9:20 Calvinists use these verses to say that God forces some people to have eternal life and forces others to have eternal death. After all, no one can resist God's will, and you have no right, as a man, to question God.

However, we must remember that the context is unbelievers. God's will is for ALL men to be saved, including those who end up in hell (I Timothy 2:4). This means that, if not resisting God's will means that I have no free will, God would force all people to be saved. Therefore, we are only not able to resist God's will in light of the free-will choices that we have already made. If we choose to believe the gospel, God has promised to give us eternal life. Even if we rebel against the sanctification process that God tries to instill in us in this life, God will still give us eternal life (Philippians 1:6 and II Timothy 2:13). Conversely, if we choose not to believe the gospel, God may, in this life, either have mercy on us or He may harden us. In the case of Israel in Exodus 33, God chose to have mercy on them. In the case of Israel during Jesus' first coming, God gave the gospel to Israel through John the Baptist and Jesus, and they made the free-will choice not to believe (John 12:37-38), fulfilling Isaiah 53:1. Because of this, God hardened their hearts so that they could not believe (John 12:39-40), fulfilling Isaiah 6:10. In the former case of believers, there is no injustice with God, because He saw our faith and rewarded us based on that faith. In the latter cases of unbelievers, there is no injustice with God, because He saw their unbelief and will punish them forever in the lake of fire, even if He does decide temporarily to be merciful to them while they are on earth.

9:21 Note how this verse says "the same lump." Based upon what we just learned in 9:20, there are two lumps. One lump is believers, and the other is unbelievers. All people make the free-will decision as to what lump they will be a part of. If they choose to believe God, we already know that God will give them eternal life. Therefore, Paul does not talk about what happens to them. Besides, the context is unbelievers. Therefore, Paul focuses on the lump of unbelievers here. Out of this lump of unbelievers, God makes some vessels "unto honour," meaning that He is merciful unto them, and He makes some vessels "unto dishonour," meaning that He hardens them. We have already learned that God makes this decision so as to maximize the number of people who will believe, and He is not unjust in His decisions with the unbelievers, because all of these people have already decided not to believe God.

9:22-24 Because the lump, in 9:21, is all unbelievers, all of the vessels made, in 9:21, whether they be "unto honour" or "unto dishonour," are "vessels of wrath" (9:22), because they will all ultimately end up in the lake of fire. Here, Paul is talking about apostate Israel. Some were made "unto honour" in Exodus 33, because God proclaimed His name to the Gentiles by showing mercy unto them. Others were made "unto dishonour" in Matthew – Acts, because God hardened them in order to save the Gentiles. However, because they are all unbelieving Israel, i.e., of the same lump, they will all spend eternity in hell, making them all "vessels of wrath."

The "longsuffering," of 9:22, refers to the fact that Israel was in unbelief throughout her whole history. Under the power of the Holy Ghost, Stephen recounted Israel's history in Acts 7:2-50, leading to the conclusion: "Ye stiffnecked and uncircumcised in heart and ears, ye do always resist the Holy Ghost: as your fathers did, so do ye" (Acts 7:51). Therefore, God shewed mercy on Israel, i.e., the vessels of wrath, in Exodus 33, and they continued in their apostasy from then until Acts 7.

This passage gives us two reasons why God shewed mercy to these "vessels of wrath fitted to destruction" (9:22). First, He shewed His wrath and made His power known (9:22) by the five cycles of chastisement that Israel went through (Leviticus 26:14-39). The result was that, when God set aside Israel and called Paul in Acts 9, the Gentiles believed the mystery gospel, and the body of Christ was formed. In other words, the reason that God suffered long with unbelieving Israel from Exodus 33 through Acts 7 was so the Gentiles would fear the Lord so that they would believe the gospel when it was presented to them through Paul.

The second reason God suffered long with Israel is so He could "make known the riches of His glory on the vessels of mercy" (9:23). In other words, by inserting the dispensation of grace in the middle of Israel's program, Israel will see that they need to believe the gospel of the kingdom in order to have eternal life. Thus, after the rapture takes place, Israel will be saved (11:26). Revelation 7:3-4 mentions that 144,000 Jews are saved by the midway point of the tribulation period. We never see such a large group of believers in Israel's history. Why? Because they have to be provoked to jealousy by Gentile salvation (11:11) during the dispensation of grace before they will believe the gospel that God gives to them in their program. Thus, God's longsuffering, during Israel's program, accomplishes salvation in the mystery program, which leads to salvation in the prophecy program. (This is also seen grammatically in that the second reason is given after a colon, which shows that it is really part of the first reason.)

9:24 defines the vessels of mercy as those who God called. This includes all believers from all dispensations, because we are all part of the same "lump" of believers. We know that Paul is referring to both programs because Paul says, "not of the Jews only, but also of the Gentiles" (9:24). Then, he quotes two passages from Hosea to show that "the Gentiles" refers to those saved during the mystery program (9:25-26). Then, he quotes Isaiah 10:22 to show that "the Jews," who are vessels of mercy, are the believing remnant of Israel's program (9:27). Now, this is not to say that Jews cannot be saved today or that Gentiles cannot be saved during Israel's program. But, God uses the term "Jews" here to define all believers in Israel's program, and "Gentiles" here to define all believers in the mystery program. This is also the case in 11:25-26.

Note also that the vessels of mercy were "afore prepared unto glory" (9:23). This goes back to God's foreknowledge. Before God made the world, He knew who the believers would be. Therefore, "before the foundation of the world" (Ephesians 1:4), God chose the body of Christ to be in Him. Also, "from the foundation of the world" (Matthew 25:34), God prepared a kingdom for believers from Israel's program. This means that God had the end result in mind when He created the heaven and the earth (Genesis 1:1). That is why God is called "the Father of glory" (Ephesians 1:17).

We should also note that 9:22-23 is another argument against Calvinism's predestination. If we believe in predestination and no free will of man, God has condemned some to hell and given eternal life to others, and there is nothing we can do to change that. If that is the case, God would just let man live out His predetermined plan and then execute wrath and mercy in the end, as He had prescribed. 9:22, though, says that God is "willing to shew His wrath," "make His power known," and endure "with much longsuffering the vessels of wrath" just so "He might make known the riches of His glory on the vessels of mercy." This shows that it takes God's wrath for Gentiles to make the free-will choice to believe the gospel and have eternal life. If Calvinism's predestination is true, God would skip the whole showing of His wrath until the end on judgment day.

Another argument against Calvinism's predestination is that it is always a minority of people who are saved. Since God gave His Son so that we might have life, it would make better sense that God would predestinate the majority of people to be saved, and only a minority would go to hell. In other

170

words, if God forces people into heaven or hell, why not force the majority into heaven, since the price of His Son was so great in order to give man eternal life?

9:25-26 Paul now quotes two passages from Hosea to show that God planned the body of Christ all along. The first quote is from Hosea 2:23. There, the context is that the Gentiles will become God's people in God's kingdom on earth in Israel's program. While that is true, the Holy Ghost, through the pen of the apostle Paul, now says that this verse also applies to the current dispensation of grace. (The Holy Ghost could not have revealed this until Paul, because it was part of God's "hidden wisdom" (I Corinthians 2:7) until then.)

The second quote is from Hosea 1:10. The context, there, is clearly Israel finally entering into God's kingdom on earth, but the Holy Ghost, through Paul, says that this verse also says that the Gentiles, who were not God's people in Israel's program, are now God's people in today's dispensation of grace.

The fact, that the Holy Ghost applies scripture to the Gentiles, that was originally meant for the Jews, is another proof that God had the Gentiles in mind all along, even when He was supposedly speaking only to the Jews. Acts 17:30 says that God "winked at" the times of the Gentiles' ignorance during Israel's program. These "winks" may be seen in that God "spoke" to the Gentiles at the same time He spoke to the Jews. In other words, the Gentiles were ignorant until the Holy Ghost could reveal His knowledge to them once the mystery was revealed to Paul.

9:27-28 At the same time, Paul does not want us thinking that God is through with Israel. God made promises to Israel (9:4), and "He will finish the work" (9:28). Paul quotes Isaiah 10:22 that says that a remnant of Israel will be saved. The context refers to the tribulation period when the Antichrist is trying to convert all of Israel to his apostate religion. It is important to note this context, because there is no "remnant" of Israel right now, since Israel's program was set aside 2,000 years ago. However, when God will pick up Israel's program again after the rapture, "a remnant shall be saved." When God does pick up Israel's program again, God will perform "a short work." In other words, He will not wait 1,500 years to send the Messiah like He did before. This time, it will just be however long it takes for the Antichrist to fulfill Daniel 9:26 plus the seven-year tribulation period of Daniel 9:27 before God finishes the work, i.e., saving Israel. So, why did He take so long the first time? Because He "endured with much longsuffering the vessels of wrath," i.e., Israel, so that He might save the Gentiles (9:22-23). Why will He cut the work short this time (9:28)? Because "except those days should be shortened, there should no flesh be saved" (Matthew 24:22). That is why Jesus says that He will "come quickly" (Revelation 22:20). Christianity says "Jesus is coming soon," but He never promised that. What He did promise is that, when Israel is ready, He will come quickly to bring them into the kingdom.

9:29 This quote comes from Isaiah 1:9. God then calls Israel "Sodom" and "Gomorrah" (Isaiah 1:10) and asks them: "What purpose is the multitude of your sacrifices unto Me?" (Isaiah 1:11). In other words, at the time that God has Isaiah write his book, there is only a remnant of believers left in Israel. Most of Israel is following the Jewish religion, in which they had replaced God's commandments with their own traditions (Mark 7:9). The reason this is important to note is because this is the same condition that Israel was in at Jesus' first coming and will continue to be in until Jesus' second coming.

In other words, Paul is saying that, because of God's foreknowledge that the Gentiles would be saved through God's hardening of Israel, i.e., setting aside Israel's program, and Israel will be saved in the tribulation period because they will have seen God's salvation of the Gentiles, God has not destroyed Israel, even though they deserved to be destroyed. Instead, He has saved a remnant of Israel for 2,000 years and counting so that He can fulfill His promises to Israel after the dispensation of grace has been completed. Otherwise, God would have utterly destroyed Israel, like He did Sodom and Gomorrah because, religiously speaking, they have been just like Sodom and Gomorrah for a long time (Isaiah 1:10).

Paul started Romans 9 by saying that God was not unfaithful to Israel. Rather, Israel was unfaithful to God. Now, he says that God has continued to allow a remnant of Israel to survive, in spite of their unbelief, so that He can fulfill His promises to them when they will be faithful to God after the dispensation of grace is over, because God knew that this long period of unbelief would be necessary before Israel would be saved. Therefore, instead of thinking that the setting aside of Israel means that God will not fulfill His promises to us, the setting aside of Israel should actually increase our confidence that God will place the body of Christ in heavenly places to rule with Christ for all eternity. After all, if God will keep His promises to Israel through thousands of years of their unbelief, He certainly will fulfill His promises to us at the end of our dispensation.

9:30-33 So, why did Israel fail in becoming righteous, while the Gentiles did not fail? The answer is that Israel tried to work their way into earning eternal life, while the Gentiles received it by faith. "It is not of him that willeth, nor of him that runneth, but of God that sheweth mercy" (9:16).

"The oracles of God" were committed unto the Jews (3:1-2). Rather than learning from that Mosaic law that "there is none that doeth good" (Psalm 53:1) and "there is none righteous, no, not one" (3:10), they decided to follow "after the law of righteousness" (9:31). Note that Israel did not follow after righteousness, but they followed after "the law" of righteousness, meaning that they tried to earn righteousness by their own works. They boasted to God about their performance of the law (2:23). Therefore, when John the Baptist preached "repent ye: for the kingdom of heaven is at hand"

(Matthew 3:2), the Jews said, "God, I thank Thee, that I am not as other men are, extortioners, unjust, adulterers" (Luke 18:11). Therefore, they would not take the free gift of righteousness that God tried to give them. This resulted in them receiving "filthy rags" righteousness (Isaiah 64:6), rather than "the fine linen" of "the righteousness of saints" (Revelation 19:8). Conversely, the Gentiles did not follow after righteousness (9:30). They did the evil deeds listed in 1:29-32. Therefore, when Paul preached the gospel to them, they believed, knowing that they were evil.

Therefore, although Israel had the law of righteousness, they did not receive eternal life because they sought it by works. The Gentiles did not have the law, but they received eternal life by faith, admitting that their works were evil. So, the Gentiles did not work, and they received God's righteousness, while Israel worked and they received their wage of death (6:23), instead of righteousness.

9:33 is a quote of Isaiah 8:14 and 28:16. Isaiah 8:13 tells us that the stumblingstone is the Lord Himself. Isaiah 28:16 says that the Lord is "a precious corner stone, a sure foundation." In Israel's program, God appointed the Jewish religious leaders to build His temple, but they would not use Him as part of the building (Matthew 21:42). Therefore, Jesus Christ Himself had to build the temple of the Lord (Zechariah 6:12), so that God can dwell with His people. This temple has Jesus Christ as "the chief corner stone" with scripture as the foundation and believers as the building (Ephesians 2:20-22).

The reason that Israel stumbled over the stone of Jesus Christ is because they were self-righteous. They thought that they did not need the Messiah to die for them. Instead, they expected the Messiah to come as their King, overthrow the Romans, and rule over the whole earth with them (John 6:15). In other words, Israel was looking for a King to sit in their self-righteous temple, and Jesus Christ came to die so that He could be the foundation for the Lord's temple. Israel thought they had the temple ready for Him, because of their self-righteousness, and God knew that they needed God's righteousness. Therefore, they stumbled over their Messiah, being offended that He would have to die for their sins. Then, when they stoned Stephen in Acts 7, they fell (Romans 11:11), meaning that they would not receive eternal life, because they tried to achieve it by their own merits, rather than by faith. If they remain in that fallen state, they will be ground to powder at Jesus' second coming by that same Stone they stumbled over (Matthew 21:44).

Thus, Paul has established that Israel's unbelief is why God did not fulfill His promises to Israel, not because God failed. God is love (I John 4:8), and "charity never faileth" (I Corinthians 13:8). Therefore, God cannot fail. This means that we can trust in God to fulfill His promises to us today in the dispensation of grace. In fact, He has already fulfilled them, as we are NOW justified by His blood (5:9), we have NOW received the atonement (5:11), and we are NOW holy and beloved (Colossians 3:12). That is why Ephesians 1:3 is not in the future tense: "Who HATH blessed us with all spiritual blessings in heavenly places in Christ."

We should also note that Isaiah 28:16 says that "he that believeth shall not make haste." But, Paul quotes it here, and in 10:11, as "whosoever believeth on Him shall not be ashamed." This shows the change in dispensations. In Israel's dispensation, you had the builders (the Jewish religious leaders) making the temple of God. The idea is that, if they believe, they can trust God to provide the corner stone, rather than making haste to try to find a cornerstone themselves. Progressive revelation in the dispensation of grace has revealed to us that God does the building. Therefore, instead of worrying about making haste in building, we completely trust God in His building of the temple, and we will not be ashamed in doing so, because God will build His temple perfectly. "He" is used in Isaiah, while "whosoever" is used in Romans. This indicates that there is no difference between Jew and Greek in today's dispensation, as 10:12 says, while the Jews were above the Gentiles in Israel's program (Deuteronomy 7:6). "On Him" is added in Romans because we now know that the corner stone is the Lord Jesus Christ.

10 Paul wants Israel to be saved (v. 1), but they have not believed because they have pursued righteousness on their own, rather than trusting in God to give them His righteousness (v. 3). Righteousness only comes to man by believing God (vs. 4-11). God gave Israel ample opportunity to be saved by sending them His word throughout their history (vs. 18-20), but they were "disobedient and gainsaying" (v. 21). Therefore, God will take His earthly kingdom away from apostate Israel and give it to believing Israel.

10:1-3 Israel has a zeal for God, but they do not have eternal life because they were trying to attain eternal life by their own works. In other words, they were ignorant of God's righteousness, because they were prideful in trying to develop their own righteousness (10:3). The majority of people attending "Christian" churches today fall into this same category. They have a zeal for God, but they will not have eternal life because they do not have faith in God to save them entirely by Christ's substitutionary death on the cross. Paul clearly states here that Israel is trying to obey God, but they will not receive eternal life, because their zeal is "not according to knowledge" (10:2).

These verses reject the myth that God will let all into heaven who try to be good. Most unbelievers will tell you that they will go to heaven because they try to be a good person, take care of their family, do not wrong anyone, and obey the ten commandments. They think that it would be unfair of God to send people to hell who tried to be good. However, the issue is not how hard you try, but how perfect you are. If you are perfect, God will give you eternal life (2:7). If you are not perfect, God will not give you eternal life (2:8-9). Thus, performance is the standard of fairness, not zeal. Just like it would be unfair to give a marathon medal to someone who did not complete a marathon but really, really tried to run the marathon, it would be unfair for God to give eternal life to someone who did not earn it. But, "there is none righteous, no, not one" (3:10). This means that none of us can earn eternal life. Therefore, zeal has nothing to do with it.

For example, there once were two men who were very zealous for God. So much so, that they did something that they knew would kill them, but they did it anyway, because they believed God wanted them to do it and would reward them in eternity for their deed. It may sound unfair to say that they will burn forever in the lake of fire. That is, it sounds unfair until you hear that they did their deed on September 11, 2001, and that deed was to hijack planes and fly them into the World Trade Center's towers in New York. From a religious perspective, they were heroes. After all, they never would have knowingly given up their lives if they did not believe God wanted them to do so. However, from a knowledge perspective, their deed did not reward them with eternal life and many virgins in heaven.

Similarly, Christianity is zealous for God. They can pray the rosary, light candles, pray fervently to God for forgiveness, "feel the presence" of the Lord as they sing, raise their hands in worship to God, give their life savings to the church, and many other things. They are zealous, but they are not zealous according to knowledge. Since they cannot earn eternal life and everything they do in their flesh is evil (7:18), none of these zealous deeds brings them one step closer to eternal life.

That is why eternal life must be a gift (6:23). Since a gift cannot be earned, God can set whatever terms He wants to in order for you to receive His gift. Since faith is the only thing that pleases God (Hebrews 11:6), God gives you the gift of eternal life when you believe what He has told you (3:22). In other words, eternal life comes, not by my zeal, but by my believing the knowledge that God has given me. That is why Paul says that, the reason Israel did not receive eternal life, is because their zeal was not according to knowledge (10:2). They had plenty of man's knowledge, knowing the traditions of the fathers. However, if they had studied the Old Testament, rather than their own traditions, they would not have stumbled at Jesus Christ's death on the cross for their sins. Similarly, in the tribulation period, apostate Israel will think that they are doing God service by killing believing Israel (John 16:2). They will be very zealous for God, but not according to knowledge. So, too, today, so many people follow the traditions of man, having a zeal for God. They will still go to the lake of fire, because they do not believe the gospel that it is Christ's work on the cross ALONE that saves them.

Having said that, there is nothing wrong with zeal, as long as it is based in knowledge. Jesus had the knowledge that His Father's house was supposed to be a house of prayer, and He saw it turned into a den of thieves (Matthew 21:13), and so He used His zeal for His Father's house to drive the moneychangers out of the temple (John 2:13-17). Therefore, the solution or the problem is not zeal. Rather, the solution is knowledge of God's Word and having faith in that word, in order to please God.

We can also see why Paul had such a great desire for Israel to be saved, because Paul was in this category before Jesus called him in Acts 9. Paul says in Acts 22:3 that, before Acts 9, he was "taught according to the perfect manner of the law of the fathers, and was zealous toward God." Paul was headed for the lake of fire, except that Christ saved him. Now, Paul sees Israel being zealous toward God but also headed for the lake of fire, and so his heart's desire and prayer is that they might be saved.

10:4-5 10:5 is a quote of Leviticus 18:5. If you are going to have "the righteousness which is of the law" (10:5), you must obey the law perfectly. "For whosoever shall keep the whole law, and yet offend in one point, he is guilty of all" (James 2:10). Therefore, "cursed be he that confirmeth not all the words of this law to do them" (Deuteronomy 27:26). Since "all have sinned" (3:23), all are guilty of disobeying the law. Therefore, God did not give Israel the law for them to obey it. Rather, He gave them the law so that they would understand that they are sinners and need to trust in God to impute His righteousness to them. That is why 10:4 says that Christ is the end of the law, meaning that, once someone comes to Christ by believing the gospel, the law ends for that person because he has learned the lesson of the law that he is a sinner. "The law was our schoolmaster to bring us unto Christ, that we might be justified by faith. But after that faith is come, we are no longer under a schoolmaster" (Galatians 3:24-25). Therefore, 6:14 says, "ye are not under the law, but under grace."

10:6-8 These verses lead up to 10:9-10, which are often taken out of context and misunderstood. Therefore, it is important that we understand 10:6-8 so that we can understand 10:9-10. Doing so is no small task, since 10:6-8 is a quote of Deuteronomy 30:12-14, but the Holy Ghost adds parenthetical references that come to conclusions that the reader of the verses in Deuteronomy would never come to without the Holy Ghost's interpretation.

Deuteronomy 30:10-12 says, "If thou shalt hearken unto the voice of the LORD thy God, to keep his commandments and his statutes which are written in this book of the law, and if thou turn unto the LORD thy God with all thine heart, and with all thy soul. For this commandment which I command thee this day, it is not hidden from thee, neither is it far off. It is not in heaven, that thou shouldest say, Who shall go up for us to heaven, and bring it unto us, that we may hear it, and do it?"

The verses in Deuteronomy are clear that God is commanding Israel to obey His law with all their heart and soul. They are told that "the word is very nigh unto thee, in thy mouth, and in thy heart, that thou mayest do it" (Deuteronomy 30:14). In other words, Israel has no excuse, because God has given them the law to obey. It is clear what they need to do. However, Romans 10:6-8, with the Holy Ghost's interpretation, says that

Deuteronomy is not speaking about Israel obtaining righteousness by them obeying the law. It is saying that it is "the righteousness which is of faith" (10:6). It is not saying that the law is with them, but it is "the word of faith" (10:8). According to the Holy Ghost's interpretation in Romans, those verses are really saying that "this commandment" (Deuteronomy 30:11) is not the law, but it is Christ ("bring Christ down from above" (10:6) and "bring up Christ again from the dead" (10:7))!

How is that? Because "Christ is the END of the law for righteousness to every one that believeth" (10:4). Remember that "the law was our schoolmaster to bring us unto Christ, that we might be justified by faith" (Galatians 3:24). God gave Israel the commandment to obey the law with all their heart and soul. If they had learned the lesson of the law, their response would be "We can't do that!" Why? Because "the heart is deceitful above all things, and desperately wicked" (Jeremiah 17:9). Therefore, even if Israel did somehow obey all of the commandments of the law, they could not do so out of a heart of love, because their heart is wicked. That is why Jesus said that the great commandment of the law is to "love the Lord thy God with all thy heart, and with all thy soul, and with all thy mind" (Matthew 22:37 and Deuteronomy 6:5). It is the great commandment, because it is impossible for sinful man to do at any time. Therefore, it causes the believer to have faith in God.

Israel's problem was that they thought they would be righteous on their own by obeying the law. They said, "all that the Lord hath spoken we will do" (Exodus 19:8). Israel did not recognize their own sinful condition. That is why God told them, "circumcise therefore the foreskin of your heart, and be no more stiffnecked" (Deuteronomy 10:16). In other words, because of Israel's unbelief, God gave Israel an impossible standard (the law) so that they would learn to trust in God to save them, rather than their own flesh.

For example, let's say that a father and his three year-old son live in the city on a very busy street. The son keeps trying to run outside. The father says that he can go outside any time he wants, except that he must ask his father, and his father will hold his hand while he is outside. The son is defiant and keeps insisting that he can go outside by himself. So, the father puts a deadbolt on the door, and only the father has the key. Because the son can no longer get outside of the house on his own, the father hopes that the son will learn the lesson that his father must be with him outside to keep him safe.

Applied to Israel, the law is that deadbolt. Israel insisted that they could be righteous on their own, and God knew that they would go to hell if He left them alone. Therefore, he put a deadbolt on the door to eternal life, and said, "I am the door" (John 10:9). "No man cometh unto the Father but by" Christ (John 14:6). The response that the father wanted from the son was, "without you, I could die. Will you open the door for me and keep me safe outside?" The response that God wanted from Israel was, "I cannot obey the law myself. Will you do it for me and keep me safe in the spirit realm?"

When Israel gets to that point of trusting in the Father to save them, God says, "And the Lord thy God will circumcise thine heart, and the heart of thy seed, to love the Lord thy God with all thine heart, and with all thy soul, that thou mayest live" (Deuteronomy 30:6). Then, "thou shalt return and obey the voice of the Lord, and do all His commandments which I command thee this day" (Deuteronomy 30:8). (This is the new covenant when God promises to put His Spirit within them and cause them to walk in His statutes and do them (Ezekiel 36:27).) These verses lead up to the passage of Deuteronomy 30:12-14 that Paul quotes. Therefore, when God tells Israel that the word is in their heart to do it (Deuteronomy 30:14), He means that the end or goal of the law is to give them righteousness by them believing that God will obey the law for them through Christ's perfect obedience of the law (10:4). If we have learned and believed the doctrine of Romans 1-9, we should now know that the commandment, of Deuteronomy 30, is not for Israel to obey the law, but it is for them to trust God to do it for them. Therefore, Deuteronomy 30:12-14 is really telling Israel that salvation is in their midst. All they have to do is stop trying to earn righteousness on their own, trust in God to give them His righteousness, and He will do all the work of the law for them through Christ. In other words, get God to open the door and go with them into the Promised Land!

Therefore, when Deuteronomy 30:12-13 says that the commandment is not in heaven or beyond the sea, what it is really saying is that Christ will obey the law for them if they have faith in God to save them. Therefore, they do not have to do anything on their own (such as go to heaven or go beyond the sea) to get that righteousness. God will do it for them if they believe.

Note also that the Holy Ghost says that "who shall ascend into heaven?" means to ascend "to bring Christ down from above" (10:6). And, "who shall descend into the deep?" means to descend "to bring up Christ again from the dead" (10:7). Therefore, the questions are really asking, "Who has the power to leave this world and enter into life in heaven so that they can be the Christ to live a perfect life?" And, "who has the power to leave this world and go beyond death so that they can be the Christ to conquer death for sinful man?" The answer is "no one." God will have to do these things Himself. He will create the virgin birth of His Son so that He can live a perfect life on earth. Then, Jesus will die and conquer death for man, going beyond Satan's sea, as the substitutionary sacrifice for our sins.

Thus, righteousness does not come by man's works. Salvation is by Christ's death, burial, and resurrection. Apostate Israel wants to do the work to get this accomplished. However, instead of Israel doing the work to bring Christ to earth or to go down into hell and conquer death themselves, they are to believe the word of faith that was preached to them. That is, they are to have faith in God and His law covenant with them, and let God take care of the details. Therefore, God intended the law to generate the faith response Israel

178

was supposed to have, rather than Israel obeying the law and bringing about salvation themselves.

As a side note, Deuteronomy 30:13 refers to conquering death as going "beyond the sea," while 10:7 refers to it as descending into the deep. This tells us that "the sea" is a metaphor in the Bible for Satan's realm. That is why, when Satan resurrects the Antichrist as a beast for the last half of the tribulation period, we are told that the beast will "rise up out of the sea" (Revelation 13:1). We are also told that Satan's religious system of Babylon "sitteth upon many waters" (Revelation 17:1). That is also why God tells saved Israel that He will "cast all their sins into the depths of the sea" (Micah 7:19) so that He will "remember their sin no more" (Jeremiah 31:34).

10:9-11 Christians like to quote 10:9-11 as support that you have to confess your sins publicly and make Jesus the Lord of your life in order to be saved. Right dividers will respond that Paul is talking about Israel (10:1) and so this "gospel" belongs to Israel's program; it is not for today. The truth is that Paul is talking about Israel, but he is talking about Israel in the dispensation of grace, since he uses the present tense. By understanding this, along with what we have already learned, we will learn that 10:9-11 is not saying what either side claims.

First, we need to recognize that 10:9 is a continuation of 10:6-8. In 10:5, Paul quoted Leviticus 18:5 to show that the righteousness of the law for Israel required them to obey the law perfectly. Then, in 10:6-8, Paul quoted Deuteronomy 30:12-14 to show Israel that their law also showed them how to be saved. That is, the law showed them their need for a Saviour, and that they were to trust in God to fulfill the law for them. This is "the word of faith" (10:8) to Israel. Paul says that this word of faith is in their heart and in their mouth (10:8), which he took straight from Deuteronomy 30:14.

Deuteronomy 30:6 tells Israel to circumcise their heart. Then, they will "love the Lord thy God with all thine heart, and with all thy soul, that thou mayest live." In other words, eternal life comes to Israel by loving the Lord with their heart and soul. If God circumcises Israel's heart, they will do all His commands (Deuteronomy 30:8). They will turn to God with all their heart and soul (Deuteronomy 30:10). Then, the word of faith will be in their heart and in their mouth (Deuteronomy 30:14). Obviously, God is talking about their spiritual heart and their spiritual mouth, since He does not want to literally cut them open, take a knife, and circumcise their physical heart.

Note how God tells them to love God with their heart and their soul (Deuteronomy 30:6,10. Also seen in Deuteronomy 4:29, 6:5, 10:12, 11:13, 11:18, 13:3, 26:16, and 30:2), but He switches to heart and mouth in Deuteronomy 30:14. That is because, spiritually speaking, the soul is the mouth of man, while the spirit is the heart of man. Therefore, when you believe with your heart, your spirit is made alive in Christ (Ephesians 2:1). The Holy Ghost can then communicate sound doctrine to your spirit (I

Corinthians 2:12-14). Your spirit then communicates these things to your soul (Ephesians 3:16), and you use your soul to "speak" for your spirit by yielding your body "as instruments of righteousness unto God" (6:13). Therefore, if you love God with all your heart and soul, you will live a perfect life, which is what Israel will do under the new covenant (Ezekiel 36:26-27).

To understand this better, let us look at Jesus Christ as an example. Jesus Christ had daily Bible studies with God the Father. "He wakeneth Mine ear to hear as the learned" (Isaiah 50:4). "Faith cometh by hearing, and hearing by the Word of God" (10:17). Thus, Jesus Christ had faith in the Father, and He learned God's Word from Him. "The Lord God hath given Me the tongue of the learned" (Isaiah 50:4). Obviously, God did not give Him a new, physical tongue. Therefore, this is a spiritual tongue. Jesus Christ lived by "every word that proceedeth out of the mouth of the Lord" (Deuteronomy 8:3) by God putting His words in His mouth (Deuteronomy 18:18). Therefore, He said, "I do nothing of Myself; but as My Father hath taught Me, I speak these things" (John 8:28). Note how doing things is equated to speaking things. Jesus further said, "I speak that which I have seen with My Father: and ye [the Jewish religious leaders] do that which ye have seen with your father" (John 8:38). He "saw" these things in those daily Bible studies that He had with His Father. Note again how "speak" and "do" are equated, since Jesus said that He "speaks" what He has seen, and the Jewish religious leaders "do" what they have seen.

In summary, Jesus Christ had faith in the Father, which resulted in His Father teaching His spirit (heart) the things of God. This would be "every word that proceedeth out of the mouth of the Lord" (Deuteronomy 8:3). In other words, God took His soul (mouth) and imparted it to Jesus' spirit so that Jesus' soul (mouth) (Deuteronomy 18:18) would only speak (do) the things that His Father wanted Him to speak (do). Thus, Jesus Christ believed God with His heart (spirit), and His mouth (soul) confessed these things to be true because He lived only by God's word (heart and soul together).

For further proof that the mouth is the soul, we will look at two more verses. Joshua 1:8 says, "this book of the law shall not depart out of thy mouth; but thou shalt meditate therein day and night." If the mouth were literal, God WOULD want the book of the law to depart out of their mouth. After all, He told them to teach the law to their "children, speaking of them when thou sittest in thine house" (Deuteronomy 11:19). Now, how are they going to teach the law to their children if the law is not supposed to depart out of their mouths? Were they supposed to use sign language? Obviously, "not depart out of thy mouth," means "not depart out of thy soul." Also, the only way they can meditate on the law is if it is internal. You cannot meditate on or deeply think about something that is not internal. Therefore, the "mouth" of this verse must be the soul.

Also, note Proverbs 13:3: "He that keepeth his mouth keepeth his life." The only way you keep your life is by keeping your soul. Your physical mouth does not defile your soul, because Jesus said, "that which cometh out of the man, that defileth the man. For from within, out of the heart of men, proceed evil" (Mark 7:20-21). Therefore, you keep your life by keeping your soul, which is mouth in Proverbs 13:3.

Now that we understand what the heart and the mouth are, let's apply this to Israel, and what they are supposed to do, according to 10:9-11. They are supposed to "confess with [their] mouth the Lord Jesus" (10:9). Leviticus 26:40 does say that Israel must "confess their iniquity." I John 1:9 also tells them that they need to confess their sins in order to be forgiven. Matthew 3:6 says that the way Israel confessed their sins was by being water baptized by John in the Jordan River. Therefore, according to that verse, the way they confessed with their mouth (soul) was by being water baptized.

The next part of 10:9 says that they also need to "believe in [their] heart that God hath raised Him from the dead." Obviously, this is belief in their spirit, not in their literal, physical heart. This would be the "repentance" part of the gospel (Matthew 3:8,11). Repenting means to change their mind (Numbers 23:19). They change their mind about trusting in their own righteousness and trust in God to impute His righteousness to them. Thus, they have believed with their heart. Then, they are water baptized, which is them confessing their sins with their mouth or soul. That is why Peter told them to "repent, and be baptized...for the remission of sins" (Acts 2:38).

What I have shared explains what Israel was to do in their program, but, in Romans 10, Paul is speaking to Israel in the dispensation of grace. Israel's gospel today is the same gospel as the Gentiles' gospel. That is why Paul said, "the word of faith, which WE preach" (10:8). Therefore, 10:9 is Paul's gospel. That is why they are to confess "the Lord Jesus," rather than confess their sins, and they are to believe in Jesus' resurrection, instead of believing that God will save them through the law covenant.

So, how would Jews (or Gentiles) do these things today? The gospel today is to trust in Jesus' death, burial, and resurrection as atonement for sin (I Corinthians 15:3-4). That covers "believe in thine heart that God hath raised Him from the dead" (10:9). How do they "confess with [their] mouth the Lord Jesus?" This is a very important question since 10:10 says that "with the mouth confession is made unto salvation." In other words, without confessing, they are not saved.

10:11 sums up what needs to be done in order to be saved by saying that "whosoever believeth on Him shall not be ashamed." This shows that, whatever confession entails, it is accomplished when they believe. 10:11 is a quote of Isaiah 28:16. We already saw Paul quote this verse just 11 verses prior in 9:33. The context of Isaiah 28:16 is that Israel has made a covenant with death (Isaiah 28:15) because they are trusting in their own works to save them. In order to get them out of that covenant with death, Jesus will have to die for them. Then, death will be satisfied (I Corinthians 15:54), and "your covenant with death shall be disannulled" (Isaiah 28:18). In dying for them, Jesus Christ becomes the Lord over death, which is why Paul calls Him "the LORD Jesus" (10:9). In today's dispensation, when we believe the gospel, we are spiritually baptized into Christ's death (6:3-4). Thus, the way we "confess with [our] mouth the Lord Jesus" (10:9) is by being baptized into Christ's death. In doing so, our soul confesses that Jesus is the Lord over death, because we have now been made "dead with Christ" (6:8). I Corinthians 12:13 says that the Spirit baptizes us into Christ's death. As we learned in 6:3-4, this is a spiritual baptism, not a fleshly baptism. Colossians 2:10-12 says that we are complete in Christ because we have been spiritually circumcised, which involves our spiritual baptism, as well.

Colossians 2:16-17 goes on to say that the things under the Mosaic law were a shadow of things to come. The Mosaic law includes physical circumcision and physical baptism, and these have now been replaced by spiritual circumcision and spiritual baptism. It is no coincidence, then, that, under that Mosaic law, God said their soul would be cut off from His people if they were not circumcised (Genesis 17:14), and that Israel had to be water baptized in order to be saved. Jesus said, "he that believeth and is baptized shall be saved" (Mark 16:16). In today's dispensation, since the shadow is gone and the body of Christ is here, believing the gospel accomplishes both spiritual circumcision and spiritual baptism, which is why Paul sums up 10:9-10 with the simple statement: "Whosoever believeth on Him shall not be ashamed" (10:11), which is a quote of Isaiah 28:16 to show that our covenant with death is disannulled when we believe that Jesus died for our sins, was buried, and rose again.

In summary, when you believe in Jesus' death, burial, and resurrection as atonement for your sin (I Corinthians 15:3-4), you have believed in your heart (spirit). Then, the Holy Ghost is given unto you (5:5). He then spiritually circumcises you, giving you God's righteousness (10:11), which means He has quickened your spirit from the dead (Ephesians 2:1). This includes spiritually baptizing you into Jesus' death (Colossians 2:11-12). When He does this, your mouth (soul) confesses that Jesus is Lord over death, giving you salvation (10:11) from the lake of fire. Therefore, recognizing that you are a sinner and trusting in Jesus' death, burial, and resurrection as atonement for your sin is what gives you the gift of eternal life. Confessing "the Lord Jesus" does not mean that you have to make Him Lord of your life, and it does not mean that you have to stand before a church and start confessing that you are a sinner or confess specific sins that you have committed. All you have to "do" is believe the gospel (10:11), and God does everything through you.

Because this was such a long explanation, I will now quote 10:9-11 and insert comments that explain what we have covered here.

"That if thou shalt confess [be spiritually baptized] with thy mouth [soul] the

Lord Jesus [His death counts for you], and shalt believe [Paul's gospel] in thine heart [spirit] that God hath raised him from the dead, thou shalt be saved. For with the heart [spirit] man believeth unto righteousness [alive in Christ]; and with the mouth [soul] confession [spirit baptism] is made unto salvation [from hell]. For the scripture saith, Whosoever believeth [the mystery gospel] on him shall not be ashamed."

10:12-13 Acts-9 dispensationalists often use 10:12 to say that, in Israel's program, Israel had favored-nation status with God, and that Gentiles would be saved by blessing Israel. However, now in the dispensation of grace, the Gentiles can be saved by going to God directly, because God has taken down the middle wall of partition between Jews and Gentiles (Ephesians 2:14). This is true. However, the focus in these verses is more on ISRAEL'S ability to be saved in the dispensation of grace than on the Gentiles being saved. In other words, in Israel's program, Gentiles had to bless Israel in order to be saved (Matthew 25:31-46). In the dispensation of grace, the reverse is not true, i.e., Israel is not saved by blessing the Gentiles. Rather, because "there is no difference between the Jew and the Greek" (10:12), the Jews are able to be saved by going to God directly, just like the Gentiles can do. Therefore, if individuals in Israel believe the mystery gospel, they will become part of the body of Christ in the dispensation of grace. This is important to note, because Christians, when they hear right division for the first time, often think we are saying that Jews and Gentiles have different gospels TODAY that they have to believe in order to be saved, and that is NOT what we are saying.

If the nation of Israel, as a whole, will call on the name of the Lord, they will be saved. This is a quote of Joel 2:32. The funny thing is that the context of Joel 2:32 is that this will take place for the Gentiles "in mount Zion and in Jerusalem" during the millennial reign on earth. The Holy Ghost now says through Paul that this verse also applies to the Jews in the Gentiles' dispensation. This shows that the Holy Ghost's offer to the Jews, in Acts 2:21, is still applicable, except that they will now be saved as part of the body of Christ, rather than as part of Israel's program. This shows that God answered Stephen's prayer of, "Lord, lay not this sin to their charge" (Acts 7:60), as Israel's program was put on hold, by allowing unsaved Jews to become part of the body of Christ by believing Paul's gospel.

10:14-16 Even in the dispensation of grace, the problem with Israel is still not with God, even though He has set aside Israel's program for now. The problem is with Israel's unbelief. Israel needs to call on the Lord, by believing in Jesus' death, burial, and resurrection as atonement for their sins, in order to be saved. Since they do not believe, they will not call on the Lord to save them.

"Faith cometh by hearing, and hearing by the word of God" (10:17). "How shall they hear without a preacher?" (10:14). Some people will say that these two verses teach that you cannot be saved without a preacher. Therefore, we must go to the "unreached peoples" with the gospel. However, 10:14 does not say that you cannot hear without a preacher. It just asks the question of how shall they hear without a preacher. So, the question goes, "If someone is by himself on a deserted island with a Bible in hand, can he believe the gospel?" The gospel is found in I Corinthians 15:3-4. Therefore, he does have the gospel. However, no one can understand the things of God with the natural mind, because they are spiritually discerned. This means that you have to have the Holy Ghost within you before you can ascertain which one of the gospels in the Bible is applicable to you, and you do not have the Holy Ghost until you are saved (I Corinthians 2:12-14). Therefore, the chances of stumbling upon the gospel in I Corinthians 15:3-4 by yourself and believing it are probably remote. But, I am not sure that such a situation of a person by himself on an island with a Bible he can read has ever arisen. Even if it has, it is not really important because, even without the Bible, a person can still be saved. We learned, in 1:19-20, that all men know of God's eternal power and Godhead "so that they are without excuse" (1:20) on judgment day. If they believe in what they know about God, they will have eternal life with Him, even if they have never heard of Jesus' death, burial, and resurrection as atonement for sin.

However, in the context of Romans 10, we are not dealing with that unlikely scenario. Instead, we are dealing with Israel. Since it is highly unlikely that Israel would hear the gospel of grace without a preacher, God sent Paul to deliver this gospel to them (Acts 9:15). Preaching the gospel is a wonderful thing. Although everyone has the internal witness of God, people usually will become "vain in their imaginations, and their foolish heart [will be] darkened" (1:21), such that they will ignore this internal witness. When someone preaches the gospel, it resonates with the internal witness. Now, that person must either believe the gospel, confirming that God's internal witness is true, or he must go further into denial by excusing himself (2:15). Although most will choose the latter, the fact, that some will choose the former, means that it is always good to share the gospel to those who are willing to listen, when you have the opportunity to do so, because it may mean the difference between eternity in heaven or eternity in hell for them.

This does not mean that you have to be an "ordained minister." God has made all believers today ambassadors for Christ to beseech people to be reconciled to God (II Corinthians 5:20). Therefore, we do not need to wait for an inner impression to be "called to the ministry." We have all been sent (10:15). That is because many people will never enter a church. Even if they do, they probably will not hear the gospel for today from the pulpit. Also, they are more likely to believe the gospel you give them, if they see the love of Christ coming through you, which they probably will not see from a pastor in church. Therefore, all believers should take advantage of the opportunities they have to present the gospel so that others may be saved.

That is why God says that the feet of the gospel preachers are beautiful. This is true, spiritually speaking, because they have used those feet to travel to wherever they are and proclaim the gospel. Paul is quoting Isaiah 52:7, which says, "How beautiful upon the mountains are the feet of HIM that bringeth good tidings." The "him" turned out to be John the Baptist at first and then the Lord Jesus Christ after him. In Romans, this is changed to "How beautiful are the feet of THEM that preach the gospel of peace." This turns out to be many people, such as Paul, Silas, Barnabas, John Mark, Aristarchus, etc. In spite of these people preaching the gospel to them, Israel does not believe, fulfilling Isaiah 53:1, which Paul also quotes here.

Note that Paul says that "they have not all OBEYED the gospel," and the support of that statement is "Lord, who hath BELIEVED our report" (10:16). In other words, obedience is equated to believing. We also learned this in 6:17-18, which says that belief is an obedience of the gospel from the heart, which makes us free from sin. This helps us understand that obedience does not always mean obeying the law, as Christianity tries to condition us to think. For example, I Peter 1:22 says that the little flock purified their souls by obeying the truth. Therefore, when the Bible mentions obeying, we need to ask the question: "Obey what?" If the answer is "obey the gospel," then we know that means believing the gospel.

Also, note that the gospel that is proclaimed is the gospel of peace. Those, who believe, are justified by faith and have peace with God (5:1), such that God's wrath will not come upon them (1:18).

The summary of these verses is that, even though God sent preachers to the Jews in the dispensation of grace, they still did not believe the gospel. Israel, as a whole, continues in unbelief to this day, not because of a lack of preachers giving them God's Word or a lack of power of God's Word, but because of their hard hearts toward God.

Finally, note the phrase "how shall they hear without a preacher?" (10:15). Today, the amount of preaching found in churches has decreased, while the amount of singing has increased. Also, the quality of preaching has decreased, as it is rare to hear a clear, gospel message preached from pulpits today. Moreover, young people say they want the church to mentor them, rather than preach at them. That statement means that they want church leaders to teach them how to live. However, without a preacher, they will not hear the gospel. Without hearing the gospel, they do not have the Holy Ghost within them. Without the Holy Ghost, everything they do will be fulfilling the lusts of the flesh. Therefore, a mentor may teach them to live more moral lives, but morality is not God's goal. God's goal is for "all men to be saved, and to come unto the knowledge of the truth" (I Timothy 2:4). Therefore, the current call, to get away from the Bible and preaching and have more hands-on application between leaders and lay people, is going against God's will. In fact, it hardens people to the gospel, because their response to the gospel would be: "I don't need to believe that. I'm okay with God, because I do good things and go to church." Paul told Timothy to commit sound doctrine "to faithful men, who shall be able to teach others also" (II Timothy 2:2). He did not say, "put the Bible on the shelf and start mentoring the people in the church." We should let God do the "mentoring" through the preaching of His Word, rather than having church leaders teach people in the church to live decent, moral lives.

10:17-18 Although speaking about Israel's program, we can also apply these verses to the mystery program today. The reason is because, regardless of the dispensation you are in, God requires faith. Hebrews 11:6 says, "But without faith it is impossible to please Him." The faith, that pleases God, comes by hearing the Word of God. Christians will sometimes try to redefine the word "hearing" to meet their false doctrine. For example, they may say that a preacher has to present the gospel to you. Then, "God has to knock on your heart's door," or "the Holy Spirit has to draw you to God before you can believe" that gospel message. By making such statements, they really are saying that they believe in Calvinism's pre-destination. After all, if the Holy Spirit has to draw you to God, then it is up to God to decide who to draw and who not to draw. This goes against God's statement at the end of the Bible that "whosoever will, let him take the water of life freely" (Revelation 22:17).

In 10:18, Paul asks the question of Israel, "Have they not heard?" The answer is, "Yes verily, their sound went into all the earth" (10:18). Paul is quoting Psalm 19:4, which says, "Their line is gone out through all the earth, and their words to the end of the world." The context of this quote is that God had declared the gospel in the stars (Psalm 19:1-3), which explains why the wise men knew the King of the Jews had been born by seeing His star in the east (Matthew 2:1-2). But, why would Israel have to rely upon the gospel in the stars when God had given them His law (3:1-2)? Because the Jewish religious leaders were not teaching them God's law. They were teaching them the traditions of the fathers (Mark 7:7-9). They were teaching them to try to earn their way into God's kingdom, rather than teaching them God's Word that their own "righteousnesses are as filthy rags" (Isaiah 64:6). Therefore, although Israel had been given God's instructions, the common people in Israel were not taught those instructions by their leaders. They were "as sheep having no shepherd" (Matthew 9:36). This means that, even though the oracles of God were committed unto the Jews (3:1-2), they were a lot like the Gentiles during Israel's program in that they had to feel after the Lord in order to find Him (Acts 17:27) due to the pastors, who destroyed and scattered the sheep (Jeremiah 23:1).

Even in this condition, God says that Israel "heard" the gospel through everything that He gave them in creation. "He left not Himself without witness, in that He did good, and gave us rain from heaven, and fruitful seasons, filling our hearts with food and gladness" (Acts 14:17). Therefore, Israel cannot blame their lack of entering into God's kingdom on not hearing God's Word, even if the religious leaders did not give them the law. Applying this to today's Christian churches, not only does God not need to "pull on your heart's strings" in order for you to hear the gospel, but you also do not need to actually hear about Jesus' death, burial, and resurrection in order for God to consider that you have heard the gospel. God has already "preached" the everlasting gospel to you through His internal witness of Himself that is confirmed by the world that He created. That is why John 1:9 says that God "lighteth every man that cometh into the world." Since all people have God's light so that they may believe, there is nothing more that God has to do. He does not need to knock on your heart's door. Such a statement implies that God is a beggar, when He is really "the blessed and only Potentate, the King of kings, and Lord of lords" (I Timothy 6:15).

In other words, God's omnipotence allows Him to give the gospel to everyone ever born, even though Satan and his forces and man's flesh are very much contrary to God's gospel to them. Thus, everyone has the internal witness of God. Those, who believe this internal witness, will want to know more. In Israel's case, believers in "the everlasting gospel" (Revelation 14:6) could then seek out the scriptures in the Hebrew tongue, so that God could reward them for their diligence (Hebrews 11:6). When they hear this gospel and believe it, they receive the gift of eternal life. This speaks to the power of "the everlasting gospel" (Revelation 14:6) within them that, when they have faith in God about what they know, God would give them the opportunity to have more faith in what they do not yet know. Similarly today, when someone believes the gospel of grace, he has further opportunity to have faith by believing what God says in His Word as the Holy Ghost teaches it to him (I Corinthians 2:9-13). He then has the opportunity to think soberly according to this greater "measure of faith" (12:3) that he now has so that the Holy Ghost can teach him even more.

Now, when 10:!7 says that "FAITH cometh by hearing," most people think this is referring to man's faith in the gospel. While that could be true, the more likely explanation is that the "faith OF Jesus Christ" (3:22) comes to the one who hears. In other words, the gospel is proclaimed by someone, who uses the word of God. A person hears that word and believes it. Then, the faith OF Jesus Christ comes upon that person because he has believed the gospel, such that he is now saved. The reason I say this is that, wherever Christ's faith is mentioned in Paul's epistles, the belief of the gospel by man is always mentioned along with it. For example, Galatians 2:16 says, "we have believed in Jesus Christ, that we might be justified by the faith of Christ." Therefore, when we hear the gospel and believe it, faith comes to us, and that faith is the faith of Christ. We also see both our belief and Christ's faith here, as belief is found in 10:16, while faith is in 10:17.

10:19-21 The next question is "Did not Israel know?" The answer is given with three verses quoted from the Old Testament and shows that Paul is referring to the Jewish religious leaders, when he mentions "Israel" here. A more detailed way of phrasing the question would be: "Since Israel had God's Word, didn't the Jewish religious leaders know that God would not save them if they did not believe?" Based on Deuteronomy 32:21 and Isaiah 65:1-2 (the three verses that Paul quotes), the answer is "yes, they did know."

The Deuteronomy 32:21 passage tells the religious leaders that God will provoke them to anger with "a foolish nation." Deuteronomy goes on to say that God will cause them to be hungry, killed by beasts, killed by the sword, scattered, and chased by this nation (Deuteronomy 32:22-31). Using a fleshly mind, a person would take this to mean that God would punish Israel with a nation like Assyria or Babylon. Then, only after Israel has been beaten within an inch of her life, would Israel come crawling back to God in repentance. However, as we will soon see, the "foolish nation" is really a nation of believers that comes out of apostate Israel ("Come out of her, My people, that ye be not partakers of her sins" (Revelation 18:4).) Since the little flock does not do to apostate Israel the things mentioned in Deuteronomy 32:22-31, this means that those things will take place spiritually speaking. Moreover, Isaiah 65:1 comes along and says that God is actually found of a nation that was not called by His name. Thus, "Esaias is very bold" (10:20) to mention that the foolish nation, not only will anger Israel, but it will also find the Lord itself.

Jesus Christ puts His knowledge of Old-Testament scripture together to say that "the kingdom of God shall be taken from you [Israel] and given to a nation bringing forth the fruits thereof" (Matthew 21:43). Christianity latches on to this verse and says, "See, we are spiritual Israel. God has given the Gentiles the kingdom today." However, it cannot refer to the Gentiles becoming spiritual Israel, because it says "nation," not "nations." Jesus gives the answer in Luke 12:32 by saying, "Fear not, little flock; for it is your Father's good pleasure to give you the kingdom."

Therefore, Deuteronomy says that God will use "a foolish nation" to punish Israel for their unbelief, Isaiah says that nation will find the Lord, and Jesus says that the foolish nation is the little flock and God's kingdom will be taken from apostate Israel and be given to believing Israel.

The reason that believing Israel is called a foolish nation is that God gave His law and His word, not to them, but to their religious leaders. It was then the job of the religious leaders to communicate that word to the rest of Israel. However, God says, regarding these leaders, that "they that handle the law knew Me not" (Jeremiah 2:8). God says that the "pastors have destroyed My vineyard" (Jeremiah 12:10), which is Israel (Isaiah 5:7). Because of this, God promised to "gather the remnant of My flock...and...bring them again to their folds....And I will set up shepherds over them which shall feed them" (Jeremiah 23:3-4). Therefore, Jesus Christ went to the tribes of Israel located in Galilee, which was called "Galilee of the Gentiles," because the Jews in Galilee were not followers of the Jewish religion (Matthew 4:13-15). In other words, God still went to Jews, but He went to Jews outside of the Jewish religion. Therefore, they were "foolish" regarding the Jews' traditions, but they were wise to believe God's Word to them. This shows that, even in Israel's program, God makes "foolish the wisdom of this world" (I Corinthians 1:20).

With this point in mind, Paul is going to use the progressive revelation of God to take things even one step further. Isaiah 65:1 specifically says that it is "A NATION" that finds the Lord, and we have seen that this refers to the little flock of Israel. However, Paul, in quoting Isaiah 65:1, does not use the term "nation." That is because Paul uses this verse, by the inspiration of God, to say that even the little flock of Israel has been set aside right now. Thus, Paul is even bolder than Isaiah. God revealed to Paul that He had set aside Israel's program and started the dispensation of grace with the body of Christ.

The question, then, is "hath God cast away His people." The answer is "God forbid. For I also am an Israelite" (11:1). In other words, God will still save Jews today, if they believe the gospel of grace given to Paul. Paul will then spend chapter 11 explaining that God's plan all along had been to start Israel's program, set aside Israel's program, start the body of Christ, seat the body of Christ in heavenly places, and then resume Israel's program before Israel is finally saved. Why? Because the Gentiles had to see God punishing Israel before they would fear God (9:22-23). Then, when God gives the gospel of grace to them through Paul, they will believe it (Acts 28:28). Then, after the rapture of the body of Christ, Israel will become jealous of the eternal life that the Gentiles received (11:11), "and so all Israel shall be saved" (11:26). Thus, God rejected the Gentiles at the Tower of Babel (Genesis 11), He rejected the Jews at the stoning of Stephen (Acts 7), He had mercy on the Gentiles with the body of Christ, beginning in Acts 9, and He will have mercy on the Jews, beginning after the rapture of the church. This is Paul's conclusion in 11:30-32.

Next, Paul quotes Isaiah 65:2 to show that God offered salvation to Israel from the time the nation was born to the time that He set them aside at the end of Acts 7. However, they never received God's salvation because they were "disobedient and gainsaying" (10:21). Disobedience is in terms of not obeying the gospel, which we learned, in 10:16, means that they did not believe the gospel. "Gainsaying" simply means that they said things for gain. I Timothy 6:9-10 says that those, who want to be rich, will err from the faith, because they will say things to get gain, rather than preaching the truth. Jesus said that the Jewish religious leaders did this, as they devoured "widows' houses" (Matthew 23:14). Therefore, riches in this life is all that they will ever get (Luke 6:24). They will not believe the gospel so that they can have true riches in God's kingdom.

This did not happen because of a lack of trying on God's part. Isaiah 59:1-2 says, "Behold, the Lord's hand is not shortened, that it cannot save; neither His ear heavy, that it cannot hear: But your iniquities have separated between you and your God." They were "children in whom is no faith" (Deuteronomy 32:20). In other words, because apostate Israel went after the riches of this world, they did not believe God and will not enter God's kingdom. Therefore, the answer to the question of "Did not Israel know?" is, "Yes, Israel knew, and they still did not believe, because they esteemed the riches of this world greater riches than the reproach of Christ (Hebrews 11:26). By contrast, the little flock of Israel did not know, in the sense that God's Word was not taught to them by their leaders, and they believed anyway!"

11 There are two main lessons to learn from this chapter: 1) We are not spiritual Israel, and 2) We should take advantage of God's mercy to us by reading and believing God's Word.

Regardless of Israel's disobedience (10:21), God has NOT cast away Israel (vs. 1-2). Because of this, God has kept a remnant of Jews alive (v. 5), until the time when they will believe God, which is after the dispensation of grace is over (vs. 25-26). Right now, Israel is blind to the truth because of their unbelief (vs. 8-10). Through Israel's fall, God has given salvation to the Gentiles to provoke Israel to jealousy (v. 11). Paul wants Israel to be saved now, because, if Jews start getting saved, it means that the rapture must take place soon because God must be starting up Israel's program again soon (vs. 13-14).

Paul sums up God's master plan with the olive-tree illustration (vs. 16-24). This illustration shows that Israel had life in Christ, i.e., in the olive tree, in their program, but God broke them off from His olive tree (v. 17), due to their unbelief (v. 20). With the dispensation of grace, God is now giving the Gentiles a chance to be part of His olive tree (v. 17). God will graff Israel back into the olive tree (v. 23), once "the fulness of the Gentiles be come in" (v. 25). This should cause Gentiles to fear, such that they should believe the gospel and the truth of God's Word so that they can continue to be part of God's olive tree (v. 20).

God did things this way because man, in his pride, will not believe God until God concludes all in unbelief first (vs. 30-32). In other words, man will not take God's grace until he experiences God's judgment for his sin first. Only God is wise enough to come up with this plan (vs. 33-35). Since God was alone in creating His wise plan, all things end up being in God, and God receives all the glory (v. 36).

11:1 "Hath God cast away His people?" (11:1). The key part of this question is "HIS people." Because apostate Israel was in unbelief, God said that they are "not My people" (Hosea 1:9). However, Paul says that God hath not cast away His people, because Paul is a Jew, and He is part of God's people. The reason Paul was saved, while most of Israel was not, was because Paul believed God, while most of Israel did not believe God. Therefore, "His people" are the ones who believe God, and God has not cast them away. God only cast away the part of Israel that was not "His people," while He will still fulfill His promises to the part of Israel that is His people. ("They are not all Israel, which are of Israel" (9:6).) That is why Hosea 1:10 goes on to say that "in the place where it was said unto them, Ye are not My people, there it shall be said unto them, Ye are the sons of the living God."

11:2-5 God "foreknew" His people. We talked a lot about foreknowledge in chapters 8 and 9. Basically, God knew, before the foundation of the world (Ephesians 1:4), that, in the end, there would be a believing remnant of Israel to enter God's eternal, earthly kingdom. Because God knew this, He made sure that there would be a surviving remnant of Jews, who could believe, after the dispensation of grace is over.

Paul gives an example from I Kings 19 to demonstrate this. Elijah had called fire down from heaven to consume the sacrifice, while the prophets of Baal were unsuccessful in their attempt to do the same. This showed Israel that Jehovah is their God, yet they killed God's prophets and dug up His altars. Elijah said to God, "I am left alone, and they seek my life" (11:3). God's response was that He had reserved to Himself 7,000 men who had not bowed down to Baal (11:4).

The application is that it may appear that all of Israel had rejected their Messiah, but God had reserved a remnant who did not take part in that apostate act. You may think that Paul is referring to the believing remnant of Israel, but he is not. We know this for two reasons. First, in the case of Elijah, God did NOT say that He had reserved to Himself 7,000 men who were trusting in God to save them, which is why they did not bow down to Baal. Rather, God said that there were 7,000 men who had not bowed down to Baal. They may or may not have been believers. We just know that they did not commit the sin of bowing down to Baal.

Second, we know that Paul is not referring to the believing remnant of Israel because 11:5 says that "there is a remnant according to the election of grace." Because the word "grace" is used, Christians take this verse to mean that there are Jews who are believers today in the dispensation of grace. While it is true that Jews today are part of the body of Christ, this verse cannot be referring to these people for two reasons. First, if they are members of the body of Christ, God does not consider them to be Jews any more, because, in the body of Christ, "there is neither Jew nor Greek" (Galatians 3:28). Second, the body of Christ will be raptured up at the end of this dispensation. Therefore, Paul cannot be referring to saved Jews of the body of Christ, because that remnant will not be around for the resumption of Israel's program.

God's grace is not exclusive to the dispensation of grace. Grace is God giving you something good that you do not deserve. If they were believers, the remnant would be based upon faith, not upon "the election of grace." If it is based upon faith, those people have already died, which means, again, that this remnant is no longer around, and so God does not have an Israel on which to be merciful in the future.

Therefore, this remnant must be of physical Jews from each tribe, because God says that at least 12,000 Jews from each of the 12 tribes of Israel will be sealed as believers, halfway through the tribulation period (Revelation 7:4). This remnant will survive until the kingdom of heaven is at hand, not because they deserve to survive, but because God had grace on them, not completely wiping out the Jews in the meantime. The remnant must be a large group since 144,000 of them will believe during the first 3 ½ years of the tribulation period (Revelation 7:4-8).

Christianity says, "Those are not physical Jews, but they are spiritual Jews." In saying so, they do not believe God's Word. Also, if they are spiritual Jews, how does God determine which tribe each person belongs to? Christianity also says that today's Jew has no idea what tribe he belongs to. Even if that is true, that still does not mean that God does not know what tribe each Jew belongs to. By contrast, Satan knows that God has promised to save a remnant of physical Jews, and he knows that, if God does not do so, He cannot fulfill His promises to Israel. That is why there is a long list of Jewish massacres/holocausts over the last 2,000 years, and yet they still survive as a people, because "there is a remnant according to the election of grace" (11:5).

11:6 Paul is making the point that the remnant of Israel, who will be around for the at-hand phase of the kingdom, will not survive because they worked to stay alive as a nation. If works were the standard, none of them would have survived. That is because "all have sinned" (3:23), and "the wages of sin is death" (6:23). Therefore, the result of their work is death. That is why the election has to be by grace, which takes away the pride of man.

This is a very important verse to keep in mind because it shows that grace and works are mutually exclusive. Regardless of denomination, the Christian religion believes they work for their salvation. Some teach that you have to confess your sins to either a priest or to God in order to maintain your salvation. Others say you have to live a "godly life," as they define it, in order to maintain your salvation. Still others say you are eternally secure unless you do something really bad, like murder someone, which demonstrates, they say, that you were never saved in the first place. Regardless of the view taken, works are involved. Yet, Ephesians 2:8-9 says, "For by grace are ye saved through faith...; not of works, lest any man should boast." If the comeback is: "Yes, I'm saved by grace through faith, BUT _____," 11:6 is the verse to share. The Lord Jesus Christ did everything for us, and it is by God's grace that we are saved. If we add works to maintain our salvation, then salvation is no longer by grace, as this verse clearly shows that grace and works do not mix.

In the context of what Paul is saying, Israel should have been destroyed as a nation when they crucified the Lord Jesus Christ, but God has kept them alive because His foreknowledge tells Him that Israel will finally believe after the dispensation of grace is over. Therefore, a remnant has survived, according to God's grace.

11:7-8 God did not cast away His people (11:1). Rather, based on His foreknowledge that Israel will be saved once He resumes His program with them (11:2), God set them aside, but is keeping a remnant of Jews alive until that time (11:5).

Paul will soon begin to address what God is doing in the meantime, i.e., in the dispensation of grace. First, we need to note that Israel did not obtain eternal life because of their unbelief (10:16). This is important to note because it means that the Gentiles must believe the gospel God has given them in order to receive eternal life. Just like Jews are not automatically saved in Israel's program because they are physical Jews, Gentiles are not automatically saved in the body of Christ's program because they are physical Gentiles.

We are then told that "the election hath obtained" eternal life, "and the rest were blinded" (11:7). Since the subject is Israel, this means that God divided the nation into two groups—apostate and believers—just as Jesus said God would do (Matthew 21:43). Therefore, "the election" refers to believers in Israel's program. As mentioned in 8:33, election does not mean that God used His sovereignty to cause certain people to be saved. Rather, as I Peter 1:2 says, election is "according to the foreknowledge of God the Father." God foreknew that a believing remnant would come out of Israel, and so God gave them the kingdom. Now, when Paul says that "the election hath obtained it" (11:7), he does not mean that God's kingdom is already being run on earth. He just means that, because they believed the gospel that God gave them, they will be part of that kingdom when it is instituted on earth.

Meanwhile, unbelieving Israel was blinded (11:7). Isaiah 29:10 explains why. God did not give Israel "the spirit of slumber" because He did not want them to be saved. Rather, Isaiah 29:13 says that Israel drew near to God with their mouth, "but have removed their heart far from Me." In other words, Israel used God's name and His Word, but they did not believe God's Word, keeping their "desperately wicked" heart intact (Jeremiah 17:9). This means that they blasphemed God (2:24). Therefore, God disassociated Himself from them as much as He could, which means that He caused them to slumber. They slumber "unto this day" (11:8), which I would take to mean that they will continue in unbelief until the day when they will be saved, which is after the dispensation of grace is over (11:25-26).

11:9-10 These verses are a quote of Psalm 69:22-23. Psalm 69:21 says that "in My thirst they gave Me vinegar to drink," which Israel fulfilled when Jesus was on the cross (Matthew 27:48). Therefore, these verses are God's punishment upon the nation of Israel for crucifying their own Messiah. In fact, Psalm 69:26 specifically says this.

Note how 11:9 says that "their table" will be "a snare..., a trap..., a stumblingblock, and a recompense unto them" (11:9). "Their table" would be what the Jewish religious leaders prepared for Israel to feast upon spiritually. They laid "aside the commandment of God" (Mark 7:8), "teaching for doctrines the commandments of men" (Mark 7:7), making "the word of God of none effect" (Mark 7:13). Thus, they were ensnared by their own religion, such that they stumbled over their Messiah, crucifying Him in unbelief, when they should have accepted His sacrifice for their sins by faith. (By contrast, God prepares a table for the believing remnant to feast on (Psalm 23:5) so that they will endure unto the end of the tribulation period and be saved (Matthew 24:13).) They have now been recompensed for this by 2,000 years and counting of unbelief that is based upon their religion. Therefore, not only is the dispensation of grace the Gentiles' opportunity to be saved, but it is also Israel's punishment for using their wickedness to kill their Messiah (Acts 2:23).

Verse 9 ends in a colon, which tells us that verse 10 is the definition of how they are recompensed. They are recompensed with darkened eyes and with their back alway bowed down. This means that, as long as Israel views God through their religion, they will not be saved.

11:11 "All have sinned, and come short of the glory of God" (3:23). Because of this, God Himself had to provide the solution for man to have eternal life with Him. Thus, Jesus Christ was born of a virgin (Matthew 1:23), lived a perfect life (I Peter 2:22), and was the sacrifice for man's sin (3:24-25). When Jesus did this, He confronted man's sin. Now, man is forced to make a choice. He can either continue with his filthy-rags righteousness and go to hell (Isaiah 64:6), or he can recognize that he is a sinner and believe the gospel in order to have eternal life with God. But, he must make a choice about what he will do with Christ's death.

Spiritually speaking, Christ is the Rock (I Corinthians 10:4). Israel could choose to be broken by the Rock so that they would be saved, or they could choose to stumble on the Rock, fall, and be ground to powder by the Rock at His second coming (Matthew 21:42-44). For the former, the Lord Himself is their sanctuary. For the latter, He is "a stone of stumbling and...a rock of offence" (Isaiah 8:13-14). The latter was true for Israel because they sought righteousness by their own performance, rather than by faith (9:32-33). Therefore, when 11:11 says that Israel stumbled, it means that they stumbled over the cross. Because they were self-righteous, they were not looking for their Messiah to die for their sins. They did not think that was necessary. They only looked for Him to be their king. Therefore, when they saw Jesus, they tried to take Him by force to make Him their king (John 6:15). And, when He would not go along with that, many abandoned Him (John 6:66).

Therefore, Israel stumbled at the cross when they crucified their Messiah. Paul asks, "have they stumbled that they should fall?" (11:11). The answer is "God forbid." Why? Because, if they are fallen on the ground when Christ comes, they will be ground to powder (Matthew 21:44), meaning that they will go to hell. The next part of the verse says "through their fall," which means that, although they did not stumble so that they would fall, they fell anyway.

After the cross, according to Luke 13:6-9, God gave Israel a one-year grace period before He would set them aside. This grace period is the ministry of the Holy Ghost, found in Acts 2-7. In Acts 4, the religious leaders arrest Peter and John (Acts 4:3) and command them not to speak or teach any more in the name of Jesus (Acts 4:18). In Acts 5, the religious leaders arrest the apostles (Acts 5:17-18), beat them, and tell them again not to speak in Jesus' name (Acts 5:40). Then, in Acts 7:54, the religious leaders start gnawing on Stephen's body and stone him to death (Acts 7:59). This is the three-fold rejection of the Holy Ghost. Therefore, Jesus stands up and pronounces judgment upon Israel (Acts 7:55-56). Christianity says that Jesus stood up to welcome Stephen into heaven, not to judge Israel. However, scripture makes no mention of Jesus standing to welcome Stephen into heaven. Scripture DOES mention that Jesus was to sit on His Father's right hand UNTIL His foes are made His footstool (Acts 2:34-35 and Psalm 110:1). Scripture goes on to say that the reason that He stands is to "judge the people" (Isaiah 3:13). Therefore, if we are to believe scripture, we will reject Christianity's assertion and recognize that Jesus' standing on the right hand of God, in Acts 7:55-56, signals the fall of Israel and the setting aside of Israel's program.

Therefore, Israel stumbled at the cross, and they fell at the stoning of Stephen. Then, Paul says that "through [Israel's] fall salvation is come unto the Gentiles to provoke [Israel] to jealousy" (11:11). This part of the verse proves a couple of Christianity's teachings to be incorrect. 1) Christianity says we are spiritual Israel today. In other words, Christianity says that God made promises to Israel, but those promises now apply to the Gentiles, because Israel was in unbelief. This cannot be true because this verse says that the reason salvation came to the Gentiles through the fall of Israel is to provoke Israel to jealousy. In other words, God did not give up on Israel in Acts 7. Rather, God recognizes that they have fallen on the ground, and He wants to prevent them from being ground into powder at Jesus' second coming. Therefore, salvation goes to the Gentiles so that Israel might become jealous of the Gentiles' salvation and want to be saved themselves. 2) Scripture clearly says that Israel stumbled over Jesus Christ, which means that Israel's fall must have come after the cross. If their fall was not at Acts 7, when was it? The only other time could have been at the end of Acts, but Romans was written around Acts 20:1-3. There is no other event, in the first 19 chapters of Acts, that more clearly represents the fall of Israel, than the stoning of Stephen. Therefore, Israel's fall must have taken place at the stoning of Stephen.

In 9:22-23, we learned that God suffered with unbelieving Israel throughout their whole history so that the Gentiles would fear God. That way, when God offers them salvation in the dispensation of grace, they will believe. Now, in 11:11, we learn that the Gentiles' salvation will result in the Jews' salvation, because they will get jealous of the gift of eternal life and want it for themselves after the rapture of the body of Christ.

11:12 Now, we have already identified the fall of Israel as being at the stoning of Stephen in Acts 7. So, when does the diminishing of Israel take place?

Just before Stephen was stoned to death, he said, "Lord, lay not this sin to their charge" (Acts 7:60). God started the dispensation of grace with Paul in Acts 9, and He commissioned Paul to go to "the Gentiles, and kings, and the children of Israel" (Acts 9:15). Therefore, God answered Stephen's prayer by having Paul go, not just to the Gentiles, but also to the Jews. As Paul's apostolic journeys are recorded in Acts 9-28, we see him go "to the Jew first, and also to the Gentile" (2:10 and 1:16). Acts 17:2 says that, "as his manner was," Paul went to the synagogue of the Jews once he arrived in Thessalonica. So, Paul would preach the gospel of grace to the Jews when he first arrived in a city, then, after the Jews rejected his message, he would go to the Gentiles.

I Corinthians 1:22 says that "the Jews require a sign." Therefore, God gave the sign gifts to the Gentiles during the diminishing away period of Israel. This was God's way of provoking Israel to jealousy so that they might be saved during the dispensation of grace. That is why you see accounts, like Acts 19:11-12, where "God wrought special miracles by the hands of Paul."

Just like there was a threefold rejection of the Holy Ghost by Israel in Acts 2-7, there was also a threefold rejection of the gospel of grace by Israel in Acts 9-28. In Acts 13:46 Paul says, "It was necessary that the word of God should first have been spoken to you: but seeing ye put it from you, and judge yourselves unworthy of everlasting life, lo, we turn to the Gentiles." In Acts 18:6 Paul says, "Your blood be upon your own heads; I am clean: from henceforth I will go unto the Gentiles." Finally, in Acts 28:28 Paul says, "Be it known therefore unto you, that the salvation of God is sent unto the Gentiles, and that they will hear it." With this final rejection, the book of Acts ends, because Acts is concerned with Israel, and they have completely diminished away by this point.

Because Israel has diminished away, the sign gifts of their program have also gone away. Whereas Paul was healing people left and right in Acts, after Acts was over Paul says, "Trophimus have I left at Miletum sick" (II Timothy 4:20). He was not able to heal Trophimus because the sign gifts had gone away. Similarly, he told Timothy to "use a little wine for thy stomach's sake and thine often infirmities" (I Timothy 5:23).

Therefore, we have seen that Israel's stumble at the cross led to their fall at the stoning of Stephen which led to their diminishing away during the dispensation of grace in Acts 9-28. Israel was supposed to be a kingdom of priests to the Gentiles so that they might be saved (Exodus 19:5-6). Yet, Israel's unbelief still led to spiritual riches for the Gentiles, because Gentiles were now being saved directly by God and they were given the riches of God's grace (Ephesians 1:7). This shows that, even the chronic unbelief of Israel was not able to snuff out God's power to save the Gentiles. Paul's point is that, since the Gentiles were "blessed...with all spiritual blessings in heavenly places" (Ephesians 1:3) in spite of Israel's stumble, fall, and diminishing away from God, just think of how great the Gentiles' blessing will be in God's kingdom on earth when Israel actually believes God and is the kingdom of priests for God to them that God intended all along for Israel to be!

11:13-14 Paul was not one of the 12 apostles. In order to be one of the 12, he would have had to have been a believer from the time of John's baptism through Jesus' resurrection (Acts 1:21-22). Paul was an unbeliever, persecuting the believing remnant of Israel (I Timothy 1:13) and Jesus Christ (Acts 9:4-5), until the Lord called him in Acts 9. It is a good thing that Paul is not one of the 12, because the 12 apostles are promised to sit on twelve thrones judging the twelve tribes of Israel (Matthew 19:28).

Therefore, if Paul was one of the 12, he could not be "THE apostle of the Gentiles" (11:13). While there were other apostles to the body of Christ after Paul was made the apostle of the Gentiles (see Ephesians 4:11), Paul had an official calling from the Lord Jesus Christ that no one else had, because "a dispensation of the gospel [was] committed unto [him]" (I Corinthians 9:17). Jesus Christ Himself revealed the mystery to Paul (Galatians 1:11-12 and Ephesians 3:2-4), appearing to him with instructions for this dispensation on multiple occasions (Acts 26:15-16). Because this dispensation is the primary dispensation in which Gentiles are saved (11:25), Paul is THE apostle of the Gentiles.

Christianity will claim that Paul's statement is egotistical, but the opposite is actually true. The fact, that God only needed 1 apostle for the body of Christ, as opposed to 12 in Israel's program, shows that the Lord Jesus Christ did indeed triumph over Satan's forces with the cross (Colossians 2:14-15) and received ALL power in heaven and earth as a result (Matthew 28:18). Therefore, Paul's statement speaks of God's power, not of Paul's pride. Because of the Lord Jesus Christ's omnipotence (I Timothy 6:14-16), He sent Paul to "Gentiles, and kings, and the children of Israel" (Acts 9:15). Recognizing this, Paul magnifies his office (11:13) from being "the apostle of the Gentiles" (11:13), in hopes that it will include Israel. Note that Paul does not say that he magnifies himself, but he magnifies his office.

In other words, the Lord Jesus Christ sent Paul to both Gentiles and Jews (Acts 9:15), but he is only "the apostle of the Gentiles" (11:13), because the Gentiles are going to be saved in this dispensation, while Israel will be saved after the rapture (11:25-26). At the end of his ministry to the Jews, Paul said that his ministry fulfilled Isaiah 6:9-10 in that Paul was sent by God to the Jews to preach the gospel to them, but they could not hear and understand that message because "the heart of this people is waxed gross, and their ears are dull of hearing, and their eyes have they closed" (Acts 28:27), which occurred when they rejected their Messiah (John 12:37-40). The fact, that Paul calls himself "the apostle of the Gentiles," then, even though he also went to the Jews, is a clue that Paul knew all along that the Jews would not believe the mystery gospel.

Nevertheless, Paul's desire is for Israel to be saved (10:1). Therefore, he magnifies his office, which means he draws attention to it. By drawing attention to it, he hopes that he will provoke Israel to emulate the Gentiles (11:14). Paul knows that all of Israel will not be saved until after the rapture (11:26), but, if he magnifies the fact that God has set aside Israel's program and is saving Gentiles now, he may provoke some Jews to believe the gospel of grace so that at least some of them will be part of the body of Christ.

When you think about it, calling Paul to be "the apostle of the Gentiles" (11:13) is the ultimate slap in the face for Israel. Spiritually speaking, the Pharisees were as low as you could go. Jesus said that they were children of the devil (John 8:44), who spent their lives making the next generation of Pharisees twofold the children of hell that they were (Matthew 23:15). Jesus called them "serpents" and a "generation of vipers" that had no capacity to escape the damnation of hell (Matthew 23:33). Meanwhile, Paul was a Pharisee (Acts 26:5), and he was the worst of them all. He "persecuted the church of God, and wasted it" and profited in that religion above many of the other Pharisees, because he was more zealous of the Pharisees' religion (Galatians 1:13-14). This made him the chief of sinners (I Timothy 1:15), such that he was not even fit to be called an apostle (I Corinthians 15:9). But, God's grace came along, gave him eternal life in heavenly places, and made him God's apostle of the Gentiles.

What this should teach Israel is that their religion will lead them to the deepest part of hell, but God's grace can exalt them to a high position in heavenly places. What's more, God had called Israel to be a kingdom of priests to the Gentiles (Exodus 19:5-6). 1,500 years passed, and, not only had Israel not become that kingdom of priests, but they also were not even going to be part of God's kingdom (Matthew 5:20). Then, God's grace is shown to Paul, and, by himself, he is leading Gentiles into God's kingdom. This should show Israel that they should emulate Paul by abandoning the Jewish religion and believing the gospel of grace.

Thus, God had already given the sign gifts to the Gentiles to provoke Israel to jealousy (11:11). Now, Paul tries to provoke Israel even further by magnifying his office as "the apostle of the Gentiles" (11:13) so that at least some Jews might see that religion gets them hell, while faith in God gets them heaven.

11:15 Now, we see why Paul had such a great desire for Israel to be saved (9:3-4 and 10:1). It was not just because he was a Jew, but it was also because Paul understood the entire plan of God. God's plan, as we have already seen, was to start the nation of Israel and to punish them for their wickedness so that the Gentiles would fear God. Then, God set aside Israel's program and offered grace to the Gentiles for them to be saved. Once "the fulness of the Gentiles be come in" (11:25), God will resume Israel's program again and "all Israel shall be saved" (11:25-26), when they see the salvation that God gave the Gentiles at the rapture. Israel will then be God's kingdom of priests to the Gentiles. After that, the dispensation of the fulness of times will begin when all things will be reconciled to God in Christ (Ephesians 1:10).

Paul is looking at this ultimate goal of having all reconciled back to God. He recognizes that, if he can provoke at least some Jews to emulate him, they will be saved as part of the body of Christ. This may snowball into all of Israel being saved. Since that takes place after Israel's program starts up, Paul can hasten the rapture of the body of Christ if Israel's salvation starts now.

In other words, Paul wants Israel to be saved because their salvation means that the Gentiles have already been saved (11:25-26), the heavenly places are reconciled back to God, and God's kingdom on earth can begin with both Jews and Gentiles blessed in God's earthly kingdom. Therefore, Paul does not just want Israel to be saved so that they can have eternal life, but he also wants them to be saved because it means Satan and his forces being destroyed forever and God ruling over all heaven and earth.

To understand this better, we will look at a similar situation. Matthew 3:5-6 says that many Jews came to John in the wilderness to be baptized by him. John is often called "the Baptist" because of this. However, John did not baptize everyone who came to him. He told the Pharisees that, before he would baptize them, they needed to "bring forth therefore fruits meet for repentance" (Matthew 3:8), but Matthew 3 focuses on him baptizing people because repentance plus baptism equaled salvation (Acts 2:38). Therefore, if John baptized them, they must have repented first. Similarly, in 11:15, Paul is looking toward the end. Although he is "the apostle of the Gentiles" (11:13) and his message is saving the Gentiles, his heart's desire is for Israel to be saved, because that means that the fulness of the Gentiles has also come in (11:25-26), meaning that Satan's rule will soon be over.

Put in the words of 11:15, since the casting away of Israel meant the reconciling of the world back to God through the dispensation of grace, the receiving of Israel means so much more. It means life from the dead for Israel in God's kingdom on earth. In other words, if Paul can get the salvation ball rolling with Israel, it means that the rapture of the body of Christ will soon happen, because Israel's salvation, as a whole, takes place after the body of Christ is raptured up. So, getting Jews saved means that God can wrap things up quicker, because Israel's salvation is the last piece of the puzzle before Jesus' second coming. Therefore, if Israel is saved, God's kingdom on earth will start, death will be swallowed up in victory (I Corinthians 15:54), and God will rule over both heaven and earth for all eternity. That is why Paul says that the receiving of Israel means so much more than them being cast away, because it means that EVERYTHING is reconciled to God.

11:16 Paul will now explain God's master plan to reconcile heaven and earth back to Himself by using the illustration of an olive tree.

The olive tree is a type of the Holy Ghost and the spiritual life that man has in God. This is seen by looking at various verses throughout scripture. In Exodus 27:20 and Leviticus 24:2, olive oil is used to keep the lamp always burning in the temple. In Exodus 30:24-25, olive oil was used as "holy anointing oil". Various things in the temple were made of olive trees (I Kings 6:23,31-33). David said that Saul could not touch him because he was "like a green olive tree in the house of God" (Psalm 52:8). In the kingdom, Israel's beauty is to be as the olive tree (Hosea 14:6). Jesus descended from the Mount of Olives at His triumphal entry (Luke 19:37). The two witnesses are called "olive trees" (Revelation 11:4. See also Zechariah 4:11-12). Jesus' second coming will be upon the Mount of Olives (Zechariah 14:4).

By contrast, the vine represents the national life of Israel. God said, "the vineyard of the Lord of hosts is the house of Israel, and the men of Judah His pleasant plant" (Isaiah 5:7). That is why Jesus gave four parables about God's kingdom on earth with a vineyard in them (Matthew 20:1-16, 21:28-32, 21:33-44, and Luke 13:6-9), and why Jesus told believing Israel "I am the vine, ye are the branches" (John 15:5).

The fact, that Paul uses an olive tree and not a vine or vineyard, shows that he is not talking about Israel's program. Rather, he is talking about man having life in God, regardless of dispensation. If we do not see this, we can be easily persuaded by reform theology to believe that we are spiritual Israel today. If God started Israel's program and then made the body of Christ spiritual Israel today, his illustration would be of a vine, not an olive tree. Since Paul is talking about an olive tree, he is talking about life in Christ.

Granted, God did call Israel "a green olive tree" (Jeremiah 11:16), as well, but that is what God called them when He created them. Since they went into unbelief right away, God told them: "the holy flesh is passed from thee" (Jeremiah 11:15). They were still God's vineyard, as long as the nation of Israel existed, but they were no longer God's olive tree, when they went into unbelief.

With that background, we will now look at what 11:16 is saying. Since God started with Israel as His green olive tree (Jeremiah 11:16), James 1:18 says that God's intention was for Israel to "be a kind of firstfruits of His creatures." God gave Israel favored nation status (Deuteronomy 7:6) and wanted them to be a kingdom of priests to reconcile the earth back to God (Exodus 19:5-6). However, because of Israel's unbelief, the firstfruit was not holy. Therefore, the lump, i.e., the Gentiles, also was not holy.

Now, remember what we learned in 9:20-24. There, we learned that God started with a lump of unbelievers (9:20-21). With the unbelieving Gentiles, He set them aside at the Tower of Babel and started the nation of Israel with Abram in Genesis 12. With Israel, as unbelievers, He "endured with much longsuffering...that He might make known the riches of His glory on...us, whom He hath called, not of the Jews only, but also of the Gentiles" (9:22-24). So, God started with a lump of unbelievers—Jews and Gentiles—and treated the Jews and Gentiles differently so that He could create a lump of believers by saving people today in the dispensation of grace.

Therefore, the firstfruit of the olive tree that is holy, in 11:16, ends up being the body of Christ in the dispensation of grace, and the lump that is holy is Israel after the rapture of the church. This explains why Paul wants Israel to be saved. Because the Gentiles in the body of Christ are holy, Paul wants Israel to become part of that body so that "the holy lump" of believing Israel after the rapture will come sooner.

Next, 11:16 talks about the root being holy. Since Paul is talking about God's olive tree, which is "the tree of life," the root must be holy. This root is the Lord Jesus Christ (Isaiah 53:2). Jesus told the little flock that He is the vine, and they are the branches. If they abide in Him, they bear fruit. If they do not, they are cast away and burned (John 15:5-6). Of course, Paul is talking about God's olive tree, not Israel as His vine. However, the same analogy applies to God's olive tree. If Israel had faith in God in their program, it means they were abiding in God's olive tree. Therefore, they were holy. If they did not have faith, it means that their root was of the serpent (Isaiah 14:29), and they were not holy.

11:17 Since most of Israel was of their father the devil (John 8:44), most of the branches of God's olive tree were broken off. Note that He did not break off all of Israel. He only broke off "SOME of the branches" (11:17). In other words, the believing remnant of Israel is still saved and is part of God's olive tree, while unbelieving Israel has been broken off.

Next, Paul says "thou, being a wild olive tree, wert graffed in among them" (11:17). "Thou" refers to the Gentiles. At the Tower of Babel, the world united against God (Genesis 11:4-6). Because of that, God gave the Gentiles "over to a reprobate mind" (1:28). Then, God started the nation of Israel with Abram in Genesis 12:1-3. Jeremiah 11:16-17 says that God planted Israel as His "green olive tree." From 9:3-4, we learned that the promises, that God made to Israel, still belong to Israel. But, we then learned that "they are not all Israel, which are of Israel" (9:6). Only the Jews with faith in God were part of God's Israel (Galatians 6:16) and part of His olive tree. Thus, Isaac and Jacob were part of the olive tree, but Ishmael and Esau were not (9:7,13).

By contrast, the Gentiles, in Israel's program, were not the natural olive tree. Since God had given up on them at the Tower of Babel, God had not given them the Mosaic law and did not give promises to them. However, just like "they are not all Israel, which are of Israel," we can also say that, in Israel's program, "they are not all Gentiles, which are of the Gentiles." In other words, just because God gave up on the Gentiles, it does not mean that they could not be saved, just like it does not mean that all physical Jews were saved, just because Israel was God's chosen people. The Gentiles still had the conscience to tell them that they are not perfect (2:14-15). They also understood God's eternal power and Godhead (1:19-20). Therefore, the Gentiles could find God by feeling after Him (Acts 17:27). (Rahab is an example of a saved Gentile in Israel's program (James 2:25).)

Now, in Acts 7, God looked at His natural olive tree (Israel) and saw that most of them were unbelievers. He then looked at the wild olive tree (Gentiles) and saw that they would believe the gospel of grace if it was presented to them. Therefore, God pronounced judgment upon Israel, due to their unbelief, and cut all of unbelieving Israel out of His olive tree. In Acts 9, God then gave Paul the mystery gospel, thereby graffing in the Gentiles to God's olive tree. Just like Rahab, as a Gentile, received eternal life outside of God's original planting of Israel, the body of Christ does the same today. That is why we are called a "wild olive tree." Yet, because of Israel's unbelief and the Gentiles' belief, we are now part of God's olive tree as if we had been there all along.

This means that we partake "of the root and fatness of the olive tree" (11:17). Remember that the root is Christ. This means that our lives are hid with Christ in God (Colossians 3:3). This means that Christ ministers nourishment to us through His Word so that we can increase with the increase of God (Colossians 2:19). Remember that the olive tree is the Holy Ghost, and we have been given the Holy Ghost (5:5), Who teaches us the things of God (I Corinthians 2:9-13). So, by being graffed into the olive tree, we can come unto the knowledge of the truth, whereas, if we stayed as a wild olive tree, we would have still had eternal life in God because we had faith in what God revealed to us, but we would not have the ability to read God's Word to grow in Christ. Therefore, the reason that we were graffed in was so God could increase our faith so that we would be better able to serve Him for all eternity in heavenly places. This reason leads to 11:18.

11:18 "There is none righteous, no, not one.... There is none that seeketh after God.... There is none that doeth good, no, not one" (3:10-12). Because of this, the body of Christ was not graffed into God's olive tree due to anything good we did. Rather, we were graffed in because we believed in the finished work of Christ. Therefore, we should not boast against the branches. In fact, 3:27 told us that boasting is excluded by the law of faith, because our salvation is "not of works, lest any man should boast" (Ephesians 2:9). That is why Paul said, "God forbid that I should glory, save in the cross of our Lord Jesus Christ" (Galatians 6:14). In other words, if you are going to glory, "glory in the Lord" (I Corinthians 1:31 and II Corinthians 10:17).

Unfortunately, most of Christianity has the attitude that they are better than non-Christians. While saved people are seated together with Christ in heavenly places (Ephesians 2:5-6), our flesh is still just as vile after we are saved as it was before we were saved (Philippians 3:21). Therefore, if we boast in ourselves, we will fail to meet up to our high standard, bringing dishonor both to ourselves and to God. We saw this earlier in Romans with the Jewish religion. They made their boast of God in their own righteousness, and the result was that they dishonored God because they broke the law (2:17,23).

We need to remember that we are branches in God's olive tree. The branch is nothing in itself. It is sustained by the root. The fact, that we are told that the root has to bear us up (11:18), is another proof that the root is Christ. We should be receiving nourishment from the root (Colossians 2:19), the Lord Jesus Christ, so that we bear the fruit of the Spirit (Galatians 5:22). If we boast, we are not allowing Christ to live in us (Galatians 2:20), such that Christ has to bear us up. In other words, because you are "accepted in the beloved" (Ephesians 1:6) and "your life is hid with Christ in God" (Colossians 3:3), Christ must abide faithful to give you eternal life because "He cannot deny Himself" (II Timothy 2:13). Therefore, if you believe the gospel and then start boasting against the branches, instead of you producing fruit for Christ, Christ has to support you. Christ did not die to put you on life support. He wants you to be a fully functioning member of the body of Christ in heavenly places for all eternity, which you are not doing if you boast against the branches.

Remember the lesson of Israel. God says that we are told of the unbelief of Israel so that we could learn not to "lust after evil things," "be...idolaters," "commit fornication," "tempt Christ," or "murmur" against God (I Corinthians 10:6-11). Israel did all of these evil things, and they still made their boast of God, saying that they would have eternal life with God based upon their own performance (2:17). As a result, instead of being a kingdom of priests to the Gentiles, the name of God was blasphemed among the Gentiles through them (2:24). Today, in the dispensation of grace, we are called to be "ambassadors for Christ" (II Corinthians 5:20). Yet, for the most part, the name of God is blasphemed among unbelievers through Christianity. Why? Because Christianity has boasted against the branches. In other words, they have an uppity attitude of superiority based upon their own "good works," when they should be allowing the love of Christ to constrain them not to judge others based upon the flesh (II Corinthians 5:14-16). In other words, Christians need to recognize that their nourishment comes from Christ, not from themselves. This is a lesson that Israel failed to learn, and the result was that they were cut off from life in Christ. How much longer will the longsuffering of God wait today before the Gentiles are cut off from God's olive tree, resulting in the resumption of Israel's program?

11:19-20 The statement of 11:19 is one of pride. It assumes that the body of Christ is better than Israel, because Israel was broken off, while the body of Christ was graffed in. Paul explains in 11:20 that no one is better than anyone else. The reason why this took place is because the body of Christ had faith while Israel was in unbelief. Since we are no better than Israel, we should fear God. In other words, if we are the best, we can be highminded and know that nothing will happen to us. However, since "all have sinned, and come short of the glory of God" (3:23), none of us deserve our position with God. Therefore, we should seek to please God so that He continues to work through the body of Christ.

For example, if I get a job because I earned it, I can be confident that, as long as I do a good job, I will continue to have the job. However, if I get a job because of connections, I need to fear and make sure I do not disrupt my connection so that I do not lose my job. Similarly, God, in His grace, gave the body of Christ eternal life and wants us to "work" for Him in heavenly places for all eternity. If we expect God to continue to pour out His grace in this dispensation, we need to please Him by reading and believing His Word. This will ensure that we do not lose our connection with Him. That is not to say that we can lose our salvation, but it is to say that, if we want to continue to have our favored position with God, we need to allow Christ to live in us so that we produce fruit so that God will continue to pour out His grace upon the body of Christ. If we, as a whole, "frustrate the grace of God" (Galatians 2:21), Christ does not produce fruit through us. There is, then, no purpose in God continuing the dispensation of grace, and so He will start Israel's program again.

11:21-23 A good example to understand what is going on here is the book of life. In Revelation 3:5, God says that the one, who overcomes, will not have his name blotted out of the book of life. The implication is that God writes everybody's name in the book of life when they are born, and He only blots their names out when they die in unbelief. That is why John 1:9 says that God "lighteth every man that cometh into the world."

Now, we have said that the olive tree represents life in God. When God created Israel, He said they were His green olive tree (Jeremiah 11:16). That means that all members of Israel were part of that tree, just like everyone born is part of the book of life. When individual members of Israel died in unbelief, they were no longer part of His olive tree, just like their names were also blotted out of the book of life.

At the same time, because God gives life to everyone when they are born, the

Gentiles in Israel's program also had life in God. However, they were the "wild" olive tree, because God saw their unbelief and gave them over to a reprobate mind at the Tower of Babel in Genesis 11. As we have previously explained, they could feel after God and be saved, but they did not have God's law and did not have favored status with God like Israel did. Thus, they were wild, in the sense that they were not being cultivated by God, as opposed to Israel, which was still under God's law and prophets. Then, in Acts 7, God's longsuffering with unbelieving Israel stopped. He cut them out of His olive tree. Then, in Acts 9, God graffed the wild olive tree, i.e., the Gentiles, into His natural olive tree. So, basically, God cut off the branches of unbelieving Israel and graffed in all Gentiles.

Granted, this graffing in also included Jews, because the middle wall of partition between Jew and Gentile has been taken down today (Ephesians 2:14). However, Paul calls the body of Christ today "Gentiles" (11:25), because it is primarily Gentiles who are saved today, just like it is primarily Jews who are saved before the millennial reign in Israel's program (11:26). Just like God gave the Gentiles over to a reprobate mind at the Tower of Babel due to their unbelief, God blinded Israel (11:7) from seeing the truth, when they rejected their Messiah, due to their unbelief (John 12:40). This is seen in that, according to Acts 28:26-27, Paul's ministry to them fulfilled Isaiah 6:9-10, which says that Israel could not see because their hearts were fat. Moreover, "the Jews require a sign, and the Greeks seek after wisdom" (I Corinthians 1:22). Today, the sign gifts have ceased because God's perfect word has come to us (I Corinthians 13:8-10). Since the Jews are spiritually blind and there are no more physical signs for them today, very few Jews are saved during the dispensation of grace, just like very few Gentiles were saved in the Old Testament.

As such, in the dispensation of grace, Jews have experienced God's severity and Gentiles have experienced God's goodness (11:22). That is not to say that God has condemned Jews to hell today and Gentiles to hell in the Old Testament. We should look at things from an eternal-life perspective, rather than an eternal-damnation perspective, because eternal life is God's perspective, since God wants all men to be saved (I Timothy 2:4) such that He puts all men's names into the book of life when they are born.

The fact is that God gave Adam life, and he would only lose that life by disobeying God. Adam disobeyed God and so did all of his descendants. "All have sinned, and come short of the glory of God" (3:23). That is because man's heart is desperately wicked and is the most deceitful of all things (Jeremiah 17:9). When God treated everyone the same at first, the result was that "every imagination of the thoughts of [man's] heart was only evil continually" (Genesis 6:5). Therefore, when God treated everyone the same, the whole world rebelled against Him. Apparently, only Noah had faith in God (Genesis 6:9). The same thing happened again in Genesis 11, and five generations passed until Abram came along and had faith in God.

Therefore, we should not think of God as being a mean, vindictive God, Who condemns entire groups of people to hell. Rather, we should see that man is utterly wicked. God offered eternal life to all those who had faith in Him, but only one person came along every now and then with a faith response to God. Therefore, God had to act to get man to believe the gospel. So, He created racial tensions and favored the Jews above everyone else, because they were fewest in number (Deuteronomy 7:7). That way, God could show that His great love and grace are able to overcome man's utter wickedness.

First, God concluded the Gentiles in unbelief at the Tower of Babel. Then, He declared the Jews in unbelief at the stoning of Stephen in Acts 7. By concluding all in unbelief, He could have mercy on all (11:32). In other words, the Gentiles would not believe until both the Gentiles and the Jews were concluded in unbelief, and the Jews would not believe until they were concluded in unbelief and the Gentiles were concluded in belief. We will get into this more when we get to 11:32. For now, suffice it to say that God had mercy on the Gentiles when He started the body of Christ in Acts 9 because He knew that the Gentiles would believe the gospel. There will come a point when "the fulness of the Gentiles be come in" (11:25). At that time, God will cut off His goodness from the Gentiles and be good to the Jews so that they will be saved (11:26). Paul's point, in 11:22-23, is that the Gentiles should not boast against the unbelieving Jews, because, once Gentiles stop believing the mystery gospel, God will cut off the Gentiles and start Israel's program again. Therefore, we should fear the severity of God as motivation to continue in the goodness of God by reading and believing God's Word and allowing the Holy Ghost to teach it to us. In other words, even God's severity shows His love, because, without fearing God's wrath, the earthly and heavenly places would not be reconciled back to God because man would not have faith in God. That is why "the fear of the Lord is the BEGINNING of knowledge" (Proverbs 1:7). Abiding in His grace, then, is the end or goal of knowledge.

Therefore, when Paul says that the Gentiles may also be cut off, He is not referring to them losing their salvation, because they already have the atonement now (5:11). Rather, he is referring to the cutting off of the grace dispensation, just like the natural branches being cut off refers to the cutting off of Israel's prophecy dispensation. Therefore, Paul is warning Gentiles not to boast about being direct recipients of eternal life from God, because God will bring an end to the grace dispensation and "cut off" the Gentiles from having direct access to God when He resurrects the middle wall of partition in Israel's program after the rapture of the body of Christ. That is when Israel will be graffed back into the olive tree so that they may be saved.

Therefore, 11:16-23's discussion of the olive tree shows God's timeline of salvation through dispensations. In 11:16, God had the prophecy program to Israel. In 11:17, He cut off Israel and began the grace dispensation, due to Israel's unbelief. In 11:22, the Gentiles' fulness is come in, and the grace dispensation ends. In 11:23, Israel believes in God, and Israel's prophecy dispensation resumes.

11:23-24 "God is able to graff them in again" (11:23) is a statement that refutes reformed theology's teaching that we are spiritual Israel today. In other words, if it is true that we are spiritual Israel today and God is fulfilling Israel's promises to the body of Christ, then God would not be able to graff Israel in again. Instead, God's response would have to be "Sorry. Too late. You snooze; you lose. You should have trusted Me before. Now, the Gentiles get the kingdom, and you do not." NO! That is not true, because "God is able to graff them in again" (11:23).

It shows the pride of man that Christianity would claim that God will fulfill His promises to us today because Israel was in unbelief at Jesus' crucifixion. Paul just said, "boast not against the branches" (11:18), which means that the Gentiles should not boast against the Jews. Yet, that is exactly what Christianity does when it says that we are spiritual Israel today. Apparently, this pride was also a problem for the Romans, since Paul addresses it here.

In fact, Paul says, in 11:24, that, if God can take us, as a wild olive tree, and graff us into His natural olive tree, God is certainly able to take the broken-off branches (Israel) from the natural olive tree and graff them back into the natural olive tree. After all, original branches are a better fit that branches from a different tree. Therefore, we should have the same attitude as Paul, which is that we should want Jews to believe the gospel, because, if Jews start becoming members of the body of Christ, and the body of Christ is mostly Gentiles, then the fulness of the Gentiles must be right around the corner, which means we will get to go to heaven soon. Instead, Christianity says we are spiritual Israel today, and they appease their guilty consciences over stealing Israel's promises away from them by creating the political nation of Israel and sending money to them, because they were God's chosen people before.

Also, note that 11:24 says that God's olive tree is "a GOOD olive tree." The "wild olive tree" is never called "good." That is because Jesus Christ is the root of God's olive tree, and He provides nourishment to us through His Word. In other words, God's olive tree can grow and prosper (Colossians 2:19), while the wild olive tree was just a temporary tree until it could be graffed into God's tree.

In summary, God started His olive tree with Israel. Therefore, the firstfruits were Israel, but they were not holy at first (11:16), because the holy flesh fell off of Israel due to their unbelief (Jeremiah 11:15). Therefore, the lump also was not holy (11:16). God broke off the branches of the tree (Israel) (11:17) in Acts 7, and graffed in the Gentiles in Acts 9 (11:17). The root and fatness of the olive tree is the Lord Jesus Christ (11:16-17). He is the One Who gives us life and brings forth fruit through our lives. Because of this, we should not boast against unbelieving Israel (11:18). If we do, we are not allowing Christ to produce fruit through us. Therefore, He has to bear us up (11:18). Knowing that our life in Christ is dependent upon God's goodness, we should fear the Lord (11:20). Since the olive tree is life in God and not Israel, we know that if the Gentiles, as a whole, stop having faith in God, God will cut off unbelieving Gentiles and graff in believing Israel (11:23-24). This will take place when "the fulness of the Gentiles be come in" (11:25), which is at the rapture.

11:25-26 Blindness has happened to Israel IN PART, because there was still a believing remnant in Israel's program. That is why "SOME of the branches be broken off" (11:17), but not all of them. That is not to say that Israel's program continued, because all those saved after Paul and until the rapture are part of the body of Christ. "In part" just means that some Jews believed the gospel of the kingdom before God set aside Israel's program in Acts 7.

Christians always want to know when the rapture will take place. The answer is that the rapture will take place when "the fulness of the Gentiles be come in" (11:25). "Fulness" can be either in terms of quantity, quality, or both. Quantity is the most popular view, just because most of Christianity does not understand the quality argument because they do not know the advanced, mystery doctrine found in Ephesians - Colossians. The quantity view is that the rapture will take place when the world gets so bad that not another person on earth will believe the gospel. Thus, the Gentiles are full in terms of quantity. This is probably true, since God wants "ALL men to be saved" (I Timothy 2:4). Therefore, if there is another person that would be born and believe the gospel, God will let the world continue on so that that person will be saved.

The quality view speaks to the purpose for us being with Christ in heavenly places for all eternity. Before the fall of man, Satan fell himself, being prideful, thinking that he would be God (Isaiah 14:12-15). He took 1/3 of the angels with him (Revelation 12:4), and he seemed to take more of the higher ranking angels with him, since only Michael and Gabriel remained of the top-level angels (Daniel 10:21), which is probably why they are the only angels mentioned by name in the Bible. Because of this, God says that the heavens are unclean (Job 15:15). God needs to fill their positions—thrones, principalities, powers, mights, and dominions (Ephesians 1:20-21 and Colossians 1:16). Ephesians 1:22-23 says that the body of Christ is "the fulness of [Christ] that filleth all in all." In other words, Christ will fill all positions in heavenly places, that are currently occupied by Satan and his fallen angels, with the body of Christ. Just like any company's organizational structure, the higher positions have higher qualification standards. Therefore, the more sound doctrine you build up in your inner man, the higher the position you are qualified for. Therefore, from the quality view, "the fulness of the Gentiles" is when God has people qualified for every position that Satan and his fallen angels currently have. For example, if there are 12 thrones and 1,200 principalities, "the fulness of the Gentiles" is not come in until 12 people qualified for the "throne" position and 1,200 people qualified for the "principality" position are in the body of Christ.

Between quantity and quality, the quality view makes the most sense, because it is in the context of this governmental structure that Ephesians 1:22-23 says, "The fulness of Him that filleth all in all." In other words, since "fulness" is used in the context of quality in Ephesians 1:22-23, it makes the most sense that "the fulness of the Gentiles" (11:25) is also a reference to quality.

This also explains why so few people have even heard of the mystery, much less have believed it and learned advanced mystery doctrine. II Timothy 3:13 says that "evil men and seducers shall wax worse and worse." Why? Because, as God gets closer and closer to filling those top positions, Satan has to ratchet up his attack on sound doctrine to keep people from filling all of those top positions. If he is successful, the rapture will never come. But, we know that God will be successful. Why? Because "all scripture...is profitable...that the man of God may be perfect, throughly furnished unto all good works" (II Timothy 3:16-17). In other words, regardless of how deceptive Satan is, he cannot stop God's Word from strengthening members of the body of Christ with the necessary sound doctrine built up in the inner man to occupy the top positions in heavenly places. Therefore, the sooner you start learning mystery doctrine and telling others about it, the sooner the rapture will come. (That is why I am writing this commentary!)

Once the fulness of the Gentiles be come in, "all Israel shall be saved" (11:26). This does not mean that all physical Jews will be saved, because "they are not all Israel, which are of Israel" (9:6). Rather, "ALL Israel" would be all "the Israel of God" (Galatians 6:16), which is all the Jews who will believe the gospel of the kingdom. Since the fulness of the Gentiles happens at the rapture, Israel's program resumes once the rapture takes place. The events of Daniel 9:26 will take place, and then the Antichrist makes a seven-year covenant with Israel (Daniel 9:27). This seven-year covenant is the tribulation period. At least 144,000 Jews are saved halfway through the tribulation period (Revelation 7:4). Then, the rest of the lost sheep of the house of Israel, how many ever that is, are saved during the last half of the tribulation period (Revelation 12:17).

This is in fulfillment of Isaiah 59:20, which Paul quotes here. The context of that verse is that God is coming to fight for the believing remnant of Israel "when the enemy shall come in like a flood" (Isaiah 59:19). The time "when the enemy shall come in like a flood" is during the tribulation period. Therefore, the time, when "the Deliverer" comes out of Sion to get rid of ungodliness in Israel (11:26) is at Jesus' second coming.

Note that the original quote, in Isaiah 59:20, says that the Redeemer comes to those "that turn from transgression in Jacob," while the Holy Ghost changes this quote in Romans to say that "the Deliverer...shall turn away ungodliness from Jacob" (11:26). This shows that, the way Israel turns from their transgression is by repenting and being water baptized for the remission of sins (Acts 2:38). In other words, since "there is none that doeth good, no, not one" (3:12), Israel is incapable of ceasing from sin. Instead, they believe the gospel of the kingdom, and then the Lord Jesus Christ turns away their ungodliness by giving them a new spirit under the new covenant to cause them to obey the law (Isaiah 59:21 and Ezekiel 36:26-27). Similarly today, we cannot turn from ungodliness, as preachers try to tell us to do ("Turn from your sin!"). We must believe that Jesus paid our sin debt for us, and then we can allow Christ to live through us (Galatians 2:20), doing God's works through our bodies (Ephesians 2:10) that we present as living sacrifices to God (12:1).

Note that 11:26 also gives a great definition of who "all Israel" (11:26) is. As we just learned, the ones, from whom the Lord Jesus Christ turns ungodliness, are the believing remnant of Israel, while the Antichrist and apostate Israel will be punished by Him (Isaiah 59:17-19). Therefore, "all Israel" would be all of believing Israel.

Now, going back to the first part of 11:25, note how what Paul says is EXACTLY what mainstream Christianity has done. First, they have invented the idea that they are spiritual Israel. This would be "their own conceits" or their own inventions. Then, they have become wise in their own conceits because they are ignorant of the mystery that blindness in part has happened to Israel until the fulness of the Gentiles be come in. After all, if we are spiritual Israel, the fulness of the Gentiles coming in is really the same as all Israel being saved. Therefore, in this view, Israel must not really be blind right now, which contradicts 11:25. Or, if they are blind, they certainly will not see in the future, because today's Gentiles see in their place. Either way, it would be impossible for Israel to be saved AFTER the Gentiles come in!

Paul is saying that, the reason he explained the olive tree, was so the Gentiles would not think that God is done with Israel. Instead, because of the hardness of Christianity's heart, they have turned Paul's olive-tree explanation into a support for their own conceits. In other words, Paul clearly shows how Israel was part of the olive tree (11:16), then they were cut out and the Gentiles were grafted in (11:17), but then, after the rapture, Israel will be grafted back in (11:23-24), proving that God is NOT done with Israel. Yet, Christianity says that the olive tree proves that God IS done with Israel! Thus, they are wise in their own conceits and blind to the truth.

11:27 This verse is a continuation of the quote from Isaiah 59 that was seen in the last verse. Basically, it says that, when God delivers believing Israel from the Antichrist and apostate Israel, He will set up His new covenant with them, and it is at that time that God takes away their sins.

Acts 3:19-21 confirms that Israel's sins are taken away from them at Jesus' second coming. If you do not use a King James Version, you will not notice this from Acts 3:19-21. (Some modern versions also keep you from seeing this here in 11:27.)

This is a good proof that we are NOT under the new covenant today. Of course, Jeremiah 31:31 says that the Lord "will make a new covenant with the house of ISRAEL, and with the house of JUDAH." He also says there that, at that time, He will "forgive their iniquity, and...remember their sin no more" (Jeremiah 31:34). This should be a big enough clue that we are not under this covenant today. However, conceited Christianity comes along and says "we are spiritual Israel today." If that is the case, then we have to wait until Jesus' second coming to receive atonement of sins. However, 5:9 says that we have "NOW [been] justified by His blood," and 5:11 says that "we have NOW received the atonement." Therefore, Reformed Christianity's blindness to the mystery dispensation that God started with Paul in Acts 9 brings up a whole host of problems.

When you tell a lie, you have to tell another lie to explain the first lie. Then, you have to tell a third lie to explain the second lie. That is why Christianity changes the truth of God into a lie by using different Bible versions, church history, Greek and Hebrew to change word definitions, and other tactics so that God's Word is no longer their authority. They can then say, "Oh, that passage doesn't say that God will save Israel in the future," when it is clear that it does say that. Then, Christians, who attend their churches, stop reading their Bibles because they cannot understand them. After all, if the Bible does not mean what it says, then I must go to my pastor to find out what the Bible says. Therefore, I might as well stop reading the Bible. William Tyndale, Martin Luther, John Knox, Erasmus, and many others risked their very lives translating God's Word into the English language so that all Christians could read the Bible for themselves. Now, Protestantism has voluntarily discarded God's perfect Word in their language (the KJV) in favor of man's opinions so that they can follow the lusts of their flesh, rather than walking in the Spirit.

11:28-29 The gospel says that Israel's righteousness is as filthy rags (Isaiah 64:6). Therefore, they need to believe what God has told them in order to be saved. This makes Israel enemies of the gospel because they boasted in their own righteousness (2:17 and 9:31-32). The Gentiles now see that Israel is no longer God's chosen people, due to their unbelief. This shows the Gentiles that they need to believe Paul's gospel, and so Gentiles started believing the gospel in the grace dispensation, when they would not believe it in Israel's program (11:30). This is what is meant by: "As concerning the gospel, they are enemies for your sakes" (11:28).

"For the gifts and calling of God are without repentance" (11:29) is yet another example that we are not spiritual Israel today. Christians will say, "Well, God will fulfill His gifts and calling, but He will do it through us."

However, this goes against God's Word. God promised that Israel would be saved only by going through "the refiner's fire" of the tribulation period (Malachi 3:2-3). "THEN shall the offering of Judah and Jerusalem be pleasant unto the Lord" (Malachi 3:4). According to I Corinthians 3:13-15, the only fire the body of Christ goes through is the judgment seat of Christ, not the tribulation period, while Israel will still go through the fire of the tribulation period (I Peter 1:7).

Also, one of "the gifts" of God to Israel is the law (9:4). Once they get into God's kingdom, they are to be a kingdom of priests to the Gentiles (Exodus 19:5-6). That is their "calling." They will go to the Gentiles, and teach them to obey the Mosaic law (Matthew 28:19-20). Believing Gentiles will say to the Jews, "We will go with you: for we have heard that God is with you" (Zechariah 8:23). They will then go with the Jews to Mount Zion, where God dwells, and learn the Mosaic law (Isaiah 2:2-3). Therefore, one of the gifts and calling of God to Israel is for them to teach the law to the Gentiles. If we are spiritual Israel today, then we need to teach the world to obey the Mosaic law.

However, in the dispensation of grace, God has told us: "Ye are not under the law, but under grace" (6:14). God has blotted "out the handwriting of ordinances that was against us, which was contrary to us, and took it out of the way, nailing it to His cross" (Colossians 2:14). Therefore, instead of telling us to teach the law, God "hath committed unto us the word of reconciliation" (II Corinthians 5:19). This "word" is that, if we believe in Jesus' death, burial, and resurrection as atonement for our sins, we are reconciled to God and have eternal life with Him (I Corinthians 15:1-4). In other words, we are "reconciled to God by the death of His Son" (5:10).

Since "the gifts and calling of God are without repentance" (11:29) and we are not to follow the gift and calling of Israel today with regard to unbelievers, we must not be spiritual Israel today. This is also explained by the statement: "As touching the election, they are beloved for the fathers' sake" (11:28). God made promises to Abraham, Isaac, and Jacob—the fathers—that He would make of them a great nation and bless the Gentiles through them (Genesis 12:1-3, 26:24, and 28:13-14). This makes Israel elect of God to receive these promises. So far, Israel does not deserve to receive God's promises, but God has left a remnant of Israel around "according to the election of grace" (11:5). In other words, in spite of the fact that Israel is in unbelief, Israel is still beloved, "as touching the election...for the fathers' sake" (11:28).

This means that the unbelief of Israel actually helps everyone out. First, it helps out the Gentiles today, because we believe as a result of Israel being enemies of the gospel. Second, it will help out all believers in Israel, because God can fulfill His promises to Israel because He has kept them alive, in spite of their unbelief, because God elected Israel to be His people, and "the calling of God [is] without repentance" (11:29). Again, this shows that we are not spiritual Israel today. If we were, 11:28 would read, "As concerning the gospel AND the election, they are enemies for your sakes and for the fathers' sakes." Israel would not be beloved, and Jews would no longer exist today.

11:30-32 God gave man paradise, and man disobeyed God so that he would be like a god himself (Genesis 3:5-6). God gave Israel the land, but Israel wanted to be the boss. Therefore, Israel created their own gods (Exodus 32:3-4). These examples show that, man's pride is so great that, if God gives man something by grace, man exalts himself, believing that he earned what God gave him. This means that, in order to give man eternal life, God must first show man his failing so that man's pride does not get in the way of God's grace.

At the Tower of Babel, God concluded the Gentiles in unbelief, showing the Gentiles that they are not worthy of eternal life. Then, God called Abram and started the nation of Israel. Then, at the stoning of Stephen in Acts 7, God concluded Israel in unbelief. This means that all people have now been concluded in unbelief. Since "all have sinned and come short of the glory of God" (3:23), no one can earn eternal life. Since both Gentiles and Jews have now rejected God's grace, God could now destroy the whole earth, as He did in Noah's day. The problem with that is that the heaven and the earth would still be unreconciled to God, because no one believed God. Therefore, instead of standing up and judging the world in Acts 7, Jesus Christ stood up to offer grace and peace. In other words, the Gentiles obtained mercy from God, due to the unbelief of Israel (11:30).

The Gentiles will then be saved through the dispensation of grace. Then, when that dispensation is over, Israel will see that God gave the Gentiles eternal life by His mercy. Therefore, God will then give Israel mercy so that they also may be saved (11:31). Therefore, God must eliminate man's pride first before He can have mercy on all (11:32). In other words, God cannot just give man eternal life because man will not handle it responsibly. God must first let man fall in unbelief before man will accept God's free gift of eternal life to him.

This is not unlike an addict. You can try to help an addict all you want to, but it will not do any good until he recognizes that he has a problem and that he cannot solve that problem on his own. Only then will he accept help from you. Similarly, man has a sin problem. He must first recognize that he is a sinner and has no capacity within himself to overcome that problem (7:18). Only then will he believe the gospel, accepting God's free gift of eternal life to him.

Thus, we now see the purpose of God in playing favorites. The whole world was in unbelief in Genesis 11, but God only concluded the Gentiles in unbelief, while offering mercy to Abram in Genesis 12. Initially, this seems unfair to the Gentiles. However, God's mercy to the Jews made the Gentiles jealous of their position with God. Therefore, when God removed the Jews from their favored position in Acts 7, the Gentiles began believing Paul's gospel. Now, God's blinding of the Jews (John 12:39-40) in today's dispensation may seem unfair to the Jews. However, God's mercy to the Gentiles will make the Jews jealous of their position with God. Therefore, when God raptures up the body of Christ and makes Israel His people again, they will begin believing the gospel of the kingdom. Therefore, God plays favorites, not because He likes one group of people above another group, but because He must do things this way in order for man to overcome his pride and believe the gospel in order to have eternal life with Him.

Therefore, the judgment that God showed the Gentiles (9:13) when He called Israel to be His people was really the only way God could provoke the Gentiles to believe God. Similarly, the judgment God shows to Israel in this current dispensation is really the only way God can provoke the Jews to believe God (11:11). Therefore, God does not hate anyone, as "God so loved the world" (John 3:16). Rather, He judges groups of people at different times so that all might accept His love for them. It is sort of like having two kids and punishing one by not giving him attention so that he will come to you, say he is sorry, and receive your love again. He needs to feel your wrath temporarily in order to see how important your love is.

11:33 Just understanding what Paul said in 11:30-32 is no small task, as very few Christians ever allow the Holy Ghost to teach them that, as seen by the prevalent idea in Christianity that we are spiritual Israel today. Since we need the Holy Ghost to teach us what God is doing, and, even then, it is difficult to understand, it would be impossible for any of us to figure out God's plan with human wisdom, much less actually come up with His plan ourselves! In fact, Lucifer was created "full of wisdom" (Ezekiel 28:12), and he still had no idea that God's plan all along was to redeem man by having Jesus Christ die on a cross (I Corinthians 2:7-8). Therefore, we must say with Paul "O the depth of the riches both of the wisdom and knowledge of God!" (11:33).

The Psalmist said that God had "beset [him] behind and before, and laid [His] hand on [him]" (Psalm 139:3). In other words, God protected him from going to hell. How did God do this? The Psalmist said, "such knowledge is too wonderful for me; it is high, I cannot attain unto it" (Psalm 139:4). But, now we CAN know the answer, because it has been revealed to us by the Holy Ghost. However, because God's plan is so deep in wisdom and knowledge, on our own, His judgments are unsearchable and His ways are past finding out (11:33). This makes Him "the only wise God" (I Timothy 1:17).

A good way of understanding this is by looking at the Bible. We have God's perfect word today, and so few people even understand a small percentage of it. Why? First, the natural man cannot understand the things of God, because they are spiritually discerned (I Corinthians 2:14). Therefore, you must believe God's gospel to you before you can even begin to understand what you are reading, because it takes the Holy Ghost teaching the Bible to you as you read it. A good example of this is found in "a man of Ethiopia" (Acts 8:27). About one year prior, Jesus had died, was buried, and rose from the dead. This man must have known that this was a significant event. Moreover, he had a Bible, and he was reading where it said, "His life is taken from the earth" (Acts 8:32-33). So, he lived at the time that Jesus died, he found an Old-Testament scripture that spoke of Jesus' death, and he went to Jerusalem where Jesus died, which shows that he probably believed that Jesus was the Messiah. If anyone could have understood by natural means what had gone on, this man would have. Yet, he told Philip, "How can I [understand], except some man should guide me?" (Acts 8:31). The man knew the event happened, God gave him the information about the event, and he still did not understand! But, Philip was able to cause him to understand, because Philip had the Holy Ghost to teach him.

Therefore, you must have believed God's gospel in order to have the Holy Ghost. Second, you then must believe God's Word over your ideas in order to understand the Bible when you read it. That is why so few people understand even a portion of scripture. How much more, then, are God's judgments unsearchable and His ways past finding out (11:33) when He kept them a secret until revealed to Paul!

11:34 God is "the beginning and the ending" (Revelation 1:8). The Lord possessed wisdom "from everlasting, from the beginning" (Proverbs 8:12,22-23). No one else was there when God made His plan. Therefore, He had no counseller, and no one knew His mind (11:34). Since "all things were made by Him; and without Him was not any thing made that was made" (John 1:3), everyone and everything is lower than God. I cannot even figure out what another person thinks. I certainly cannot figure out what the mind of my Creator!

11:35 When Satan said, "I will be like the most High" (Isaiah 14:14), he had no idea what that meant and no way of achieving that goal, even though he was "full of wisdom" (Ezekiel 28:12). Certainly, then, since I am a fallen man, I cannot achieve to God's level. God makes the wisdom of this world out to be foolish (I Corinthians 1:20). Therefore, I cannot give anything to God; He can only give to me.

11:36 Therefore, all things are "of Him, and through Him, and to Him" (11:36). For example, for us to have eternal life, we have to receive the righteousness that is OF God. That righteousness comes THROUGH the death, burial, and resurrection of Jesus Christ. We are then given TO Him to be part of His body, "the fulness of Him that filleth all in all" (Ephesians 1:23). Since all things are of, through, and to Him, God receives the eternal glory.

Now, that is not to say that sin, evil, murder, etc. are of God. All of those things are not really things, because they will pass away. Revelation 21:4-5 says that "there shall be no more death, neither sorrow nor crying, neither shall there be any more pain: for the FORMER THINGS are passed away…. Behold, I make all things new." When God made the world, He saw that "it was very good" (Genesis 1:31). Since then, He has allowed Satan, man, and sinful things to prevail on this earth for over 6,000 years so that we would have faith in God. Once all have faith who will have faith, God gets rid of the former things of sin, and makes all things new, and those new things are now "beautiful" (Ecclesiastes 3:11), which shows that faith has been added to God's very good creation to make it beautiful. Therefore, it took us suffering through the temporal things in order for us to have faith in the eternal things.

Paul says that "we look not at the things which are seen, but at the things which are not seen: for the things which are seen are temporal; but the things which are not seen are eternal" (II Corinthians 4:18). If we are not to look at the temporal, God must not look at them either. In fact, He cannot look at them, because "Thou [God] art of purer eyes than to behold evil" (Habakkuk 1:13). Thus, the evil things of this world, because they are temporal, are not even considered by God to be real things. That is how God can say all things are for, through, and to Him, without including all of the evil things of this temporal world.

12 Because God's mercies are still being poured out upon us in the dispensation of grace (11:30), we should present our bodies as living sacrifices to God (v. 1), so that God can live in us. We will then be transformed by Christ's mind, rather than being conformed to the things of this world (v. 2). This also leads to sober thinking according to the sound doctrine we know (v. 3). Sober thinking is important since every member of the body of Christ has a different job to do (vs. 4-5). This included the use of supernatural gifts for the Romans (vs. 6-8). For us today, these gifts are not needed because we have God's completed Word. Therefore, we can show God's love to others (v. 9), even when they are our enemies (vs. 17-20). In so doing, it may give us an opportunity to share the gospel with them so that they may be saved (v. 21).

12:1 Note that Paul beseeches us. This means that he is strongly encouraging us to present our bodies as living sacrifices. Since Paul is the apostle of the Gentiles (11:13), he has the authority to command us to do this, but that is not what grace living is all about. When you were a child, your parents commanded you to do things. When you became an adult and started your own family, you still may have gone to your parents for advice, but they no longer commanded you to do something, because you were now mature enough to make your own decisions. Similarly, when we believed the gospel, we were adopted by God as full-grown sons (Galatians 4:1-7). Therefore, Paul beseeches us, rather than commanding us.

A great example of this is found with Philemon. Paul says that he could have enjoined or directed/commanded Philemon to receive Onesimus. However, for love's sake, he beseeched him instead, not as the apostle of the Gentiles, but as "Paul the aged" (Philemon 8-9). In other words, Paul knew that Philemon would use the sound doctrine of the mystery dispensation to act in the correct way, because he was a mature saint of God. Similarly, if you have read and believed the first 11 chapters of Romans, you are a mature saint of God, who can be beseeched to allow Christ to live in you, rather than commanded to do so.

Paul now begins giving practical application of the doctrine that has been learned in the first 11 chapters of Romans. All of this doctrine is tied into "the mercies of God" (12:1). We learned, in 11:30-32, that God must conclude us in unbelief before we will accept God's mercy, because we will not recognize our failure in meeting God's perfect standard until we see God's punishment. Our life in Christ, then, is just a continuation of God's mercy upon us.

Given the mercy God has shown us in giving us eternal life and making us dead to sin and alive to Christ, we should present our bodies as living sacrifices to God. Remember what we learned in Romans 6-8 that "in my flesh dwelleth no good thing" (7:18), and "our old man is crucified with Him" (6:6). Therefore, we should yield our flesh "as instruments of righteousness unto God" (6:13). In other words, presenting out bodies as living sacrifices means to count the flesh as dead and allow the Holy Spirit to use our flesh to serve God. This is the only way that our flesh, that can do nothing but sin, can be used as a holy vessel for God.

Yes, Paul does say that, when we present our bodies as living sacrifices to God, our bodies are "holy" (12:1). That is not to say that our flesh is holy, because our corruptible bodies are still vile, according to Philippians 3:21. However, "as the elect of God" we are "holy and beloved" (Colossians 3:12). In other words, if we yield our bodies "as instruments of righteousness unto God" (6:13), Christ has taken our flesh and sanctified it "with the washing of water by the word" (Ephesians 5:26). In other words, Christ neutralizes the vileness of our flesh by sound doctrine, because we are not using our flesh to satisfy its own lusts. Thus, Christ uses the word to make our bodies holy sacrifices for God to use. Without this, our bodies would not be "acceptable unto God" (12:1) to use, because God is holy Himself (I Peter 1:16).

Note also that this is our "reasonable service." Most Christians think that "reasonable" means that "serving God with my body is the least I can do to pay Him back for all He has done for me." However, this kind of thinking flies in the face of the doctrine Paul just taught us in Romans 6-8. Rather, "reasonable service" means service based upon reason. We reason out the doctrine we learned in Romans 6-8 to come to the conclusion that we cannot serve God in the flesh. Then, we use the doctrine we learned in Romans 9-11 to conclude that we need to take advantage of the mercies of God while they are upon us. We do this by sacrificing our flesh for God to use, rather than us trying to use our flesh to serve God ourselves, which we learned in Romans 6-8 is an impossibility, even after we are saved. This is important to grasp at this stage, because Paul is going to talk about our service for the remainder of Romans, and we cannot serve God unless we present our bodies as living sacrifices for God to use.

Contrast this "mercy" thinking with how most people view Christianity. Unbelievers often think of the Christian life as boring, because Christians should not do the evil things of the flesh. Therefore, they reason that they will become Christians later in life, but not now. Even among believers, most Christians think that God saved their souls to give them eternal life, and that is it. The only reason they try to do good deeds is so they look good to their Christian friends and stay "in the club." Thus, most all people, both unbelievers and believers, will not serve God at all in their entire lives. Unbelievers wait until later in life, and believers wait until they get to heaven.

However, Romans 1-5 has taught us that we will not have eternal life unless we trust in Jesus' death, burial, and resurrection as atonement for our sin. Romans 6-8 taught us that, even after we are saved, we cannot serve God in our flesh, no matter how hard we try. Romans 9-11 taught us the urgency of allowing Christ to live in us, since God can cut off the dispensation of grace at any time. Therefore, the reasonable conclusion of the first 11 chapters of Romans is to present our bodies as living sacrifices to God so that His mercies can live through us, such that others are saved and come to the knowledge of the truth (I Timothy 2:4).

12:2 When God saved us, He made us alive in Christ (6:11), giving us Christ's mind (I Corinthians 2:16) and the Holy Ghost (5:5). As we read God's Word, the Holy Ghost teaches our spirit the spiritual things of God (I Corinthians 2:14), which renews the mind of Christ within us to the things of God. As such, our mind is transformed from the "fleshly mind" (Colossians 2:18), sin-nature way of thinking to the "mind of Christ" (I Corinthians 2:16), new-nature way of thinking. As such, we decide to "put off" the things of the flesh (Colossians 3:8-9), and we "put on the new man" (Colossians 3:10). If we do this, we have been "transformed by the renewing of [our] mind" (12:2). In other words, we have presented our bodies as living sacrifices to God, such that our bodies are changed into something that is "holy," as we learned in 12:1. However, if we do not build up sound doctrine in our inner man, we will continue fulfilling the lusts of the flesh. We will then be "conformed to this world" (12:2).

In other words, when God saved us, He changed us on the inside. We can then choose to allow Him to transform our behavior to match who we are on the inside, or we can choose to use our vile flesh (Philippians 3:21) to conform us, or make us look like, the world, even though we are different on the inside. The sad thing is that, because Christianity has chosen the latter option, very few people have Christ living through them, and so the world mocks Christians as those with arrogant attitudes, thinking they are better than others, when their actions are often worse than the rest of the world, because they use grace as an excuse for sin to abound in their lives (6:1). Then, because Christians are focused on the flesh, they think that others will become Christians if they make their services more appealing to the flesh. Thus, they conform themselves to the world even more, when they should be transformed by the renewing of their mind.

However, if we choose to be transformed, we will "prove what is that good, and acceptable, and perfect, will of God" (12:2). Note that we do not DO the will of God, because Christ has to do God's will through us. Rather, we just walk in the good works that God has for us to walk in (Ephesians 2:10), and Christ lives the practical application of the doctrine in us (Galatians 2:20). People then see "that the excellency of the power [is of] God, and not of us" (II Corinthians 4:7), "proving" that God's will is for "all men to be saved, and to come unto the knowledge of the truth" (I Timothy 2:4). Then, the world will want to believe the gospel, because of the transformation it has made in our lives. But, this involves too much suffering in the flesh for most people. Therefore, churches choose to conform to the world, get new people to come to their services, and then brag about the work they are doing for the Lord, when the truth is that they are blaspheming God's name by satisfying the lusts of the flesh in the name of the Lord.

Also, presenting our bodies a living sacrifice does not mean literally giving our bodies over to be burned. Paul said that doing that profits nothing, if it is not done in love (I Corinthians 13:3). Moreover, you would not be making "a LIVING sacrifice" if you were dead or killed in the process!

12:3 The grace given unto Paul is "as a wise masterbuilder" (I Corinthians 3:10). In other words, God gave Paul mystery doctrine to build up the body of Christ in sound doctrine so that the will of God is done through us. At the same time, we need to keep in mind that "knowledge puffeth up, but charity edifieth" (I Corinthians 8:1). Your "flesh lusteth against the Spirit" to try to keep you from doing "the things that ye would" (Galatians 5:17). Therefore, as the Holy Spirit teaches you more sound doctrine, the danger can be for pride to rear its ugly head. That is why Paul warns us that, when the Holy Ghost teaches us sound doctrine through His Word, we should not think above the measure of faith that we have. In other words, we should not think that we are the expert and can now serve God in our flesh. Regardless of how much we yield the sin nature over to Christ, the sin nature remains with us and is not any less vile than it always has been. Therefore, we must think soberly, meaning that we are to think rationally and "die daily" (I Corinthians 15:31) to the flesh. In other words, we need to set aside our good emotions of what good people we are for reading our Bibles and how we must know better than others. Instead, we need to think through Romans 6-8 that our flesh is no better off than it was before we were saved. Therefore, we need to continue to yield our flesh over to God as a living sacrifice for Him to use for His purposes, rather than us trying to use our flesh for His purposes.

For example, I know that, as a believer, I should not let filthy communication come out of my mouth (Colossians 3:8). If I hear an unbeliever at work cussin' up a storm, my flesh will want me to chastise that person, because of the knowledge I have. However, sound doctrine tells me that that unbeliever cannot help but sin because in his flesh dwells no good thing (7:18). Therefore, I should use the love of Christ to judge that he is dead in his sins (II Corinthians 5:14). As such, I will not correct him, but will look for an opportunity at a later time to share the gospel with him. When that opportunity comes, he might listen and believe, whereas, if I had corrected him, he probably would not believe because I had shown him a "better-than-thou" attitude before. Therefore, charity edifies in the latter situation and God is lifted up, while knowledge puffed up in the former situation and God is made by me to look bad.

"The measure of faith" does not mean that God limits the amount of faith He gives to people. We are saved by faith (3:28), and we are supposed to live by faith (1:17). Our faith is increased the more we read God's Word rightly divided and believe the sound doctrine that the Holy Ghost teaches us as we read. Therefore, what Paul is saying is that thinking soberly means living by faith in God, using whatever "measure" of faith that we have right now. If we think according to that measure, we will not be thinking too highly, which means that we will walk after the Spirit (8:1-5). Then, the more we read and believe God's Word, the greater our "measure" of faith will be, which means we can walk in the Spirit even more so, as time goes on. Paul just wants us to keep in mind that we should not think higher than the doctrine that we know, because that is a way that the flesh can deceive you into serving yourself.

12:4-5 In 5:12, we learned that death has passed upon all men because we are all in Adam. In 5:15, we learned that all believers have been placed into Christ. (Our identity in Adam or in Christ is also stated succinctly in I Corinthians 15:22.) Now, for the first time, we are told how we are in Christ, i.e., we are in His body. This is not just an illustration that Paul is using, because he says, in I Corinthians 12:27, that "ye ARE the body of Christ, and members in particular."

It is vital for us to understand this, because it shows our identity. My "life is hid with Christ in God" (Colossians 3:3). (By the way, saved Israel is "in Christ" by being His wife (Revelation 21:9-10), and God said that, upon marriage, the two become one flesh (Genesis 2:23-24). Therefore, Christ's wife (saved (Israel) is just as much a part of Christ as His body is.) This also helps us understand that "Christ liveth in me" (Galatians 2:20). Christ is the head of the body (Ephesians 1:22, 4:15, and 5:23). Therefore, we must hold the head to receive nourishment from Christ (Colossians 2:19).

In the natural world, there are people who are paralyzed from the neck down. Their body parts look normal, but they are not able to function because they cannot receive instruction from the head. Similarly, if we do not read AND believe God's Word rightly divided, we receive no nourishment from Christ, and our labor is in vain. That is why, just after "Christ liveth in me" in Galatians 2:20, Galatians 2:21 says that, if we put ourselves back under the law after we are saved, we "frustrate the grace of God," and "Christ is dead in vain" to us.

In other words, before we are saved, we are part of "the body of sin" (6:6), and that body produces death (6:23). However, once we are saved, we are baptized into Christ's death (6:3). In other words, Christ paid the death penalty of sin for us so that we could now be taken out of death and be placed into His life (6:4). If we receive nourishment from Him, then we operate in His body, and we are under "the law of the Spirit of life in Christ Jesus" (8:2). If we decide to operate in our sin nature and not in Christ, we are still in Christ, but we are like a paralyzed body part. We are of no use to God, and we are a hindrance to the rest of the body of Christ.

Today, most of the body of Christ is paralyzed, refusing to receive nourishment from Christ. As a result, they are a hindrance to those who read and believe God's Word rightly divided. That is why this commentary is so long. I have had to write pages upon pages to explain away false doctrine popularized by Christianity and to go into more detail on what the verses are really saying in order to overcome preconceived notions from paralyzed body parts. This is the issue that Paul now addresses in 12:4-5.

12:3 said that we are to think soberly according to "the measure of faith" or the doctrine that we have built up in the inner man. In 12:4-5, Paul shares why this is important. Since we are all members of the body of Christ, if members think more highly than what they know, they are of no use, just like paralyzed body parts. In other words, if they espouse doctrine that is not sound doctrine for today, they are operating in the body of sin, rather than in the body of Christ. They are then not doing their part in the body, and the rest of the body has to make up for them, in order for the body to function properly.

For example, let's look at baptism. God's Word for us today says that "Christ sent me not to baptize, but to preach the gospel" (I Corinthians 1:17). It also says that the Spirit baptizes us into the body of Christ when we are saved (I Corinthians 12:13). Thus, today's baptism is a dry baptism that happens automatically when we believe. Since there is only "one baptism" (Ephesians 4:5) today, God does not recognize water baptism today, and so we should not be water baptizing people. We proved this sound doctrine by looking at just 3 verses.

However, the Baptist organization has declared that all believers should be water baptized as an outward manifestation of an inward work of grace. As such, they have thought more highly than they ought to have thought, because they went beyond the measure of faith that they had and went into apostasy. And, because they, along with all other Christian denominations, have so greatly influenced the body of Christ with their bad doctrine, it is extremely rare that a member of the body of Christ will believe that water baptism is not for today by just looking at the three verses mentioned. I will likely have to go through the context to explain that Paul is not saying, in I Corinthians 1:17, that others baptized for him. I will have to explain that ALL the Corinthians were baptized by the Spirit, in I Corinthians 12:13, which means that it cannot be talking about water. I will have to go over Romans 6:3-4 and Colossians 2:10-12, as well, as further proof that today's baptism is a dry one by the Spirit. Then, when they bring up Matthew 3:13-17 as support for water baptism, I will have to explain right division. I will also have to give Old-Testament verses to show how water baptism applied to Israel's program only, and why it was especially for the at-hand phase of the kingdom. I will also have to show that Christ was water baptized as part of that program, instead of being water baptized as an example to us today. And, assuming that the other person has not gotten angry and walked away from me before I get a chance to finish, I probably will not be believed, anyway. Instead, I will be accused of taking verses out of context and changing meanings to fit my theology. That person will probably think I am part of a cult and will not have anything to do with me after that. And, all of this happens because Christianity has drunken thinking, according to the lusts of their flesh, going beyond their measure of faith, to hinder the body of Christ from getting nourishment from the head. Therefore, Christianity, as a whole, is in apostasy, because Christians have failed to obey 12:3.

Different people have different measures of faith based upon their time in God's Word rightly divided. If we would just spend our time giving others the sound doctrine that we know and not speak of things that we have not learned yet, all of this confusion in Christianity would be eliminated. It would also result in many more people believing the gospel and receiving the gift of eternal life. Instead, on the rare occasion when an unbeliever actually shows interest in the afterlife, churchgoers do not even know the gospel to share with them so that they might be saved, which means that the churchgoers are not even saved themselves. Instead, they tell the unbeliever to go to church with them, where they also will be indoctrinated into a religious program that is void of life in Christ, due to the apostasy of the church! This shows how important it is for us to obey 12:3!

With regard to all members not having the same office (12:4), this simply means that there are jobs for novices to do, and there are jobs for those more advanced in the doctrine to do. For example, if someone new to the church comes in, someone, who is real personable, may want to talk with him a little bit to find out if he is saved or not. If he is saved, the person in the church may refer him to a deacon to explain basic right division. The bishop then gives the message for the day. After the service is over, the initial person in the church may go back to him to find out if he has any questions. The initial person may then refer the visitor back to the bishop if he has questions. As can be seen, the greeter can be a novice, the deacon needs to know advanced doctrine, and the bishop needs to know even more advanced doctrine. Of course, there are other novice offices, such as coordinating where to meet or planning conferences, and there are more advanced offices, such as taking care of the finances. If all members of the body of Christ work together in their respective offices, everything will operate smoothly, just like all members of the natural body need to work together.

By contrast, what is often seen in churches today is that no one talks to the new person, or, if they do, nothing is mentioned about salvation. The deacons do not know right division or sound doctrine, and so about all they do is take up the offering. The bishop also does not know sound doctrine, and so he gives a greater time for singing so people feel good. When he does finally speak, he just gives new-age philosophy, or, if he does use scripture, it is changed to fit church doctrine, rather than using scripture to establish church doctrine. The result is that the new person either comes back because he likes the social club, or he never comes back, because he wanted to learn how he can have life with God, and no one, from the least to the greatest in the church, bothered to mention that to him. It is no wonder, then, that the body of Christ is largely paralyzed today!

12:6 Now, Paul talks about using spiritual gifts to help other members of the body of Christ. Since they are "gifts," they are not things that are learned through work. In Ephesians 4:7-12, we are told that, after Jesus' ascension, He supernaturally gave gifts to the body of Christ. These gifts are to remain "TILL we all come in the unity of the faith" (Ephesians 4:13), which is when God's Word is completed. I Corinthians 13:8-10 confirms this to be the case, saying that "when that which is perfect is come, then that which is in part shall be done away." The context shows that the "perfect" is the Word of God, and the "part" are the supernatural gifts. Therefore, once God's Word was completed, these supernatural gifts were done away with. Colossians 1:25 says that the information, that the Lord gave to Paul, "fulfil[ls] the word of God," which means that complete mystery doctrine is what fulfills the word of God, not Hebrews – Revelation.

The last information that Paul received was written after Acts 28, which means that the spiritual gifts passed off the scene at the conclusion of Acts. Acts 28 is also important for another reason. That is when Paul told the Jews that he had fulfilled Isaiah 6:9-10 by going to the Jews with the mystery gospel (Acts 28:25-27). He would now go to only the Gentiles (Acts 28:28). This means that, at the end of Acts, the Jews have now diminished away (11:12). Since "the Jews require a sign, and the Greeks seek after wisdom" (I Corinthians 1:22) and the sign gifts were given to the body of Christ to provoke the Jews to jealousy (11:11), the gifts pass off the scene at the end of Acts. Therefore, after Acts 28, Paul left Trophimus sick (II Timothy 4:20), while, before Acts 28, "God wrought special miracles by the hands of Paul," such that the sick were healed (Acts 19:11-12).

Since we have God's completed Word today and the Jews have diminished away, we no longer have the supernatural gifts mentioned here by Paul. They have been done away with. For example, the teachers in the body of Christ today have to study and be a workman for God (II Timothy 2:15), while the body of Christ, at the time Romans was written, had people with the supernatural gift of teaching (12:7).

In the context, Paul mentions these gifts to show how the Romans were to use those gifts to help each other. Note how 12:6 says that they "prophesy according to the proportion of faith." This is like what we just learned about "the measure of faith" (12:3). I Corinthians 12:8-11 says that the Spirit gives different gifts to different people. I Corinthians 12:28 says that there is a hierarchy of gifts, with speaking in tongues being the least of the gifts. I Corinthians 14:5 says, "Greater is he that prophesieth than he that speaketh with tongues." I Corinthians 12:31 says that they are to "covet earnestly the best gifts." Putting all of these verses together, we learn that the greater "the proportion of faith" (12:6) that a person has, the greater the gift he will receive. All gifts can profit the body of Christ (I Corinthians 12:7), but the higher gifts can profit the body more than the lower gifts do.

The Spirit gave a member of the body of Christ the highest gift he could handle. At first, this was tongues, because tongues, by itself, does not communicate anything. Once the person used tongues after the Spirit and got more sound doctrine in his inner man, he could handle a higher gift, and so the Spirit may have given him the gift of prophecy at that time. The gifts in the body differ "according to the grace that is given to [each person]" (12:6), and the Spirit's grace was based upon "the proportion of faith" (12:6) that each member of the body of Christ has in sound doctrine.

Today, we know that these gifts have passed off the scene (I Corinthians 13:8-10), and that "faith, hope, [and] charity" remain (I Corinthians 13:13). Therefore, we know we can use these three to think soberly. Faith, as we have already talked about, has to do with believing God's Word and allowing the Holy Ghost to live through us. Hope has to do with the confident expectation that God will change our vile bodies into glorious bodies at the rapture (Philippians 3:21); therefore, we do not trust in the flesh. Charity is love in action, and God's love is shed abroad in our hearts by the Holy Ghost when we go through tribulations (5:3-5). Thus, God's Word works in us a greater "gift" to the body of Christ than the supernatural gifts God gave ever did.

12:7-8 Since these gifts are not in operation today, it can be hard to imagine what these gifts look like. "Prophecy" (12:6) is speaking what the Lord has said. Because they did not have God's completed Word, God used prophets to speak sound doctrine to them that was not yet in God's Word. This is seen in Paul's statement: "If any man think himself to be a prophet, or spiritual, let him acknowledge that the things that I write unto you are the commandments of the Lord" (I Corinthians 14:37). In other words, a prophet would speak the Lord's words to the body of Christ.

Since the ministers are said to "wait on our ministering" (12:7), ministry probably refers to ministering to the physical needs of the body of Christ. This is also seen in Acts 6:1, where taking care of widows is referred to as "the daily ministration."

"Teaching" (12:7) would be taking the sound doctrine, that has already been revealed to the body of Christ, and explaining it to them. "Exhortation" (12:8) is a step beyond teaching. Now that they have been taught the sound doctrine by the teacher, the exhorter urges them to believe and apply the sound doctrine to their lives. The gift of giving is to be done with simplicity (12:8). In other words, he is to do so with no strings attached. What is being given is not specified. It may be money, time, or even spiritual wisdom. The ruler is to do so with diligence (12:8). I would say that the ruler is the bishop. This is based on I Timothy 3:4-5, which says that the bishop must rule his own house well, or else he will not be able to take care of the church of God. Therefore, the ruler or bishop should spend a great deal of effort (diligence) making sure that the messages that he preaches and the things he does for the church are for the edification and the proper functioning of the body as a whole. I would also see the gift of mercy as belonging to the bishop or perhaps the deacons, depending on the matter (12:8). It is interesting that Paul starts out all of his epistles with "grace and peace" from God, except for I Timothy, II Timothy, and Titus. There, Paul starts out with "grace, mercy, and peace." Mercy is added because those are the pastoral epistles. God shows mercy to the pastors because they will not do things perfectly, since they still have the sin nature. Similarly, the rest of the body of Christ will also sin and do things incorrectly, and so the bishop and the deacons, i.e., the church leaders, need to show mercy to the body of Christ, as God has shown mercy to them in their positions.

12:9-10 "Dissimulation" is doing something with a false appearance. Therefore, they are to love without a false pretense. I Corinthians 13:4-8 gives a detailed description of what charity (the love of God) is. Included in this list is: "Seeketh not her own." "God commendeth His love toward us, in that, WHILE WE WERE YET SINNERS, Christ died for us" (5:8). God's love does not have strings attached. He does not love because we deserve it or because He is trying to get us to do Him a favor (we can't anyway!). Since God's love is supposed to be shed abroad by the Holy Ghost (5:5), we should allow God's love to come through us to others without seeking something in return. It may be that "the more abundantly I love you, the less I be loved" (II Corinthians 12:15), and people may speak "against us as evildoers" (I Peter 2:12). Regardless, if we share God's love without any ulterior motives, people, who are genuinely looking to us as examples of God, will ask "a reason of the hope that is in you" (I Peter 3:15), giving us the opportunity to share "the hope of the gospel" (Colossians 1:23).

Therefore, if we present our bodies a living sacrifice (v. 1), allow God to transform our minds (v. 2), and think soberly about who we really are (v. 3), God's love will then be given to others through us, such that it is without dissimulation. We will be kind to other members of the body of Christ, even preferring their welfare over ourselves. This is the practical application of the sound doctrine that is taught to us by the Spirit.

This shows the importance of sound doctrine. Actions do not change doctrine, but doctrine changes actions. Jesus said, "That which cometh out of the man, that defileth the man. For from within, out of the heart of men, proceed evil thoughts, adulteries, fornications, murders," etc. (Mark 7:20-21). Therefore, when Paul says to "abhor that which is evil; cleave to that which is good" (12:9), he is primarily talking about sound doctrine, not good or bad deeds. This is like the command of I Thessalonians 5:21 to "prove all things; hold fast that which is good." When someone teaches you doctrine, you should abhor the doctrine that is not in line with God's Word rightly divided, while you cleave to the good doctrine. If you do that, God's love will proceed from you without dissimulation. Otherwise, if you "play church," you will act good, but the "love" you show others will not be God's love. Rather, it will be the love of yourself, which does not save or edify anyone.

12:11 People like to put their Christianity in a box. They go to church on Sunday to justify their bad behavior on Saturday night. It is like they "pay their Christian dues" by going to church on Sunday, so that they can behave badly the rest of the week. 12:11 is contrary to this type of thinking.

First, it tells us not to be "slothful in business." This shows that being a Christian is not about attending church. Rather, it is about learning sound doctrine so that Christ can live in us. This is how people are saved. Typically, your co-workers spend more time with you than anyone else. Therefore, if they see you are different, they will take notice. For example, most all employees complain. They may act nicely in front of their bosses and their customers, but, once that person leaves, they start complaining to their co-workers about the boss being lazy or not understanding or the customers being rude. However, if they see you, day in and day out, with the same positive attitude all the time, they will see that are you "fervent in spirit; serving the Lord" (12:11), giving you an opportunity to share the gospel with them. Therefore, the practical application of walking in the Spirit in the workplace is that we will not be lazy, we will have a good attitude as we work, and we will work as if the Lord is our master, because He is (Ephesians 6:5). This is the only way that God's genuine love will come through us to others so that they may be saved and come unto the knowledge of the truth (I Timothy 2:4).

12:12 I Thessalonians 5:16 says to "rejoice evermore." That is not a suggestion. It is a command. The way we do it is by "rejoicing in hope" (12:12), meaning that we have the confident expectation that God will rapture us up, changing our vile flesh to be like His glorious body (Philippians 3:21). We will then "set [our] affection on things above, not on things on the earth" (Colossians 3:2), and we will rejoice. However, if we get caught in the mire of how bad the world is and how unfair everything is, we will just be miserable and be conformed to this world (12:2). God has not called us to change the world. Rather, He has called us to be delivered "from this present evil world" (Galatians 1:4). We can then rise above the world (Galatians 4:3), considering it to be dead unto us (Galatians 6:14), and be ambassadors for Christ (II Corinthians 5:20) so that others may be saved from this evil world.

Therefore, by having our focus on the eternal, we can rejoice in hope. Since the world is now dead to us, we will also be patient in tribulation. Something that is dead cannot harm you. Since "the world is crucified unto me, and I unto the world" (Galatians 6:14), tribulation should have no effect on us. "The Lord is on my side; I will not fear: what can man do unto me?" (Psalm 118:6), or, as Paul said, "If God be for us, who can be against us?" (8:31). Sure, from a fleshly perspective, tribulation is tough, but it is just temporary. Therefore, Paul can say, "For our LIGHT affliction, which is but for a moment, worketh for us a far more exceeding and eternal weight of glory" (II Corinthians 4:17). Therefore, we can patiently endure the world's afflictions, "while we look...at the things which are not seen," because they "are eternal" (II Corinthians 4:18).

Finally in this verse, Paul tells us to continue "instant in prayer" (12:12), which is very similar to "pray without ceasing" (I Thessalonians 5:17), which is found right after "rejoice evermore" (I Thessalonians 5:16). This shows that the way we set our affections on things above and look at the eternal is by praying without ceasing. That is not to say that we are always on our knees or have our eyes closed. Rather, it is saying that, because we have internalized God's Word, instead of using our conscience to make decisions, we should talk or pray God's Word to God in our minds so that our decisions are based upon God's Word instead (Ephesians 6:17-18). After all, man's fall was that he ate of the tree of the knowledge of good and evil. This knowledge caused him to be a god (Genesis 3:5,7). In other words, instead of having faith in what God told him, man would now make his own decisions based upon his conscience. Therefore, if we internalize God's Word, pray it, and allow Christ to live in us instead, we have allowed God to override our conscience, thereby reversing the sin curse in our lives. This is what life in Christ is all about! However, if we are not "instant in prayer" (12:12) nor "pray without ceasing" (I Thessalonians 5:17), our decisions will be based upon our conscience, usurping God's authority in our minds, which means we will be in sin. That is why Paul will later say, "whatsoever is not of faith is sin" (14:23), because it is of Adam instead of being of Christ.

12:13 If we are patient in tribulation, God's love will be shed abroad in our hearts (5:3-5). We will then be willing to help fellow Christians out. Galatians 6:10 says to "do good unto all men, especially unto them who are of the household of faith." We need to take care of those of our own house first (I Timothy 5:8). Then, we can take care of the saints.

12:14 Paul says to "bless them which persecute you." You may think he is talking about unbelievers persecuting you. However, the context, of 12:13-16, is the saints. Also, 12:18-21 deals with enemies, which would be unbelievers. Therefore, Paul is probably talking about people in the church persecuting you, which means that they probably persecute you with false doctrine. It is sad to say that most believers do not walk in the Spirit. When they do see someone walking in the Spirit, they may persecute him as a way of feeling better about themselves. Paul says that we are to continue to show love to these saints, even if they treat us badly. Moreover, if you do good to them while they are doing bad to you, they may believe God's Word over their own doctrine. Even if they do not, other people in the church are more likely to side with the sound doctrine that you are giving, because they see you have a better attitude than the other person. Therefore, blessing them which persecute you within the church has the effect of leading the church into the knowledge of the truth.

12:15-16 How can we "rejoice evermore" (I Thessalonians 5:16) and weep at the same time? The rejoicing evermore refers to rejoicing in our position in Christ. 12:15 is referring to having such love for our brothers and sisters in Christ that we rejoice and weep as they rejoice and weep. Our love for the fellow saints goes beyond emotions though. It goes to the intellect as well, since we are to be of the same mind.

In 12:3, we learned that we are not to think higher than what we know to be true from God's Word. That is why Paul says to "mind not high things" (12:16). "The end of the commandment is charity out of a pure heart, and of a good conscience, and of faith unfeigned" (I Timothy 1:5). When we get puffed up in our knowledge and think that we IN OURSELVES are the authority, charity is replaced with pride, our faith in God's Word becomes faith in ourselves, and our conscience is seared with pride (I Timothy 4:2). Then, whatever we speak is "vain jangling" or noise, and we do not know what we are talking about (I Timothy 1:6-7).

However, if we think soberly, according to the measure of faith that we have in God's Word (12:3), then we can all be of the same mind (12:16), meaning that we all are trying to help each other out, rather than trying to exalt ourselves above others. Then, instead of minding high things, we will "condescend to men of low estate" (12:16), meaning that we will give sound doctrine only to those who are less knowledgeable than us, rather than giving false doctrine to try to exalt ourselves above others. By speaking only what we know, we can bring the weaker brethren up to our level. Paul will go into greater detail on this point in Romans 14.

By contrast, if we are high minded, we will be "wise in [our] own conceits" (12:16). We already saw an example of this in 11:25, where reformed Christianity teaches that we are spiritual Israel today, and the result is that they fail to see the mystery. Therefore, they cannot serve God, which shows that DOCTRINE MATTERS! Therefore, it is extremely harmful to the body of Christ when Christians become prideful and get others caught up in their false doctrine. In fact, false doctrine is so serious that, when Paul saw Hymenaeus and Alexander teaching false doctrine, he called it blasphemy and kicked them out of the church (I Timothy 1:19-20)! That is why Paul told the Galatians that "if ye bite and devour one another, take heed that ye be not consumed one of another" (Galatians 5:15).

12:17 It appears that Paul now shifts his focus from interactions within the body of Christ to interactions of the body of Christ with unbelievers.

If you live godly, you will suffer persecution (II Timothy 3:12). The flesh's reaction is to stick up for itself by fighting back. However, in the spirit, you do not have to fight back. Since the spirit of an unbeliever is dead (Ephesians 2:1), he does not have the capacity not to fight back. Therefore, when someone renders evil to you, rather than using the flesh to fight back, you have a tremendous opportunity to show the love of God to him by "contrariwise blessing" (I Peter 3:9). The way you do this is by not getting upset. That way, your emotions do not get in the way. Second, be kind to the person (Ephesians 4:32). Third, if you see that the person is willing to listen, present the gospel to him. Jesus said to "bless them that curse you" (Matthew 5:44). The reason you want to do this is because unbelievers only bless those who bless them (Matthew 5:46-47). Therefore, if you return good for evil, the other person will notice that you are different, which may or may not open up the opportunity to share the gospel. However, if you return evil for evil, he will not believe the gospel because he will see you as not being any better than he is.

Providing "things honest in the sight of all men" (12:17) means that you are transparent. A great example of this is in finances. The Corinthians were going to take up a collection for the poor saints in Jerusalem. Paul told them that, when the money is ready, they need to appoint someone to go with Paul to Jerusalem so that he can verify that Paul did not take some of the money for himself. Paul says that the reason, that they should do this, is so they can provide for honest things in the sight of the Lord and in the sight of men (II Corinthians 8:21). Applied to today, a church provides their finances honest in the sight of all men when they publish income statements and balance sheets, just like the corporate world is required to do. Also, if they are going to support missionaries or other causes in other countries, they need to have someone from the organization in the other country to verify that what the church says they are giving is what they are actually giving. In this way, no one will be able to bring an accusation against the church for being a money laundering scheme.

Of course, providing things honest in the sight of all men does not just apply to money, but it also applies to all other matters in which the body of Christ deals with unbelievers. We need to be completely transparent, even if it means that we are taken advantage of by the unbelievers (12:19). That is because our goal should not be to gain as many material possessions as possible, but our goal should be to lead others to be saved and to come unto the knowledge of the truth (I Timothy 2:4). If this means that we get cheated out of some money, a piece of property, or other things, or we are treated like dirt, so be it.

12:18 This is one of the most difficult commands for us to follow today in the dispensation of grace. Christianity thinks they are doing good if they obey the 10 commandments, but that is the law. We "are not under the law, but under grace" (6:14). God has given us His grace so that His love can come through us, such that all quarrelling with all people stops. It often takes a whole lifetime to get to this point. That is why the verse says, "as much as lieth in you" (12:18), because it can take a lifetime for the sound doctrine to strengthen you with might in the inner man (Ephesians 3:16), such that you do live peaceably with all men. If you do, it is the best testimony that a believer can have with an unbeliever, because only a believer can live peaceably with all men.

Note also that the verse says, "if it be possible." Regardless of how much sound doctrine is within you, it still may not be possible to live peaceably with others. For example, Jesus Christ was the perfect man, yet there was great strife between him and the Jewish religious leaders. That is because it is up to each person as to how he will respond to the love of Christ being shared with him.

12:19 Note how this verse starts with "dearly beloved." Paul is reminding the Romans that they are "accepted in the beloved" (Ephesians 1:6). Since their lives are "hid with Christ in God" (Colossians 3:3), there is no need to seek vengeance upon anyone. This is a great example of what the grace life is all about. Christianity refers to eternal security as "easy-believism" or as an excuse to continue to live in sin (6:1). However, what the grace life is really about is that, with Christ living in you (Galatians 2:20), you now have the ability to show Christ's love to all you meet so that they may desire to have life in Christ, as well.

Again, since your focus with others should be on their spiritual edification, rather than trying to get out of them what you want in the flesh, when you are wronged, you should "avenge not yourselves" (12:19). Go ahead and allow others to pour their wrath upon you. That is not to say that you should intentionally allow someone to walk all over you. However, it is to say that you have the eternal perspective. You recognize that God is offering "grace and peace" to the world right now (1:7). You also recognize that you are Christ's ambassador to reconcile people back to God (II Corinthians 5:20). An ambassador brings peace between two parties. He is not a war agent. Therefore, we should let people mistreat us when we show God's love to them, recognizing that, when the time comes, the Lord "will repay" (12:19) with vengeance, since He is "a man of war" (Exodus 15:3).

"Vengeance is Mine" comes from Deuteronomy 32:35 which says that "their foot shall slide IN DUE TIME." In other words, there is "a time of war, and a time of peace" (Ecclesiastes 3:8). Right now is a time of peace with God. The time of war with God will come later at Jesus' second coming.

12:20 This is a quote of Proverbs 25:21-22. Now, if I am to "recompense to no man evil for evil" (12:17), "live peaceably with all men" (12:18), and "give place unto wrath" (12:19), why would I feed my enemy if doing so heaps "coals of fire on his head" (12:20)? In other words, wouldn't I be harming my enemy by feeding him, if doing so heaps coals of fire on his head? Christians usually think of heaping coals of fire on his head as making the person angrier and angrier at you. Therefore, you get your revenge on them by doing good to them. However, Paul said, "avenge not yourselves" (12:19). Therefore, the standard interpretation of heaping coals of fire cannot be true. The answer must be that heaping coals of fire on his head is a GOOD thing for him, rather than a bad thing, since 12:21 says that you "overcome evil with GOOD."

What this phrase really means is that, by doing good to someone who does evil to you, you are getting him to realize that he is not a good person. This helps him realize that he is headed for the lake of fire. Therefore, by your doing good, you are heaping coals of fire on him in the sense that you are giving him an opportunity to see that you are a saint of God, while he is headed for hell. It is as if he can see the coals of fire from hell being poured out upon him as you do good unto him. The reason this is good is because he can see this now, which means that he can do something about it now. He can believe the gospel and receive God's gift of eternal life to him. Thus, doing good to someone, who is your enemy, is like an intervention of an addict. In an intervention, you show the other person that he has a problem and needs helps. Similarly, by doing good to your enemy, you show your enemy that he has a sin problem that only God can solve for him.

12:21 This verse shows that you overcome evil with good. In 1:18-32, we learned of the downward spiral of sin. The more you sin and deny the things of God, the greater your sin becomes over time. Therefore, if you do evil to me and I do evil back to you, you will do a greater evil back to me. Evil becomes worse and worse, and no good ever comes out of it. However, if I show the love of Christ to an unbeliever, he can see how "the goodness of God [leads him] to repentance" (2:4), because God's goodness is coming through me to him. He may then believe the gospel and be saved. If that happens, then evil is overcome with good. Even if that does not happen, God will pour His vengeance out upon the person. Since God is good (Matthew 19:17), His judgment of that person will be good, and so the person's evil is still overcome with good. If evil is overcome with good now, the person has eternal life with God. If evil is overcome with good at the judgment, the person has eternal damnation in the lake of fire. Therefore, it is better that we heap coals of fire on his head now, instead of him actually burning in the lake of fire forever after the Great White Throne Judgment (Revelation

13 In order to obey God, we need to subject ourselves to God's governmental structure. This includes both Satan in the heavenly structure and men ruling in the earthly structure (vs. 1-2). Therefore, subjecting ourselves to rulers is based upon God having ordained the governmental structure, rather than based upon the worthiness of the individual rulers over us. On the earth, this means that we need to pay our taxes and other governmental fees, as well as fearing and honoring the law men over us (vs. 5-7). Our relationship with society should be that we love everyone (v. 8). We do so with God's love. Therefore, we give them the truth, rather than accepting, with a non-judgmental attitude, the lies that men follow (vs. 9-10). We need to do this because, in view of eternity, our lives on earth are short. Therefore, we need to get the sound doctrine of Paul's epistles in our inner man so that the Lord Jesus Christ will live through us so that others are saved and come unto the knowledge of the truth (vs. 11-14). If we do not do this, we will sleep spiritually, and God's kingdom will not be advanced through us.

13:1-2 "The higher powers" (13:1) are all the powers over you. We normally think of government. However, this also must mean that we are subject to spiritual powers. Therefore, we need to be subject to Satan. Now, before you accuse me of committing blasphemy and being a Satan worshipper, let us examine what scripture says. Jude 9 says, "Michael the archangel, when contending with the devil he disputed about the body of Moses, durst not bring against him a railing accusation, but said, The Lord rebuke thee." Michael is a high-ranking angel, and angels are higher than humans in our current state (Psalm 8:4-5). The devil must have been wrong about the body of Moses. Yet, because the devil ranked higher than Michael, Michael was subject unto the higher powers and said "The Lord rebuke thee," rather than Michael rebuking the devil himself. Further, angels will not even bring railing accusations against ungodly men, even though the angels are "greater in power and might" than they are (II Peter 2:10-11).

Satan is "the god of this world" (II Corinthians 4:4). He is "the prince of the power of the air" and has the world following an ungodly course (Ephesians 2:2). Therefore, we need to respect Satan as a higher power in that we do not try to overthrow him, even though he is leading people astray. This means that it is not our job to go on moral crusades to try to get people to stop taking drugs, stop having pre-marital sex, stop having abortions, etc. Moral crusades undermine the authority of Satan as the god of this world, because we are trying to change the world. This means that we are resisting the ordinance of God (13:2), because God has ordained Satan as the god of this world (13:1).

Instead, we are ambassadors for Christ. We should present the gospel to unbelievers when we have the opportunity. Then, if they believe, they join God's side. In this way, we say to Satan: "The Lord rebuke thee." But, if we rebuke Satan ourselves by trying to interfere with his course via moral crusades, we disobey God, we create an attitude that we are better than unbelievers which hurts our ability to reconcile people to God, and we stop focusing on what God has called us to do.

(Moral crusades also usually backfire. For example, in the late 1800s and early 1900s, the Woman's Christian Temperance Union strove to get rid of alcohol in the United States. They succeeded in that an amendment was made to the Constitution. However, they failed in that an indirect result of their efforts was that more women began engaging in promiscuous behavior and dress, which was their flesh's way of rebelling against the new law. On top of that, their amendment was later repealed. Therefore, not only do moral crusades rebel against the higher powers, but they also produce unintended results, even when they are "successful.")

Moral crusades also show a lack of faith in God, because God said, "Vengeance is mine; I will repay" (12:19). This shows that who is right and who is wrong is not the issue. After all, we are all wrong in the sense that we have all sinned (3:23). Therefore, if you are looking for justice, then God needs to send you to hell, right along with the people you are judging. However, since God is pouring out grace and peace today, we should, as His ambassadors, look for opportunities to point others to God's grace and peace.

That is not to say that we should not be grieved with what goes on in the world. Jesus was grieved over the hardness of Israel's hearts (Mark 3:5), and He wept over the unbelief of Israel (John 11:35). Remember, we are not to be conformed to this world, but we are to be transformed by having our minds renewed by sound doctrine (12:2). Therefore, we should be grieved when we see the unbelief of this world, but that does not mean that we should try to stop people from sinning, because they cannot. Paul will soon say that "whatsoever is not of faith is sin" (14:23), which means that unbelievers always sin. Therefore, any victories over a particular sin will just result in that person engaging in a different sin, or he will still commit that sin in his heart, if not in his actions.

When we look at a person, we should ask ourselves: "Is he in Adam or is he in Christ? If he is in Adam, I need to look for an opportunity to share the gospel. If he is in Christ, I should share sound doctrine with him." In fact, the love of Christ constrains us to judge people in this way (II Corinthians 5:14-16). Either way, I do not try to stop people from sinning, because the unbeliever cannot stop sinning and the believer stops sin by having sound doctrine work in his life, not by telling him to stop sinning. Because Christians do not understand their identity in Christ, as defined in Romans 6-8, they try to stop sin, rather than trying to stop unbelief.

Therefore, we need to respect the power of Satan as the god of this world. At the same time, we should not confuse respect with conformity to the world.

233

Learning to respect Satan's power in this world now gives us the proper perspective when it comes to those over us in our government. We should always obey those over us in our government, provided that doing so does not go against a command given us in Paul's epistles (see also Titus 3:1). The reason is because all those over us are ordained of God. This does not mean that they act as God would have them to act, nor does it mean that we agree with how they are ruling. It just means that God has allowed them to rule over us, which means we need to respect them.

A great example of this is found in Acts 23. There, Paul is smitten in the face by commandment of the high priest (Acts 23:2). Paul responds, "God shall smite thee, thou whited wall," because he was smitten contrary to the law (Acts 23:3). Paul is correct that, by smiting him, the high priest broke the commandment of Leviticus 19:15. However, the high priest is still a power over him. When Paul finds out that he is the high priest, Paul does not say, "When he stops disobeying the law, I will stop disobeying the law." Rather, he says, "I wist not, brethren, that he was the high priest: for it is written, Thou shalt not speak evil of the ruler of thy people" (Acts 23:5 and Exodus 22:28). In other words, although the high priest was in the wrong by smiting Paul, Paul was equally in the wrong by speaking evil of the high priest. Paul should have been subject to the higher power, even though the higher power was wrong in what he did.

Since we are subject to God and those over us are ordained of God, we are to be subject to those ruling over us as well, unless doing so means disobeying God (Acts 5:29). Complaints from Christians about their rulers usually come from not understanding Romans 6-8. Christians generally try to serve God in the flesh by imposing legalism in serving God. They then try to get their rulers to obey their legalism, because it makes the Christians feel morally superior to the unbelievers. Christians may also complain about rulers because they do not like the immorality that they allow. Regardless of the reason, our priority should be on allowing Christ to live through us, which includes obeying those in authority over us, regardless of how corrupt they may be. Since God has allowed them to rule, we should to. If we do not, we are seen as being judgmental, which brings up the defenses of the other party against our judgment. Since God is not judging today, we should not be judging either. Therefore, if we do not say anything about specific sins but get the person to recognize that all have sinned, including himself, the unbeliever can focus on God's grace, rather than defending against judgment, so that he may become a believer.

Receiving damnation does not mean that we lose our salvation because we disobey rulers. Our salvation was settled by Jesus' sacrifice on the cross. Paul stopped talking about that in Romans 5. Rather, the damnation Paul is talking about is simply the punishment you will receive from rulers if you disobey their commands, as explained in 13:4.

13:3-4 Rulers are a terror to evil works, not to good works. If the Christian is walking in the Spirit, he will only do good works. Therefore, he has no worry over what rulers can do to him. Of course, there are exceptions, where rulers persecute Christians, but that is when religion gets mixed up with politics. Religion is a terror to good works, while rulers are usually just a terror to evil works. We see this with Jesus and Paul, for example. Both suffered great persecution from religious leaders, while secular leaders had no problem with them. Rulers, if they do not have a religious agenda, are concerned with keeping the peace. This is how they are "the minister of God to thee for good" (13:4), because they help combat the evil that would hinder the gospel from going out. God established four institutions for mankind in Genesis: 1) Free will, 2) Marriage, 3) Family, and 4) Nations. He did not establish nationalism until the Tower of Babel in Genesis 11, and He did so to protect the first three institutions He established. Therefore, government is ordained of God, making rulers ministers of God.

Again, do not confuse respect with conformity. God has called us to "fight the good fight of faith" (I Timothy 6:12), not fight the fight of morality. Therefore, when Hitler gassed the Jews and FDR imprisoned the Japanese, the Christians' job was not to put a stop to them or right their wrongs. The Christian is an ambassador for Christ. Therefore, he is to fight the spiritual battle against Satan's forces so that people may be saved and come unto the knowledge of the truth (I Timothy 2:4). He is not to fight the moral battle of right vs. wrong. When Christians get involved with morality, they stop fighting for faith and start fighting for the flesh, which means they have stopped fighting for Christ. ("We wrestle not against flesh and blood" (Ephesians 6:12).) Therefore, they are not being ambassadors for Christ.

13:5-6 The two reasons given for obeying those over you are: 1) So that you do not incur their wrath, and 2) "For conscience sake" (13:5). 14:20,23 says that you sin if you go against your conscience. "Ye are not under the law, but under grace" (6:14). "All things are lawful unto me, but all things are not expedient" (I Corinthians 6:12). We have already learned that we should act as mature, adult believers in Christ. Therefore, although we can do whatever we want, we sin if we go against our own conscience. Since we are "dead to sin" (6:2), we should always obey our own conscience.

For these same, two reasons, we should pay our taxes (13:6). We should also pay our taxes because governmental rulers are God's ministers, and they work as such. Since "the labourer is worthy of his reward" (I Timothy 5:18), we should "reward" him by paying what we owe him, which is our taxes. In other words, God has set up rulers to protect the four divine institutions that God set up: 1) Free will, 2) Marriage, 3) Family, and 4) Nationalism. Therefore, they should be paid for their work, even if we do not think they are doing a good job. The flesh may say, "I didn't vote for him; I don't like his policies; He is no good, etc." However, the spirit says, "I owe him a debt." This shows how different grace thinking is from the flesh's thinking!

13:7-8 Some Christians say that we should never go into debt on anything, because 13:8 says, "Owe no man any thing." However, Paul never says that. Everything, in 13:7, has to do with what we are required to give to the government. It says nothing about voluntary payments. The government is to receive the money that they require of us, which is tribute and custom. They are also to receive fear from us, which means that we should obey the law, because we fear the punishment of disobedience. We are also to honour them, which means that we respect the authorities over us.

Then, in 13:8, Paul says that the only debt that we owe to society is that we love them. Again, this has nothing to do with financial transactions. Even if we try to apply this to loans, we still do not owe anyone anything, as long as we pay the agreed-upon amount of the loan. For example, if I buy a house and agree to $1,000 payments for 30 years, I still do not owe anything, as long as I make the agreed-upon payments. If you try to say that I owe, you also have to consider all other bills as things I owe. Therefore, even if I paid cash for the house, I could not have electricity, water, trash pickup, and homeowners' insurance, because I would owe those bills. I could not even buy the house, because I would "owe" property taxes. I could not rent a house, because I would owe rent, according to the rental agreement. Therefore, Paul cannot be saying that we are not allowed to enter into credit transactions.

Another reason why this cannot apply to loans is because God authorized loans for Israel in the Old Testament. "If thou lend money to any of My people that is poor by thee" (Exodus 22:25) means that God authorized loans. Leviticus 25:36-37 and Deuteronomy 23:19-20 also express the same thing.

Probably the reason why some Christians focus on not taking out loans is because they do not want to obey what this verse is truly saying, which is that our debt to society is to love them. "The love of Christ constraineth us" to judge all people as dead in their sins (II Corinthians 5:14), which means we can no longer judge people after the flesh (II Corinthians 5:16). Therefore, no matter how good of a person I am, I cannot judge myself to be any better than the vilest of people on earth, because "all have sinned" (3:23), and "there is none that doeth good, no, not one" (3:12). Granted, I am seated with Christ in heavenly places and unbelievers are not, but my flesh is no better than unbelievers' flesh (Ephesians 2:5-6). This is a reality that very few people will admit to.

For example, a lawyer told Jesus that the way to inherit eternal life was to love God and love his neighbor. Jesus said that he was correct. Then, "willing to justify himself, [he] said unto Jesus, And who is my neighbour?" (Luke 10:25-29). Jesus then told him that the vilest of people is his neighbour (Luke 10:30-37).

What this shows is that the law is not just some list of commands that you check off and obey by rote. Rather, the law is obeyed by loving God and others. The problem is that the law tells me what to do, but it does not give me the ability to perform the law. Since "in my flesh dwelleth no good thing," "how to perform that which is good I find not" (7:18). We have already learned that "God through Jesus Christ our Lord" (7:25) has given us His Spirit so that Christ in me can perform the law perfectly through me. In other words, my flesh cannot share God's love with others, but the Holy Ghost can share God's love with others through me (5:5).

Note also that Paul does not say that love "obeys" the law; he says that love "fulfills" the law (13:8). Fulfilling the law means that it accomplishes the purpose of the law. God wants the law's purpose accomplished through us, but, as Romans 7 taught us, we could not accomplish the law's purpose when we were under the law. Therefore, we had to be put under grace (6:14), have our requirement to fulfill the law blotted out (Colossians 2:14), and have the Holy Spirit work through us in order to fulfill the purpose of the law.

13:9 The first five of the 10 commandments show how to love God, while the last five show how to love each other. Since Paul is talking about our relationships with others, he only quotes the latter 5 commandments.

Because Christianity is so focused on the law, they want to know which of the Old-Testament commandments we need to obey today. They will say that we need to obey all moral laws, or they will say that we only need to obey the laws that are mentioned in the New Testament. Such an attitude shows that they have not learned the sound doctrine of Paul's epistles! "When we were children [we] were in bondage under the elements of the world" (Galatians 4:3). Now, we have been redeemed from being under the law and have received the adoption of sons (Galatians 4:5-6). Therefore, "ye are not under the law, but under grace" (6:14). We have been freed from the law of sin and death and have been put under the law of Spirit and life (8:2). Therefore, if you are asking what commandments to obey, you are asking the wrong question.

Rather, you should recognize that you have eternal life right now, which means that your performance is no longer an issue. You are an adult son of God, rather than a child. A child asks, "What do I have to do?" in an effort to see what he can get away with. An adult asks, "What can Christ do through me?" in an effort to allow the love of God to come through him to others. That is why Paul lists the latter five commandments of God, and then says that they are all "briefly comprehended in this saying, namely, Thou shalt love thy neighbour as thyself" (13:9). In other words, you are free from trying to comprehend all of the "do's and don'ts" of the law, because, now that you have learned basic mystery doctrine, you understand that the whole law is "briefly comprehended" in the commandments to love God and love others. Just like an adult does not have to keep in mind the specific laws that his parents put him under when he was a child because he knows how to live on his own, you do not have to compile a list of what you should or should not do living in grace.

Christians rarely understand that they are not under the law today, and, when they do, the first thing they ask is how do they live in grace. It is very simple. Love God, and love others. Just read and believe God's Word rightly divided, allow the Holy Ghost to teach it to you, and Christ will automatically share His love to others through you. The lesson of the law was not for you to obey the law. The lesson of the law was for you to learn that you cannot obey the law. Now that you have learned that lesson, you are no longer under the schoolmaster of the law, freeing you up to live by the faith of Jesus Christ (Galatians 3:24-25).

This is an especially important concept to understand when it comes to so-called "gray" areas or contradictory elements of the law. For example, let's say that someone invited me over to dinner, and he cooked me a steak. I did not like the steak because it was tough to chew. Should I lie, and say that I liked it, so that I do not hurt his feelings? The love of Christ constrains me to share the gospel with him if at all possible. Since that possibility will probably be diminished by me telling the truth, I should lie and tell him that I liked the steak. Christianity will say, "Oh, but lying is breaking one of the 10 commandments." Again, that is not the focus. The focus is sharing the love of Christ with him.

Now, let me share a Biblical example with you. The government of Jericho told its citizens to let them know if they see any spies from Israel. Rahab, a citizen of Jericho, hid Israel's spies. Therefore, she disobeyed her government's command. Not only that, but she also lied about where the spies had gone. Titus 3:1 says "to obey magistrates." Therefore, she broke the law of her land, and she broke God's law. Yet, James 2:25 says that God justified Rahab BECAUSE she lied. Why? Because she responded to the law of faith. In other words, God is not interested in people trying to obey His law. Rather, He gave His law so that people would stop trusting in their flesh and start having faith in God. The love of Christ then constrains us to operate by the law of faith. Therefore, we should never ask, "What does the law say?" Rather, we should look at "the law of the Spirit of life in Christ Jesus" (8:1), which is the law of faith in God's Word. Christ will then live His Word out naturally in us. The Christian asks, "Yeah, but what do I do?" The answer is, "You don't do anything! You just read and believe God's Word and walk in the good work that God wants you to walk in" (Ephesians 2:10). You may ask, "But, how do I do that?" Again, you are missing the point.

You never have to ask the question, "How do I sin?" because it happens naturally in your flesh, due to your sin nature. Similarly, in Christ, you never have to ask the question, "How do I serve God?" because Christ naturally serves God for you through your body, since you have now been made "partakers of the divine nature" (II Peter 1:4). In other words, by presenting your body as a living sacrifice to God (12:1), you are allowing God to do through you what comes naturally to Him. If this is not a good enough answer for you, then it means that you are trying to serve God in your flesh.

For example, let's say that you want to build a house, but you must first move a 3,000-pound rock out of the way. You ask me, "How do I move the rock?" I tell you, "I will bring my excavator over and move the rock for you." That is the answer to the question. If you respond with, "But I want to move the rock. I do not want you and your excavator to do it," you have not learned the lesson, which is "YOU cannot move the rock. It is too heavy. You must let me operate a machine that will move it for you." Similarly speaking, YOU cannot serve God. Christ must serve God through you. You just let Him do it. Colossians 3:16 says, "LET the word of Christ dwell in you richly in all wisdom." When you recognize your flesh cannot do anything for God in itself, you stop striving and you just LET God's Word dwell in you so that Christ can live God's Word through you. Stop saying, "I want to serve God," and start saying, "I want Christ to serve God through me."

13:10 People complain about there not being any peace on earth. There will not be peace until God's millennial reign on earth. The way He accomplishes peace is by putting a new heart and the Holy Spirit within Israel so that they obey the law perfectly (Ezekiel 36:26-27), and He rules with a rod of iron (Revelation 2:27) over the Gentiles in order to enforce His law. If men want peace today, they need to have government that strictly enforces God's law, but people do not like the strictest governments today, because they are not able to fulfill the lusts of their flesh. People want to do the evil desires of their hearts and have peace at the same time, which is an impossibility.

Therefore, this verse does NOT say that God's law is fulfilled when we live in harmony with others. Rather, it says "love worketh no ill to his neighbour" (13:10). This means that, the way the love of God comes through my life to others, is when I look out for the spiritual well-being of all those around me. If they are unbelievers, love says, "I want them to be saved." If they are believers, love says, "I want them to come unto the knowledge of the truth" (I Timothy 2:4).

By contrast, living in harmony says, "Peace, brother. I will not say anything or do anything that will offend you or cause you to be upset. Therefore, if you want to be a Hindu, that's great. Everyone must find his own path to God." Such a response works ill to my neighbour, because it does not give him the gospel so that he might be saved. The response of love may be, "How is the Hindu religion working for you? How do you right the wrong of making a mistake in your religion? I have learned that no religion leads you to God because we all make mistakes from time to time. The good news is that Jesus Christ lived a perfect life so that you do not have to. If you just believe that He died, was buried, and rose again as atonement for your sins, God will give you eternal life. You can stop trying to earn it yourself." This latter response will probably result in strife between me and the other person. We will not be able to live in harmony. However, it is the response of love, because it is meant to help him spiritually, rather than working ill to him spiritually. Therefore, love fulfills the law of God, and it does not fulfill the purpose of man, which is pure, unadulterated selfishness packaged as "love" so that I can be prideful in what a great person I am.

Jesus said, "I came not to send peace, but a sword. For I am come to set a man at variance against his father, and the daughter against her mother" (Matthew 10:34-35). That is because "the Word of God is quick, and powerful, and sharper than any twoedged sword, piercing even to the dividing asunder of soul and spirit, and of the joints and marrow, and is a discerner of the thoughts and intents of the heart" (Hebrews 4:12). Love will share God's Word to others, which will pierce them. Because of this, harmony may be destroyed. Therefore, love is sharing the truth with others; love is not tolerance of bad doctrine that will either lead someone to hell (non-Christian) or keep someone from taking a position in heavenly places in Christ (Christian).

13:11-14 "Knowing the time" is not a reference to knowing when the rapture will take place, because no man knows when that event will take place, since no prophecy has to be fulfilled for the rapture to take place. All we know is that the rapture will happen when "the fulness of the Gentiles be come in" (11:25). Rather, Paul is referring to the time in an individual's life. Psalm 90:10 says that we get to live about 70 to 80 years. Even if you are saved as a child, you have, at the most, about 80 years to do God's will on earth, which is for "all men to be saved, and to come unto the knowledge of the truth" (I Timothy 2:4). When compared with all eternity, that is a very short time. Therefore, "the day is at hand" (13:12). Our time to do God's will on earth gets shorter each day, because "now is our salvation nearer than when we believed" (13:11).

Therefore, "it is high time to awake out of sleep" (13:11). "Ye are all the children of light, and the children of the day: we are not of the night, nor of darkness. Therefore let us not sleep as do others; but let us watch and be sober" (I Thessalonians 5:5-6). Obviously, Paul is talking about spiritual sleep, as in the parable of the ten virgins (Matthew 25:5). Before we were saved, we were "dead in trespasses and sins" (Ephesians 2:1). Once we are saved, we are "alive unto God" (6:11). If all we do is follow the lusts of our flesh and the course of this world, then our spirits are not being used. Since our spirits are alive but not being used, they must be asleep. Since we are "of the day" (I Thessalonians 5:5), we should be awake, spiritually speaking. This means that we should be reading and believing God's Word and following after the things of the Spirit. God's light can only shine through us to a dark world while we are on this earth. People can only be saved through God's light shining through us for 80 years or less. That period is "but for a moment" (II Corinthians 4:17) when compared with eternity. Therefore, "it is high time to awake out of sleep" (13:11).

Given this eternal perspective, the urgency we feel to allow Christ to live in us should be like the urgency that a college football player feels about turning pro and making millions of dollars. One injury could end his career. Even if he remains uninjured, he still probably will not make millions per year for more than 10 years. Similarly, one accident could end our lives in the flesh. Even if we live a long life, 80 years is nothing compared with eternity. Therefore, there should be a great sense of urgency to allow Christ to live through us on this earth, while we are still on this earth. We need to stop sitting on our hands, and start using them to turn the pages of the Bible. By being edified in God's Word, God's love will come through our lives to others; thus, accomplishing God's will through us.

With regard to "the armour of light" (13:12), we need to understand that, because "the Lord is a man of war" (Exodus 15:3), and our lives are "hid with Christ in God" (Colossians 3:3), we are in a war. "We wrestle...against spiritual wickedness in high places" (Ephesians 6:12). "We do not war after the flesh: (For the weapons of our warfare are not carnal, but mighty through God to the pulling down of strong holds" (II Corinthians 10:3-4). Therefore, "the armour of light" consists of spiritual weapons for a spiritual war. We just learned, in I Thessalonians 5:5, that we are "children of light." Well, that same passage also mentions some of our "armour of light." It tells us to put "on the breastplate of **faith** and **love**; and for an helmet, the **hope** of salvation" (I Thessalonians 5:8). I Corinthians 13:13 says that faith, hope, and love are the three things that will abide forever. Romans – Galatians teaches us faith in God, Ephesians – Colossians teaches us the love of God, and I and II Thessalonians teaches us the hope of salvation. Therefore, "the armour of light" is really the sound doctrine found in Paul's epistles used by Christ in us as we read and believe that doctrine. Thus, awaking out of our sleep means that we just need to read and believe Paul's epistles. This is "the simplicity that is in Christ" (II Corinthians 11:3).

While our fight, using the armour of light, does occur in the world, the battle must first be won against our own flesh. Paul compares this fight to running a race. He says that, in order to win, you have to be temperate in all things, which means that you have to be certain about how to win the race. This means that he must keep his body in subjection to mystery doctrine. When the internal battle is won, people may believe the gospel when he presents it to them. If he has not won the internal battle between his flesh and his spirit, the world will cast him away (I Corinthians 9:24-27). Thus, "the works of darkness" lose when we use "the armour of light" (13:12) to "fight the good fight of faith" (I Timothy 6:12). But, if we are spiritually asleep, our spirit does not fight that internal battle, the flesh wins, and God's will is not done through us.

"The day" refers to when we live in heaven. It is "at hand" (13:12) because "our old man is crucified with Him" (6:6) and we are "freed from sin" (6:7). Therefore, "the day" is "at hand" or within our grasp right now. In other words, we can live our lives today as if we are already in heaven, which is what Paul means when he says to "walk honestly, as in the day" (13:13).

In 13:13, Paul lists three groups of two things that we should not be doing today. The first group is "rioting and drunkenness," which would be the body of Christ coming together as a group to satisfy the lusts of their own flesh. Unfortunately, we see this today in most churches. They are spiritually rioting and drunken when they sing songs to feel the presence of God, rather than as a way of teaching each other sound doctrine (Ephesians 5:18-19), and when they listen to sermons full of man's philosophies, rather than God's Word rightly divided. The second group is "chambering and wantonness," which refers to living after the lusts of the flesh among the world, as opposed to living according to the truth of God's Word (12:3). The third group is "strife and envying." Strife is contending in anger with those in the world. Why would you be angry? Because you are envious or jealous of what the world has. Therefore, these three groups show the downward spiral of sin. It first starts with bad doctrine in the church, such that Christians value the flesh over the spirit. Then, they go out in the world and live according to the lusts of their flesh. Finally, they are so desirous of the things of the flesh that they actually get jealous of unbelievers who are more successful than they are, when the believer has all things in Christ! It seems unbelievable, except when you look at Christianity. How many Christians wish they could win the lotto or be rich, even though the things of this world are only temporary?

The answer, to this downward spiral of sin in 13:13, is to "Put ye on the Lord Jesus Christ" (13:14). Then, we will not make "provision for the flesh, to fulfil the lusts thereof" (13:14). The fact, that we can actually put on the Lord Jesus Christ, is one of the most amazing statements in scripture. Our flesh is vile (Philippians 3:21), and no good thing dwells in it (7:18). Therefore, when we use our flesh, we always sin. When Jesus Christ died on a cross for our sins, He did not just forgive us of our sins and give us heaven, but He also gave us eternal life that we can experience now. That does not mean lifting your hands and singing "worship" songs so that you feel good emotions by being "in His presence" (whatever that means). Living our everlasting lives in the present means that Christ can live a perfect life through us, because we can literally "put...on the Lord Jesus Christ" (13:14), and, according to Galatians 3:27, every Christian can "put on Christ"! This means that Christ can live in every one of us (Galatians 2:20), just as if He was on the earth in human form today!

Christians say, "I wish I could have been alive when Jesus Christ was on the earth." Well, you are! He is on the earth through every one of His saints! "Oh, but I want to see all the miracles He did." Sure, it would have been nice to have seen Him heal the sick and cast out devils, but you can actually experience a much better miracle in your life today. God can take you, who were bound for hell, give you a home in heaven, and live a perfect life through you as you "put...on the Lord Jesus Christ" (13:14). Then, everyone has the opportunity to see a changed life, which is a far greater miracle than seeing a lame man walk. Moreover, the Lord's miracle of making you alive in

Christ lasts for all eternity, as opposed to the physical miracles Jesus did on earth, the effects of which ended at the person's death, if not before then. The fact, that Christians do not see that it so much better to live today than when Jesus was on earth, shows that they walk by sight and not by faith, when we are commanded to do the opposite (II Corinthians 5:7).

Jesus Christ "did no sin" (I Peter 2:22), so we will do no sin if we put on Christ. He always spoke and did what God wanted Him to do (John 8:28), and so we will always speak and do what God wants us to do if we put on Christ. Jesus could do nothing apart from God (John 5:19), and so God will always work through us when we put on Christ. Jesus and the Father are one (John 10:30), and so we are also one with God when we put on Christ.

It is wonderful to recognize that we cannot lose our salvation, because we are "accepted in the beloved," who is Christ (Ephesians 1:6). Therefore, our sins are not counted against us. However, it is astronomically more wonderful that "Christ liveth in me" (Galatians 2:20). This means that, if I present my body as a living sacrifice to God (12:1), my life will be exactly according to the will of God, because Christ will live His life through me! Note that Galatians 2:20 goes on to say that "the life which I now live in the flesh I live by the faith OF the Son of God." It is not "faith IN the Son of God," but it is "faith OF the Son of God." It is His faith, because He is living in me. That is why Paul says, "I can do all things through Christ which strengtheneth me" (Philippians 4:13). God's power in Christ triumphed over all forces in heavenly places (Colossians 2:15), raised Him from the dead, and set Him far above all powers in heavenly places (Ephesians 1:19-21). Since I am in Christ, I am also sitting far above all powers in heavenly places (Ephesians 2:5-6). This means that, if I put on Christ, nothing can stop me. "All things are yours" because "ye are Christ's; and Christ's is God's" (I Corinthians 3:21-23). Keep in mind that we are thinking in spiritual terms. I could be physically killed, as Christ was. I could be persecuted, as Christ was. It is possible that no one will be saved, even if I put on Christ, because men may make the free-will choice to remain in unbelief. However, all spiritual things are mine in Christ.

Why, then, would we not utilize this power? Why use grace as an excuse to sin? Why live in the flesh, being content with eternal life in heaven, when that life can be experienced today? If you think heaven will be so great, why not live as if you are there right now, because, as far as God is concerned, you are! He says that "our conversation is in heaven," and it is from heaven that we look for the rapture (Philippians 3:20)!

Living our eternal life right now is especially wonderful when you consider that we live in a world, where Satan is the god (II Corinthians 4:4), and nearly all of the 8 billion people in the world, including Christians, serve Satan. The light of Christ in heaven will certainly be wonderful, but it is even greater on the earth, when it shines in the midst of darkness. This means that we have a unique opportunity for Christ to live in us so that people may be saved and come unto the knowledge of the truth that we will never have once we die. It is no wonder, then, that Paul says that "it is high time to awake out of sleep" (13:11)!

Sadly, most Christians never put on Christ! A similar situation in the material world would be if I had an unlimited supply of money in the bank, and I chose to live on the street and starve to death, because I refused to touch that money. Similarly, Christians have the unlimited power of God to work through them if they just put on Christ, and most people just let that power sit within them untapped, because they will not put on Christ. What a colossal waste! And, that power is so easy to tap into. We just need to "LET the word of Christ dwell in [us] RICHLY" (Colossians 3:16). Let it happen, and enjoy the spiritual riches of putting on the Lord Jesus Christ!

14 In 13:11-14, Paul covered living in the Spirit so that unbelievers may be saved. Now, he covers walking in the Spirit so as to help edify other believers. Christ has begun a work in the weak brother to make him strong in the faith. This involves thinking soberly according to the measure of faith that he has (12:3). If I, as a strong brother, do something against the weak brother's conscience, I cause him to stumble against his weak conscience (v. 13). The result is that he begins to walk in doubt, which is sin (v. 23), rather than living by faith. This destroys the edification process in that believer (vs. 15 and 20). Therefore, I should show charity toward my brother (v. 15) and not do anything against his conscience, even though I have the liberty to do so. Then, Christ can continue to build up that weak brother so that he can take a high position in heavenly places for all eternity (vs. 10-12).

14:1 Someone weak in the faith means someone who does not have as much sound doctrine built up in their inner man, especially as it relates to how to live in the dispensation of grace, as told to us in Paul's epistles. The weaker believers are in need of sound doctrine in the fundamentals of the faith, such as knowing: 1) The blessings we have in Christ now that we are saved, 2) That our old man is crucified with Christ and has been put to death by God, 3) Christ lives in me, which means I should not try to serve God in the energies of my flesh, and 4) Walking in the Spirit involves reading God's Word rightly divided to allow the Holy Spirit to teach us the things of God and then believe those things when we learn them. Walking in the Spirit does not mean going by inner impressions.

I am supposed to receive my weaker brother but not "to doubtful disputations" (14:1). This means that I need to consider my brother's beliefs and not do or say anything that goes against his conscience, because, if I do, he may dispute with me, causing him to doubt the word of God. Being weak in the faith usually involves either trying to serve God legalistically or trying to follow Christian traditions, because most of Christianity follows these things over the Bible.

For example, a family member, who is a Christian, may think that a

Christian shows his Christianity by having a big Christmas tree in his home in December. However, God says to "learn not the way of the heathen." He then describes one of the heathen's customs as cutting "a tree out of the forest" and then decking "it with silver and with gold" (Jeremiah 10:2-4). God also says, regarding unbelievers, for us to "come out from among them, and be ye separate, saith the Lord, and touch not the unclean thing" (II Corinthians 6:17). Therefore, since the Christmas tree is a pagan symbol, sound doctrine from God's Word tells us that we should not have one in our homes. However, the Christian family member, who thinks I should have a Christmas tree at home, will be coming over to my house to celebrate Christmas. If I do not have a Christmas tree, he may be offended, think I am following a cult, and will not listen to any sound doctrine I try to give him. Since "all things are lawful for me" (I Corinthians 10:23), I have the freedom to put a Christmas tree in my house. Since the lack of a tree would offend my weaker brother and hinder him from coming into the knowledge of the truth, I should put a Christmas tree in my house for him to see, even though I know that it is a pagan symbol.

How do I know when to stand up for sound doctrine versus caving in to my weaker brother? The answer is that God's will is for him to come unto the knowledge of the truth (I Timothy 2:4). This means that I should only cave in when doing so helps him come unto the knowledge of the truth. For example, if I know that my brother will only listen to an NIV version of the Bible, I should use an NIV to show him sound doctrine. But, if I know that, while he only uses an NIV, he will have no problem reading along in a KJV if I show him verses, I should use a KJV. In other words, only cater to the weaker brother when not doing so will cause him to doubt and dispute sound doctrine with you, but, if standing your ground will not cause him to doubt sound doctrine, you should stand your ground.

14:2-3 To demonstrate the weaker-brother argument, Paul uses the issue of eating meat versus being a vegetarian. Some religious people were "commanding [people] to abstain from meats" (I Timothy 4:3). Sound doctrine says that "every creature of God is good, and nothing to be refused, if it be received with thanksgiving" (I Timothy 4:4). Therefore, based upon sound doctrine for today, I can eat whatever I want.

However, as Paul will later mention: "Whatsoever is not of faith is sin" (14:23). Therefore, if a weaker brother thinks it is not okay to eat bacon and I eat bacon in front of him, he will be offended and think that I have sinned. His view of me as being an outstanding Christian will be diminished, and so he probably will not listen to me when I try to give him sound doctrine. Therefore, I should not eat the bacon so that he may learn sound doctrine and become stronger in the faith later on. Or, as Paul puts it: "Destroy not him with thy meat, for whom Christ died" (14:15). Therefore, we should avoid everything that is considered by Christians to be sin, such as smoking, drinking, gambling, cursing, etc. This also helps our witness to unbelievers.

Also, by establishing this weaker-brother principle, Paul is getting our focus where it should be. The Christian religion is primarily focused on doing the right instead of the wrong from a legalistic standpoint. In other words, they think that the way a Christian serves God is by obeying the 10 commandments, church doctrine, and other things that a "good" Christian should do. In other words, they approach Christianity from a legalistic standpoint. For example, many Christians think that a Christian should not smoke cigarettes. They will say that the reason we should not smoke cigarettes is because "your body is the temple of the Holy Ghost,... and ye are not your own.... Therefore, glorify God in your body" (I Corinthians 6:19-20). So, the argument goes that we should not smoke cigarettes, because they do not belong in God's temple. That is not what that passage is talking about. Regardless, what Christianity has done is that they have set up some legalistic restrictions in order for a person to be "in good Christian standing" with their church.

However, as Christians, we "are not under the law, but under grace" (6:14). "The law was our schoolmaster to bring us unto Christ, that we might be justified by faith. But after that faith is come, we are no longer under a schoolmaster" (Galatians 3:24-25). In other words, God gave us the law so that we would learn that we could not do the law so that we would have faith in Christ's death in our place. Once that happens, I "am dead to the law, that I might live unto God" (Galatians 2:19). God has made us dead to "the law of sin and death" and has placed us under "the law of the Spirit of life in Christ Jesus" (8:2). In other words, the mind of Christ (12:2) thinks of how our life in Christ can be lived out, not how the death of the law can be avoided.

Therefore, we should not smoke for two reasons: 1) So that weaker brethren are not offended, and 2) So we live longer so that we have an opportunity to do God's will on this earth for a longer period of time. The conclusion is still "don't smoke," but the conclusion, from the weaker-brother argument, advances God's will, while the conclusion from the legalistic standpoint, advances my flesh, as I brag about what a good Christian I am for not smoking. Therefore, the main reason Paul brings up the weaker-brother argument is to change our way of thinking from a fleshly mind (Colossians 2:18) to the mind of Christ (I Corinthians 2:16), from law to grace (6:14), and from death to life (8:2).

You may think, "As long as I do what's right, what's the big deal?" However, why you do something is far more important to God than what you do. For example, God told Israel to bring sacrifices to the temple. In fact, Leviticus 1-7 goes over the details of specific sacrifices. Yet, when Israel brought sacrifices to God later on, He said, "I hate, I despise your feast days, and I will not smell [your sacrifices] in your solemn assemblies" (Amos 5:21). Why? Because "this people draw near Me with their mouth, and with their lips do honour Me, but have removed their heart far from Me" (Isaiah 29:13).

In other words, God wanted Israel to offer sacrifices out of an attitude of faith in His Word, rather than out a prideful, legalistic attitude. Therefore, based upon Israel's example, we can say that the Christian religion has done the same thing. Yes, they may refrain from smoking, but God does not care about that, because they do so to look good to others, rather than to advance God's will that all men be saved and come unto the knowledge of the truth (I Timothy 2:4).

14:3-4 Galatians 5:15 says that "if ye bite and devour one another, take heed that ye be not consumed one of another." This is what is going on in Christianity today, as they engage in a flesh contest to determine who is the "Super Christian" among them. These five words: "For God hath received him" (14:3) are all that is needed to remove all flesh contests and all clubs and cliques within the church.
We need to keep in mind that Christ died for us, "while we were yet sinners" (5:8), and that the only good that comes from me is when I allow Christ to live in me. Therefore, there can be no pride or boasting when it comes to God (3:27).

Since all that I have is because of Christ, the same is true for the weaker brother. Perhaps he does not stand on sound doctrine, but he does stand: "For God is able to make him stand" (14:4). Maybe he is not standing right now, but he will stand later in life as he reads and believes God's Word rightly divided. Or, he will stand at the judgment seat of Christ, because his position in heavenly places is based upon Christ's work, not his own work. Since Christ has promised to perform His good work in all members of the body of Christ (Philippians 1:6), God will cause all believers to stand in eternity. Therefore, if I judge my weaker brother as inferior, I am essentially blaming Christ, saying that He did not do as good of a job on him as He did on me. Besides, the weaker brother is God's servant. He's not my servant. Therefore, I have no right to judge him anyway.

14:5-6 Now, Paul deals with the issue of holidays or "holy days." In Israel's program, God created certain days as holy unto the Lord. The sabbath was holy (Exodus 20:8), as was all of the feast days (Leviticus 23:2). However, today, in the dispensation of grace, every day is a holy day, because, as members of the body of Christ, we are holy (Colossians 3:12). Therefore, we should not observe certain days as being holier than other days.

However, most Christians do observe holy days. They think that Christmas, Easter, and Sundays are more holy than the other days of the year. However, if we understand that our lives are "hid with Christ in God" (Colossians 3:3), then we understand that it does not really matter. In other words, since all days are holy days to be lived unto the Lord, whatever we do is unto the Lord, whether we realize it or not.

Therefore, it is more important that we be "fully persuaded" in our own minds (14:5) about what to do with holy days than to actually be correct about holy days. This shows, again, that attitude is the most important thing with God. If we are following what we think we should do, it means that we are true to the doctrine that is built up in our inner man. In other words, we are thinking soberly according to the measure of faith we have (12:3). Therefore, whatever we do, we will do it unto the Lord, rather than trying to satisfy our own flesh by looking good to others. Then, as we learn more sound doctrine, our measure of faith is increased, and we will serve the Lord according to this higher level of doctrine. But, if we just do things according to the flesh, we will never grow.

For example, if I go to church on Sunday and try to serve the Lord only on Sundays in order to please my family and look good to others, I am satisfying the flesh. My flesh will then use my "good" deed from Sunday as justification to do what I want to do on Saturday. However, if I go to church on Sunday and try to serve the Lord only on Sundays because I am fully persuaded that that is what God wants me to do, then, when I find out that every day is holy unto the Lord, I will allow God to work through me throughout the week. The key is that, as long as I do something unto the Lord, even if the Lord would want me to do something different, the Lord is pleased because He knows that I will eventually grow in faith and what I say and do will gradually become more in line with sound doctrine found in God's Word. That is why Colossians 3:17 says, "And whatsoever ye do in word or deed, do all in the name of the Lord Jesus, giving thanks to God and the Father by Him."

Similarly speaking, the KJV is God's perfect Word in English for you today. However, God would rather you use an NIV, understanding that God has preserved His Word perfectly today, than for you to use a KJV because that is what your church uses. The reason is because, if you understand the doctrine of preservation, you will learn more from the NIV as your final authority than you will from the KJV as something that your church uses. Also, if you use the NIV, you will eventually discover its errors and find the KJV is your final authority, while the one, who uses the KJV out of tradition, will not believe the perfect Word of God that he is reading, receiving less edification than the NIV person. Again, this shows that attitude is the most important thing with God. After all, "without faith it is impossible to please" God (Hebrews 11:6).

14:7-8 Remember your identity. "So we, being many, are one body in Christ (12:5). "But of [God] are ye in Christ Jesus" (I Corinthians 1:30). Because you are in Christ, whatever you do, you do "unto the Lord" (14:8). "For we are unto God a sweet savour of Christ" (II Corinthians 2:15). Regardless of what you say and do, you represent Christ. Therefore, if you live after the flesh, you "die unto the Lord." If you walk in the Spirit, you "live unto the Lord" (14:8). Whatever you do, you represent the Lord.

Because that is true, I have no right to judge my brother (14:10). Granted, each one of us will have to give an account to God (14:12). Therefore, we should walk in the Spirit, rather than fulfilling the lusts of the flesh. However, because each one of us answers to the Lord, and not to each other, we need to take care of ourselves, rather than others. For example, I understand that I am dead to sin and alive to Christ because I have been buried with Christ into His death. Most Christians do not understand this. It would be wonderful if all of them understood this, so that they would "live unto the Lord," instead of living unto their own flesh. However, they have to answer to God for this. They do not answer to me. Even if Christians live in rebellion to God for their entire lives, God knows that when the fulness of the Gentiles be come in (11:25), Christ will present to Himself "a glorious church,... holy and without blemish" (Ephesians 5:27). The reason is because Christ will be faithful to complete the good work He has begun in us (Philippians 1:6). The reason is because our lives are "hid with Christ in God" (Colossians 3:3). Since we are in Christ, He must complete the work, because "He cannot deny Himself" (II Timothy 2:13). Therefore, God knows that the body of Christ will eventually come unto the knowledge of the truth, even though it does not seem like we are doing that right now.

A good example of this is the 12 disciples. For three years, Christ gave sound doctrine to the 12. During that whole time, they had no idea what Christ was talking about to the point that they did not even understand that the Christ must rise from the dead until after He had already done so (John 20:9). Granted, Christ does chide them for not having faith, e.g., Matthew 8:26 and 16:8, but He was not worried about it. He said that "the Comforter, which is the Holy Ghost, Whom the Father will send in My name, He shall teach you all things, and bring all things to your remembrance, whatsoever I have said unto you" (John 14:26). Sure enough, in early Acts, the 12 disciples are speaking and doing the things of God.

What this shows us is that, because we are God's servants, God will make sure that we come unto the knowledge of the truth. We may not do so during this lifetime, which means that we will not be able to serve God in a high position in heavenly places for all eternity. Nevertheless, the body of Christ, as a whole, will function at the level it needs to function at for all eternity, because God will see to it that this happens.

Therefore, we should not judge other members of the body of Christ for being weak in the faith. All we can do is take care that we believe God's Word and allow Christ to live in us. What this does is that it takes the pressure off of us. We do not need to beat ourselves up over someone rejecting the gospel or over someone rejecting sound doctrine. This also keeps us from trying to force people to be saved and to come unto the knowledge of the truth. If we see that unbelievers are willing to hear the gospel, we should present it to them. However, if they will not listen, if we try to force it on them, all we will do is harden them to the gospel message. Similarly, if a weak brother is not interested in learning sound doctrine, we just need to let him continue to be weak and wait for the time when he is willing to listen. If he sees sound doctrine working through our lives, perhaps he will be willing to listen in the future. Even if that time never comes, so be it. He will learn when he gets to heaven. Since God does not force saved people to read their Bibles and they answer to God, how much more, then, should we not force weaker brethren to learn the truth of God's Word. When we do, we are trying to take control over God's servant, saying that we know better than God does.

14:9 The reason that "Christ...died, and rose, and revived" was so "that He might be Lord both of the dead and living" (14:9). When "Christ...raised from the dead," He "dieth no more" because "death hath no more dominion over Him" (6:9). In other words, He became the Lord of death. "He died unto sin," rose from the dead, and now "He liveth unto God" (6:10). Before we were saved, we were all dead (II Corinthians 5:14). Since Christ is Lord of death, He is Lord over all. Once we believe the gospel, we are baptized into Christ's death (6:3), which means that our new identity is Christ. Since Christ rose from the dead, we are also "alive unto God through Jesus Christ our Lord" (6:11). This also makes Christ the Lord of the living, since "Christ...is our life" (Colossians 3:4). Therefore, Christ's death and resurrection make Him "Lord both of the dead and living" (14:9).

Therefore, being Lord of the dead does NOT refer to those in the grave, because they are not dead if they were believers. They are only sleeping in Jesus (I Thessalonians 4:14). Also see Matthew 22:32, where Jesus says, "I am the God of Abraham, and the God of Isaac, and the God of Jacob[.] God is not the God of the dead, but of the living," meaning that, even in the grave, Abraham, Isaac, and Jacob are still living, because, as Lord of the living, Christ gave them life. Christ is not God of the dead in the sense that, while in the grave, there is nothing they can do to worship Him. However, He is still Lord of the dead in the sense that He has authority over them to judge them to hell (See Revelation 20:11-15).

We should also note that 14:9 says that "Christ BOTH died, and rose, and revived." Since the word "both" is used, it refers to two events. The first is His death, and the second is His resurrection. His resurrection is broken into His rising and His reviving, showing that He rose from the dead, and He also revived to live His life unto God. Similarly, spiritually speaking, Christ has raised us from the dead, but He did not just stop there. He has also revived us, which means that He has quickened our spirits (Ephesians 2:1,5-6) to make us "alive unto God" (6:11). In other words, if Christ just rose from the dead, He would be like a walking zombie. Since Christ also revived, He lives an abundant life (John 10:10) far above all power (Ephesians 1:19-21).

14:10 Since Christ is Lord over all, we have no right to judge our brother (14:10). All believers shall "stand before the judgment seat of Christ." (14:10). On that day, things done in the flesh will be burned, while those things done through the Spirit will be rewarded (I Corinthians 3:11-15). This shows that the things done by the weaker brethren will not harm them in eternity. Therefore, we should not judge them. Instead, we should leave it up to God to judge their works.

14:11-12 This is a quote of Isaiah 45:23. Philippians 2:10-11 gives further revelation to say that every knee shall bow "at the name of Jesus..., and that every tongue should confess that Jesus Christ is Lord."

At "the judgment seat of Christ," the body of Christ appears before Christ to be judged for the things that we did while on earth (II Corinthians 5:10). If those things were done in Christ, we receive a reward. If they were done in the flesh, they are burned up and we are not rewarded for them (I Corinthians 3:11-15). Also, all unbelievers, regardless of dispensation, appear before Christ at the great white throne judgment. Because they have not believed the gospel, they are judged by their works and cast into hell (Revelation 20:11-15). Obviously, all unbelievers will not bow down and confess that Jesus is Lord until the great white throne judgment.

However, since the context of 14:11-12 is the judgment seat of Christ (14:10), this shows that there are also some believers in the body of Christ who will not bow down and confess that Jesus Christ is Lord until the judgment seat of Christ. They will then give an account to God. Their works done in the flesh will be burned, and those done in the Spirit will be rewarded. The point, in this context, is that the fleshly deeds of the weaker brethren will be judged or burned up by Christ at that time, because Christ is their master. Therefore, we should not judge them. Rather, we should help edify them, if they are willing to be edified in sound doctrine, but we should leave them alone if they are not willing to have sound doctrine built up in their inner man, because Christ will destroy of their weakness on judgment day.

A side point to this is that there are weaker brothers, who will not confess that Jesus Christ is Lord until they receive their reward and go into heavenly places with Christ for all eternity. This is important to note because there is a segment of Christianity that says that, in order to be saved, "you must make Jesus the Lord of your life." These verses have just proved that doctrine to be false. Also, what exactly does making Jesus the Lord of your life mean? It cannot mean that I will serve Him perfectly, because no one does that. It cannot mean that I will always place Him first in my life, because no one does that either. What is meant by that statement is that you dedicate yourself to live as a Christian should. This means that you agree to live by Christianity's rules. However, that is legalism, and we all fail at that, no matter how hard we try. Therefore, while on the surface it appears that making Jesus the Lord of your life is a good thing, in actuality it is a statement of pride that means that you are agreeing to be entangled with the yoke of bondage of the law, when you should really stand fast in the liberty wherewith Christ hath made you free (Galatians 5:1).

All members of the body of Christ having to give an account of what we did is not the means by which God punishes you for secret sin that you committed. Rather, it simply means that none of us are perfect, and so Christ will separate the good things (in Christ) from the bad things (in your flesh) (II Corinthians 5:10), rewarding you for the good things and destroying the bad things, while you yourself are saved and enter into God's eternal kingdom in heaven (I Corinthians 3:11-15). Christ is not going to scold you for your fleshly lifestyle, because He recognizes that "ye are dead" (Colossians 3:3) and you cannot punish a dead man! He will just burn up those fleshly deeds so that they cease to exist, and all that remains is your life in Christ.

14:13 Therefore, we should show God's love to the weaker brethren, rather than judging them. To this, the flesh will be quick to respond: "We need to tolerate and love everyone. 'Judge not, that ye be not judged' (Matthew 7:1)." Because God knows the flesh's response, Paul goes right into what we are to judge. After all, being spiritual, we should judge all things (I Corinthians 2:15). In other words, because our spirits are alive in Christ and Christ is the judge, if we use the mind of Christ (I Corinthians 2:16), we will "judge righteous judgment" (John 7:24). Actually, Christ will judge righteously through us. Therefore, we can judge our weaker brethren, but we should not criticize them. Rather, we should judge them as weaker and seek to make them stronger.

Think of it this way. I am not a judge in the government of the United States because I have not gotten the proper training in order to judge righteously, i.e., according to the law. Similarly, in the spiritual realm, my flesh is vile (Philippians 3:21). Therefore, I cannot judge. However, Christ lived a perfect life and now has glorified flesh. As such, He is qualified to judge. Since I have the mind of Christ, I can use His mind to judge all things. Then, my judgement will be righteous.

Therefore, in the case of the weaker brother, if I use my flesh to judge him, I will condemn him, i.e., judge unrighteously. However, if I use the mind of Christ my judgment will be not to "put a stumblingblock or an occasion to fall in [my] brother's way" (14:13). In other words, I will not do or say something that will cause him to go against his own conscience. Why? Because "every man [should] be fully persuaded in his own mind" (14:5). In other words, every man needs to walk by faith. If he does not, he has sinned (14:23). I have then used my liberty in Christ to cause my brother to sin, when I should be using my liberty in Christ to increase his faith. Paul will now continue his example from 14:2-3 to illustrate this.

14:14-15 In this example, since "I know...that there is nothing unclean of itself" (14:14), I am in the position of being the stronger brother. There is a weaker brother, who thinks it is a sin to eat meat. Since his conscience tells him that eating meat is a sin, it is a sin to him, even though God's Word rightly divided says that it is not a sin. To understand this, we need to put together some things that we have already learned.

"The wages of sin is death" (6:23), and "all have sinned" (3:23), because we all have a sin nature. Therefore, all were dead (II Corinthians 5:14). Because all were dead, if God left me alone in my death, I would never recognize that I am dead, because all I see is death. Therefore, God gave everyone the conscience, which is "the law written in [our] hearts" (2:15). "The law is holy" (7:12), "but I am carnal sold under sin" (7:14). The conscience works with my sin nature to "become exceeding sinful" (7:13). That is, God gave me a conscience so that I would see my sinful condition. I then believed in Jesus' death, burial, and resurrection as atonement for my sin (I Corinthians 15:3-4), and God gave me the gift of eternal life (6:23).

In other words, eternal life only comes by faith (3:28), so as to exclude boasting (3:27). That is why Genesis 15:6 says that Abram "believed in the Lord; and He counted it to him for righteousness." Therefore, eternal life comes only "through the righteousness of faith. For if they which are of the law be heirs, faith is made void, and the promise made of none effect" (4:13-14). Therefore, law and faith are two, diametrically-opposed systems. Law plus my sin nature produces death, while believing the gospel plus the faith of Christ produces life. Therefore, "the law was our schoolmaster to bring us unto Christ, that we might be justified by faith. But after that faith is come, we are no longer under a schoolmaster" (Galatians 3:23-24).

This means that I am "not under the law, but under grace" (6:14). Therefore, "the law of the Spirit of life in Christ Jesus hath made me free from the law of sin and death" (8:2). Therefore, my identity is that I am now in Christ Jesus.

Now, back to 14:14-15. I know that it is not a sin to eat meat. My brother does not know this. How can it be a sin for him to eat meat, and it is not a sin for me to eat meat? Why should I refrain from eating meat when my brother is too stupid to know that it is okay to eat meat? Shouldn't I try to help his weak conscience by telling him it is okay to eat meat?

The answer is that the body of Christ has a life in heaven (Philippians 3:20) by faith. We now operate in a different realm. This different realm is the realm of faith and life, not sin and death. My fleshly mind (sin and death) is still with me, but I should be living in the mind of Christ (faith and life). How much of the mind of Christ I have depends upon how much sound doctrine I have built up in my inner man. Regardless, I should think soberly according to the measure of faith I have (12:3). If I think beyond that, I am using my fleshly mind.

So, the weak brother has a small measure of faith, such that he thinks that it is a sin to eat meat. I am a strong brother, and I know that it is okay to eat meat. If I eat meat in front of him, since he knows that I am a strong brother, he may eat meat himself. It is not wrong to eat meat, but it is wrong for him to eat meat, because it goes against his conscience. By going against his conscience, he has used his fleshly mind to make the decision, rather than using the mind of Christ. By using his fleshly mind, he is operating under the principle of sin and death, rather than under the principle of faith and life. His weak conscience is now defiled (I Corinthians 8:7), not because he broke a law because God says it is okay to eat meat, but because he used his fleshly mind, rather than the mind of Christ. His measure of faith has now decreased. Because Christ is doing the work to transform His mind and I have stopped that process by causing my weak brother to go against the mind of Christ, I have sinned against Christ (I Corinthians 8:12). Therefore, my weaker brother is damned (14:23), not in the sense of going to hell, but damned in the sense that I have condemned the work that Christ was doing in him. In other words, I have used my liberty to cause him to stumble against his own conscience, such that he is now operating in his fleshly mind, rather than operating in the mind of Christ.

That is why 14:15 says, "Destroy not him with thy meat, for whom Christ died." In other words, Christ died, not to just save him from his sin, but also to give him life in Christ. Christ saved him to operate in faith for all eternity so that he will judge angels (I Corinthians 6:3) and all spiritual matters under the law of Spirit and life, rather than under the law of sin and death. Now, I have come along and destroyed his growth in faith. Christ died so that He might sanctify and cleanse His church by the Word so that it will be glorious and holy (Ephesians 5:25-27). He paid the ultimate price. Shouldn't I, then, as part of His body, be willing to give up the liberty of eating meat so that Christ's work on this weaker brother is not destroyed? We are commanded to "support the weak" (I Thessalonians 5:14), not "destroy the weak."

Another key to understanding this is that 14:14 says that I "am persuaded by the Lord Jesus." In other words, I have read and believed God's Word, such that the Lord Jesus has taught me that eating meat is okay. It does not say that I "am persuaded by my stronger brother." The Lord is my brother's master, and He knows everything about the spiritual realm. I am my brother's brother, and my flesh knows nothing about the spiritual realm. Therefore, if I try to change him, it would be like a child interfering with a master sculptor.

This is why I Corinthians 8:1 says, "Knowledge puffeth up, but charity edifieth." If all I do is use my knowledge in Christ, I come across as an arrogant know-it-all, and no one will listen to me. However, if I have charity toward my brother, I recognize where he is at, and meet him at his level. Then, he continues to have faith in what Christ has done with him so far, and Christ's work of faith in his life can continue.

14:16 The first reason we should be guided by the conscience of the weaker brother is so Christ's work in that weaker brother is not destroyed (14:15). The second reason is so that Christ's work through us is not destroyed (14:16). If my weaker brother thinks that I should not eat meat and I eat meat in front of him, he will probably tell others that I am not obeying God. My "good," in this verse, is my faith in what the Lord Jesus has told me through His Word. In this case, it is the liberty that I have to eat meat. This liberty or this "good" is then "evil spoken of" (14:16) by the weaker brother. Therefore, by me eating meat in front of my weaker brother, not only does the weaker brother sin and his weak conscience is defiled, but also my ability to do God's will is hindered through the "evil" testimony given of me by my weaker brother to others.

To put this in modern terms, maybe you do not participate in a Lord's supper ordinance at a church, because you know that that is not the Lord's table that we are to observe. The Lord's table refers to fellowship with other saints over a meal. However, your refusal to take a sip of grape juice and eat a bite of cracker may cause a weaker brother to speak bad about you, like telling others that you must be living in sin, as the reason for not participating in the "communion" of the Lord. To keep this from happening, you should go ahead and participate in the ceremony.

14:17 Paul says that all things are lawful unto us (I Corinthians 6:12). The reason for this, as we described in 14:14-15, is that, as Christians, we are under the system of faith and life, not the system of law and death. Therefore, we do not need to take a moral stand on what we can or cannot do, because God has called us to operate in the higher, spiritual realm. This means that "the kingdom of God is not meat and drink" (physical realm), but it is "righteousness, and peace, and joy in the Holy Ghost" (spiritual realm). Therefore, we should pursue the latter over the former, which we do when we cater to the conscience of the weaker brother.

God's will is for all men to be saved and come unto the knowledge of the truth (I Timothy 2:4). When people are saved, they receive God's righteousness (3:21-22), and they have peace with God (5:1). When they come unto the knowledge of the truth, they have joy or "rejoice evermore" (I Thessalonians 5:16) over being forgiven of their sin, being seated with Christ in heavenly places, and everything else they have in Christ, including Christ living in them. These things are far more important than eating a steak. That is why Paul says, "If meat make my brother to offend, I will eat no flesh while the world standeth, lest I make my brother to offend" (I Corinthians 8:13).

The issue is all about perspective. Now that you have learned 13 chapters of sound doctrine, you should have the perspective of being in Christ, allowing Christ to live in you, and recognizing that the only things that are eternal are the things of God. Therefore, we should concentrate on these eternal things. As such, the things of this world should have no attraction to us, which means that what we eat should be irrelevant to us, in light of the things of God. Therefore, when we see that a weaker brother's participation in the things of God could be hindered by our participation in the things of this world, we should gladly give up worldly things for spiritual things.

Note also that this verse shows a difference between the heavenly places promised to us as part of the body of Christ in the dispensation of grace and God's earthly kingdom that is part of Israel's program. Since we have spiritual blessings in heavenly places, the kingdom of God for us is "righteousness, and peace, and joy in the Holy Ghost," while, in speaking about God's earthly kingdom, Jesus said in Luke 14:15, "Blessed is he that shall eat bread in the kingdom of God."

14:18 "In these things" (14:18) means in "righteousness, and peace, and joy." As we just saw, these things relate to God's will. Therefore, if I serve Christ in these things, I am "acceptable to God" (14:18). This is a great example of how I can yield my "members as instruments of righteousness unto God" (6:13). Presenting my body as a living sacrifice to God (12:1) does not mean to refrain from sin, as most Christians think. Rather, it means Christ living in me. In the context of 14:17, the in-Christ life is when the things of God are built up in the inner man and shown to others. In this case, it means me not exercising my liberty to eat meat in front of my weaker brother. He can then see the fruit of the Spirit and desire that, which would give me an opportunity to present sound doctrine to him. Therefore, not exercising my liberty in front of my weaker brother may get him out of the shackles of legalism so that he may be at liberty for Christ to live in him (Galatians 5:1).

This is seen by the fact that not exercising my liberty makes me "approved of men" (14:18). Because Christianity seeks after the things of the flesh, they think we should act like the world so that the world will be attracted to us. This has resulted in the world changing Christianity, not the other way around. Church attendance may go up, but numbers do not help anyone when the church does not stand for the truth, when we are called to be "the pillar and ground of the truth" (I Timothy 3:15). We are not supposed to be conformed to this world, but we are supposed to be transformed by the renewing of our mind to be like the mind of Christ (12:2). Paul will later tell us to be "wise unto that which is good, and simple concerning evil" (16:19). Therefore, being "approved of men" simply means that men will listen to what I have to say about God, because they see Christ living in me. This means that I do not follow the lusts of the flesh or conform myself to the world. Rather, "I keep under my body, and bring it into subjection: lest that by any means, when I have preached to others, I myself should be a castaway" (I Corinthians 9:27). Reach the world for Christ by having Christ live through you. Then, "the excellency of the power [will be] of God, and not of us" (II Corinthians 4:7), and men will be attracted to God.

This is not unlike parents with their children. If parents do not live by the rules they create, their children will not follow those rules. The parents can then try to become best friends with their children by letting them do whatever they want to do, and their children will like them. However, their children will be unruly. Instead, if the parents create the rules and follow the rules, their children will respect them and follow the rules. The parents then are approved of their children, in the sense that they are approved as having authority over them. Similarly speaking, if we allow Christ to live through us, we will be "approved of men" as being "ambassadors for Christ" (II Corinthians 5:20). It will then be up to men to believe Christ or not. Otherwise, if we live in the flesh, the world will like us, but they will not be saved and come unto the knowledge of the truth.

14:19 You may wonder where to draw the line with weaker believers. In other words, how do you know when to take a stand against the weaker believer and when to do what the weaker believer wants you to do?

You are to follow after two things: 1) "Things which make for peace," and 2) "Things wherewith one may edify another" (14:19). Since you are edified by coming unto the knowledge of the truth, the TEACHING of false doctrine must always be stopped. Paul told Timothy to charge people to "teach no other doctrine" than sound doctrine for this dispensation (I Timothy 1:3). Hymenaeus and Alexander had made some shipwreck concerning faith, and Paul kicked them out of the church (I Timothy 1:19-20). "A man that is an heretick after the first and second admonition reject" (Titus 3:10). Thus, there is to be no tolerance for false doctrine being taught.

However, when it comes to the conscience of the weaker brother regarding our liberty in Christ, we should "follow after the things which make for peace" (14:19). That is because it is "the God of peace" who bruises Satan under our feet when we are united in sound doctrine (16:20). In a way, you sort of distract the weaker brother from trying to spread false doctrine when you go along with his conscience. You are then free, as the stronger brother, to focus on the things that bring edification to the weaker believers so that they may come unto the knowledge of the truth and not be weak any more. Moreover, the weaker brethren are more likely to listen to the sound doctrine later on, because you were willing to go along with their conscience in practice.

Note that Paul mentions to Timothy that there were false teachers "commanding to abstain from meats" (I Timothy 4:3). Paul told Timothy to "put the brethren in remembrance" that sound doctrine says that "every creature of God is good, and nothing to be refused" (I Timothy 4:4-6). Therefore, the same issue of meats, when brought before the whole church, needs to be addressed because false doctrine must be kept out of the church because "a little leaven leaveneth the whole lump" (Galatians 5:9). However, when it comes to the actual practice of things from a weaker brother who simply has not grown to the level of maturity to understand the sound doctrine in the situation, it is best to go along with the weaker brother to keep the peace so that there will be an opportunity for edification later on. In other words, the time for edification is not when the situation is front of you. The time for edification is before the situation arises. If you try to correct the weaker brother when the situation is in front of him, his flesh gets in the way of being edified. So, yes, take a stand for sound doctrine, but do not do it to the weaker brother in the situation. In other words, you have to recognize when it is a time for peace and when it is a time for edification, because you are to pursue both. Put in terms of Paul's example, the time for peace is when the food is in front of you; the time for edification is when the issue can be discussed apart from the situation.

A good example of this comes from business. Let's say that there is a new cashier at a clothing store. The store policy is not to take back used clothing. The new cashier does not know this and tells the buyer that he can return the clothing after using it that night. The next day, he returns the clothing to a different cashier, who knows the policy, but has been told that the new cashier authorized a return. In this case, the "stronger" cashier should take the clothing back. Because this keeps the peace based upon the weaker cashier. After the situation is over, the stronger cashier can remind the weaker cashier of the store policy. This way, in the situation, the weaker cashier is not "set at nought" (14:10), keeping the peace, and is later edified by the proper policy. This keeps the weaker cashier from quitting or having a poor attitude, and it keeps him in line with what the store policy is.

14:20-21 "When I was a child, I spake as a child, I understood as a child, I thought as a child: but when I became a man, I put away childish things" (I Corinthians 13:11). Before I was saved, I was a child "in bondage under the elements of the world" (Galatians 4:3). Once I was saved, I was adopted as God's son, which means that I am no longer a child. Therefore, God took away the law and gave me His Spirit (Galatians 4:5-7). Since I am no longer a child, I should put away childish things. "Childish things" are the things of the flesh. In this context, the childish thing to put away is flaunting my liberty in front of my weaker brother.

"All things indeed are pure" (14:20) shows the concept that "all things are lawful unto me" (I Corinthians 6:12). The reason I can do anything I want to do is because God says that I am an adult son, mature enough to make my own decisions. Therefore, I should use my spiritual maturity to understand that, when it comes to the weaker brother, the issue is not what I CAN do, the issue is what will advance "the work of God" (14:20) in my weaker brother. The mature believer in Christ will recognize that I should forego my liberty to eat meat, "lest by any means this liberty of yours become a stumblingblock to them that are weak" (I Corinthians 8:9).

For example, a child may have to go to bed at 9:00 PM, because the parents recognize that he needs to get a good amount of sleep. Once that child becomes an adult, he can stay up as long as he wants to. He should not say, "I can stay up as late as I want to. Therefore, I will not go to bed." Rather, he may still choose to go to bed at 9:00 PM, because his maturity tells him that he needs to go to bed at that time in order to function well the next day. In other words, his decision is based upon sound thinking, rather than based upon the law. Similarly speaking, before we were saved, we were children

(Galatians 4:1). God had to put us under the law. Once we were saved, we became adults, and so God blotted out the law (Colossians 2:14). As mature believers, we can see that God is working in the weak believer to make him stronger, and so the mature believer will decide not to eat meat so that God's work with the weak believer can continue.

Therefore, the important matter is doing the work of God. Do not exercise your right to eat meat if it causes a weaker believer to stumble because it destroys the work of God in being able to: 1) Edify that believer, 2) Edify other believers that believer has an influence over, and 3) Have the gospel believed by unbelievers. God's work is far more important than being able to eat meat!

14:22 This verse is not saying that we should not share the gospel with others because we are supposed to keep silent about our faith. The context shows that having faith means being "persuaded by the Lord Jesus" (14:14), via sound doctrine found in His Word, that we are at liberty to eat what we want to eat. In this case, expressing this faith may cause a weaker brother to stumble, because the weaker brother's conscience tells him something different. Therefore, we should keep this sound doctrine to ourselves by not eating meat, so as not to offend the weaker brother.

14:23 Being damned, in this context, does not mean that the weaker brother will lose his salvation if he eats a piece of meat when his conscience tells him not to eat it. The damnation or condemnation is self-condemnation. In 7:14-24, we learned that, if we try to serve God in the energies of our flesh, we condemn ourselves by saying, "O wretched man that I am!" Then, in 7:25 and 8:1, we learned that Jesus Christ our Lord has delivered us from this self-condemnation if we allow the mind of Christ to work in us to serve God, rather than our fleshly mind. Similarly speaking, if a weaker brother thinks that it is a sin to eat meat and he eats meat, he has damned or condemned himself. That is not to say that he thinks he is going to hell now, but he feels guilty for going against his own conscience. He has also damned the edification process in his inner man from continuing, since he is now walking by sight, instead of by faith.

"Whatsoever is not of faith is sin" (14:23). What this means is that a weaker brother sins by doing the thing that he think is sin, even though he did not break one of God's commands. In other words, although all things are lawful to us (I Corinthians 6:12) because we are under grace (6:14), we can put ourselves back under the law so that we sin. That is why Paul tells the Galatians to "be not entangled again with the yoke of bondage" (Galatians 5:1), and, if they do, they have "fallen from grace" (Galatians 5:4). Therefore, although God has declared that "ye are not under the law, but under grace" (6:14), I can use my freedom to put myself back under the law. If I do this, I am become "a debtor to do the whole law," "Christ is become of no effect unto" me (Galatians 5:3-4), and "Christ is dead in vain" (Galatians 2:21). And, all of this starts with the stronger brother flaunting his liberty in front of the weaker brother.

Therefore, in order to get the weaker brother out from under the law, we need to obey the law of his conscience. At first, this sounds contradictory. However, when we recognize that the flesh resists correction, we understand that sound doctrine can come in later as the weaker brother reads and believes God's word. Trying to correct him at the time of eating will begin the defense mechanism of the flesh. In other words, let God work through His Word to build up the weaker brother over time, rather than trying to force him to live by your measure of faith. We can also see from experience that most of Christianity is in the flesh today, and a big part of this is because the stronger brethren are not treating their weaker brethren according to the instructions found in Romans 14 and I Corinthians 8.

Perhaps an example will help explain this. Let's say that I am a bodybuilder. Someone with a weak back comes into the gym and wants to build muscle. He sees me doing deadlifts and decides that he should do deadlifts, since I have a lot of muscle. (Deadlifts are a good back exercise but are hard on the back.) Because he has a weak back, he ends up injuring his back even more. In other words, his back is worse because he did a back exercise that he could not handle. Therefore, I should refrain from doing deadlifts in front of him and should show him something that he can do instead. Then, when his body is ready later, I can show him the deadlifts. Now, we apply this to soulbuilding. As a "soulbuilder," I know that I can eat meat. The weaker brother sees me eat meat. Therefore, he eats meat, going against his own conscience, which hurts the soulbuilding process within him because he has gone beyond what he can do. Therefore, the only "soulbuilding" I can do with him is in other sound doctrine, lest he injure his conscience and be worse off than before. Then, when his soul is ready later, I can show him sound doctrine for today regarding meat. Therefore, just like someone with a weak back should not do a hard back exercise, a weak brother should not go against his conscience, lest he stop his growth in faith.

15 Paul mentions Christ as an example of someone who did not use His liberty to please Himself (vs. 3-4). Therefore, the Romans will be using the mind of Christ (v. 6), if they do not squabble over things in the conscience of the weaker brethren. Jesus Christ came specifically to minister to the Jews (v. 8). However, because He had faith in God, He also ended up saving the Gentiles with the dispensation of grace (vs. 9-12). This shows how following God's plan is always best, since God's "ways [are] past finding out" (11:33). Therefore, the Romans should go by the conscience of the weaker brethren.

Paul has been planning to visit the Romans for many years (v. 23) but has not been able to, because the Lord Jesus Christ commissioned him to preach the mystery to the whole world (vs. 18-21). This worked out well for us, because we now have the foundational doctrine of the mystery program available to us in this letter to the Romans. This also may have worked out well for the Romans, because Paul will now go to Jerusalem (v. 25). There has been some strife between the believers of Israel's program in Jerusalem and the believers of the mystery program. Therefore, if that strife can be taken care of before Paul visits the Romans, he can come to them "with joy...and...be refreshed" (v. 32) with them.

15:1-2 God refers to following religious rules as an infirmity (15:1). In other words, religious Christians are spiritually sick, because they are trusting in man, instead of reading God's Word rightly divided and believing what it says. Since we are stronger, we are to "bear the infirmities of the weak" (15:1), meaning that we are to go along with the rules they follow so that we do not wound their weak conscience. We can then strengthen them in the fundamentals of the faith, such as learning that they are dead to sin and alive to Christ, so that they will be edified. We miss our edification opportunity when we are not willing to go along with their religious observances. This is important to remember because, as we learn God's Word rightly divided, it is so easy to blast other Christians for not believing like we do. Doing so prevents us from getting the opportunity to teach them right division and the in-Christ message so that they can get out of the bondage to the law that they are in.

15:3-4 15:3 is a quote of Psalm 69:9, referring to how Christ was scorned by the religious crowd because He chose to obey God, rather than following their religious system. Basically, the quote is saying that the Jewish religious system reproached God because they thought that their plan for self-righteousness by obeying the law was better than God's plan to impute righteousness to them by believing the gospel. Because Jesus believed in God's plan over the Jewish religious system's plan, the Jews reproached Jesus.

Paul says that this verse was written for our learning (15:4), which means that this verse applies to the situation of the dealings of the stronger brother with the weaker brother. In other words, weaker brethren reproach God by not believing sound doctrine, and the stronger brethren, who believe sound doctrine, should allow those reproaches to fall on them, much like Jesus was reproached by the Jewish religious leaders. Obviously, those reproaches fell upon Christ at the cross. By Jesus' reproach bearing, apostate Israel received a new opportunity, in Acts 2-7, to believe the gospel of the kingdom through the ministry of the Holy Ghost. Since Paul has applied Jesus' situation to ours, we can say that the reason we should bear the reproaches of the weaker brethren is because doing so will give them an opportunity to believe sound doctrine later on that will make them stronger. If Jesus did not bear the reproaches of unbelievers, the Holy Ghost would not have come. Similarly, if we do not bear with the weaker brethren, they will probably reject future attempts to give them sound doctrine. This is an application of God's statement that His "strength is made perfect in weakness" (II Corinthians 12:9). Therefore, we should seek to please others, rather than ourselves, so that they may be edified in sound doctrine, even though pleasing them means bearing with their doctrinal infirmities (15:2-

3).

15:4 also says that previously recorded scripture was "written for our learning." This supports the truth that the vast majority of the scriptures are written FOR us, but not TO us. Now, when we say this, fundamental Christianity gets upset and says that we are heretics because we do not seek to obey all of God's Word. However, the truth is that, not only do they not obey all of God's Word, but they also disregard most of scripture, while we recognize that ALL scripture is profitable for us today (II Timothy 3:16), and we gain that profit by first considering what Paul says in Romans through Philemon (II Timothy 2:7).

The way that fundamental Christianity uses the Bible is as follows. They use Genesis – Esther as children's stories with Ruth and Esther also being used for women's studies and I Samuel – II Chronicles also being used for men's studies. Job, I & II Peter, and Jude are used to show how Christians must suffer. Psalms is used for women's studies to substantiate how they are feeling about God and their lives. Proverbs is used for men's studies, as little tidbits of wisdom, primarily as warnings not to cheat on your wife. Ecclesiastes is largely ignored. Song of Solomon is only used in marriage counseling sessions. Isaiah – Malachi is largely ignored, except for a verse here and there that they can twist to apply to themselves today. Matthew – John is where most Sunday morning messages come from. They pick up what Jesus said and did to fit their doctrine. Acts is used a lot on Sunday mornings, as well, to get people to give to their missionary fund. Romans – Philemon is used sparingly and only when they can make the verses fit their doctrine. Hebrews is used to explain what the cross means to us. James is used to show how we must work to maintain our salvation. I – III John is used to emphasize the love we must have for everyone. Revelation is used to get people in the seats, since it focuses on future events. About the only commands of God, that Christianity seeks to obey, are found in Matthew – John.

By contrast, a Bible believer recognizes that all scripture before Paul's epistles were written for our learning (15:4). They were not written directly to us. These scriptures give us hope, based upon, for the most part: 1) What God says, 2) What Jesus did (15:4), and 3) What others did that we should not do (I Corinthians 10:2-11) (This includes the New Testament outside of Paul's epistles, as well.). Then, we use Paul's epistles to learn the sound doctrine for today. Thus, all scripture is profitable for everyone. We do not put books of the Bible into learning boxes that are defined by the flesh, but we let the Bible mean what it says. (By putting different books of the Bible into fleshly learning categories, Christians are taught not to believe what their Bibles literally say.) We recognize that God gave different instructions to different people in different dispensations. By doing so, we have the proper context for every scripture so that we can learn what to do and what not to do, rather than trying to change God's word to fit into pre-defined categories in order to learn lessons of the flesh that have "a form of godliness, but [deny] the power thereof" (II Timothy 3:5).

In this way, we do not look at Psalm 69:9 as a mere, historical fact of what happened to Jesus on the cross, and say, "Jesus sure did love me to endure all that He did." While that statement is true, we also learn, as Paul has taught us here, to use this verse to learn how Jesus applied sound doctrine on the cross so that we can apply that same doctrine to similar situations that we face. The fact, that sound doctrine has worked in the lives of Biblical characters, gives us comfort that sound doctrine will also work for us in our lives (15:4). This is not the comfort of a hug or a warm bowl of soup on a cold day, but it is the spiritual comfort that comes by experience.

For example, if I get incredibly sick with vomiting and diarrhea, I may think that I am going to die. Through that experience I learn that I had food poisoning that eventually went away after a few days. Then, the next time I have that, although I do not enjoy it, I can take comfort in the fact that I will not die from this. Similarly speaking, when we suffer for believing sound doctrine, we can gain comfort from reading in the scriptures that the world always persecutes those who believe sound doctrine (II Timothy 3:12). Therefore, I will not abandon sound doctrine for religion. Thus, the Old Testament is not a bunch of children's stories or a resource to pick and choose which verses we like while ignoring the others, but it is written for us to learn to take comfort that "all things work together for good to them that love God" (8:28), and I only get that comfort through the spiritual edification of the scriptures, because "all that is in the world [is] the lust of the flesh, and the lust of the eyes, and the pride of life" (I John 2:16). The world has no comfort to offer you; God is "the God of ALL comfort" (II Corinthians 1:3).

Note also that Paul says that we need patience in order to receive hope from the scriptures (15:4). That is because God has designed His Word in such a way that you must diligently study it and believe it in order to get the profit out of it that He has put in it for you. Just like a miner of precious metals and stones must go through intense labor in order to come up with the pure, finished product, you must also "diligently seek" God in order for Him to reward you (Hebrews 11:6) with the "TREASURES of wisdom and knowledge" that are hid in Christ (Colossians 2:2-3). "It is the glory of God to conceal a thing: but the honour of kings is to search out a matter" (Proverbs 25:2).

God does not just want you to learn the truth, but He also wants you to learn patience while you learn the truth. The reason is because you need patience in order to live a godly life on this earth, because you will suffer persecution for your godly living (II Timothy 3:12). Therefore, you will need to "set your affection on things above, not on things on the earth" (Colossians 3:2). In other words, you will need to have the patience to wait until after this life is over before you are rewarded for godly living here.

Thus, God's Word is a practical book, not only in what it teaches you, but also in how it goes about teaching it to you.

15:5-7 "Let this mind be in you, which was also in Christ Jesus" (Philippians 2:5). Since the last verse of chapter 13 says to "put...on the Lord Jesus Christ" and 15:5 says to be "likeminded...according to Christ Jesus," it would be accurate to say that chapter 14 is all about how to think like Christ would think toward weaker brethren.

The Father is the member of the Godhead who is "the Father of glory" (Ephesians 1:17). Therefore, the one you are to glorify is the Father (15:6). Note that we are to bring Him glory "with one mind and one mouth" (15:6). This speaks of the unity that is in Christ. Sometimes, you will hear of an ecumenical movement in Christianity, in which several churches/ denominations try to get together as one. Since every denomination believes something different, the only way this works is if they all discard their specific doctrine. In other words, they get together on fleshly terms, only agreeing to very general statements about the Bible and God, since they all have different views. Therefore, even though they say they are together, there really is no unity.

By contrast, all members of the body of Christ have been given the mind of Christ (I Corinthians 2:16). If we all use that mind, our inner man will have the same doctrine stored up in it. We can then use our mouth, which we learned in 10:9-11 is our soul, to "speak" that sound doctrine, thus bringing glory to God. This is true unity and is only seen when the body of Christ as a whole receives spiritual nourishment from our head, Who is Christ (Colossians 2:19). This is "the unity of the Spirit in the bond of peace" (Ephesians 4:3). It is a bond of peace because there are no differences in the body when we all believe the same thing. You may say, "But not everyone will believe the same thing. Everyone is at a different level of maturity." Yes, that is true. However, we just learned that the stronger brethren are to bear the reproaches of the weaker brethren when it comes to things that the weaker brethren do not know yet. This gives the weaker brethren time to learn sound doctrine. Therefore, all will agree at the weaker brethren's level of maturity, which brings peace. If we do this, "the God of peace shall bruise Satan under [our] feet shortly" (16:20), because unbelievers are looking for peace, but it is not found in the world. If they see peace in a community of believers, they will be drawn to it. Since the entire body of Christ can agree on the gospel (If they do not, they are not part of the body of Christ. We are then to mark these people and avoid them (16:17).), these unbelievers may believe the gospel and receive eternal life, thereby bruising Satan. By contrast, ecumenical efforts do not work like this, because they are following man's religion. Therefore, they do not agree on the gospel, and most of them are not part of the body of Christ.

Because of our different levels of maturity, we must "receive...one another" (15:7). Remember that "knowledge puffeth up" (I Corinthians 8:1). Therefore, the flesh of the stronger brethren will automatically find fault with the weaker brethren. That is why Paul reminds us that "Christ also received us to the glory of God" (15:7). Remember from 5:8 that Christ received us when we were sinners. Therefore, if Christ can receive sinners to the glory of God, how much more can we bring glory to God if we receive our weaker brethren, who are all saints now (1:7), thanks to the blood of Christ!

15:8 If a fellow Christian says that we need to obey what Jesus said in the gospels, we should show him this verse. This verse says that Jesus "was a minister of the circumcision." In other words, Jesus came to minister to the Jews. Why? Because God had made promises to the fathers, i.e., Abraham, Isaac, and Jacob. God started the nation of Israel with Abram and promised to make of him a great nation and to bless those who bless Israel (Genesis 12:1-3). If Jesus came to the Gentiles, as Christianity teaches happened, God's Word would not be true (15:8), because God would have skipped over Israel and went straight to the Gentiles, contrary to His promise to Abram. That is why Jesus said, "I am not sent but unto the lost sheep of the house of Israel" (Matthew 15:24).
In the context of 15:8, what Paul is saying is that, Jesus did not think to Himself: "Israel is in unbelief. I will go to the Gentiles." Rather, Jesus went to Israel IN SPITE of Israel's unbelief. Why? Because God told Him to, in order to make God's Word true, and, since "Christ pleased not Himself" (15:3), He did what God told Him to do. The application for us today is that, if we have learned the sound doctrine that Paul has taught so far in Romans, we are in the stronger-brother position in most cases, just like Jesus was. Instead of us chastising the weaker brethren, we "ought to bear the infirmities of the weak, and not to please ourselves" (15:1). Why? Because that is what God has called us to do.

Now, what ended up happening with Jesus was that, by Him going to Israel, He continued God's promises. After Jesus' ascension to heaven, the Father sent the Holy Ghost to Israel (John 14:16-17). Israel still ended up in unbelief, but, as we learned in 11:32, God had to conclude Israel in unbelief before He could have mercy upon the Gentiles. This shows the deep wisdom of God that is "unsearchable" and "past finding out" (11:33). If Jesus relied upon His Own intellect, He would not have gone to Israel. After all, why bother if they are not going to believe? However, God knew better. God knew that the Gentiles would only believe if Israel was first concluded in unbelief. Therefore, God sent Jesus to Israel to confirm the promises to Israel, and Jesus had faith in the Father's plan, doing what He told Him to do. And, by the way, once God concluded Israel in unbelief, then Jesus went to the Gentiles through Paul (Acts 9:15).

Similarly speaking, we are told to bear the infirmities of the weak. If I use my own logic, I would try to correct the weaker brethren, which is what most people do. However, because God's wisdom is deeper than mine, I need to have faith in what God tells me to do, because it will work out according to God's plan. God says that the only way Israel will believe is by seeing the mercy the Gentiles have obtained from God (11:31). Therefore, I need to set aside my fleshly way of thinking and put on the "one mind" (15:6) of Christ, which is to have faith in God, so that "the God of peace [can] bruise Satan under [my] feet" (16:20).

15:9-12 Since 15:8 ends with a colon, 15:9-12 is an explanation of how the Gentiles are saved as part of Jesus Christ's coming to confirm the promises made to Israel. Paul quotes four Old-Testament verses. First, Psalm 18:49 has the context of Israel thanking the Lord among the Gentiles and singing to the Lord for delivering them from the Antichrist. Second, Deuteronomy 32:43 has the context of the Gentiles rejoicing with believing Israel because God has avenged them of apostate Israel and will be merciful to believing Israel. Third, Psalm 117:1 has the context of the Gentiles praising the Lord in light of Israel praising the Lord for delivering their souls from death. Fourth, Isaiah 11:10 has the context of the Gentiles seeking Jesus Christ in the millennial kingdom. Thus, the way the Gentiles are saved is by a progression of events. First, they see Israel saved. Second, they rejoice with Israel. Third, they praise the Lord for what God did for Israel. Fourth, they seek God to deliver them from sin, as well. This is Gentile salvation in Israel's program.

However, the Holy Ghost, by the apostle Paul, is now saying that these verses do not just apply to Israel's program, but they also apply to the dispensation of grace. Because Paul preaches "the revelation of the mystery, which was kept secret since the world began, but now is made manifest" (16:25-26), the Holy Ghost did not reveal how these verses apply to us today until now.

Psalm 18:49 applies today in that Jesus' death, burial, and resurrection delivers us "from the violent man" (Psalm 18:48), i.e., Satan, by us believing the mystery gospel. The body of Christ then confesses the gospel among all unbelievers, i.e., the Gentiles, while the original context has believing Israel confessing the gospel among all unbelievers in their program, i.e., the Gentiles. Deuteronomy 32:43 applies today in that unbelievers should rejoice in the salvation that God has given the body of Christ. Psalm 117:1 applies today in that unbelievers should also praise the Lord for the life that believers have in Christ. Isaiah 11:10 applies today in that unbelieving Gentiles, as a result of what they see God has done to the body of Christ, will also join the body of Christ themselves by trusting in Jesus' death, burial, and resurrection as atonement for their sins.

Right dividers concentrate on 15:8 to demonstrate that Jesus Christ came to save Israel. However, by using Old-Testament quotes and applying them to the mystery program, what the Holy Ghost has just done through Paul is to show us that Jesus Christ's death, burial, and resurrection is the atonement for our sins in the mystery dispensation, just like it is the atonement for people's sins in the prophecy dispensation. You may think this is obvious, but it is only obvious because the Christian religion has taught us so. For example, Hebrews 6:4-6 says that Jesus Christ's death does not pay for the sin of worshipping the image or taking the mark of the beast (Revelation 14:9-11). Therefore, just because Jesus died for the sins of Israel, we cannot automatically assume that Jesus' death also pays for the sins of those saved in the mystery dispensation. Therefore, the Holy Ghost give us 15:9-12 to tell us that His death applies to our sins today. The Old Testament revealed that Jesus' death would justify the "many" of the prophecy dispensation (Isaiah 53:11 and Matthew 20:28), and now the Holy Ghost has revealed that Jesus' death also justifies believers in the mystery dispensation. Paul is the "due-time" testifier of this (I Timothy 2:6-7).

While this is a glorious truth to realize, the context of these verses show that, the main reason that Paul brings up these quotes, is to show how salvation works. The Gentiles will be saved in Israel's program during the millennial reign when they see Jews operating under the new covenant. The Jews obey God's law perfectly, because the Spirit causes them to do so (Ezekiel 36:26-27). Similarly today, unbelievers will be saved when they see us using the mind of Christ to walk in the Spirit (15:6), which is the body of Christ operating under our new covenant (II Corinthians 3:6). Thus, Israel's program can be applied to us today by seeing that we have been given the ministry of reconciling (II Corinthians 5:18-20) unbelievers to Christ today, while Israel will reconcile unbelievers to God in the millennial reign (Isaiah 61:5-6).

This also helps us understand God's timeline. In the dispensation of grace, God has given us the atonement now (5:11). Therefore, we can walk in the Spirit now (8:4) and all the unbelieving Gentiles, who will eventually believe, can be raptured up and enter God's heavenly kingdom at the same time that we are. Thus, the dispensation of grace ends at the rapture. In the prophecy dispensation, Israel does not receive the atonement and are not placed under the new covenant until Jesus' second coming. Therefore, the Gentiles, in that program, are not saved until God sets up His kingdom on earth. Thus, believing Jews enter God's eternal kingdom before Gentiles do. This is why God gives the Gentiles a 1,000-year period (Revelation 20:4) after Israel is saved so that they can see Israel walking under the new covenant, learn the knowledge of the Lord (Isaiah 11:9), and be saved themselves (Isaiah 11:10). Today, since unbelievers are not given a 1,000-year grace period after the rapture, it is vitally important that we walk in the Spirit BEFORE entering heaven, and not just afterward.

15:13 Since Paul refers to "the God of hope," he is referring to the "hope of eternal life" (Titus 1:2) that unbelieving Gentiles can have if they see the body of Christ walking in the Spirit and then believe in Jesus' death, burial, and resurrection as atonement for their sin. In order for unbelievers to come to "the God of hope," we must "abound in hope" (15:13). First, we must read and believe God's Word so that we will have the joy and peace that come as part of the fruit of the Spirit (Galatians 5:22-23). The joy comes from the confident expectation of our heavenly home (5:11) and from standing by faith in sound doctrine (II Corinthians 1:24). The peace comes by thinking through sound doctrine to make decisions in life (Philippians 4:6-9). Thus, if we believe God's Word and bring sound doctrine into our inner man, "the power of the Holy Ghost" will bring joy and peace into our lives such that we will "abound in hope" (15:13) in the things of God that are ours in heaven. Remember that hope causes "the love of God" to be "shed abroad in our hearts by the Holy Ghost" (5:4-5). Therefore, unbelievers ask us "a reason of the hope that is in" us (I Peter 3:15) so that they might be saved. Thus, we are good "ambassadors for Christ" (II Corinthians 5:20) when we simply read and believe God's Word, allowing the Holy Ghost to produce spiritual fruit in our lives that unbelievers will see.

15:14 The Romans are "full of goodness" (15:14) as a result of the Spirit working in their lives (Galatians 5:22). They are "filled with all knowledge" (15:14), because they have gotten this far in Paul's epistle. Therefore, they are "able also to admonish one another" (15:14). Now, you may think that Paul has just contradicted himself, because, in chapter 14, he taught the Romans to make sure they do not offend weaker brethren. Now, he is saying that they can admonish one another. This latter statement is based on them already having the knowledge of chapter 14, which is not just to "follow after...peace," but also to "follow after...things wherewith one may edify another" (14:19). In other words, a mature believer in Christ will forego his liberty so as not to offend the weaker brethren, but he will also admonish weaker brethren when they are willing to listen to corrective sound doctrine. In other words, now that the Romans know the caveat of the weaker-brother principle (Romans 14), they can keep that in mind and look for opportunities to edify others with sound doctrine, which includes admonishing weaker brethren when they will not be offended.

The reason that admonishing one another is important is because, if we are living in sin and are letting fellow members of the body of Christ continue in sin, that also detracts from having unbelievers believe the gospel. Peace among the body of Christ should not come at the sacrifice of allowing sin in our midst. Therefore, we also need "to admonish one another" (15:14).

15:15-16 The Romans were already "beloved of God, called to be saints" (1:7), and their faith was already "spoken of throughout the whole world" (1:8). So, why did Paul write the foundational epistle for the dispensation of grace to a group of people who were already known worldwide for their faith? The reason is because Paul is "the minister of Jesus Christ to the Gentiles" (15:16) so that "the offering up of the Gentiles might be acceptable" (15:16). In other words, Paul was responsible for dispensing the gospel, and all mystery doctrine associated with it (I Corinthians 9:17), so that the fulness of the Gentiles would come into the body of Christ (11:25).

Since the Romans were faith examples to the world, if Paul could get mystery doctrine working through them, all other body-of-Christ congregations would see how the doctrine works effectually in those who believe. Then, these other congregations could follow their example and also have Christ live in them. For example, if I come up with an athletic supplement that works really well, I will try to get professional athletes to use my supplement. The professional athletes need my supplement the least of all people. However, if they use it, others, who truly need it, will see how effective it is, and they will use it themselves.

Similarly, Paul was "bold" (15:15) in presenting mystery doctrine to the Romans in the sense that they did not need it as much as the Corinthians needed it. But, he did so, in order that the Corinthians (and other carnal Christians) could see the doctrine worked out in the Romans' lives and seek to allow Christ to live in them, as well. Therefore, Paul sought to impart the "spiritual gift" (1:11) of how we are saved (Romans 1-5), how Christ can live in us (Romans 6-8), how we need to make valuable use of our time since the dispensation of grace can come to an end at any moment (Romans 9-11), and how to live sound doctrine practically (Romans 12-16) to a group of people who were already considered faithful. Then, others would see how important sound doctrine is so that they also would study to show themselves approved unto God (II Timothy 2:15) so that sound doctrine could work through them also.

In summary, Paul is saying, in 15:15-16, that he chose to make the Romans the model church for all churches, because they were already faithful. Others would then see how faith in mystery doctrine accomplishes God's will of people being saved and coming unto the knowledge of the truth (I Timothy 2:4), which would make "the offering up of the Gentiles … acceptable" unto God, because they will have been sanctified by the Holy Ghost's teaching them sound doctrine (15:16). As such, Paul was practicing the principle not to "cast...your pearls before swine" (Matthew 7:6).

15:17 "He that glorieth, let him glory in the Lord" (I Corinthians 1:31 and II Corinthians 10:17). "But God forbid that I should glory, save in the cross of our Lord Jesus Christ" (Galatians 6:14). Because our flesh is vile (Philippians 3:21) and there is no good thing that dwells in our flesh (7:18), the only thing we can rightfully glory in is in the Lord. That is because everything that we accomplish, spiritually speaking, is done by Christ living in us (Galatians 2:20). Therefore, when it comes to the flesh, Paul says, "What things were gain to me, those I counted loss for Christ" (Philippians 3:7). But, when it comes to the spirit, he can glory in the Lord, and it is not pride, because Christ does the work by him (15:18).

15:18-22 Today's churches will use 15:20 to say that we should not build upon another man's foundation. Therefore, we need to raise money to go to the unreached nations with the gospel. However, there is nothing wrong with building upon another man's foundation. Paul said, "I have planted, Apollos watered" (I Corinthians 3:6). Paul even said that he "greatly desired" for Apollos to come to the Corinthians (I Corinthians 16:12). In other words, Paul greatly desired for Apollos to build upon the foundation that Paul laid.

The reason Paul would not do that is because he was in a unique situation. A dispensation of the gospel had been committed unto him (I Corinthians 9:16). He received his gospel "by the revelation of Jesus Christ" (Galatians 1:11-12), and Jesus Christ commissioned him to go to all unbelievers in the world with that gospel (Acts 9:15). Paul was the first to be saved in the dispensation of grace, and God established him as a pattern for others who would believe after him (I Timothy 1:16). As such, Paul was commissioned to all unsaved people, while the little flock of Israel was commissioned to saved Israel (Galatians 2:7-9). If Paul went "where Christ was named" (15:20), he would be going to people, who were a part of Israel's program. He would then be edifying them in doctrine for their program, which would leave the mystery dispensation without its apostle (11:13). In other words, the reason Paul would not build upon another man's foundation was because others' foundation was Israel's program and Jesus Christ commissioned him to preach the mystery gospel to those who had not heard it before "and to make all men see what is the fellowship of the mystery" (Ephesians 3:8-9).

This also explains why he would "not dare to speak of any of those things which Christ hath not wrought by" him (15:18). If he did, he would be speaking of Israel's program, and people would get confused about what they need to believe today. After all, people today believe the wrong doctrine, thinking they should follow Matthew – John, instead of Paul's epistles. How much more would have this been the case in Paul's day if he did not keep his ministry separate from the ministry of the 12 apostles!

Therefore, Paul sought "to make the Gentiles obedient" (15:18), not the Jews. Obedience means that they believe the gospel, as 6:17 says, "Ye have OBEYED from the heart that form of doctrine which was delivered you." He did this "by word and deed" (15:18), meaning that he told people that they were sinners and that they needed to believe in Jesus' death, burial, and resurrection as atonement for their sins (word). He then confirmed that his word was true "through mighty signs and wonders, by the power of the Spirit of God" (15:19) (deed). He then moved on to the next place where Christ was not named, so that more unbelievers would hear the mystery gospel.

In doing this, Paul fulfilled Isaiah 52:15 (15:21). As with Paul's Old-Testament quotes in 15:9-12, Isaiah 52:15 will be fulfilled in Israel's program. However, the Holy Ghost says, here, that Paul also fulfilled it in the dispensation of grace. In other words, the reason that Jesus commissioned Paul to go to the Gentiles with the mystery gospel was because God knew that the Gentiles would believe if they heard the gospel. Since the Jews would not go to the Gentiles, Jesus commissioned Paul to go to them.

Paul says that he finished his course (II Timothy 4:7), which means that he gave the truth of the gospel to all the world (Colossians 1:5-6). This means that his commission ended when he died. Therefore, we cannot use 15:20 as justification for us today to go to the "unreached people groups" of the world with the gospel, because we should not build upon another man's foundation. This verse is taken out of context to get people to donate to "missions" so that church leaders can get rich. I notice that today's churches have no problem publishing newsletters and spreading the testimonies of people on the mission field today, even though 15:18 says not to dare to speak of things that Christ has wrought by others. After all, if you are going to try to apply 15:20 to us today, you also have to apply 15:18!

Rather, because this passage is at the end of Romans, Paul knows that his audience knows that he had a special commission to reach all Gentiles with the gospel and all grace believers with mystery doctrine. Therefore, Paul mentions not speaking of others' work and not building upon another man's foundation, not as an example for us to follow, but as the reason why Paul wrote the epistle to the Romans, rather than going to them and telling them these things in person (15:22). As such, he was "much hindered from coming to" them (15:22), because Jesus Christ told him to go to the world with the gospel. (Note how Jesus told the apostles in Israel's program to go to the whole world and preach the gospel to every creature (Mark 16:15), but they were to start with Israel (Acts 1:8). By the time Israel's program was put on hold, not even the city of Jerusalem was saved, as seen by the apostles staying in Jerusalem (Acts 8:1). Since the Gentiles were ready to believe the gospel but the Jews were still in unbelief, Jesus transferred this commission from the 12 apostles of Israel's program to Paul in the mystery program. Therefore, the 12 confined their ministry to saved people in Israel's program (the circumcision), while Paul went to the whole world (the heathen) (Galatians 2:9).)

By the way, this commission also facilitated Paul writing down all of the instructions for this dispensation (Colossians 1:25), as we now have the foundational doctrine for this dispensation in the book of Romans, preserved for us to read and believe 2,000 years later. The rest of the mystery doctrine is also recorded for us in the rest of Paul's epistles, which were written in response to issues that came up. This also shows the practicality of sound doctrine. After all, if reading scripture does not solve problems, Paul never would have written these letters!

The problem today is that Christians say that they are studying the Bible, but they are really studying man's ideas about the Bible. They are "ever learning, and never able to come to the knowledge of the truth" (II Timothy 3:7). Therefore, Christians think that the Bible is not practical because it is of no help to them because they do not study the Bible! The truth is that Paul's epistles contain "the doctrine which is according to godliness" (I Timothy 6:3). In other words, in order to live the godly life, you must have the sound doctrine of Paul's epistles built up in your inner man. Going to church and feeling good about yourself will not cut it!

15:23-25 "Having no more place in these parts" (15:23) means that Paul has covered the whole area of Jerusalem to Illyricum with the gospel of Christ (15:19).

Paul says that he will now go unto Jerusalem (15:25), and he does arrive in Jerusalem in Acts 21:17. This means that we can read the book of Acts and determine that the book of Romans was probably written around Acts 20:1-3.

Paul's plan is to see the Romans when he goes to Spain. The Bible never records him going to Spain. However, since we know that "the word of the truth of the gospel" came to "all the world" (Colossians 1:5-6) and Paul finished his course (II Timothy 4:7), we can assume that Paul did, in fact, go to Spain after Acts 28.

However, we do know that Paul did get to go to Rome. Paul was arrested in Jerusalem, and he eventually appealed his case to Caesar (Acts 25:11). King Agrippa saw this as a bad decision, because Paul probably would have been set at liberty if he did not appeal to Caesar (Acts 26:32). However, Paul was not concerned with being free. Rather, he had "a great desire these many years to come unto" the Romans (15:23) and appealing to Caesar gave him a free trip there (Acts 28:16)!

15:25-27 In 15:20, Paul said that he strove to preach the gospel where Christ was not named. Yet, now he says that he will "go unto Jerusalem" (15:25), the very place where the 12 apostles are. However, he does not go there to preach the gospel, but he goes to bring an offering "for the poor saints which are at Jerusalem" (15:26).

In Israel's program, the Lord Jesus Christ told the believing remnant to "sell that ye have" (Luke 12:33). In Acts 2:45 and 4:34-35, we see them doing just that. The reason they sold what they had was because, if Israel believed, the tribulation period would have started right away, and their goods would have done them no good because they would not take the mark of the beast (Revelation 13:17). Since Israel did not believe, Israel's program was set aside, and the dispensation of grace began in Acts 9. This left the Jerusalem saints in a status of being poor. This gave the opportunity to the Gentiles to bless the little flock monetarily.

"The Gentiles have been made partakers of [the Jews'] spiritual things" (15:27). This does not mean that they received Israel's promises. God gave Israel promises of spiritual blessings in their program. At that time, the Gentiles were "aliens from the commonwealth of Israel, and strangers from the covenants of promise, having no hope, and without God in the world" (Ephesians 2:12). But now that God has started the mystery dispensation, saved Gentiles are "blessed...with all spiritual blessings in heavenly places" (Ephesians 1:3). Therefore, the Gentiles are now receiving eternal life and blessings from God, like Israel had in time past. The Gentiles' duty, then, to the Jews, was to help them out financially. In other words, the Jews have helped out the Gentiles spiritually by showing them what not to do (I Corinthians 10:4-11). Now, the Gentiles can show the Jews the love of Christ by helping them out financially.

In talking about the same situation with the Corinthians, Paul says that, by giving to the Jerusalem saints, the Corinthians' abundance is a supply for Jerusalem's lack and vice versa (II Corinthians 8:14). The same is true in the offering from the Macedonians and the Achaians. By giving to Jerusalem, the givers grow spiritually, because they trust in the things of God, rather than the things of this world. At the same time, the Jerusalem saints are helped out physically, and they have the opportunity to grow spiritually, as they see the love of Christ in action. Thus, all can benefit spiritually through this material gift.

15:28 "Sealed to them this fruit" (15:28) is a wonderful statement. When we believe the gospel, we are "sealed with that holy Spirit of promise" (Ephesians 1:13), meaning that our eternal life with Christ is guaranteed. We cannot lose our salvation. Therefore, if Paul seals fruit to the Macedonians and the Achaians by bringing their gift to Jerusalem, it means that, whenever we walk in the Spirit and yield spiritual fruit, it is sealed to our account so that, regardless of what we do afterward, Jesus will reward us for that at the judgement seat of Christ. In other words, that work will survive the fire of the judgment, and we will be rewarded for it (I Corinthians 3:13-14). Therefore, not only do we not have to worry about losing our salvation by living in sin, but we also do not have to worry about losing our reward in heaven, if we walk after the Spirit but later on walk entirely after the lusts of the flesh. Thus, Christ's blood removes all our guilt—past, present, and future (Hebrews 9:14).

15:29 When Paul mentions that he will "come in the fulness of the blessing of the gospel of Christ," this means that he knows that, when he comes to Rome, he will have the fulness of the mystery. When he wrote Romans, he did not have full knowledge of the mystery. That is why he said, in 8:26, that "we know not what we should pray for as we ought." By the time you get to Ephesians, Paul does know what to pray, since he has full knowledge of the mystery at that time. For Paul to be sure he will have full knowledge when he comes to Rome, he must have had a revelation from Christ regarding this, which tells us that he does have full knowledge by the time we get to the end of the book of Acts. It is just that he does not write everything down until after Acts is over. Therefore, while the Romans are probably sad that, for many years, Paul has wanted to come to them and has not been able to do so yet (15:23), they can take consolation in the fact that, when he does come, he will be able to answer all of their questions regarding doctrinal issues.

15:30-31 Today, whenever a Christian travels, it is common for other Christians to pray for "traveling mercies" for him. If anyone ever needed

273

"traveling mercies," it was Paul, as he was told on several occasions by the Holy Spirit that he would be bound in Jerusalem, e.g., Acts 21:11. However, Paul asks prayer, not for his well being, but for others. Granted, he does pray to be delivered from the Jewish religious leaders in Judea, but that is only so that he may come unto the Romans afterward (15:32).

He also wants prayer that the Jerusalem saints may accept him. This seems appropriate in light of Paul's last visit to them in Acts 15. At that time, there was "much disputing" (Acts 15:7) among them. That is because the believers of Israel's program were zealous of the law (Acts 21:20), while Paul taught that "ye are not under the law, but under grace" (6:14). Since we should endeavor "to keep the unity of the Spirit in the bond of peace" (Ephesians 4:3), Paul asks for the Romans' prayers. This seems appropriate in light of the little flock's reaction to Paul in Acts 21:17-26, where they brag about how well those under the kingdom program are doing (Acts 21:20), complain about Paul's grace message (Acts 21:21), and then end up getting him to do something under the Mosaic law, which gets him arrested (Acts 21:22-26). People under the law tend to dislike those under grace; therefore, Paul's request for prayer for acceptance among the Jerusalem saints.

15:32-33 Although we are to "rejoice evermore" (I Thessalonians 5:16), that joy refers to our position in Christ. It does not mean there will not be sorrow; otherwise, we could not "weep with them that weep" (12:15). Paul did have "continual sorrow" in his heart over Israel being lost (9:2-4). Paul's request for prayer from the Romans over his trip to Jerusalem is fundamentally so that the little flock of Israel's program would have peace with grace believers of the mystery program. That way, instead of there being an "us vs. them" mentality among those in Christ, they could all be united in doing God's will of having people saved and come unto the knowledge of the truth (I Timothy 2:4). Then, Paul could come to Rome and be refreshed by the unity in the Spirit between the two dispensations, instead of having to tell them that there is still strife between the two groups of believers. Then, the God of peace (15:33) would be with them.

Of course, even if there is not peace between the two groups of believers, the Romans can still have peace among themselves (15:13), knowing that they have been reconciled to God (5:1) and they have the opportunity to walk after the Spirit (8:2). Therefore, while having peace among the two groups of believers helps the kingdom of God in the sense that people will be more likely to believe the gospel, "the God of peace" (15:33) is still with those who choose to present their bodies a living sacrifice to God (12:1) so that Christ can live through them (Galatians 2:20). The Romans will make this choice if they have allowed Paul to impart unto them the spiritual gift of sound doctrine in the mystery program (1:11), which is the point of his epistle.

16 Paul greets all of the house churches in Rome (vs. 1-16), showing that, as long as Satan is the god of this world (II Corinthians 4:4), believers are never in the majority. We need to understand this so that we do not compromise sound doctrine in order to gain the masses. In fact, Paul says to mark and avoid those who do not teach sound doctrine, because they serve the flesh, rather than God (vs. 17-18). Although they may bring in more people, it will be at the expense of the truth, and only by abiding in the truth will God bruise Satan under the church's feet (v. 20).

The church is "the pillar and ground of the truth" (I Timothy 3:15). This means that we need to be stablished in faith. This takes place by first believing Paul's gospel and second by coming into the knowledge of the truth by learning the sound doctrine from Paul's epistles and by learning from the examples of the rest of scripture, which are "the scriptures of the prophets" (vs. 25-26). This is the plan of the only wise God (v. 27), Who will glorify us in Christ Jesus for ever (v. 27) when we allow the Holy Ghost to teach us God's wisdom (I Corinthians 2:13) so that the power (v. 25) of God comes through us (II Corinthians 4:7) to accomplish God's will (I Timothy 2:4).

16:1-2 Phebe delivered the epistle to the Romans. The idea is out there in Christian circles that Paul was a male chauvinist because he said that women are to keep silent in the church (I Corinthians 14:34). However, Paul was not a male chauvinist. He just knew the role of women that God set up for them ("The head of the woman is the man" (I Corinthians 11:3).), and that is for them to be a helper in the ministry under the direction of male leadership. Phebe is a great example of this, as she was "a succourer [or helper] of many" (16:2), and she even appears to have gone to Rome by herself to deliver the epistle. (Paul also mentions Mary as someone who helped him out (16:6).)

Note also from this passage that, just because a woman's head is the man, it does not mean that she is not allowed to work outside of the home, or that there is such a thing as "woman's work." Lydia was a saleswoman (Acts 16:14), Phebe conducted business with the Romans (16:2), and even Jesus Himself received financial support from a group of women (Luke 8:1-3)! We are not told what business she conducted, but the point is that a woman is allowed to make decisions independently of a man and even have her own business. She just needs to recognize that the man is over her spiritually, and so she should submit to his spiritual headship.

16:3-4 Even a man, Aquila, is mentioned as being a helper as well. He recognized Paul's position as the apostle of the Gentiles (11:13). Therefore, he was willing to lay down his life in order to see God's gospel of grace continue to be preached from the apostle Paul. Being a helper, then, is not a bad thing and is often the role of men in a church, as well, since many helpers are needed to do God's will.

We are not told exactly what Priscilla and Aquila did to spare Paul's life. We do know that Paul stayed with Priscilla and Aquila in Corinth, because they were all tentmakers (Acts 18:1-3). Then, they sailed with Paul to Ephesus

(Acts 18:18-19). While in Ephesus, they taught Apollos mystery doctrine (Acts 18:26), and Apollos became a great help to Paul (I Corinthians 3:6 and 16:12). Paul was in Ephesus for two years (Acts 19:10), and his time there ended with his very life being threatened (Acts 19:30-34 and 20:1). It was right after this that Paul probably wrote Romans. Therefore, Priscilla and Aquila were probably instrumental in saving Paul's life in Ephesus.

16:5 As we read through this chapter, it appears that there were several house churches in Rome (v. 5, v.10, v.11, v.14, and v.15 tell us that there were at least 5 churches in Rome). What probably happened is what happens today. When you believe the truth over the lies of religion, religion kicks you out. Very few people will believe the truth over religion's lies. The main reason is because most people, who claim to be Christians, value being accepted by a group of people over the truth. Therefore, they will not take a stand for the truth, or, if they do take a stand, they will quickly back down when threatened with expulsion. As a result, Bible believers are few and far between. Even if there are a group of them in one location, they probably cannot afford to rent a church building and maintain it. Therefore, their meetings will inevitably be in someone's house. Apparently, this is what happened with the Romans. A little group of believers in one spot started a house church themselves with God's Word and the gifts of the Spirit (12:4-8) to teach them the truth. Little churches like this cropped up all over, and they got to know each other. Paul wrote to all of them as a whole and had them pass this epistle to each other from house to house.

I Corinthians 16:15 says that "the house of Stephanas...is the firstfruits of Achaia." Epaenetus could be another name for Stephanas. However, since Paul baptized Stephanas in Corinth (I Corinthians 1:16), Epaenetus and Stephanas are probably two, different people, who were part of the original group of grace believers in Achaia.

16:7 Andronicus (v. 7), Junia (v. 7), Herodion (v. 11), Lucius (v. 21), Jason (v. 21), and Sosipater (v. 21) are listed by Paul as being "my kinsmen," meaning that they are fellow Jews. This tells us that there were Jews in the Roman church.

Andronicus and Junia "were in Christ before" Paul (16:7). However, Paul says that it was in him FIRST that Jesus Christ showed forth longsuffering as a pattern to those who would believe after him (I Timothy 1:16). This means that Paul was the first one saved in the body of Christ. Obviously, there were many people saved before Paul in Israel's program, and Andronicus and Junia are two of those people. Since they "were in Christ before" Paul, this tells us that all believers, regardless of dispensation, are in Christ. That is why Ephesians 1:10 says that both heaven (body of Christ) and earth (bride of Christ) will be reconciled back to God "in Christ." Therefore, while it is much easier to see the in-Christ message in Paul's epistles, believers, in Israel's program, are also "in Christ."

Given that Andronicus and Junia are saved Jews in Israel's program, the apostles, among whom they are of note, would probably be the 12 apostles of Israel's program, although the Lord Jesus Christ did give apostles to the dispensation of grace (Ephesians 4:11). This tells us that they were saved under the gospel of the kingdom, but they have recognized the shift in dispensations and are helping out the body of Christ in Rome. (Barnabas is another example of a saved Jew in Israel's program who helped grow the body of Christ.)

Since Andronicus and Junia were "fellowprisoners" of Paul, they were saved before Paul was, and Paul used to imprison Jewish believers (Acts 22:4), it is quite possible that Paul arrested them before he was saved.

16:8-9 Paul refers to Amplias and Satchys as "my beloved." Perhaps they are given this label because they were saved as a direct result of hearing Paul preach the gospel of grace.

16:11 In case you are wondering, Narcissus was a Greek god known for his beauty. He could not stop staring at himself, being fixated on his beauty. That is how the term "narcissism" came about. This story may come from Satan, since he covered the throne of God (Ezekiel 28:14), which has a sea of glass before the throne (Revelation 4:6). He saw himself, was fixated on his beauty, and declared that he would become God (Isaiah 14:13-14). Obviously, the Narcissus, of 16:11, is not a Greek god, but he may be mentioned by Paul as a type of all believers. Before we are saved, we are children of the devil (John 8:44), which means we are like the Greek god Narcissus. After we are saved, we are new creatures in Christ (II Corinthians 5:17), and God has "translated us into the kingdom of His dear Son" (Colossians 1:13). Therefore, God can take the vilest person, make him something new and beautiful, and bring him into His eternal kingdom.

16:12 Tryphena and Tryphosa are names of women, and so here is another example of women in the service of the Lord. If Paul was a male chauvinist, he would not have named any women. Also, the fact, that their names are so similar, may indicate that they are twin sisters, although that is pure speculation.

16:13 The phrase "his mother and mine" (16:13) leads to a lot of speculation. There are two possibilities: 1) Rufus was Paul's brother, and him and his mother became believers after Paul did and moved to Rome to get out of the persecution in Jerusalem, or 2) Rufus' physical mother was like a mother to Paul, having been disowned, possibly, from his physical mother for abandoning the Jewish religion and believing in Jesus Christ as atonement for sins. Paul never mentions his mother in any other passage. If this was his physical mother, it seems weird that her only mention would be buried here, especially since, if this were the case, she is probably a believer, since both Paul and Rufus are believers. Also, there is a Rufus mentioned in Mark 15:21. He is the son of Simon, who carried Jesus' cross. If this is the same Rufus as mentioned here, Simon, Rufus, and Rufus' mother probably became believers as a result of Simon carrying Jesus' cross. Then, Paul became acquainted with them after his conversion and she treated him like a son, since she was intimately involved with Jesus' crucifixion. Therefore, it seems likely that Paul is saying that Rufus' physical mother is like a mother to him.

16:14 Hermes is another believer in Rome, who was named after a Greek god. The Greek god, Hermes, was a messenger of the gods, which makes him like an angel.

16:16 Paul concludes four of his epistles with the command to greet one another with "an holy kiss" (Romans 16:16; I Corinthians 16:20; II Corinthians 13:12; I Thessalonians 5:26). Paul is the only one who uses this term. That is because, as members of the body of Christ, our sins have already been atoned for (5:11). Therefore, we are already holy (Colossians 3:12). As long as there is sin in the world, only members of the body of Chrsit can engage in a holy kiss. Contrast this with Israel's program. Their sins are not forgiven until Jesus' second coming (Acts 3:19-20). This means that they are not holy until then. Therefore, they are told to greet each other "with a kiss of charity" (I Peter 5:14), rather than a holy kiss.

"The churches of Christ" (16:16) is not a denomination. It just refers to the churches that Paul had been visiting. In fact, God is against denominationalism. He says that those, who boast in being part of a denomination, are carnal (I Corinthians 1:11-13 and 3:3-5). Instead, if someone asks you what church you are a part of, you should say that you are part of "the church of the living God" (I Timothy 3:15). If they like that answer, they may be willing to listen to the truth. If they do not like it, you know that you will probably not get anywhere with them.

16:17-18 Serving "their own belly" is a reference to feeding the flesh. Even in Paul's day, "all they which are in Asia" had turned away from him (II Timothy 1:15). Moreover, II Timothy 4:3-4 says that "the time will come when" the people in the church will not even "endure sound doctrine; but after their own lusts shall they heap to themselves teachers, having itching ears; And they shall turn away their ears from the truth, and shall be turned unto fables." This even took place in Jesus' day. A great multitude followed Jesus because they wanted to force Him to be their king (John 6:15). When they learned that He was going to die instead (John 6:51), "many of His disciples went back, and walked no more with Him" (John 6:66).

The truth offends people, even Christians (Galatians 5:11). Therefore, if someone preaches the truth, very few people will listen to him, which means that he will not make money. And so men abandon "the doctrine which is according to godliness" (I Timothy 6:3). Instead, they dote "about questions and strifes of words...perverse disputings of men of corrupt minds, and destitute of the truth, supposing that gain is godliness" (I Timothy 6:4-5). That way, they have "a form of godliness," but they deny God's Word (II Timothy 3:5). This is the most effective way to get money from people.

Here is what is going on. Man is sinful (3:9-12), and his conscience tells him that he is a sinner (2:14-15). Man is not interested in stopping his sin. Rather, man is only interested in appeasing his conscience. That way, he can do what he really wants to do, which is "to work all uncleanness with greediness" (Ephesians 4:19). Therefore, if a clear gospel is presented to someone, he will probably reject it. Even if he does believe the gospel, it means that he believed his conscience that he is a sinner, and he allowed God to take care of his sin problem for him. Now, instead of being his friend, the conscience is his enemy. In other words, if he continues to listen to his conscience, he will seek to obey God in his flesh, which is an impossibility (7:18). That is why the conscience is only given to us to teach us that we need to trust in Jesus' death, burial, and resurrection as atonement for our sin. Once we learn this, we are no longer under the conscience (Galatians 3:24-25), but we are under grace (6:14). But, you will never know this unless you read God's Word rightly divided and believe it. Since Christianity teaches the opposite is true and most Christians never question their church, they spend their whole lives trying to serve God in their flesh, and they are never successful.

Instead, they need to recognize that they are dead to the flesh (6:6). However, our flesh does not like this, and so it wars against our spirit (Galatians 5:17). We have to "pray without ceasing" (I Thessalonians 5:17) and "die daily" (I Corinthians 15:31) to our flesh so that we bring our bodies into subjection (I Corinthians 9:27) to "the law of the Spirit of life in Christ Jesus" (8:2). This is a great blow to our pride, a blow that very, very few Christians are willing to inflict upon themselves, because "no man ever yet hated his own flesh" (Ephesians 5:29). Therefore, if someone comes into the church and teaches the Bible without actually teaching the truth for today, he will receive tons of money. That is because the conscience is appeased by rationalizing that I am okay because I am "following the Bible," even though I am "ever learning, and never able to come to the knowledge of the truth" (II Timothy 3:7). Therefore, I am following false doctrine, and, since I am following false doctrine, my flesh is satisfied. Thus, I can appear godly to myself and to others, while still living a life of sin. Just like a Catholic may rationalize that he is okay with God by confessing his sin to a priest, fundamental Christianity rationalizes that it is okay with God by going to church and "following the Bible" when they are living after the flesh. Therefore, I can serve the flesh, while thinking I am serving the Spirit. As such, if I am confronted with the fact that I am serving my flesh, I can vehemently deny it, because I supposedly have scripture to back up what I believe. By contrast, the drug addict or the child molester will have to admit that he is a sinner, as he has no justification for his actions. As such, the Christian is more grounded in his flesh than those in prison are.

Christianity presents the ideal situation to my flesh, because I can serve the lusts of my flesh and get away with it with my own conscience and with others. And, even if there is a godly man who confronts me, I can still justify myself with scripture and feel okay about what I am doing. Then, there are "Christian support groups" to make me feel good about myself, such that I label the Bible believer as a heretic and continue on my merry way of living a life of sin. Thus, I can serve my flesh, ease my conscience, go to heaven, serve God, and live a prosperous and happy life. In other words, the sin problem has been eliminated by perverse doctrine. This is why people will throw money at preachers who are good at doing this. Therefore, you have people, who know this, and will concoct such a situation in order to get rich. That is why those, who covet money, will err from the faith and "fall into temptation and a snare, and into many foolish and hurtful lusts, which drown men in destruction and perdition" (I Timothy 6:9-10).

Thus, they "serve their own belly" by using "good words and fair speeches" to "deceive the hearts of the simple" (16:18). Since they "drown men in destruction and perdition" (I Timothy 6:9), these men must be stopped. Fortunately, it is very easy to identify them. All you have to do is compare their doctrine to God's Word rightly divided. If it is contrary to sound doctrine for today, we should "mark them...and avoid them" (16:17). However, most Christians have "simple" hearts (16:18), meaning that they do not know basic, sound doctrine for today. Therefore, they will be deceived into giving these preachers their money.

It is this deception that makes preachers of the flesh with a cloak of godliness the most dangerous people in the world. That is why Paul said that he delivered a couple of them "unto Satan, that they may learn not to blaspheme" (I Timothy 1:20). Moreover, because more and more of Christianity has turned their ears from the truth (II Timothy 4:4), "evil men and seducers...wax worse and worse, deceiving and being deceived" (II Timothy 3:13). Prostitutes will sell their bodies for money. Drug dealers will risk their lives and their freedom for money. A preacher of false doctrine sells his soul for money. However, since most people only concentrate on the flesh, it looks like he gets away with it. He is not in danger of being arrested or of being hated. Instead, people give him preferential treatment, and he is well respected (Matthew 23:6-8). All the while, he is pilfering people out of their money, and the people are happy to give it to them. As far as the flesh is concerned, being a preacher of false doctrine is the best job possible.

Basically, the Romans, and all Christians today for that matter, should compare man's teachings with the teachings of God's Word rightly divided. If they do not match, then we should avoid those teaching false doctrine. Paul calls this proving all things and holding fast to that which is good (I Thessalonians 5:21). It is the church's responsibility to believe Romans 6-8 and cast out those who come into the church teaching false doctrine. The lack of the body of Christ's following this command has resulted in widespread false doctrine being taught in the name of God all over the world today. This results in people not hearing the gospel for today and not being edified in God's Word. Thus, not following this command has caused God's will (I Timothy 2:4) not to be done on earth today.

Young people in 2017 leave the church in droves once they can get away from their parents. The reason is because Christianity is no longer "the pillar and ground of the truth" (I Timothy 3:15). These young people see their parents playing the game of appearing to be good, when they are just as bad as everyone else. Thus, they see no power in God, the Bible, and the Lord Jesus Christ to transform their lives. Therefore, they go out to the world, where at least the people are not hypocrites. If only Christianity would heed the words of Paul in 16:17-18, then the God of peace would bruise Satan under their feet (16:20). Instead, they follow the lusts of the flesh with a cloak of godliness, and the world turns away from them.

16:19 The Romans' obedience spoken abroad is their obedience of faith (1:8). In other words, they obeyed the gospel in having faith that Jesus' death atones for their sins. Thus, the first part of God's will for them has been accomplished. Paul has written this epistle so that the second part of God's will may also be accomplished in their lives, i.e., to come unto the knowledge of the truth (I Timothy 2:4). If they do this, they will be "wise unto that which is good." Some people today try to justify their actions in the flesh by saying that they need to experience sin or at least hang around with people living in sin so that they will be able to witness to them. However, God tells us here to be "simple concerning evil." We do not need to engage in evil to witness to evil. In fact, because we are still in our vile bodies after we are saved (Philippians 3:21), if we are around evil, we will usually do evil deeds, satisfy the flesh, and the ones, who we are trying to influence, will see us as hypocrites and will not believe the gospel. Psalm 1:1 says, "Blessed is the man that walketh not in the counsel of the ungodly, nor standeth in the way of sinners, nor sitteth in the seat of the scornful." Note that the progression is from walking to standing to sitting. When we walk among evil, it will not be long before we become part of that evil. Instead, we should walk in the Spirit and let God take care of working in the hearts of men so that they will want to be saved. Besides, people hanging out at bars or other evil places are not looking for the truth, or else they would not be in those places. Therefore, even if you are able to rise above evil, they still will not be interested in hearing the gospel from you.

Also, note that the word "simple" is used to contrast with "simple" in 16:18. There (16:18), "the hearts of the simple" are those who do not have basic, sound doctrine stored up in their inner man. Here (16:19), we are to be "simple concerning evil." This shows the contrast between the flesh and the spirit. If you are simple concerning evil, it means that you do not mind the things of the flesh. If you are simple in your heart, it means that you do not mind the things of the spirit. Even a cursory look at Christianity reveals that they know all about the evil things going on in the world, but they do not even know that the mystery exists, much less actually knowing mystery doctrine. This shows the carnality of Christianity today.

16:20 When Adam fell, God gave the promise of a redeemer, saying that the Lord Jesus Christ would bruise Satan's head, and Satan would bruise Christ's heel (Genesis 3:15). In other words, the cross is where Christ gave a blow to Satan's head. How did He do this? He had daily Bible studies with the Father (Isaiah 50:4-5) and He "learned...obedience by the things which He suffered" (Hebrews 5:8), such that He "did no sin" (I Peter 2:22). Since "whatsoever is not of faith is sin" (14:23), this means that He always had faith in the Father's plan over Satan's plan.

If the Romans are "wise unto that which is good" (16:19), it means that they have sound doctrine built up in their inner man, and they have faith in God's plan. Since "Christ liveth in me: and the life which I now live in the flesh I live by the faith OF the Son of God" (Galatians 2:20), when we present our bodies as living sacrifices unto God (12:1), Christ actually does God's work through us (Ephesians 2:10)!

God prepared a body for Christ to suffer in while He was on the earth the first time (Hebrews 10:5). Once you are saved "your body is the temple of the Holy Ghost" (I Corinthians 6:19) and Christ lives in you (Galatians 2:20). Therefore, when you believe sound doctrine, you yield your body to God (6:13), and Christ uses that body for God's glory. Since Christ bruised Satan's head by having faith in God's plan the first time, Christ will bruise Satan under your feet when you live by Christ's faith by having faith in the sound doctrine found in Paul's epistles. How amazing that, when the body of Christ is united in doing the will of God, God bruises Satan under our feet!

Christians will say, "I wish I was alive to see the physical miracles that Jesus did when He was on the earth." However, the greatest miracle He did was that He conquered death. Now, it is up to individuals to believe the gospel to allow Christ to conquer death for them individually, and Christ does this by living through you. Therefore, when you have faith in the sound doctrine of Paul's epistles, not only are you witnessing spiritual miracles that Christ is doing, but He is actually doing those spiritual miracles through you, as you live by the faith of the Son of God! As such, we see the same impact made for God's kingdom today as Christ made when He rose from the dead, and we are actually a part of that work! That is because, when Christ died, He brought people from Satan's kingdom into God's kingdom. When we live by the Spirit, men believe the gospel, bringing people from Satan's kingdom into God's kingdom.

People, who do not believe in eternal security, will often say that eternal security is used as an excuse to sin. While some people may use it as such, it is not God's design. God's design is that, by being saved by the shed blood of Jesus ALONE, we are freed from sin and alive unto Christ. The Holy Spirit can then live through us and accomplish the same work through us as Christ's death did, i.e., bringing people into God's kingdom and into the knowledge of the truth. Since this is only done when we have faith in God's Word through our daily Bible studies with the Father, just like Christ had with the Father, we should be motivated to die daily to the flesh and allow the Holy Ghost to teach us God's Word so that Christ can live in us every day! This is how "the grace of our Lord Jesus Christ" (16:20) is with us.

People will say that the "Amen" means that Paul was ending the epistle here. Then, he decided to add some extra verses. That is not the case. "Amen" just means "let it be so." This is seen by the fact that Paul uses "Amen" six times in Romans (9:5, 11:36, 15:33, 16:20, 16:24, and 16:27). "Amen" is just an exclamation to emphasize the point that Paul is making. In this context, "Amen" means we should allow Christ to live through us so that "the grace of our Lord Jesus Christ" is with us, meaning that Christ works the Father's will through our lives.

16:21 Lucius is probably Luke, who wrote Luke and Acts. Starting in Acts 16:10, Luke uses the word "we" in describing Paul's journeys, indicating that he travelled with Paul. Therefore, it makes sense that Paul would mention him here. Also, note that he is one of three Jews mentioned by name, again showing that God is no respecter of persons in the dispensation of grace (2:11).

16:22 Tertius is not the author of Romans. He transcribed the epistle, while Paul told him what to write (1:1). Thus, it is an epistle of Paul, being from him. However, "all scripture is given by inspiration of God" (II Timothy 3:16), and it is holy men of God who speak as they are moved by the Holy Ghost (II Peter 1:21). Therefore, God is the ultimate author of Romans.

16:23 As with Luke, Gaius was also one of Paul's traveling companions, as mentioned in Acts 19:29 and 20:4. Romans was probably written during that time.

Erastus is also mentioned around that time (Acts 19:22) as a minister to Paul. Evidentially, he continued faithfully to the end of Paul's life (II Timothy 4:20). He is "the chamberlain of the city," meaning that he took care of the court in that city, which means he probably helped others, who were persecuted for the cause of Christ.

16:24 Anything that God says is true, but, if He repeats something, it means it is important for us to pay attention. Lest we think we are somebody special in that God can bruise Satan under our feet for us (16:20), Paul reminds us that any blow to the enemy comes, not by our greatness, but by "the grace of our Lord Jesus Christ" (16:20 and 16:24).

16:25-26 In 1:11, Paul said that he wanted to impart unto the Romans a spiritual gift "to the end [they] may be established." They are established in the truth of Romans 6-8 that they are dead to sin and alive to Christ and they need to count the flesh as dead in order to serve God by walking in the

Spirit. Now that they are established, Paul wants them to continue to be stablished. (Establish means the initial establishing, while stablish means a continuance in what you have already been established in.)

In order to walk in the Spirit, the Romans will need God to continue to stablish them in Paul's gospel. In other words, they need to continue to live by faith in God (1:17) in order for God's will to be done through them. Paul uses the term "my gospel" to distinguish it from the gospel that is part of Israel's program ("the gospel of the uncircumcision" (Paul's gospel) vs. "the gospel of the circumcision" (Israel's gospel) (Galatians 2:7)). Paul's gospel is to trust in Jesus' death, burial, and resurrection as atonement for sins (I Corinthians 15:3-4), and you are justified by faith alone without the deeds of the law (3:28). The term "my gospel" is only found three times in scripture (2:16, 16:25, and II Timothy 2:8), and only Paul uses it. That is because "a dispensation of the gospel [was] committed unto [Paul]" (I Corinthians 9:17) as "the apostle of the Gentiles" (11:13), whereas the kingdom gospel for Israel's program was committed unto the 12 apostles.

Now, you may say, "Wait a minute. The next phrase in 16:25 says, 'and the preaching of Jesus Christ.' This means that Paul preached the same gospel as the 12 apostles preached." Knowing that you would think that, Paul adds that he preaches Jesus Christ, "according to the revelation of the mystery, which was kept secret since the world began" (16:25). While Peter did preach Jesus Christ in early Acts, he preached Jesus Christ as bad news to Israel. He told them, "Ye have taken [Jesus], and by wicked hands have crucified and slain" Him (Acts 2:23). God then made Jesus "both Lord and Christ" (Acts 2:36). This means that they are now subject to the wrath of God (Luke 3:7). Peter gave the gospel to them, which is to "repent, and be baptized...for the remission of sins" (Acts 2:38). Thus, Peter told them of the things that "God hath spoken by the mouth of all His holy prophets since the world began" (Acts 3:21). Luke 1:69-70 confirms this by saying that Jesus was "an horn of salvation for [Israel]...As [God] spake by the mouth of His holy prophets, which have been since the world began." In other words, Jesus does bring salvation to Israel, but they receive that salvation by repenting and being baptized.

By contrast, Paul spoke "the mystery, which was kept secret since the world began" (16:25). Therefore, Paul must have spoken something different from Peter. As with Israel, Jesus brings salvation to us. However, we receive that salvation by believing in Jesus' death, burial, and resurrection as atonement for our sins. Thus, the preaching of Jesus Christ to us is good news, while the preaching of Jesus Christ to Israel in Acts 1-7 was bad news.

Furthermore, the Old Testament never says that the Messiah would die on a cross. This was "hidden wisdom, which God ordained before the world unto our glory: Which none of the princes of this world knew: for had they known it, they would not have crucified the Lord of glory" (I Corinthians 2:7-8). Once the cross happened, God could reveal the mystery to man, and He chose to reveal it to Paul, beginning in Acts 9. Jesus Christ Himself revealed the mystery gospel to Paul. He did not receive it from man, which means Peter or any other man did not teach it to him (Galatians 1:11-12).

Fundamental Christianity will tell you that the mystery is not a new gospel or new doctrine. It is just that the Gentiles will be saved like the Jews. They get this from Ephesians 3:3-6, which says that God revealed to Paul "the mystery...Which in other ages was not made known unto the sons of men...That the Gentiles should be fellowheirs." The word "that" means that God gave Paul the mystery so that the Gentiles would be saved. It does not mean that the mystery itself is that the Gentiles should be fellowheirs. We also know this by the fact that Gentile salvation in Israel's program was God's plan all along. Isaiah 49:6 says that the Messiah would be "a light to the Gentiles, that [He] mayest be [God's] salvation unto the end of the earth." Since this is prophecy, it cannot be mystery. Thus, God had taught by the prophets that the Gentiles would be fellowheirs with the Jews. What is different about the mystery is that God makes the Gentiles fellowheirs with the Jews by going to the Gentiles directly with the gospel, rather than using the Jews as a kingdom of priests to them (Exodus 19:5-6). He does this because of Israel's unbelief, as we learned in Romans 11 (11:30). Therefore, the mystery is the gospel and the doctrine found in Paul's epistles, and it is through the mystery gospel that the Gentiles are fellowheirs with the Jews. The mystery CANNOT be Gentile salvation, since Gentile salvation is also part of God's plan in the prophetic scriptures.

Thus, Paul did preach Jesus Christ, but he did so according to the new information that Jesus Christ gave him, and not according to the red letters found in Matthew – John. We can also see this by examining the red letters themselves. Jesus taught a conditional salvation. For example, He said, "But if ye forgive not men their trespasses, neither will your Father forgive your trespasses" (Matthew 6:15). Contrast this with Ephesians 4:32, where Paul said, "And be ye kind one to another, tenderhearted, forgiving one another, even as God for Christ's sake hath forgiven you." Jesus' message was that God would forgive them after they forgave others, and Paul's message is forgiving others because God has ALREADY forgiven you. These are clearly two, different messages.

You may say, "But Paul is speaking in his epistles and Jesus was speaking in Matthew – John. Therefore, 'the preaching of Jesus Christ' must be the red letters." Such a view fails to understand the Bible. John 1:1 says, "In the beginning was the Word." John 1:14 identifies the Word as Jesus Christ. Therefore, every word of the Bible is really the preaching of Jesus Christ. Paul says, in Galatians 1:11-12 that Jesus Christ gave him his gospel. Jesus also told Paul that He would make Paul a minister of the things which He would show him (Acts 26:16). Paul also said that the words in his epistles "are the commandments of the Lord" (I Corinthians 14:37), and Acts 2:36 tells us that God made Jesus to be Lord. Therefore, "the preaching of Jesus Christ" (16:25) today comes from Paul, just like "the preaching of

Jesus Christ" came from Moses to Israel in the wilderness and it came from Jesus Christ Himself to Israel in Matthew through John. In fact, the preaching of Jesus Christ is more authoritative from Paul, because he is in Christ. Therefore, when Paul says, "be ye followers of me" (I Corinthians 4:16), he is not being egotistical. Rather, he is saying that, because he is in Christ and he preaches Jesus Christ, then you follow Christ by following Paul. Therefore, what is viewed as pride in Paul is really the opposite—it is Paul being in Christ, such that you can follow Christ by following Paul. Therefore, if you want to know what Jesus Christ says to you today, you need to read Paul's epistles, because "the mystery" that He revealed to Paul "was kept secret since the world began," and it is only revealed to us through Paul.

Another objection is raised by fundamental Christianity when we get to 16:26. This verse says that the mystery "NOW is made manifest, and by the scriptures of the prophets." So, the argument goes that what Paul preached was not new information, because it was contained in the Old-Testament prophets.

Before addressing this argument, we should mention that, in order to understand the Bible correctly, you have to believe that the Bible is always true, because God says it is true (John 17:17) and God cannot lie (Titus 1:2). Therefore, when God says that the mystery "was kept secret since the world began" (16:25), then it was not known by man until given to Paul in Acts 9. End of discussion. You cannot say that statement is untrue just because the next verse says that the mystery is "now...made manifest...by the scriptures of the prophets." In other words, since we know God's Word is true, the mystery was kept secret until revealed to Paul, and it is now made manifest by the scriptures of the prophets. Both statements must be true. You cannot pick one or the other to be true!

This means that "the scriptures of the prophets" are one of two things. The first possibility is that they are the Old-Testament scriptures, and Paul is saying that, although the mystery was kept secret, information about the mystery is found in the Old Testament. That information was not made manifest to man until given to Paul. This is a possibility in light of I Peter 1:10-12, which says that the details of Israel's salvation, while being contained in the Old-Testament prophets, were not revealed to Israel until after the cross. If 16:26 is referring to the scripture of Old-Testament prophets, then Paul is saying the same thing about the mystery, i.e., that the mystery is in the Old-Testament prophets, but it was not revealed to man until given to Paul. This also makes sense in light of Acts 15:13-18. There, James quotes Amos 9:11-12 to say that these verses refer to the mystery. Without the Holy Ghost revealing this, there is no way that man would know that that passage refers to the mystery, which is why James says, "Known unto God are all His works from the beginning of the world" (Acts 15:18). In other words, James is saying that only God knew that Amos 9:11-12 referred to the mystery at the time it was written. It was still a mystery to man until Jesus Christ revealed it to Paul.

The second possibility is that "the scriptures of the prophets" refers to Paul's writings. Paul says that God gave prophets to the body of Christ until the time (Ephesians 4:11) when we reach "the measure of the stature of the fulness of Christ" (Ephesians 4:13), which would be when the Word of God was completed. According to I Corinthians 14:37, one of the prophet's jobs was to identify which of Paul's writings are scripture and which are not. We know that Paul wrote at least four letters to the Corinthians, but only two of them made it into the Bible. That is because only two of them are "the scriptures of the prophets." Under this view, God revealed the mystery to the Romans, both by verbal communication to Paul and by written communication through Paul with the prophets identifying which of Paul's epistles are "thus saith the Lord," and which ones are not part of the revelation of the mystery.

One problem with this view is that only I and II Thessalonians, I and II Corinthians, and possibly Galatians have been written by this time, and the Romans may not have had those books yet. Even if they did, they probably would not think of them as being "the scriptures of the prophets," because the prophets are generally considered to be the writings of Isaiah – Malachi. Regardless of which view you take, 16:26 CANNOT be saying that believing Israel in the Old Testament knew the information that Paul presented, because 16:25 says that it was a mystery and 16:26 says that it has only NOW been made manifest. Therefore, what Paul preached was not revealed to man until the Lord Jesus Christ revealed it to Paul, beginning in Acts 9.

Having said all of that, I believe the truth is really secret option #3. If you take the whole grammatical structure of 16:25-26 into account, Paul is saying that the Lord has the power to stablish the Romans by three things: 1) "My gospel", 2) "The preaching of Jesus Christ, according to the revelation of the mystery," and 3) "By the scriptures of the prophets," meaning all of the scripture, both Old and New Testament, outside of Paul's epistles. This appears to be what Paul is saying because this is the divine outline by which God's will is done in us. The first part of God's will is for us to be saved (I Timothy 2:4), which happens today by believing Paul's gospel. The second part of God's will is for us "to come unto the knowledge of the truth" (I Timothy 2:4). Our first priority should be to learn the sound doctrine found in Paul's epistles (see II Thessalonians 2:15 and I Timothy 1:3). At the same time, "all scripture...is profitable" (II Timothy 3:16) to us, but we must first learn the sound doctrine found in Paul's epistles before we can gain understanding in all things (II Timothy 2:7). Therefore, God's design is for us to believe Paul's gospel, learn sound doctrine in Paul's epistles, and then learn from the examples found outside of Paul's epistles (I Corinthians 10:1-11), which would be the rest of the Bible or "the scriptures of the prophets." If we do all of these things we will be stablished in the faith, which is the real subject of 16:25-26.

Therefore, rather than looking at these verses as a point of debate between right dividers and mainstream Christianity, we should really view them as God's outline by which God's will is done in us. In other words, "the commandment of the everlasting God...for the obedience of faith" has now been "made known to all nations" (16:26) through Paul, and that commandment is for us to believe Paul's gospel, and then come into the knowledge of the truth by learning the sound doctrine in Paul's epistles and then by learning the rest of God's truth found in the scriptures outside of Paul's epistles.

Now, when God started the kingdom program, He made Israel His chosen nation. Deuteronomy 7:6 says, "For thou art an holy people unto the LORD thy God: the LORD thy God hath chosen thee to be a special people unto Himself, above all people that are upon the face of the earth." In the mystery program, however, this middle wall of partition between Jew and Gentile was broken down (Ephesians 2:14), such that the gospel of grace is now "made known to all nations" (16:26), not just the nation of Israel, so that all people might have faith in it for salvation.

At the same time, faith does not stop with salvation. The mystery also sanctifies the body of Christ (Ephesians 5:25-27). That is why Paul mentions "the OBEDIENCE of faith" (16:26). The obedience of faith is to first believe the gospel and second to learn mystery doctrine so that Christ can live in us. In other words, faith does not just say, "I thank God for saving me. Now, I will continue to sin so that grace will continue to abound in my life" (6:1). God forbid (6:2). Faith says, "I am now just, and so I will now live by Christ's faith (1:17, Habakkuk 2:4, and Galatians 2:20) by reading Paul's epistles to learn sound doctrine and by reading the rest of the Bible as examples so that I will walk after the Spirit. This is the complete obedience of faith.

16:27 Only God is wise enough to reconcile both the earth and the heavenly places back to Himself through two, different programs, one of which He kept secret for 2,000 years after revealing the first one in Genesis 12. I Corinthians 2:9 confirms this by saying, "Eye hath not seen, nor ear heard, neither have entered into the heart of man, the things which God hath prepared for them that love Him." That is because God's ways and thoughts are higher than our ways and thoughts (Isaiah 55:8-9), such that "His ways [are] past finding out" (11:33). This shows how wise God really is.

A wise man may come up with an idea that others have not thought about before. Once his idea is shared, people understand it. However, God is so wise that, not only did He come up with a plan to reconcile the heaven and the earth back to Himself that no one ever thought of, but His plan is also so wise that the wisest man cannot even understand it. "For it is written, I will destroy the wisdom of the wise, and will bring to nothing the understanding of the prudent" (I Corinthians 1:19). "The world by wisdom knew not God" (I Corinthians 1:21). It took the foolishness of the preaching of the cross to save us (I Corinthians 1:18). Then, it takes the Holy Ghost to teach us the things of God (I Corinthians 2:10,13).

Note that glory is tied to God's wisdom. He receives glory for ever because of His wisdom. However, this glory is not His alone, because He receives glory "through Jesus Christ" (16:27). Since all believers are "in Christ" (12:5), we also receive God's glory, which is why Ephesians 1:3 says that God has "blessed us with all spiritual blessings in heavenly places in Christ." Since glory is tied to wisdom, the more of God's wisdom we allow the Holy Ghost to teach us, the more of God's glory we receive in Christ. Therefore, God is not selfish in receiving glory, because He shares it with those, who are willing to believe the gospel, and they receive more glory as they allow God to teach them His wisdom.

This is the conclusion of Romans, as it should spur us to continue to allow the Holy Ghost to teach us the things of God found in the remainder of Paul's epistles. That is why the next chapter, I Corinthians 1, talks of the wisdom of God versus the foolishness of man, while the chapter after that, I Corinthians 2, talks of how we can learn that wisdom. Thus, Paul has begun to reveal the mystery in Romans, and he has given us motivation to learn the rest of the mystery in his remaining books.

So, on to I Corinthians...

Manufactured by Amazon.ca
Bolton, ON

31586457R00160